REAP THE WHIRLWIND

REAP THE WHIRLWIND

The Untold Story of 6 Group,
Canada's Bomber Force of World War II

Spencer Dunmore and William Carter

M&S

*To our families and to all
those who served in 6 Group*

Canadian Cataloguing in Publication Data

Dunmore, Spencer, 1928 –
Reap the whirlwind

Includes bibliographical references and index.
ISBN 0-7710-2924-1 (bd.)
ISBN 0-7710-2926-8 (pa.)

1. Great Britain. Royal Air Force. Bomber Command.
Group, No. 6 – History.   2. World War, 1939-1945 –
Aerial operations, Canadian.   I. Carter, William S.
II. Title

D792.C2D85   1991   940.54'4971   C91-095158-6

Design by Marisa Mendicino

Maps by James Loates

The text of this book has been printed on acid-free paper
Printed and bound in Canada

McClelland & Stewart Inc.
The Canadian Publishers
481 University Avenue
Toronto, Ontario
M5G 2E9

They have sown the wind and
they shall reap the whirlwind.

Hosea 8:7

"They sowed the wind and now
they are going to reap the
whirlwind."

Sir Arthur Harris

CONTENTS

FOREWORD

This is an important book because it deals with a chapter of Canadian history that is little known – even among Canadians. It is the story of 6 Group, the Canadian bomber force of World War II, a formation that the politicians in Ottawa saw as a political symbol of the new, independent Canada, and that the RAF chiefs regarded as an unfortunate "colonial" venture doomed to failure. Above all, it is the story of the young Canadians who found themselves thrust into the fiercest aerial war in history. Very few of those who survived a tour of operations in No. 6 (RCAF) Group of Bomber Command have written about their experiences. Thus, the authors have done a great service in telling these stories, retrieved from official files and obtained in personal interviews, for they bring out the ongoing fear of taking off from airfields in England, sometimes under dreadful meteorological conditions, to face the determined defences of Nazi Germany. The difficulties they encountered, the acts of pure heroism, and the terrors of trip after trip are recorded here.

In its difficult early days, the Group regularly recorded the highest casualties and the worst "early return" rates in Bomber Command. Eventually, however, time and experience gave the Canadians the maturity they needed to make their group one of the finest. The demands of operations brought out the best in the true spirit of a team effort, which ultimately resulted in victory and, perhaps, made the loss of so many heroic aircrew a little easier to bear.

Lieutenant General R. J. Lane DSO DFC* CD

INTRODUCTION

The weather was perfect that Friday morning, May 25, 1917. The entire population of Folkestone, Kent, seemed to be out, thronging the main street, enjoying the sunshine. For many of them it was pay day, the high point of the week.

At the distant sound of pulsating aero-engines, the pedestrians stopped and looked up. Those possessing the keenest eyesight soon spotted the aircraft high in the clear sky, at least twenty of them, circling like eagles, the sun glinting on their broad wings. Most thought the aircraft were British. They were mistaken. Moments later, bombs burst in the centre of the Folkestone, killing ninety-five townsfolk and injuring nearly two hundred. The Toronto *Globe* reported indignantly that the raid had occurred while "streets were crowded with shoppers, promenaders and workers returning to their homes." The paper described the attack as "the most ambitious airplane raid yet undertaken by the Germans on Great Britain."[1]

In the context of the daily slaughter in the trenches a few miles away across the Channel, the raid on Folkestone was a minor incident. Yet it stunned the population of Britain, precipitated a crisis in the British government, and set in motion a chain of events that culminated in the creation of a force which, little more than a quarter-century later, would wreck Germany from end to end.

The Folkestone raid was by no means the first aerial attack on a British town; for more than two years, the Zeppelins had been in action. At first, their monstrous presence in the night sky had alarmed the population, but the defenders soon had the measure of the slow, suicidally inflammable airships. German aircraft had also ventured across the Channel, dropping bombs here and there.

But this was the first time that a *formation* of bombers had been seen. A few days after the Folkestone raid, the Gothas mounted more attacks, against London as well as smaller targets such as Sheerness, Harwich, and Felixstowe. They flew through English skies with apparent impunity. Outraged, the British called the bombing "Hunnish," the latest example of the enemy's depravity. While the raids caused limited damage and casualties, their effect on Britain's politicians was remarkable. Officialdom rapidly became convinced that if the raids continued, they would lead to widespread panic in "working class" districts. (Apparently, the possibility of panic in Belgravia never occurred to anyone in authority.) Cabinet ministers pictured hordes of citizens running wild in the streets, demanding that the government get out of the war to stop the bombing. The honourable gentlemen needn't have worried. Although some London districts reported considerable concern, there was no panic. It was, Britons told themselves, another example of the stouteartedness of the national character; lesser folk (i.e., foreigners) would probably have wavered, but not the British. It was all very heartening. Nevertheless, more anti-aircraft guns soon encircled the capital, and a couple of scout squadrons left their airfields in France and took up residence near London, ready to take on any more Gothas that might put in an appearance.

The success of the German raids prompted another, even more significant action by the British: the creation of a bomber formation charged with the responsibility of attacking strategic German targets far behind the lines. It was to be an "independent" force, that is, not under the control of the Army or Royal Navy (RN), as were the Royal Flying Corps (RFC) and the Royal Naval Air Service (RNAS). In command was Major-General Sir Hugh Trenchard, formerly head of the RFC in France. Known as the 41st Wing, the new force consisted originally of two RFC squadrons flying single-engined DH4s and FE2Bs plus an RNAS unit equipped with the big new twin-engined Handley Page 0/100. In May 1918, after mounting more than a hundred raids, the 41st Wing became part of the Independent Air Force. By the end of the war it had developed into a formation of ten squadrons.

Even in those early days, the airmen demanded bigger bomb loads and greater range. In response, the Handley Page factory at

Cricklewood, a north London suburb, produced the V/1500, a 126-foot span, four-engined behemoth manned by a crew of six. Capable of taking to the air carrying 7,500 pounds of bombs, the V/1500 could fly all the way to Berlin and back. But it never got the chance. The war ended just as the first models rolled off the production line. Confidently, the airmen told each other that a few score V/1500s could have knocked Germany out of the war, avoiding all that ghastly blood-letting on the Western Front. They were convinced that they had in their hands the weapon that would decide future wars. Hadn't the prescient Mr. H.G. Wells already come to the same conclusion in his novel *The War in the Air*? The aeroplane would alter the character of war for all time. It would destroy an enemy's means of waging war by demolishing his factories. And, of even greater importance, it would wreck the morale of his people. Masses of bombers would supersede huge armies; indeed, there would be no need for troops, except as occupying forces to go in once the bombers had done their work.

In the inter-war period, the airmen worked diligently and successfully to convince politicians that the concept of an independent bomber force was still correct. Squadrons of fighters would protect Britain while the bombers were busy laying waste to the enemy's cities and destroying the morale of entire populations. The Italian General Giulio Douhet had predicted it all in his book *The Command of the Air* – although it's hard to imagine how much damage the RAF's "heavies" of the period would have done even to undefended targets. They were biplanes: the Virginia, bearing a disquietingly close family resemblance to the Vimy that had tottered across the Atlantic back in 1919, and the Heyford, an antediluvian-looking Handley Page design of the early Thirties that entered service at a time when more forward-looking air forces, including the *Luftwaffe*, were taking delivery of stressed-skin monoplanes with retractable undercarriages. Not until late in 1936 did the Royal Air Force receive its first monoplane bomber, the Fairey Hendon. And even that was considered an interim design and equipped only one squadron. Fortunately, the British aircraft industry was working on more promising bombers: Handley Page's HP52, which became the Hampden, the AW23 from Armstrong Whitworth, which was developed into the Whitley, and, best of all, the Vickers Type 271, which would achieve fame as the Wellington. Simultaneously, the Air Staff began to consider specifications for a generation of even larger bombers, the aircraft that eventually became the Stirling, the Halifax, and the Manchester/Lancaster.

In July 1936, as Germany busily re-armed, the outdated Air Defence of Great Britain organization was finally abolished. Four functional Commands took its place: Bomber, Fighter, Coastal, and Training. Bomber Command, the direct descendent of the strategic bombing force of the Great War, comprised four groups initially: 1, 2, 3, and, curiously enough, 6, a training group. When war came in September 1939, Bomber Command had grown to five operational groups – 1, 2, 3, 4, and 5 – plus the non-operational 6, all under the command of the austere but capable Air Chief Marshal Sir Edgar Ludlow-Hewitt.

Most people in Britain expected the declaration of war to be followed immediately by intense aerial bombardment. It didn't happen. For several months, and for their own reasons, Britain and Germany scrupulously avoided bombing each other's cities. Formations of RAF heavy bombers attacked ships and naval installations in daylight. It was a tenet of faith at the Air Ministry that such formations could protect themselves against attack by enemy fighters because of the much-vaunted power turrets with which most of the bombers were equipped. Unfortunately, no one seems to have taken the trouble to compare the performance of the British bombers' .303-inch Browning machine guns with that of the 20 mm cannons carried by all German fighters. The Messerschmitts could stand off, out of the range of the bombers' defensive armament, and fire at will. Before the war was more than a few weeks old, the RAF's best, most experienced bomber crews were being shot out of the sky. Losses rapidly became insupportable. It was a bitter disappointment. But worse was to follow. The Air Ministry decided that, if its heavy bombers couldn't survive by day, they would bomb by night. But it soon became embarrassingly obvious that the vast majority of Bomber Command's aircrews couldn't find their targets by night, let alone hit them. While the heavies floundered in the hostile darkness, the Command's light bombers continued to operate by day. During the invasion of France and the Low Countries, hapless Fairey Battle and Bristol Blenheim crews died by the score in desperate attacks on German troop concentrations, road junctions, and bridges.

In the fall of 1940, Bomber Command settled down to its primary task, that of destroying the enemy's industrial and military facilities. In those days, before the introduction of radio and radar navigation aids, the bomber crews flew by moonlight to enable their navigators (then called observers) to pinpoint their positions by visual means. They flew singly or in relatively small groups, often attacking several targets at night. The theory was that by such means they would cause the maximum amount of disruption over as wide an area as possible. Although this seemed to be the most expedient way to utilize the limited bomber force available, it had one overwhelming disadvantage: it gave the defences too much time to concentrate on individual aircraft. Casualties mounted alarmingly. In 1941, the RAF lost one bomber for every thirty tons of bombs dropped.[2] And the truth was that Bomber Command wasn't hurting Germany – notwithstanding the ebullience of the newspaper prose describing airfields and port facilities as "smashed" and "obliterated." British Prime Minister Churchill's patience was dwindling. He had supported the bombing campaign from the start, despite intense pressure from the other Services. Now he wanted results: the sort of cataclysmic blows that the airmen used to talk about with such confidence in the palmy days of peace.

In August 1941, the prime minister received a chilling report from D.R.M. Butt of the War Cabinet Secretariat. Lord Cherwell, Churchill's scientific adviser, had ordered Butt to appraise the current performance of Bomber Command by studying the bomber crews' logs and target photographs. Butt's findings sent shock waves through the Air Ministry. He declared that, of the crews who claimed to have attacked their primary targets (about one-third didn't even claim to have found them), only one in three came within five miles of the aiming point. On Ruhr targets, only one in *ten* got that close.[3] The senior air officers stoutly refuted Butt's findings, pointing out that lack of photographic evidence of an attack didn't necessarily mean that an attack had failed and that Butt's investigation had taken place during unusually poor weather. But the damage had been done. Churchill was bitterly disappointed. And alarmed. Everything depended on the bomber. In 1940, he had written of the need for an "absolutely devastating exterminating attack by very heavy bombers from this country upon the Nazi homeland. We must be able to overwhelm them by this means, without which I do not see a way through."[4]

A major part of the country's resources had been committed to the construction of bombers and airfields and the training of crews. A gigantic organization had been established, everything based on the practicality of strategic bombing. But when would the effort start to pay off? Soon, the first of the electronic navigational aids would emerge from the factories. They would help the bombers find cities in the darkness. But would they enable them to hit individual factories? Or power plants? Or stations? No one was very hopeful.

Late in 1941, the Air Staff decided upon another approach: *area*-bombing, wiping out vast urban areas, destroying entire cities and all the industrial facilities and workers' dwellings they contained, systematically wrecking the enemy's nerve centres until nothing was left but huge piles of rubble. How could any nation continue to resist under such punishment? How long would the population have the will to keep fighting? How long, in fact, would Germany last? The Chiefs of Staff declared: "We must first destroy the foundations upon which the German war machine rests – the economy that feeds it, the morale which sustains it, the supplies which nourish it and the hopes of victory which inspire it."[5]

A successful area-bombing campaign was a tall order for a force that had so far failed to do much more than spoil the Germans' sleep for a few nights. A force of *four thousand* bombers would be needed, Churchill was told. Such a force would bring about Germany's collapse within six months. But the airmen had claimed too much too often. They didn't get their four thousand bombers, but they did get another chance to prove that bombing could make a substantial contribution to victory.

The area-bombing campaign began officially on February 14, 1942, shortly before the appointment of Sir Arthur T. Harris as Air Officer Commanding-in-Chief Bomber Command. An Air Ministry directive named the "morale of the enemy civil population and in particular, of the industrial workers"[6] as the primary objective of the campaign. Interestingly, the Germans had named the same goals when they planned their attacks on Britain in the Great War. In both conflicts, each side saw morale as their enemy's Achilles' heel. Allied leaders perceived German workers as downtrodden drudges who laboured in a state of seething discontent, obedient only because of brutal repression by Hitler's Praetorian Guard, the *Schutzstaffel*, more commonly known as the SS. A few heavy raids on key cities would bring the whole rotten structure crashing down, they believed. The "Jerries" would never display the same courage and tenacity under bombing as had the citizens of London and Coventry, Manchester and Sunderland. Events soon proved the fallacy of such predictions.

In his memoirs, Harris declared, "I was unable to begin any real bomber offensive for a whole year after I took over the Command for lack of aircraft, proper equipment and trained crews, and also because I was compelled to use what force I had for many other purposes besides the strategic bombing of Germany."[7] The year would, however, be notable for highly destructive incendiary raids on Lübeck and Rostock in March and April and the famous thousand-bomber raids on Cologne, Essen, and Bremen in May and June 1942. There would also be changes in equipment, with the twin-engined bombers giving way to the four-engined "heavies." Tactics would change too, with "streams" of bombers speeding through target areas, overwhelming the defenders with numbers. Of equal importance, the aircrews began to use a new navigational tool, "Gee," the forerunner of a great range of electronic devices that would help make a truly effective force out of Bomber Command.

In the second half of 1942, two new bomber formations came into being. The first was the Path Finder Force (PFF), originally and perhaps more accurately called the Target Finding Force, commanded by a brilliant Australian, thirty-two-year-old Wing Commander (later Air Vice-Marshal) Donald C.T. Bennett. Manned by some of the most experienced crews in Bomber Command, the PFF had the task of finding the targets and "marking" them with bombs and flares called "target indicators" (TIs), literally circumscribing large, illuminated areas into which the "Main Force" bombers would drop their bombs. The Pathfinders achieved group status as 8 (PFF) Group in January 1943.

The second of the new formations was No. 6 (RCAF) Group, Canada's contribution to the strategic bombing campaign and the only non-British group ever to serve in Bomber Command. The Canadian Bomber Group came into being at a turning point in the air war. The years of experiment and uncertainty were over. The strategic bombing campaign was at last moving into high gear, with the British and their newly arrived American allies eager to prove what their bombers could accomplish.

The Canadian airmen of 6 Group would be in the thick of the battles to come.

1

INTO BATTLE

"Where are the Canadian memorials to the aircrew? We have more memorials to the six hundred men killed in the Boer War than we have to the 18,000 Canadian airmen killed in World War II."

Wilbur Pierce, DFC, pilot, 433 Squadron

On December 31, 1942, as the clock ticked its way toward twelve midnight, airmen of eight RCAF bomber squadrons in England wished each other a happy new year. All agreed that 1942 had been a strange year, a bloody nightmare at the beginning, with everyone reeling from the shocks of Pearl Harbor and Hong Kong, the Japanese invasion of Burma, and German Field Marshal Rommel's counter-offensive in the desert. Would anything ever go right for the Allies? Not yet, it seemed. In February, the Germans had pulled off the cleverly planned and brilliantly executed "Channel Dash," with the battle cruisers *Scharnhorst* and

Gneisenau slipping out of their harbour at Brest and purring off to Germany, protected by vile weather and British inter-Service incompetence. It was the ultimate humiliation for the Brits, having the Jerries sailing cock-a-hoop through the English Channel with all the might of the RN and the RAF powerless to do a thing about it. Catastrophe after catastrophe. What else could go wrong? The answer came a few days later. The Commonwealth forces at Singapore surrendered to a numerically inferior Japanese army. Then the Americans raised the white flag on Bataan. Allied fortunes had touched rock bottom.

As the year progressed, however, the tide, in its unhurried way, began to turn. In the Middle East, at El Alamein, British General Bernard Montgomery launched the attack that stopped Rommel's *Afrika Korps* in its tracks. A month later came the three-pronged landings in North Africa, Operation *Torch*. In Russia, the vast armies of the Soviet Union and Nazi Germany attacked and counter-attacked, slaughtering each other in mind-numbing numbers. The German Sixth Army hacked and blasted its way to the outskirts of Stalingrad. Its commander, General Friedrich von Paulus, had hoped to give German Chancellor Adolf Hitler the city as a Christmas present. The Soviets had other ideas. They counter-attacked, throwing the Germans back, eventually surrounding them. Short of food, warm clothing, ammunition, and medical supplies, the German troops had to fight for their lives. Paulus asked permission to initiate a strategic withdrawal. Hitler refused, declaring that the *Luftwaffe* would supply the Sixth Army with everything it needed. Hadn't Hermann Göring, its corpulent commander, promised that the job could be done? He had indeed but, ill-equipped for such a mission, his airmen failed. The Sixth Army faced annihilation.

In the Far East, the hitherto invincible Japanese suffered their first setbacks. In May, the Battle of the Coral Sea halted their advance on Australia. Then came Midway in June. The American giant was starting to hit back, hard.

In Britain, every other brick wall bore painted signs: SECOND FRONT NOW! Communist sympathizers accused the Allies of unwarranted delays in invading Europe. In August 1942, a force of Canadian troops supported by small numbers of British and Americans launched an attack on the port of Dieppe. They were repulsed, bloodily. Some claimed that the Canadians were sacrificed for no other reason than to demonstrate how tough and costly an invasion was going to be, and how it would take time, lots of time, to make sure it succeeded.

Yes, 1942 had indeed been an odd year. A pivotal year. And now 1943 was about to dawn.

The airmen at the Canadian bomber squadrons had something else to celebrate: as of one minute past midnight, they would become part of a new organization, 6 Group. To most of them it was an event of only passing significance. What aircraft would the Group fly? Where would it be based? Who would run it? These were the things that really mattered. Besides, how Canadian would it be? The existing RCAF bomber squadrons were full of British, with a sprinkling of Australians, New Zealanders, South Africans, Rhodesians, and Americans. Canadians seemed to be heavily outnumbered in their own units. It had been like this since the first ops of the Canadian bomber squadrons eighteen months before. On the night of June 12/13, 1941, four Wellington bombers of 405 Squadron had taken to the air from the grass field at Driffield, Yorkshire. Each aircraft carried one 1,000-pound bomb, four 500-pounders, and two 750-pound canisters of incendiaries. The target was Schwerte, near Dortmund, in the thick of the Ruhr – "Happy Valley" to the aircrews. One of the Canadian Wellingtons developed engine trouble soon after take-off and returned to Driffield. The others pushed on into the deepening darkness. En route, they joined forces with eighty RAF Whitleys to bomb the railway marshalling yards. For the period, it was a sizable operation. But uncommonly quiet. Only spasmodic flak. No enemy fighters. Just the usual searchlights piercing the blackness, swaying in lazy-looking arcs. The Wellingtons returned safely to Driffield, the last one touching down at 0530. The crews reported that, in spite of ground mist and industrial haze, they had identified the target and bombed it successfully. But had they? Air raid sirens had wailed in Schwerte during the early hours, but no aircraft flew over and no bombs fell on the town.[1] The 405 Squadron crews had presumably bombed something that night, but no one was quite sure what.

In the intervening months, the Canadian bomber squadrons had soldiered on, attached to RAF groups. Now Canada had its own bomber group, the first non-British formation of this size ever to become part of RAF Bomber Command, an impressive symbol of the new, *independent* Canada. But symbols don't win wars. The "acid test" would come over the dangerous skies of Germany.[2]

Initially the new Canadian Group consisted of eight squadrons, most of them hastily assembled to meet the January 1, 1943, deadline. Five had Yorkshire bases: 408 Squadron at Leeming, 424 at Topcliffe, 425 and 426 at Dishforth, and 428 at Dalton; three more were based in nearby County Durham: 419 and 420 at Middleton St. George and 427 at Croft. The longer-established squadrons, 408, 419, and 420, were under-strength, having given up many of their most experienced crews to help form the new units. Everything seemed to be in short supply: tools, ground-handling equipment, experienced tradesmen, cans of this, barrels of that. And Canadians. Eventually, however, Canadians would largely replace the RAF and other Commonwealth aircrew and ground and administrative staffs who had predominated initially.

And what of the aircraft of 6 Group? Six squadrons flew the twin-engined Vickers Wellington bomber, affectionately known to the crews as the "Wimpy." The type had been in service since before the war; it was a pleasant aircraft to operate, good-natured and utterly reliable, though shatteringly noisy. Veterans who flew the Wellington in action still recall its ability to absorb horrific damage and remain aloft, thanks to its geodetic "basket-weave" construction. The Wellington was unusual among modern aircraft in having a fabric skin stretched over its metal framework, through which the clumsier members of the ground crews frequently stuck their boots. The Wellington carried a crew of five: pilot, navigator, bomb-aimer, wireless operator, and gunner. The Mark IIIs equipping the Canadian squadrons were powered by Bristol Hercules radial engines of 1,500 horsepower. The aircraft had a range of about 2,000 miles. Its top speed was in the region of 250 mph and it had a service ceiling of 22,000 feet. The Wimpy's defensive armament consisted of four Browning .303 machine guns in the rear turret and two in the nose turret. The Wellington could carry 4,500 pounds of bombs, a formidable load back in the early Thirties when the aircraft first flew. However, the recently introduced four-engined bombers had made the Wimpy obsolete;

it would soon disappear from the ranks of Bomber Command's first-line aircraft, although Canadians would continue to operate the type for several months.

The Handley Page Halifax was one of the new generation of Bomber Command aircraft. It equipped two of 6 Group's squadrons, 419 and 408. In service for two years, the Halifax was still plagued by technical problems. The type's shortcomings angered Harris. In letters to Air Chief Marshal Sir Charles Portal, Chief of the Air Staff, he regularly excoriated Frederick Handley Page and everyone else responsible for the aircraft. Powered by the famous Merlin in-line engine, the Halifax in its then-current Mark II and V versions carried a crew of seven: pilot, navigator, bomb-aimer, flight engineer, wireless operator, and two air gunners. Hydraulic failures were daily occurrences. Far more serious, however, were the chronic lack of power (for some reason the Merlin that served the Lancaster, Spitfire, and Mosquito so superbly was never a success in the Halifax) and the fatally flawed tail unit, which was likely to stall at low speed due to a condition known as rudder overbalance. Among the crews of Bomber Command, the Halifax quickly gained a reputation as a killer. Take the approved evasive action – the famous "corkscrew" – and there was every chance that your rudders would lock, completely overpowering the ailerons, and that you would find yourself in an uncontrollable spin. One can only guess at the number of crews killed before these faults were corrected.[3] In 1942, Bill Swetman of Kapuskasing, Ontario, flew the Halifax II as a relatively inexperienced sergeant pilot with 405 Squadron. "It was a catastrophe," he recalls. "When you were fully loaded there were only about twenty knots between cruise and stall speeds."

Harris demanded that the production of Halifaxes be cancelled and turned over to Lancasters. But the complex assembly lines couldn't be turned on and off at short notice, even for "Bomber" Harris. Much to his disappointment, the Halifax would remain in service for the rest of the war. But the makers worked energetically to rectify its faults, ripping out gun turrets, installing new fins and rudders, applying various types of exhaust shrouds (the aircraft was dangerously visible to night fighters because of the bright glow of its four exhausts), and removing such weighty items as fuel-jettisoning devices and balloon-cable cutters. The Halifax had gone into service too soon. Most airmen loathed it in its original form, although others grew perversely fond of it despite its flaws, much as some RFC airmen had a curious affection for the egregious RE8 of Great War fame. Eventually, the Halifax became a vastly improved weapon, able to carry some twelve thousand pounds of bombs with defensive armament consisting of eight .303 machine guns in power-operated turrets, plus a single gun in the nose. Hercules XVI radial engines replaced the Merlins.

In the months to come, the splendid Avro Lancaster would be flown by some squadrons of the Canadian Group; indeed, by May 1945 it would be the dominant type. But the majority of 6 Group aircrew veterans flew the Halifax; it was the workhorse that saw them through the toughest, most costly phases of the war.

The creation of 6 Group had prompted the mandatory exchange of courtesies between Harris and Air Officer Commanding 6 Group, Air Vice-Marshal G.E. Brookes. Brookes signalled: "We are proud to be part of Bomber Command and will do our utmost to maintain its high tradition."[4]

The RCAF's Air Officer Commanding-in-Chief overseas, Air Marshal Harold "Gus" Edwards, was equally effusive: "We feel that this is one of the great moments in the life of our air force. The RAF has nurtured a child to be its grown-up equal."[5]

Those were the public words. The private words had been less diplomatic – even hostile. From the start, Harris had been opposed to the formation of 6 Group. He had little regard for Brookes. In December of 1942 he had written to Portal, commenting on the fact that the amiable, talkative Canadian commander was nicknamed "Babbling Brook": "I am frankly alarmed at the prospects of that [Canadian] Group."[6] Harris was equally critical of Edwards; in August he had written to Portal: "For your purely personal information (and please do not quote this, even to the source) 'Boom' [Trenchard] expressed a positive horror of Edwards the other day, and described him as an appalling fellow quite unsuited for any sort of Command."[7] Such harsh comments exemplified the patronizing attitude of many senior RAF officers and demonstrated a lack of understanding of the difficult position in which Brookes and Edwards found themselves as a result of the Canadian government's politicking.

Harris had the highest regard for the Canadians aircrews' verve and courage – if not for their offhand attitude to the niceties of military courtesy. But he wanted the Canadians in the existing RAF groups; at all costs he wanted to avoid the administrative nightmare of creating a brand-new group for the sole purpose of satisfying a lot of political demands from Ottawa. Understandably impatient with anyone or anything that interfered with his energetic prosecution of the war, Harris said no to the creation of 6 Group. But Whitehall said yes; it was politically desirable. Whereupon, the Canadians demanded to be equipped with Lancasters. But here Harris drew the line. In September 1942 he wrote to Portal: "I fail to see why we should give these people, who are determined to huddle into a corner by themselves on purely political grounds, the best of our equipment at the expense of British and other Dominion crews."[8]

When they had been laying the administrative groundwork for 6 Group, the Canadians had made do with temporary headquarters at RAF Linton-on-Ouse, Yorkshire. But Edwards soon found more suitable quarters at Allerton Park, four miles east of Knaresborough, Yorkshire. The main building, an impressive, seventy-five-room baronial mansion, Allerton Hall, was the ancestral home of Lord Mowbray; it dominated an enormous estate of two thousand acres. Edwards reported to Ottawa that the owners were none too pleased about having to turn the place over to the Canadians: "We are having a little trouble getting Lord Mowbray to give up his home. Although he knows that in the end he has no other alternative, he is putting obstructions in our way and, generally speaking, making trouble."[9] Edwards eventually got Allerton Hall. The Canadians promptly renamed it "Castle Dismal."

While there is no doubt that Edwards conducted the negotiations with all the courtesies, it is not unreasonable to suppose that he derived a little private satisfaction from the task. Imagine, a Lancashire lad who had worked in a coal mine telling a real live lord to get packing! Edwards had unquestionably come up the hard way. Born in Chorley on Christmas Eve 1892, he emigrated to Canada with his family as a boy. The Edwards family settled on the east coast. They found the New World as tough as the one they had left. At the age of eleven, Edwards was working in a Nova Scotia coal mine, a "trapper boy" responsible for the mine's primitive ventilation system. The sheer dreadfulness of the job was probably a blessing in disguise, for it convinced Edwards that he must work with all his energy to improve his lot in life. He became addicted to his school books, tirelessly studying for an hour or two in the mornings before he went to the mine and for a minimum of three hours in the evenings. At eighteen, Edwards was an electrician at the British Empire Steel Corporation, a bright lad with a future. Fascinated by all things technical, he built one of the first radio sets in Nova Scotia.

When war broke out in 1914, Edwards was twenty-two. Like so many of his generation, he had become captivated by the new science of flight. He joined the RNAS and became a pilot. Commissioned, he went to France, only to be shot down and taken prisoner. Typically, Edwards used the two years of captivity to learn German and French, becoming fluent in both languages. But fate had a nasty shock in store for him on his release from captivity. During his repatriation medical, a medical officer informed Edwards that he had tuberculosis. Shattered, the young airman felt his world disintegrating around him. What should have been one of the best times of his life was unquestionably the worst. Bleakly, he wondered what sort of future lay in store for him. He wandered about London, not knowing, not caring where he was. "I just walked down the street in blackness," he said. "Then I heard my named called and saw Seton Broughall of Toronto." Seton was a former prisoner of war, a cheerful extrovert, just the sort of friend Edwards needed at that moment. Seton immediately suggested a binge to spend some of the several hundred pounds in back pay the two of them had accumulated while imprisoned. Afterwards, Edwards claimed that the binge changed his life, for it gave him a sense of priorities. In a curious way, it also set in motion his conversion from a shy introvert to a man possessing plenty of self-confidence – the latter no doubt bolstered by a visit to a Harley Street specialist who informed him that his lungs were sound; the MO had erred.

While digesting this splendid news, Edwards began to regret having spent so much of his back pay. Reports from Canada told of tough conditions with little work for ex-servicemen. Edwards decided to delay his return. He heard about an expedition being mounted to assist the beleaguered White Russian armies in their vain attempt to oust the Bolsheviks. Within a few weeks he was flying DH4s in the snowy wastes of Russia. The expedition was short-lived. In 1920, Edwards returned to Canada. He found too many ex-servicemen chasing too few jobs. For a time, he operated a winch on the recently opened Welland Canal, a tedious occupation but better than none. Fortunately, the Canadian government chose that time to create its own air force. Edwards sent in his application without delay. Although he was accepted with the rank of flight lieutenant, he soon found that opportunities were limited in the tiny, post-war force. When, in 1937, he commanded the RCAF honour guard at the Coronation of King George VI, he observed sourly that, as Canada's junior service, the airmen marched *behind* the Royal Canadian Mounted Police!

The outbreak of World War II found Edwards in charge of the RCAF's Personnel Division, a highly intelligent, well-read, and capable individual in his mid-forties, intensely proud of the RCAF and his adopted country, Canada, a practical man who enjoyed French-polishing furniture and working on a blacksmith's anvil, yet one also devoted to poetry and the opera. A tough-talking, outwardly severe man, Edwards exuded self-confidence but was rarely seen without his cap, being sensitive about the baldness that had afflicted him since his twenties.

When he went to England in 1941, Edwards had attained the rank of air vice-marshal. He immediately set out to make the British public aware of Canada's contribution to the air war, despatching batches of press releases describing actions in which Canadian airmen were involved. To some extent, his good intentions backfired. Most British editors wrote up the stories thinking they were the *first* actions of Canadian airmen in the war. Edwards soon set them straight.

In England in 1942, he was the RCAF's chief negotiator, responsible for many of the final arrangements for the creation of 6 Group. He proved to be a formidable adversary at the conference table, able to hold his own with the likes of Portal and Harris.

Some of the old colonial attitudes still lingered, and Edwards had to keep reminding the senior RAF officers that Canada, in spite of strong emotional ties to the Old Country, was independent. No longer was it merely a supplier of manpower, obliged to do whatever London demanded. Evidently, he made the point effectively. Harris was later quoted in a message deliberately "leaked" to the RCAF: "I will get that so and so Edwards out of this country if it is the last thing I do."[10]

The man selected to lead the new Canadian Group was also an Englishman by birth, forty-nine-year-old George Eric Brookes. He had sailed for Canada as a young man of sixteen, finding work as a steam and hot-water heating apprentice and fitter. When war came in 1914, he joined the 5th Canadian Field Ambulance. He soon transferred to the RFC, qualifying as a pilot. He began his active service in February 1917. Like Edwards he was to have a brief career at the front. In April (the "Bloody April" of legend), he was shot down and seriously wounded, spending the rest of the war recuperating in England. Returning to Canada after the Armistice, he joined the newly formed Canadian Air Force at the same time as Edwards. He received service number C42. A superb pilot and instructor, he spent most of the inter-war years in training jobs. Thus it surprised many when he was selected to lead the Canadian Bomber Group.[11]

A man of engaging personality, Brookes was well liked by his contemporaries. But the years in Training Command had done little to prepare him for the command of an operational group in the intensely demanding European Theatre of Operations. He had no experience of modern combat, a fact that became glaringly obvious in countless staff meetings at Castle Dismal. In many ways, Brookes was the archetypical Canadian commander of the period: a man in a key job for which he had neither the experience nor the training. Many critics would later postulate that the principal reason for the creation of 6 Group was to create important jobs for the RCAF's senior officers and to provide reasons for promoting them beyond their capabilities. There is little doubt that some officers compared Brookes unfavourably with the thoroughly "operational" RAF commanders, men who had been in the thick of the air war since the earliest days, completing at least one or two tours of operations, men who had earned the respect of their crews the hard way. The majority of Brookes's most experienced airmen had served under such commanders before they joined 6 Group. Inevitably they compared RAF and RCAF senior officers to the disadvantage of the latter. It would be a problem to plague the Canadian Bomber Group in the months to come.

Yorkshire, January 1943. Vile weather immobilized 6 Group's aircraft. Did it ever do anything here but rain, sleet, and snow? Bomber Command telexed no orders on the first of the month. But on the second day a "Gardening" (mine-laying) operation was scheduled. Then cancelled. The weather. What else?

Veterans of those early days recall the scheduling of some fifteen operations in January. Each meant going through all the preparations, the air tests, the bombing-up, the pre-op meals – precious fried eggs and bacon, reserved for operational crews only – the briefings at which the "Met man" droned on with such totally unwarranted assurance about the weather, "Dim," the intelligence officer, babbled endlessly about the importance of the target, and the CO did his earnest best to give the impression that it was a simple little job and no one should have the slightest trepidation about any part of it. Then came the nail-biting rides out to the dispersals, the forced humour, the waiting, the wondering, the frequent relieving of one's bladder. In many ways, the rituals that preceded ops were the worst part. In the air, you were usually too busy to worry.

The Canadian Group flew an operation of modest proportions on the night of January 3/4, a Gardening trip involving a dozen crews. Their orders were to lay mines off the Frisian Islands. Met had less than encouraging news: low stratus cloud likely in the north of England, equally poor conditions over Germany plus thick cloud, continuous rain and the danger of icing in the area to be mined. For once, the nail was struck squarely on the meteorological head. Conditions became so poor that half the force never took off. But six Wellington IIIs of 427 Squadron got away from their base at Croft, each carrying two mines. Within moments of leaving the ground, they had vanished into the overcast. The sound of their engines trailed away. Silence. The ground crews began the vigil that would be such a part of their lives throughout 6 Group's operational history.

Three of the Wellington crews couldn't find their targets in the grim conditions. They returned to Croft. The three remaining Wimpies soldiered on, succeeded in locating their pinpoints, and dropped their mines. They turned for home. All returned safely, although one Wellington suffered minor damage from flak. None encountered any enemy fighters.[12]

Thus did 6 Group begin its operational career. It was a gentle initiation that did little to prepare the crews for the murderous operations ahead.

The frightful January weather precluded more ops – or indeed *any* flying – for days on end. The aircraft stood immobile on their hardstandings, dripping tarpaulins shrouding engines and cabins while long-suffering ground crews kept working, striving to maintain serviceability because there was no telling when the weather might change. But it was as if nature itself was determined to put a stop to the killing in the air. The skies remained grey; the rain and sleet and snow continued to fall.

For the airmen, the lull in activity gave them an opportunity to take a closer look at the area in which officialdom had planted them. Many Canadians objected vociferously to the Group's location. It was, they said, just another example of the Brits saving the best areas for themselves and the Americans, haughtily tossing the topographical scraps to the Canadians. But in fact there really wasn't anywhere else to put the Canadians. Their group, being the last formed, had to be situated in what space was left. Although Edwards boldly suggested that 6 Group take over one of the RAF group's bases in Lincolnshire – *and* their Lancaster aircraft – it's unlikely that he ever believed it would happen.[13] In the great scheme of things, 6 Group was relatively unimportant. Besides, the Canadians weren't alone in Yorkshire; the RAF's 4 Group was based there throughout the war.

Yorkshire, the Canadians (and Australians and New Zealanders, *et al.*) discovered, was Britain's largest county, covering some

six thousand square miles, divided into three sections called "rid-
ings." North Riding, West Riding, East Riding. No South Riding.
The inquisitive soon discovered that "riding" came from the old
English word "thriding," meaning a third. Yorkshire extended
from the North Sea in the east almost to the Irish Sea in the west. It
was at once a bleak and a beautiful place with its craggy moors and
rolling pastures, its heather-covered hills, its dour cities, its marvel-
lously warm and cosy villages that seemed to be so much a part of
the landscape that they might have sprung up out of the dark earth.
To those Canadians interested in things historical, the city of York
was awesome, once a Roman capital, the place where the Emperor
Constantine was crowned in 306 AD. You could walk along a wall
that the Romans had built; you could shop in streets that had
changed little since the Middle Ages. The literary-minded discovered that the famous Brontë sisters had lived most of their lives in
Yorkshire, residing in a parsonage possessing about as much charm
and warmth as the guard room at Trenton. Windswept moors
surrounded the place like an angry sea. Everything in Yorkshire
seemed to be made of the same grey-brown stone: magnificent
mansions, depressing mill towns, farmers' walls, outhouses. Sturdy,
no-nonsense stuff. The adjectives might well have been applied to
the people of Yorkshire. In their steady-eyed way, they regarded the
"Colonials" with the wariness that they reserved for all strangers,
whether they hailed from Winnipeg or Wimbledon.

Both sides had to get to know one another. And when they did,
with remarkably few exceptions, they came to share a warm
mutual regard that survives to this day. For the Canadians, the
immediate challenge was to figure out what the Yorkshire people
were talking about. Like sailors, they kept saying "aye" instead of
"yes." Most shopgirls called you "loov" – and it was up to you to
find out the depth of feeling behind the term. "Gradely" meant
great or just good, depending upon the tone in which it was
uttered. A "cuddy" was a left-handed person. The word "clag"
meant low cloud and fog to every airman, but to the Yorkshireman
it meant "to stick." A "nessy" was an outside "privy." To "mash"
tea was not to pound it into oblivion, simply to make it. But the
Yorkshire folk had problems of their own. Where, they wondered,
were the "boondocks" the Canadians kept talking about? And
what was a "back forty"? Nice enough lads, the Canadians, but

why were they always putting things "on the back burner" and referring to "height*th*" and getting themselves "hog-tied"?

Most of the Group's squadrons were situated in the Vale of York in unnerving proximity to one another because of hills to the east and west. On a southerly wind, smoke from the Leeds–Bradford industrial area would travel along the Vale, drifting across the airfields, an irritation in daylight, often a deadly hazard at night.

The hills of Yorkshire and Durham killed many Canadians. Soon after 6 Group became operational, a Wellington of 427 Squadron descended cautiously through the patchy mist that so often formed in the region. Perhaps the pilot had neglected to set his altimeter to Croft's barometric pressure; perhaps he simply wasn't where he thought he was. We will never know. The aircraft hit the high ground above Black Intake Moor. All the crew died instantly. Fragments of the aircraft are still to be found in the area. A Halifax of 420 Squadron smashed into the ground near Shill Moor, killing everyone aboard. A Lancaster of 408 Squadron collided with the hill near High Mowthorpe.[14] In the two and a half years of 6 Group's war, scores of smashed aircraft would litter the craggy hills, the victims of mist or smoke, inaccurate navigation, sometimes mechanical failure and battle damage, but more often, a fatal lack of experience. Icing conditions often lurked in the clouds over Yorkshire. While air temperatures hovered around the freezing mark, the clouds themselves could be colder; a passing aircraft would be the catalyst to set the deadly process in motion. The chilly droplets of moisture from the cloud would adhere instantly to wings and tail unit, propellers, antennae, and windows. An aircraft might be iced up within minutes. The crew could do nothing about it (wartime bombers carried no de-icing equipment) except find a safer, drier part of the sky. Not only could the ice add tons of weight to aircraft usually loaded to capacity and beyond, but it formed a coating that literally changed the shape of the flying surfaces. An aircraft can only stay aloft when its wings and tail are able to shape the speeding air to create lift. Iced up, a thirty-ton bomber was so much metal and rubber, high explosive and fuel, tumbling out of the sky, the crew unable to do anything but jump for their lives.

*   *   *

The Canadian Bomber Group mounted its second operation on the night of January 9/10. Another Gardening op. Again the weather was marginal, the Met prediction being considerably more optimistic than conditions warranted. The Wellingtons of 420, 425, and 427 Squadrons joined the Halifaxes of 408 and 419, making a force of forty bombers that headed out toward their dropping points close to the Frisian Islands, Kattegat, and German Bight.

It turned out to be an eventful night for Flying Officer Pat Porter and his crew from 419 Squadron. George Sweanor, the bomb-aimer, a native of Sudbury, Ontario, recalls that their Halifax "bumped along through numerous rain storms trying to avoid in the dark both the menacing waves just beneath us and, just above us, the solid clouds that had perfect conditions for aircraft icing." Sweanor saw cloud forming a "solid blanket" with bases below one thousand feet and tops at twenty-five thousand feet, weather considerably less attractive than that predicted.

Sweanor and the gunners, Scottie Taylor and Danny London, tried to ease the strain on Porter's eyes by looking for whitecaps "to estimate how high we were above the water."

Stretched out in his compartment in the Halifax's nose, Sweanor suddenly saw a dark shape ahead. "I opened my mouth to shout a warning but before a word could leave my lips, Kitty (K-Kitty, the aircraft's call sign) was filled with cordite fumes as two streams of tracers joined just above us. In this new light I could see German flak ships firing at us: two were to port, one to starboard."

Sweanor told Porter to dive. He did. But the cone of fire followed the aircraft down while the two air gunners blazed away in reply.

"As the waves were about to slap us," Sweanor says, "I told Pat to level out, and we raced on, barely missing another flak ship as we sped by at mast-top level. Darkness again engulfed us . . . we were through! Cordite fumes and a few holes remained to remind us that we had been very close to a watery grave." Closer, in fact, than they knew, for Porter had closed the throttles when he dived and, in the excitement of the moment, had neglected to open them again. In the nick of time, he thrust the levers forward and hauled the aircraft away from the choppy sea.

The rest of the trip was relatively quiet for K-Kitty and her crew. After locating their aiming point, they dropped the mines and turned for home. On their way they saw "a big explosion just above the sea behind us."[15] No doubt it marked the end of one of the four Bomber Command aircraft lost that night. It may well have been the 419 Squadron Halifax flown by Sergeant F.H. Barker, for Barker and his crew never returned from the sortie. They were 6 Group's first casualties. At Middleton St. George, the sad little routines began: the Service Police accompanied the padre to the missing men's quarters to collect and sort through their belongings before sending them home. The clerks processed the necessary paperwork. The CO penned letters to the aircrews' next of kin. Most COs tried valiantly not to let these letters become routine, although it was difficult, for in the months and years ahead there would be so many of them, and in all too many cases, the CO, try as he might, had no recollection of ever laying eyes on the individuals in question. But he would write that the man was a "valued and popular member of the squadron . . . engaged in an operation of great importance to the war effort." Seldom would a CO tell parents that their son went missing on a routine trip. (Six weeks after Barker's Halifax went missing, the body of Sergeant D.A. Watson, the crew's bomb-aimer, washed ashore in Sweden. He was buried with full military honours near Grebbtad on February 19.)

Mine-laying was one of Bomber Command's major tasks throughout the war. During 1943 alone, Bomber Command "planted" some one thousand "vegetables" every month. The Canadian Group contributed 911 sorties in 1943, laying close to fifteen hundred mines. The sorties cost the Group nineteen aircraft. Bomber Command as a whole laid 13,837 mines during the year, losing 125 aircraft. Thus, for every 111 mines laid, Bomber Command lost one aircraft. But the tireless statisticians had worked out that for every forty-two mines laid, an enemy ship was sunk or damaged.[16] Unspectacular though sea mining may have been, in the callous economics of war it was an excellent investment.

On the night Barker and his crew were lost, the briefing officer at Middleton St. George had instructed the crews to release their mines from an altitude of between 500 and 1,000 feet while flying at precisely 200 mph. Accuracy was vital; the crews were told to bring their mines back to base if they were unable to find the aiming point.[17]

Late in 1942, Bomber Command began to use an electronic navigational aid known as "Gee." At the time of 6 Group's first ops, it had become standard equipment throughout Bomber Command. The device relied on radio impulses transmitted from England by three stations situated one hundred miles apart on a "base line" two hundred miles long. Station A, the "Master," controlled the pulses from stations B and C, the "Slaves." Aboard the bomber, the navigator watched the cathode ray tube of his Gee box, noting how long pulses from B and C stations took to arrive. Then he pinpointed the intersection of the lines on a special grid superimposed on a map. In about a minute, he had determined his precise position.

Originally conceived as a blind-bombing device, Gee proved insufficiently accurate for that purpose. But it became an indispensable navigation aid, providing crews with excellent fixes up to three or four hundred miles from England. Beyond that range, its readings became progressively less accurate. Thus, the device could not normally be used with much confidence beyond the Ruhr. Moreover, since August 1942, the Germans had been jamming the system by sending radio signals interfering with its pulses. These radio countermeasures reduced the effective range of Gee to the Dutch coast. In response, the British introduced Gee Mark II which provided a short-term respite from the enemy's jamming. It came into service in February 1943 and by the end of March it equipped 60 per cent of Bomber Command's aircraft.[18]

When 6 Group became operational, its Wellingtons and Halifaxes were immediately pressed into service for mining sorties. The Wellington proved itself admirably suited to the task, being able to carry two Mark IV, 1,500-pound mines. The Halifax, despite its greater size and power, could do little better, because of the design of its bomb bay. Eventually, a mine was developed specifically for the Halifax, the Mark V, 1,000-pound model; the Halifax could accommodate four of them.

Gardening was a demanding business. The 1943-vintage mines had to be dropped from low level; if they fell too far, they broke up when they hit the water. The Canadian Group would eventually become Bomber Command's Gardening specialists.

Harris was furious. Just when the area-bombing campaign was about to begin in earnest, it had to be postponed. The RN again, damn them. Few bodies of men irked Harris more frequently and violently than their Lords of the Admiralty. Now they had succeeded in convincing Churchill that all available bombers should be employed to bomb the U-Boat bases "with the object of effectively devastating the whole area in which are located the submarines, their maintenance facilities and the services, power, water, light, communications, etc. and other resources upon which their operations depend." Lorient, St-Nazaire, Brest, and La Pallice were the bases named, with Lorient being a test target. If the raids against that port proved effective, the campaign would continue; if not, it would be cancelled.[19]

No one could dispute the importance of Lorient. Located in the Bay of Biscay, it provided the U-Boats with a haven well away from the dangerous waters around the British Isles. Lorient boasted concrete pens large enough to accommodate at least twenty U-Boats, plus drydocks, extensive stores of machinery, fuel, and all sorts of weapons, power facilities, railways, and barracks.[20] At this stage of the war, the U-Boats were still chalking up a horrifying toll of Allied shipping. Their bases were vital targets. But it was essential that they be bombed with little or no damage to the cities themselves or their inhabitants. When asked whether Bomber Command could do the job, Harris said no, emphatically. His crews had neither the equipment nor the training to hit individual targets in darkness. "Until we get the Mark XIV sight, we are virtually unable to do accurate bombing at night," he declared. "Therefore, as was evidenced in our attacks on Brest, about one bomb in five hundred aimed at the docks might hit a submarine or might hit one of the few workshops engaged in submarine repairs, if we are lucky. All the rest of the bombs would either go in the water or kill Frenchmen in the town."[21]

He advocated intensified sea-mining. The RN disagreed. Harris could scarcely contain his ire. A year earlier he had urged a series of attacks on the U-Boat bases which at that time were under construction. His recommendation had been ignored. But now that the enemy had succeeded in protecting their vessels with countless tons of concrete, the admirals wanted the job done.

On the night of January 14/15, 122 aircraft of Bomber Command took off to attack Lorient. Among them were fourteen aircraft from 6 Group, a combination of Halifaxes from 408 Squadron and Wellingtons from 426 Squadron. Two returned early for technical reasons. This was the first bombing operation undertaken by 6 Group, an event of some significance for Brookes and his staff at Castle Dismal: at last the Group was engaged in the task for which it had been created. While many of the crews involved had participated in bombing ops with other groups, for others it was the first, an important step in the career of every airman in Bomber Command. Galvanized by that disquieting combination of nervousness and eagerness that afflicted all "sprog" (freshmen) crews, they approached the target. Skippers did their best to sound confident as they ordered their gunners to watch out for fighters. Bomb-aimers settled down over their sights, frowning in concentration as they prepared for the task ahead. Apart from some smoke that drifted across their field of vision, visibility was reasonably good with only a little broken cloud.

The defences opened up. Flak was like a succession of electric lights snapping on and off in mid-air, the nearest ones emitting a dull "woof" that was just audible over the roar of the engines. A sharp stink of explosive. An occasional patter as spent fragments of flak hit the fuselage. Searchlights swept the night sky, towering columns of light that looked as if they would topple over but never did.

"Steady . . . left, left . . . right . . . steady. . . ."

Bombs gone!

The bombers bounded upward, relieved of the great weights in their bellies. Wide-eyed, the crews watched the dull red eruptions far below. *Their* bombs. Fires spread like a rash. To the sprogs on their first ops, it looked like hell down there. But when they got back to base, they listened as the experienced crews airily described the bombing as "somewhat scattered." At Leeming, Yorkshire, all 408 Squadron's Halifaxes returned safely, but a

Wellington of 426 Squadron, BK165, commanded by Pilot Officer George Milne, disappeared over the North Sea on the way home, its fate a mystery to this day.[22] More gear to be sorted and despatched, more letters to be written by the CO, Wing Commander S. S. Blanchard – who was himself destined to die on operations one month later.

Another 6 Group Squadron, 424, based at Topcliffe, had a frustrating evening. Initially the crews had expected to go on a Gardening operation. Briefed and fed, they zipped and buttoned themselves into their gear. Take-off had been planned for 2200 hours. But Group HQ ordered 424 to cancel its plans for mine-laying and join the bombing attack on Lorient. There followed one of those frenetic interludes that never received any publicity but were grindingly hard on everyone concerned. The armourers worked in the darkness at top speed to remove the sea mines and substitute high explosive bombs. They managed to complete their arduous and often dangerous work in time for the second aircrew briefing of the day. Now take-off was set for 2220 hours. The weather began to deteriorate. Local icing was reported. The planned op was cancelled. Frustrated, the crews clambered out of their aircraft and pulled off their flying togs. Having accomplished absolutely nothing, they could go to bed knowing that they would have to go through it all again the next night or the night after that.[23]

Between mid-January and early April 1943, Bomber Command mounted fourteen attacks on Lorient and St-Nazaire, a total of 3,170 sorties. Thirty-eight bombers didn't return, 1.19 per cent of those despatched. Nine more Bomber Command aircraft crashed in England on take-off or landing.[24] In comparison with later raids, the losses were minuscule. But so were the results. The raids failed utterly to interfere with the Germans' operations in any meaningful way. As far as is known, they resulted in the destruction of not a single U-Boat; neither did they cause significant damage to the submariners' vital services. Bomber Command succeeded only in destroying much of Lorient and St-Nazaire and in creating a seething backlash of hostility among the French citizens. Mercifully, the campaign was cancelled in April.

As far as Harris was concerned this was "one of the most

infuriating episodes in the whole course of the offensive." He points out in his memoirs that the U-Boat pens were the only worthwhile target in Lorient and St-Nazaire but "they were impervious to Bomber Command's current inventory of heavy bombs." It was, Harris said, a "hopeless misuse of air power on an operation which could not possibly achieve the object that was intended." He lamented the useless devastation of two "perfectly good French towns."[25]

The Canadian Bomber Group's first attack on Germany took place on January 15, a modest daylight incursion (known as a "Moling" operation) by half a dozen Wellingtons of 420 Squadron against Norden, north of Emden. The plan was to use cloud cover to conceal the bombers' approach. But the cloud began to break up en route. The sortie was cancelled and the bombers recalled. Five of the Wellingtons turned for home. The sixth did not receive the recall order and attacked the target alone. Remarkably, it survived the attentions of the defences and returned safely to base at Middleton St. George. On January 23, another Moling operation took place, this one against Esens, twenty miles northwest of Wilhelmshaven. Six Wellingtons were involved. All returned safely.

Not until January 30 did 6 Group lose any aircraft over Germany. The occasion was the tenth anniversary of Hitler's rise to power. On that day, Bomber Command sent a force of Wellingtons and Bostons to targets in Germany and Holland. It was yet another Moling operation, a daylight incursion, using cloud cover to keep out of sight of fighters and flak. The Canadian Bomber Group contributed eleven Wellingtons from 424, 425, 426, and 427 Squadrons. The target: Oldenburg. It was a disappointing day. Six of the eleven Canadian bombers returned early because of lack of cloud cover; three others failed to find their primary targets and bombed alternatives. One of the many American airmen in the RCAF at that period, Pilot Officer Sidney Leon Murrell of Gainesville, Texas, bombed Westerstede, northwest of the target from an altitude of only 2,000 feet. His Wellington had been attacked by a German fighter en route to the secondary target. On the way home, two Me 109s tried for fifteen minutes to shoot the Wimpy down. Murrell's gunners fought back, forcing one of the fighters to break off. The second fighter eventually followed his comrade with "smoke pouring from the fuselage." Aboard the Wimpy, cannon shells had started a fire behind the navigator's seat but the crew put it out. Murrell landed safely in England and later became the recipient of the Distinguished Flying Cross (DFC), 6 Group's first – and the first to be won by an American – for his "keenness, determination and fine fighting spirit."[26]

The day's operations cost two 6 Group Wellingtons and their crews. One was flown by Pilot Officer C.J. Bennett of 427 Squadron, the other by Flight Lieutenant R.H. Lowe of 426 Squadron. The last message received from Lowe, an SOS at 1629 hours, reported that he had to "ditch" (alight on the sea). A radio fix indicated that the message had been transmitted over Heligoland. One of 425 Squadron's crews reported having seen two German fighters attacking a Wellington in that area. It seems likely that it was Lowe's aircraft. His loss was serious; an experienced skipper and a deputy flight commander, he had no fewer than fifty-six ops to his credit. Flying Officer G.D. Fitzgibbon, the wireless operator/air gunner, had completed thirty-six ops. Also aboard the ill-fated aircraft was 426's navigation leader, Flight Lieutenant A.T. Sprosen.[27]

The beginning of February saw 6 Group's participation in an unsuccessful attack on Hamburg by 263 Bomber Command aircraft. Forty-six Canadian aircraft took off on the night of February 3/4. But more than half of them – twenty-five aircraft in all – turned back before reaching the target. The aircrews couldn't be blamed. Over the North Sea, icing conditions became dangerous. Only nineteen 6 Group bombers reached Hamburg – to be confronted by ten/tenths cloud with tops as high as 18,000 feet. The crews dropped their bombs on the Pathfinders' skymarkers and crews reported the glow of fires "seen through cloud." But the German night fighters shot down sixteen, more than 6 per cent of the force. Two 6 Group Halifaxes were numbered among the casualties, one from 408 Squadron, another from 419 Squadron.

The following night, 6 Group visited Italy for the first time. Fifteen Canadian aircraft joined 173 RAF bombers in an attack on the Fiat works at Turin. Returning crews reported large fires; in the exceptionally clear conditions they could be seen many miles away. The raid resulted in "serious and widespread" damage to the target as well as twenty-nine deaths and fifty-three injuries among the citizens. The Canadian Group's Operations Record Book (ORB) described the results as "very satisfactory" with "well concentrated" bombing and many fires and explosions. An unidentified Halifax pilot commented vividly: "It was just like somebody swishing a white paint brush up and down the town and criss-crossing the area with parallel lines. The white lines of fire slowly turned to red as the fires took hold, and among them were the flashes of high explosive bombs."

The crews encountered irresolute opposition. Crews thought the flak batteries more numerous than on the last attack in December 1942, but "not up to the German standard"; the Italian crews handled the guns "with little skill." The raid cost Bomber Command three Lancasters, but no 6 Group aircraft were lost.[28]

On the night of February 14/15, Bomber Command mounted an attack by 243 aircraft on Cologne. Fifty-five bombers from 6 Group joined the force in this unsuccessful raid. One didn't return, a Wellington of 426 Squadron flown by the highly regarded CO, Wing Commander S.S. Blanchard. Blanchard "had built up his squadron to an efficient unit, and had won the respect and admiration of all" in his four months of command. His replacement was an RAF officer, Wing Commander Leslie Crooks, who would himself die on operations the following August.[29]

Later in the month, on the night of February 24/25, 6 Group mounted its largest raid of this period. The target was Wilhelmshaven. A force of 338 aircraft attacked the city; 6 Group contributed ninety-eight bombers: twenty-seven Halifaxes and seventy-one Wellingtons. The operation failed. Thick cloud completely obscured the target. The Pathfinders' skymarkers "quickly disappeared," according to crew reports. The raid was categorized as "minor" by city officials, inflicting little damage and slight injuries on three people. The Canadian Group suffered no losses that night.[30]

Interestingly, many crews rated the raid as quite successful, reporting fires and considerable damage, presumably observed through gaps in the cloud. But how accurate were the crews' reports? How accurate *could* they be? From twenty thousand feet one fire looks very much like another. If crews took decoy fires to be the genuine article, it was hardly surprising. At night, with flares and searchlights dazzling them, with smoke and clouds obscuring vision, with everyone constantly on the lookout for enemy fighters, conditions for detailed observation could hardly be worse.

Back at Dishforth after the Wilhelmshaven raid, an aircraft landed with a bomb hung up in the bomb bay due to a malfunction of the electrical release switch. The moment the aircraft touched down, the 500-pound bomb broke free and went bouncing across the airfield. The disposal squad dealt with the errant missile, but the process took so long that the Gardening sorties scheduled for that evening had to be cancelled – or "scrubbed," in the parlance of the day.[31]

On the night of March 1/2 the target was Berlin. The Canadian Group contributed twenty-two Halifaxes from 408 and 419 Squadrons to a force of over three hundred. Bomber Command rated this raid as only partially successful, although the crews of the fourteen 6 Group aircraft that bombed the German capital reported "huge fires" in the target area; they considered the operation "a great success." The Canadians lost two aircraft; Bomber Command as a whole lost seventeen, more than 5 per cent of the force. At that stage of the war, Bomber Command considered 3 per cent losses "acceptable"; the training units and factories could quickly make them good.

During the period from January 1 to March 4, 1943, 6 Group mounted seventeen mine-laying operations, losing thirteen aircraft: four Halifaxes from 408 and 419 Squadrons and nine Wellingtons from 420, 424, 425, 426, and 427 Squadrons. The Group attacked Lorient nine times and St-Nazaire once. The ten operations cost eleven aircraft and their crews: two Halifaxes from 408 Squadron and nine Wellingtons from 420, 424, 425, 426, and 427 Squadrons. The latter was the hardest hit with five aircraft missing.

Attacks on Germany in the same period resulted in the loss of thirteen aircraft: two Halifaxes from 408 and one from 419, plus ten Wellingtons, from 420, 425, 426, and 427 Squadrons. 426 Squadron was the unlucky unit, losing four.

In total, however, the Canadian Bomber Group's casualties had been light during its first two months of operations. Far less satisfactory were the Group's records of serviceability and early returns. In January, an average of 64 per cent of the Group's aircraft were ready for operations on any given day, a far from impressive figure. But in February the rate was even worse, a mere 59 per cent.[32] The statistics detailing 6 Group's serviceability, flying accidents, and early returns and losses would make increasingly depressing reading in the months to come, causing a crisis in confidence at Castle Dismal – and at Bomber Command HQ, High Wycombe.

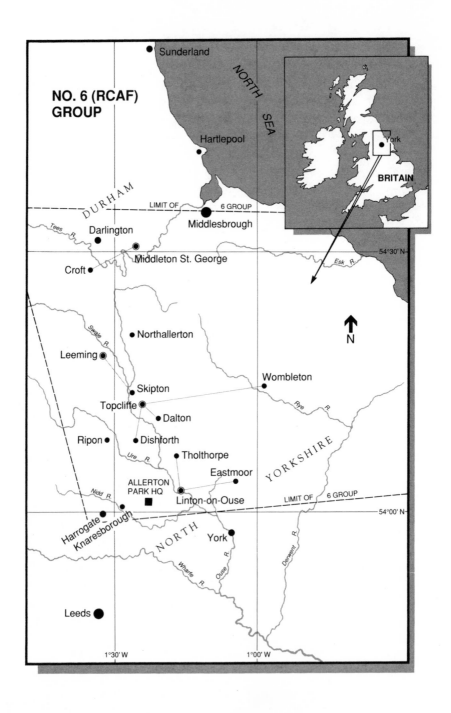

NO. 6 (RCAF)
GROUP

Sunderland

NORTH SEA

York

BRITAIN

DURHAM

LIMIT OF   6 GROUP

Tees R.

Darlington

Middlesbrough

Hartlepool

54°30' N

Middleton St. George

Croft

Esk R.

Swale R.

Northallerton

N

Leeming

Wombleton

Skipton

Topcliffe

Rye R.

Dalton

Ripon

Dishforth

Tholthorpe

Ure R.

YORKSHIRE

Eastmoor

ALLERTON
PARK HQ

Linton-on-Ouse

LIMIT OF   6 GROUP

Nidd R.

54°00' N

Harrogate
Knaresborough

NORTH

York

Wharfe R.

Ouse R.

Derwent R.

Leeds

1°30' W   1°00' W

2

PATRIOTISM AND PARSIMONY

"The hangar exploded into a roar of boos. Startled, I turned to ask, 'Who is this guy?' . . . Finally a groundcrew flight sergeant enlightened me. 'It's Mackenzie King,' he said."[1]

J. Douglas Harvey, DFC, pilot, 408 Squadron

Credit for the creation of 6 Group has to go to one of the oddest, most contradictory individuals ever to occupy public office in Canada. In turn a bore and a wit, astute politician and eccentric mystic, William Lyon Mackenzie King occupied the prime minister's residence for close to a quarter-century, from 1921 to 1926, again from 1926 to 1930, and from 1935 to 1948. An ardent patriot who became a sycophant in the presence of British royalty and American presidents, a spiritualist who regularly discussed his problems with his dead mother and his equally dead pet terriers, a trencherman and a connoisseur, he manipulated colleagues and enemies alike with Machiavellian skill. A lifelong bachelor, he kept falling in and out of love with a bewildering variety of women, most of them married. It was his unshakable conviction that he had been chosen by the Almighty to save Canada from its many enemies both within and without – just as it was the un-shakeable conviction of many of his fellow members of Parliament that he should have occupied a psychiatric ward, not the PM's residence. A puzzle, King, a survivor, an individual who craved power as others crave wealth, a numbingly tedious speaker who would probably never have achieved public office if he had had to make a speech in front of a television camera. This was the unlikely author of a formation unique in the annals of Bomber Command and the RCAF. King himself had little interest in things aeronautical. He saw 6 Group as he saw everything else, in political terms. The creation of the Canadian Bomber Group was the solution to a pesky problem.

In the late Thirties, as the world drifted inexorably towards war, King pondered long and hard. What role would Canada play in the coming conflict? What would be the best way to support Britain, the Mother Country? He remembered all too well the Canadian Corps' ghastly casualties in the Great War. And the conscription crisis of 1917, that monumental political nightmare that threatened the very substance of Canada. The crisis polarized public opinion as never before in the country's fifty-year history. In the simplest possible terms, English Canadians favoured conscription; French Canadians didn't. The bitter arguments and animosity resulted in a schism that hadn't healed by the outbreak of World War II.

The more King thought about it, the more he liked the idea of focusing most of Canada's war effort on the air force. As he saw it, the RCAF would remain a volunteer force principally involved in training aircrew in Canada, with a relatively small contingent serving overseas. Casualties would surely be light. So there would be no pressure to introduce conscription, with all its nightmarish political implications.[2] It seemed to be a politically astute solution to a complex problem.

But not for long. In the 1943/44 period, the Canadian rifle companies in Italy and Northwest Europe suffered crippling casualties. Half-trained men had to make up the gaps in the line.

Wounded men found themselves back in action before they had fully recovered. The shortage of properly trained troops exploded into a national scandal. In its wake, like a ghastly spectre from the past, the conscription crisis of 1944 emerged to haunt King, and it proved just as divisive as its ancestor of twenty-seven years before. What's more, the losses of aircrew in the European theatre – primarily those in Bomber Command – proved to be far heavier than King and his advisers had ever thought possible. Of approximately thirty thousand Canadian war dead, about half were RCAF personnel; two-thirds of these died while flying with Bomber Command, 4,272 being killed while with 6 Group.[3]

But all that was far in the future. In 1939, the Canadian government had embarked upon the acrimonious and tortuous wranglings that led eventually to the creation of the British Commonwealth Air Training Plan (BCATP) – "The Plan." When these negotiations began on October 31, the British and Canadian governments approached the table with quite different views about how the RCAF should be employed. The Riverdale Mission, headed by British industrialist Lord Riverdale, saw the RCAF as a convenient manpower pool for the RAF. Riverdale seems to have been guilty of monumental insensitivity, imperiously taking for granted that the Canadians would, *of course*, be willing to go along with whatever Britain asked. Mackenzie King testily scribbled in his famous diary: "It is amazing how these people have come out from the Old Country and seem to think that all they have to do is tell us what is to be done. No wonder they get the backs of people up on this side."[4]

King set out to convince the British negotiators that Canada was talking about rendering *voluntary* aid, not fulfilling some obligation to its suzerain. Although Canadians might serve in RAF squadrons, he vowed that there should be an *identifiable* Canadian presence in the Allied air armada.

Thus was born the policy that came to be known as "Canadianization." It was enshrined in Article XV of the BCATP Agreement[5] – although the interpretation of the Article would lead to such bickering that it nearly resulted in the premature demise of The Plan as a whole. Money was the problem. Who was to pay the airmen in the RCAF squadrons serving in RAF groups overseas? King had already stated that Canada would bear the cost of a complete RCAF contingent overseas.[6] But he felt differently about the so-called Article XV squadrons. As they were operating under RAF control, they should be paid for by the British, he asserted. To King, a balanced budget was a sacred trust and minor events like Great Depressions and World Wars were no excuse for red ink. He was horrified by the way the costs of The Plan kept escalating.[7] When the training plan had first been proposed, the aim had been to train two thousand pilots a year plus "as many observers and air gunners as possible."[8] Under the expanded plan suggested by the Canadian and Australian High Commissioners to Britain, Vincent Massey and Stanley Bruce, a yearly minimum of thirty thousand aircrew, including twenty thousand pilots, would be trained in Canada.[9] The Canadian share, some $350 million over three years, was awful enough – but *another* $750 million for the upkeep of those Article XV squadrons? No, it was far too much for King to swallow in Canada's pre-Keynesian era.[10]

Thus, the conflict between King's patriotism and his fiscal caution set the stage for 6 Group's problems three years later. Despite all King's much-vaunted political acumen, he placed his own side in a no-win position. The British Chancellor of the Exchequer, Sir John Simon, proposed the designation of certain RAF squadrons as "Canadian." RCAF aircrew would be posted to such units as they were trained, but most of the ground crew would be RAF. Simon preferred not to ask Canada to contribute more than the $350 million already agreed on for the BCATP; yet he was equally reluctant to abandon Britain's position that the Dominions should pay for the upkeep of their squadrons overseas.

Although the bargaining became heated at times, the negotiators eventually came up with a compromise. The Canadian government would limit the number of Article XV squadrons to match the Canadian contribution to the BCATP.[11] The delegates heaved sighs of relief. Not until later did the Canadians discover that they had been outmanoeuvred. They had lost almost every vestige of control over their own squadrons. Their only victory, if it can be so described, was that Britain "recognized" Canada's right to form an RCAF contingent overseas.

While the talks dragged on, Canadians were already flying and fighting with the RAF. They were the young men who had enlisted in the RAF before the war. Most had previously tried to join the RCAF, a tiny, stiflingly exclusive club in which everyone knew everyone else and to which only the most overqualified had the slightest chance of gaining entry. Just before the war, the RCAF possessed a grand total of twenty-nine aircraft that could be described as modern: nineteen Hawker Hurricane fighters and ten Fairey Battle light bombers. The rest of Canada's air force, a motley collection of such types as the Atlas, the Wapiti, the Siskin, and the Stranraer, wouldn't have looked out of place on the Western Front twenty years before.

In mid-1941, more talks took place between the hard-drinking, card-playing C.G. "Chubby" Power,[12] the Canadian minister of national defence for air, and H.H. Balfour, the British under-secretary of state for air. Power's visit to Britain represented yet another Canadian attempt to gain a reasonable measure of control over Canadian airmen overseas. Among the issues Power brought up were the provision of ground crews for the Article XV squadrons and the formation of the Canadian bomber organization that would eventually become 6 Group. The first matter was soon dealt with; Canada offered to send one thousand ground personnel to man the Article XV squadrons.[13] But the creation of a bomber group posed more difficult questions. So, although the delegates agreed in principle to set up a group, for the moment it was decided simply to increase the size of bomber squadrons from the then-current sixteen aircraft per squadron to twenty-four, with no new squadrons to be formed until all existing units had been brought up to strength.[14]

Meanwhile, Canadian graduates of the BCATP were arriving overseas in significant numbers. The formation of the first four Article XV squadrons proceeded in 1941: 405 Squadron in April, 408 in June, 419 and 420 in December. To 405 Squadron went the distinction of carrying out the first raid by a Canadian bomber squadron in World War II, the operation against Schwerte in June 1941. The Hampdens of 408 Squadron went into action in August of that year with a raid on the dockyards at Rotterdam.

In May/June 1942, at the Ottawa Air Training Conference, the British and Canadian delegates agreed on the formation of ten more RCAF squadrons. In addition, the Canadian government at last declared its willingness to pay the salaries and benefits of all RCAF personnel overseas. What's more, the delegates agreed that the Canadian Bomber Group should be formed as soon as possible.

Balfour informed Sir Archibald Sinclair, British secretary of state for air, that "there is a big drive for general Canadianization. In fact the Minister [Power] said today that the ideal they [the Canadians] aimed at was a separate Air Force organization operated comparable to that of the Americans . . . I believe we shall be able to surmount Canadianization difficulties, meeting them on many minor points, but giving away nothing in principle if we act swiftly."[15]

What irritated the British was that the Canadians were insisting on the formation of 6 Group in spite of the fact that, as yet, only four RCAF bomber squadrons had come into being and there seemed little chance of forming any more until the end of 1942. One can sense – and perhaps sympathize with – the impatience of the British. Didn't they have enough problems? Disasters on every front. Bad news by the acre in every newspaper. Strident demands from the Soviets for a Second Front and for equipment of every kind. Chilling losses of shipping in the Atlantic. Endless technical difficulties with the new four-engined bombers. And now . . . the Canadians, *demanding* this, *insisting* on that. Things were a damned sight simpler when Dominions were colonies and knew their place.

Eventually, however, the negotiators agreed that the four RCAF bomber squadrons already operational, 405, 408, 419, and 420, would be located in the same RAF group, stationed in close proximity to one another. As new RCAF bomber squadrons were formed, they would be posted to the same group. In addition, RCAF officers were to be "double-banked" at RAF groups, observers who would learn the workings of a group and be ready to take over when the Canadian Group at last came into being.[16]

There is no doubt that Canadianization took a major step forward with the Ottawa Air Training Conference. But it left the RCAF far short of the autonomy envisioned early in September 1939 when the two governments agreed in principle to the formation of a Canadian-funded RCAF contingent overseas.

Harris objected to the proposed addition of as many as ten new Canadian squadrons by year-end. He referred to the Canadian airmen as "good crews" but considered that the current expansion policy would give credence to allegations apparently rife in the United States at the time that the Mother Country was "fighting with the bodies of Colonial and Dominion personnel in preference to British." In Harris's view, the addition of ten new RCAF squadrons would give Canada a disproportionate number in Bomber Command.[17]

The Air Ministry didn't agree, pointing out that, in addition to the seventeen squadrons scheduled for creation in Bomber Command between June and December 1942, another twenty-six squadrons – none of them RCAF – would be formed in other Commands and overseas. Also, if the acceptable proportion of the RCAF element under Harris was calculated according to the number of aircrew personnel instead of squadrons (only 9.8 per cent RCAF), then the RCAF was actually *under*-represented: 25 per cent RCAF to 65 per cent RAF aircrew. As it happened, external circumstances made the discussion academic. The Americans failed to supply aircraft in the numbers originally promised; as a result, Bomber Command had to trim its expansion plans by 22 per cent. The RCAF had little choice but to reduce its own plans accordingly. Now there would be seven instead of ten new squadrons. The formation of 6 Group would not be delayed, however. It was decreed that the five existing squadrons and the seven new units would constitute a force large enough to be an efficient group.[18]

By the end of October 1942, 408 and 419 Squadrons had become operational; the former was trading its twin-engined Hampdens for Halifaxes; and 424 was in the process of being formed at Topcliffe, Yorkshire. At Skipton-on-Swale, 420 Squadron was also replacing Hampdens, with Wellington IIIs. Two more squadrons, 425 and 426, had been formed at Dishforth; both would fly Wellingtons until mid-1943. In November, three more squadrons, 427, 428, and 429, were formed on Wellingtons at Croft, Dalton, and East Moor respectively. A further two squadrons had been planned for December, but only one materialized, 431 Squadron, which flew Wellington Xs from Burn, Yorkshire, until moving to Tholthorpe in mid-1943.

The units were in place. The politicians were happy. They could point to a signal achievement, the creation of the first non-British group in Bomber Command. What better proof of Canada's emerging power? What more cogent answer to all those who carped about Canada's subservience to Britain?

But it's one thing to type up a list of squadrons and call it a group, another to send them into battle. Too many of the units had been formed in haste. They would be thrust into action when the air war was reaching a pitch of ferocity that no one could have imagined a year before. The new 6 Group squadrons weren't ready. The airmen would pay for the politicians' haste.

In Liverpool and Greenock, the ships kept arriving and disgorging their cargoes of airmen, usually accompanied by even larger cargoes of troops, Canadian and American. For most of the young Canadian airmen, this was a fabulous adventure, a trip to Europe at someone else's expense! For many, it was the first time they had travelled out of Canada. Volunteers to a man, they were of the generation that used to be referred to as "air-minded" – which usually meant that they could tell the difference between a Hurricane and a Heinkel and could talk at length about the exploits of Canada's Great War hero, Billy Bishop, now an air vice-marshal. They had sat on the edge of their seats while *Dawn Patrol* and *Hell's Angels* flickered across the movie screen. They had devoured the aviation pulps of the period: *Battle Aces*, *Sky Riders*, *Air Stories*, all of which, for a mere twenty cents a copy, regaled their readers with the exciting if improbable exploits of Buzz Benson, Carbunkle Pinkham, and other fabulously skilled and intrepid fictional aviators of the period.

But before enlisting, remarkably few of those air-minded young Canadians had been inside an airplane, let alone up in one. Not until 1937 did the country have its national air carrier, Trans-Canada Airlines. In those days, the cost of air travel placed it far beyond the reach of ordinary Canadians. Only tycoons and movie stars could afford it. If you wanted to fly from Montreal to Vancouver and back, TCA would be glad to oblige – for a staggering $225, two to three months' wages for the average worker, if he was lucky enough to be working. The Great Depression still held the country in its cruel grip. Even those lucky Canadians with jobs had little money to spare for luxuries like air travel. For as long as most of the RCAF's recruits could remember, the talk had been of bread lines and pogey, Bennett Buggies (engineless autos drawn by horses), and tumbling wheat prices.

Then came war. The famous BCATP – known in Britain to this day as the Empire Air Training Scheme – started in a small way, at the half-dozen RCAF airfields then in existence. Simultaneously, construction began on scores of new fields: Boundary Bay, High River, North Battleford, Neepawa, Mont Joli, Debert *et al.* The students poured in: British, Australians, Americans, New Zealanders, Norwegians, French, Belgians. On those small fields, most of them miles from the nearest town, they learned their craft.

The first students of The Plan trained under appalling conditions. Most of the airfields were still under construction. Bulldozers and graders tortured the terrain until it looked like No Man's Land. In the prairie provinces, the fine-grained silty soil reacted with moisture to become a devilish substance called gumbo. It had a rubbery consistency. It stuck to boots with extraordinary tenacity. And once firmly established, it seemed to breed. In no time at all, a bit of gumbo on a boot could become a ten-pound load on each foot.

The cooks had no kitchens, the MOs had no dispensaries, the latrines had no toilets. There were no lights. Or running water. No one had the right nuts and bolts to assemble the crated Ansons and Battles that had been shipped over from Britain, because British and North American screw threads weren't interchangeable. But the training went on anyway.

For the most part, the aircraft initially used for elementary training were biplanes, Tiger Moths and Fleet Finches, both manufactured in Canada. To supplement the domestic supply of aircraft, the Americans sent Fairchild Cornell monoplanes and Stearman biplanes, Harvard advanced trainers, as well as twin-engined Cranes. There were some odd birds too: the Yale, a trainer similar in appearance to a Harvard but possessing a fixed gear, and the Hawk, a radial-engined fighter. Both types had been ordered by the French, then sent to Canada in 1940. The BCATP people were glad to have them even if their instruments were in metric and their throttles were set up the Continental way, i.e., backward to increase power, forward to cut power, the opposite of the North American and British systems. Curiously, none of the instructors or students experienced much trouble with the unfamiliar controls.

The majority of aircrew volunteers wanted to be pilots – *fighter* pilots. Secretly, every one fancied himself as another Billy Bishop. The name was still one to be reckoned with. The great man himself frequently officiated at "wings" ceremonies, where students received their aircrew badges. Chester Hull, later to become CO of 428 Squadron and a post-war general in the Canadian Armed Forces, had his wings pinned on by Bishop. A plump, avuncular man with a jolly smile, Bishop was the RCAF's public relations figurehead. Doug Scanlan, a bomb-aimer who later flew a tour with 415 Squadron of 6 Group, recalls the hero's words to a graduating class about to go overseas. In his engaging way, Bishop told the fledgling airmen that it was their duty to kill the enemy, but there was no need to hate him; the enemy was just doing his job as they were doing theirs.

Most aircrew volunteers would not become pilots, however. And the majority of those selected for pilot training would not become fighter pilots. From 1942 on, the need was for bomber crews. Many hundreds would find their way to the squadrons of 6 Group.

An aircrew selection board consisted of two or three officers. They decided whether a man's destiny was in the clouds or on terra firma. And they had no time to waste. Should the hopeful recruit fail to impress those stern-visaged officers within a few minutes, he had, in the vernacular of the day, had it. He didn't get a second chance.

Successful candidates wore white flashes in their wedge caps, a badge almost as cherished as aircrew wings themselves. But many a self-satisfied wearer of the white aircrew-trainee flash discovered to his dismay that the girls in town actually seemed to be *avoiding* him! Only later did trainees learn that ground staff were in the habit of letting it be known locally that the white flashes were a means of identifying servicemen who had contracted VD!

Student pilots found themselves on an assembly line. You conformed to the required pattern or you were out. With pilots, the training process lasted anywhere from twenty-five to fifty weeks. In the early days, a pilot might be on operations within six to nine months of starting his training. Later, the average was closer to eighteen months. It all began at a manning depot with a succession of interviews, lectures, tests, and countless hours of drilling. Then an hour or two was spent in the Link trainer, the 1940s' version of today's simulators. If the pupil showed little aptitude for coordinating its controls, his chances of becoming a pilot had usually shrivelled and vanished before he had even climbed out of the contraption.

Pilot trainees met real airplanes face to face at Elementary Flying Training School (EFTS), although the diminutive biplanes with open cockpits and fixed landing gear were a far cry from the Spitfires everyone wanted to fly. But they were adequate for the task at hand: teaching students the mysteries of heavier-than-air flight, making them comprehend how the stick and rudder pedals could combine to tame the bewildering barrage of forces that kept trying to make the little craft do anything but what you wanted it to do. It was a little like learning to ride a bicycle all over again, only in three dimensions, none of which was solid. The instructors explained it all: drag and lift, longitudinal stability, angle of incidence, stalling, spinning, side-slipping: why they happened, what you were supposed to do about them. In the classroom, it all made sense. But it was only when you found yourself up there, squeezed into that knot-hole of a cockpit, trussed up in flying gear, being blasted by hurricane-force winds, deafened by a clattering motor a couple of feet away, feeling the wilful little airplane wandering off to one side or the other, its wing inexplicably sagging, its nose for some reason on the rise, that you really found out once and for all whether you could fly. On average, one pupil in four washed out during elementary flying training. Some cried openly when they heard the news. But instructors seldom changed their minds; they knew that letting a borderline case slip through would probably jeopardize someone else's life six months or a year down the line.

At Service Flying Training School (SFTS), the trainees progressed to bigger, more powerful trainers, often Harvards for those selected as fighter pilots, Oxfords or Cranes for those headed for multi-engined futures. But a posting to a Harvard school was no guarantee that you would end up on Spitfires. The air force's increasingly rapacious appetite for bomber crews led to many a Harvard-trained pilot finding himself learning to fly multi-engined aircraft when he arrived overseas.

Students came to know the BCATP's aircraft intimately – and to love them or loathe them. Every type had its own personality. The ubiquitous Canadian-built Tiger Moths, Finches, and Fawns were aptly named, fluttery little things, light, with lots of wing which made them tricky in windy weather. They had to be *flown* constantly. The Tiger Moth had a fuel tank perched on the centre section struts immediately above the front cockpit. If you turned a Tiger over on the ground – and plenty of students did – you might observe the struts piercing the tank and fuel splashing over the hot engine, and you. Other elementary trainers were American-built: the Stearman biplane, an attractive and pleasant aircraft to fly although possessing something of a reputation for ground-looping, and the Fairchild Cornell, a low-wing monoplane of handsome appearance but widely believed among the students to be structurally unsound. The Harvards could be spiteful; at low speeds they sometimes dropped a wing and snapped into a spin. If you could handle a Harvard you could progress to high-performance, awesomely powerful fighters. The twin-engined Ansons were incredibly docile, the Oxfords and Cranes less so, which was just as well, for multi-engine students would soon graduate to far more demanding equipment.

Students destined to become navigators learned the basics of their demanding trade at Initial Training School (ITS). Later, at Air Observer School (AOS), they went on interminable "cross-countries," attempting to find their way about by "dead reckoning" (from deduced reckoning). In theory nothing could be simpler – a piece of cake. You plotted your course on a map, calculated your speed, applied a wind factor, and off you went. But as the instructors pointed out, on ops it was seldom that easy. Compasses and airspeed indicators were only *relatively* accurate instruments; furthermore, only the most experienced pilots were capable of flying really accurate courses. Add to this the fact that the wind had an annoying habit of changing direction and speed just after take-off, and mix in a few diversions that might be necessary to avoid enemy action, not forgetting of course that once overseas it would all have to be done in total darkness, over intensely hostile enemy territory. Hardly surprising, then, all those stories of sprog crews getting hopelessly lost on their first ops. Radio bearings from ground stations could be useful, although they were vulnerable to interference by bad weather and the enemy. Astro-navigation was another system then in use. All bombers had transparent astro domes from which navigators could use their sextants to obtain sightings. But it took an experienced and skilled navigator to calculate his position accurately from the stars. And sextant sightings took time. Once you had completed the many calculations involved, you might have flown as much as a hundred miles from where you figured you were.

During his training, the student navigator spent sixty or seventy hours in the air, rapidly learning what a world of difference existed between plotting courses in comfortable, *static* classrooms and in bouncing, swaying, deafening aircraft. A remarkably large proportion of student navigators suffered from air sickness. Many never managed to rid themselves of the problem throughout their air force careers. Gallantly, they went out on ops night after night, quietly vomiting into paper bags, going back to their calculations, never complaining.

Of the thirty-seven graduates from the first AOS of The Plan, the majority went to Bomber Command. Two out of three were killed on operations.

Early in the war, the navigator/observer was responsible not only for finding the target but also for dropping bombs on it. It soon became obvious that wartime navigation was a full-time job. So a new aircrew category came into being, that of air bomber, more commonly referred to as bomb-aimer, the man responsible for what was the point of the whole business: getting the bombs on the target. The first British bomb sights had been notoriously inadequate, but from mid-1943 on, the Mark XIV sight took over. It was an efficient sight, an airborne computer that took essential data and decided the moment at which the bombs should be dropped. The bomb-aimer provided the wind direction and speed, the terminal velocity of the bombs being dropped, the aircraft's air speed, its course and height, as well as the target's height and the sighting angle. In addition to dropping the bombs, he assisted the navigator by map-reading and operating various items of radar equipment.

Before 1942, the training of wireless operators and air gunners had been somewhat haphazard. Many of these tradesmen went overseas never having laid eyes on the equipment they would use on ops. Later, however, they received twenty-eight weeks of wireless and six weeks of gunnery training.

Until late in the war, the flight engineers in 6 Group came principally from the RAF. When the Flight Engineers' School (FES) finally opened at Aylmer, Ontario, it graduated nearly two thousand flight engineers, all of whom went to 6 Group.

The BCATP was undoubtedly one of the major accomplishments of World War II. Without it, the air war might not have been won. Producing 131,553 aircrew, the Plan cost more than two billion dollars. Of this, Canada paid about $1.6 billion, the United Kingdom paid $54 million and supplied equipment worth another $162 million, Australia paid $65 million, and New Zealand contributed $48 million. The rest was provided by the American Lend-Lease Act of 1941, which gave the president the power to sell, transfer, lend, or lease necessary war supplies to nations important to the defence of the United States.[19]

Few airmen missed the opportunity of having themselves photographed within hours of receiving their brand-new aircrew wings. They had graduated. They were ready for the serious business of war. Almost. There still existed the possibility of the powers-that-be deciding that this man or that would make a good instructor. The excitement and dangers of overseas or a steady, relatively safe job, probably for the duration? The vast majority prayed for overseas. It was, after all, the reason they had enlisted in the first place. They shook hands with the unlucky ones who had to stay, promising to keep in touch, saying they expected to see them "over there" before long. They had their embarkation leave, kissed mothers, daughters, aunts, nieces, and girlfriends and told them not to worry. *It* would always happen to the other guy. They hoped.

Wartime Britain was a world of blackouts, air raid shelters, shortages, queues, sandbagged doorways, taped windows, posters talking about saving food, posters talking about not travelling unnecessarily, posters talking about not talking. For the Canadian airmen, it was simultaneously exciting and, yes, just a trifle disillusioning. They had expected plucky little Britain to look a bit more *battered*. Hadn't the press at home churned out reams of copy about the brutal punishment being inflicted on the diminutive island? Whole towns reduced to rubble. Untold numbers of families forced to sleep in air raid shelters or subway stations. Yet the fact was, the majority of places looked downright *normal*. It was only in the big cities that you saw real damage. And even there, it seemed to be less extensive than the papers had led you to believe. Coventry was still *there*, nine-tenths of it, yet most Canadians at home believed it had been wiped off the map.

The arrival times of batches of Canadian airmen were supposed to be top secret. The airmen themselves were repeatedly lectured about the absolute necessity for security. Ed Moore, from Edson, Alberta, a bomb-aimer who later flew with 426 Squadron, arrived in Britain early in 1943. After being warned once more not to let anyone know that he had just landed, Moore went to a welcome party. "Our hosts had assembled a very presentable group of young ladies to greet us," he writes. "Late in the evening, Lord and Lady Liverhue, our hosts, gave us a welcome speech starting with . . . 'Since this is your first day in England, we are. . . .'"

Many of the Canadians expected to be shipped immediately to operational squadrons. Instead they found themselves in a south coast seaside resort town called Bournemouth. The climate was mild and the female company quite captivating, although the competition was fierce with so many airmen on the loose. Comfortably ensconced in the town's best hotels, the Canadians enjoyed excellent service and meals as good as strict rationing would permit. The only snag was, there was nothing to do but wait. Bournemouth, the airmen discovered, was a sort of reservoir in the aircrew production line. Here fresh supplies of pilots, navigators, bomb-aimers, wireless operators, and air gunners were literally stockpiled until needed. It was a pleasant interlude, a paid vacation, spoiled only by an irrational impatience to get on with whatever fate had in store. Bournemouth had its dangers, however. From time to time German raiders, usually Me 109s and Fw 190s, would come streaking at wave-top level across the Channel to lob their 250 kg bombs into the town and blaze away with cannon and machine guns before turning tail and heading for home. The careers of more than a few Canadian airmen ended suddenly and violently in Bournemouth.

Some Canadians stayed in Bournemouth for weeks, even months. Joe Widdis, a bomb-aimer who would later join 429 Squadron, remembers: "At Bournemouth we were housed in a very nice hotel . . . We were there about two months doing nothing which seemed a terrible waste of our time." Jim Gunn, a navigator who joined 428 Squadron, was there even longer, remembering "three glorious months in Bournemouth." Some began to believe that their names had been lost in the shuffle. No such luck. Inevitably the orders arrived. It was time to move on. Time to discover how much you still had to learn before you were ready to fly on ops.

First AFU, the Advanced Flying Unit. Here the Oxfords with camouflaged upper surfaces and yellow undersides waited to take the Canadians on their first flights in wartime Britain, usually in mist and rain with visibility that was appalling, far below the minimums permitted in Canada. There were lectures, too. About wireless procedures. About balloon barrages. About Pundits and Occults – navigation aids – and a hundred other mysteries never encountered in the friendly skies of Canada.

After AFU came OTU, the Operational Training Unit, where in subtle but important ways, every airman ceased to be an individual and began to think of himself as part of a crew. The creation of the crew was a significant moment in any airman's career. Recognizing this, the authorities showed rare good sense and left the crewing-up process largely in the hands of the airmen themselves. In most cases, it was as simple as ushering groups of pilots, navigators, bomb-aimers, wireless operators, and air gunners into a large room, often a hangar, and telling them to "get on with it."

There followed a curious ritual: young airmen standing in awkward clusters, trying not to glance too closely at one another, yet attempting to do precisely that. Some of the bolder types simply selected crew members by the look of them, relying totally on first impressions. It was as good a method as any. Steve Puskas of Hamilton, Ontario, a pilot who later served with 429 Squadron, recalls the rite vividly. At his OTU, five pilots were introduced to five navigators. All the navigators were officers. But only two

pilots, not including Puskas, were commissioned. Feeling somewhat self-conscious, Puskas asked the nearest navigator if he
wanted to "crew up." The man shook his head; no, he was thinking of flying with *him*, he said, indicating another pilot. Puskas
waited until all the other airmen had crewed up; he discovered
that Jasper Still, the navigator with whom he had conversed,
remained unattached. "His" pilot had teamed up with another
navigator. So Still and Puskas joined forces after all. (The pilot
Still had originally favoured was lost early in his tour of operations.)

It was a haphazard system; one could only guess how these
strangers would function as a team, how they would react to the
emergencies inevitable in any tour. Harry Shotton of Windsor,
Ontario, a pilot who later joined 420 Squadron, thought the
crewing-up process absurd. When his turn came to form a crew, he
simply waited until the other crews were established, then took
those who were left; they became his crew. On the other hand,
some Canadian airmen never went through the crewing-up process; it all depended on the current need for certain trades. Jim
Moffat of Castleton, Ontario, an air gunner, went straight from
Bournemouth to a Heavy Conversion Unit where he met and
joined his already-assembled crew and travelled with them to 427
Squadron.

An airman's first loyalty belonged to those with whom he flew.
The crew met the need of a man to identify with something bigger
and more important than himself. The crew was the band of
comrades with whom he would enter the dangerous world of
operational flying. A frightening world. Every man had heard the
stories. About the squadrons that were "bad luck outfits" and
hadn't had a crew complete a tour in six months. About the
"rogue" aircraft that were assigned to sprog crews because no one
else would have them. About the terrifying "Scarecrows" – often
called "Scare*crews*" – that the Germans were said to send up to
explode with frightful pyrotechnics for the sole purpose of
unnerving anyone in the immediate vicinity. About the night
fighters that cruised unseen beneath the bombers, waiting for the
right moment to destroy them with upward-firing guns. About the
chances of getting through a tour.

Poor meals, ropey aircraft, and haughty RAF officers and NCOs seem to be most Canadians' memories of OTUs. For example, Frank Hamilton of Mazenod, Saskatchewan, a pilot who later went on to join 424 Squadron, recalls food of miserable quality at Pershore, appallingly monotonous servings of mutton and Brussels sprouts. Pershore was particularly disliked by all new arrivals; not just Canadians, but British, Australians, and New Zealanders too. Although they wore sergeants' stripes, the airmen found themselves barred from the Sergeants' Mess, being relegated to an Aircrew Mess. Each man was provided with a spoon – no knife, no fork, just a spoon. Like inmates of some Dickensian gaol, they had to carry their spoons in their greatcoat pockets and use them for every meal.

The final stop in the training process was the Heavy Conversion Unit (HCU), the "finishing schools" where the crews learned to operate the aircraft they would fly on ops. In most cases, by mid-1943, the crews graduated to Lancasters or Halifaxes. These were the four-engined heavy bombers that, as every newspaper reader knew, were nightly carrying the war to the Germans in their homeland. The crews acquired two additional members: a mid-upper gunner, and a flight engineer whose chief responsibility was the operation of the aircraft's engines and its fuel, electrical, and hydraulic systems. Many of the flight engineers who flew with 6 Group in its first eighteen months were remustered RAF ground "types" who tended to be older than the average aircrewman. Some arrived at the HCU with amazingly little flying time. In fact, when Stanley Fletcher reported to 1664 HCU at Croft Spa in October 1944, he had *never* flown, despite the presence of an aircrew badge on his "best blue" tunic. "Most crews joined up together at a big crewing session," he remarks. "Not in this case. Dammy [Flying Officer Harold Damgaard] already had his own Wellington crew with all their training and an op on the marshalling yards at Beauvais behind them. All he wanted was a flight engineer ... so he looked around the room, saw me and came across ... 'I would like you to be my flight engineer.' I nodded my assent." Fletcher adds: "Thankfully, no one asked me how many flying hours I had in my log book." John McQuiston of 415 Squadron acquired a flight engineer who said he had been a gigolo in civvy street. His nerve may have been steady on terra firma; it wasn't in the air. The first time he flew with McQuiston, he could only hang on to a bulkhead, quivering with fright. He was quietly returned to ground duties. When Steve Puskas and his crew arrived at HCU, they were on the lookout for a Canadian flight engineer. But Puskas had no choice in the matter; he found that an RAF flight engineer, Jack Phillips, had been assigned to the crew. Having heard of their preference, Phillips apologized for not being Canadian. Embarrassed, the crew welcomed him into their ranks.

Before going to an operational squadron, sprog crews undertook various exercises designed to prepare them for the realities of operational flying. "Bulls-eyes," for example: trips over London and other British cities in which they learned how tricky it was to evade searchlights and night fighters. Such crews also flew "Nickels" in which they were required to find a target, usually in France, sometimes in Germany, and drop leaflets. Nickels were the culmination of most crews' training, although some HCU crews took part in minor raids, diversionary ops designed to take the defenders' attention away from the main attacks.

But even if you weren't involved in a major raid, Nickels could be deadly. Wireless operator Wally Loucks, who had grown up on an Indian reservation near Peterborough, Ontario, has vivid memories of just such a sortie. He and his crew had almost completed their training at 1664 HCU when they were briefed for a Nickel on the evening of March 21, 1944. They took a veteran Halifax II, LK930, that had seen service with 428 and 429 Squadrons before being relegated to training duties. Loucks says the crew were "still jittery" after a forced landing five days earlier. Near the French coast, a radio message recalled the aircraft. The skipper, Ray Collver, turned back as ordered. But as he did so something went violently wrong with the starboard outer engine. "We had a runaway prop," Loucks says, "but whether it was caused by mechanical trouble or enemy action no one was sure." So fierce was the vibration that the starboard inner engine failed. Navigator Ralph Pilkington remembers fragments of fuselage falling on his navigation table in the Halifax's nose, the result of metal rubbing against metal.

Remarkably, Collver managed to coax the crippled bomber back to England. But he couldn't make it to the base at Dishforth, Yorkshire. Over Derbyshire, the vibration intensified. The aircraft seemed to be in imminent danger of breaking up. Collver ordered the crew to bale out. Pilkington, Loucks, and Peel, the bomb-aimer, escaped through the nose hatch. By the time they had gone, the aircraft was too low for anyone else to jump. Collver almost managed to pull off a miraculous forced landing in the dark mid-way between the villages of Scarcliffe and Palterton. He put the big aircraft down with its wheels still retracted. The Halifax went skidding over the rough ground. But the darkness concealed a hillock ahead. The Halifax was still travelling rapidly when it hit. The shattering impact threw Collver clear, but three of the crew – Carl Starnes, the rear gunner, Russell Pym, the RAF flight engi-neer, and Bill Andrews, the mid-upper gunner – were still inside.

The noise of the crash woke two brothers, George and Albert Calow, who lived nearby. They hurried outside and found the wreckage wreathed in flames. At great personal risk they dragged the three crewmen clear of the blaze.

The three members of the crew who baled out were extraordi-narily lucky. Wally Loucks says he seemed to hit the ground the instant he pulled the parachute's rip-cord. Dazed, unable to see where he was, he stumbled about in the darkness until he came to a cottage. He knocked at the door. An elderly lady appeared at an upstairs window. Loucks asked to be admitted. The lady refused and told him to go and report to the local Home Guard. Loucks tottered off. Luckily he came across a police station. There he found out what had happened to his crew-mates. Collver, the skipper, was injured but alive; so were Pilkington and Peel who had jumped with Loucks. Pilkington later recounted that he had found a country policeman and had been obliged to wait, in shock, while the constable consulted his manual to find the cor-rect way to deal with downed airmen.

The three airmen dragged from the burning wreckage did not survive in spite of the gallantry of the Calow brothers, both of whom received the British Empire Medal (BEM).

The airmen who came through the crash of LK930 recovered from their various injuries and went to fly with 6 Group, all completing their tours and returning safely to Canada. (By curi-ous coincidence, some years after the war, Loucks was visited by an insurance salesman who turned out to be the brother of Bill Andrews, the mid-upper gunner on the ill-fated Halifax.)

Three airmen died when LK930 crashed in Derbyshire, yet according to air force records, there were no operational casualties that night. The anomaly is easily explained. Bomber Command's practice was to define operational casualties only as those incurred beyond Britain's shores. Thus, the many aircraft that crashed on take-off or landing were never included in the operational totals despite the undeniable fact that they were engaged in ops. By such means, the chilling tally of bomber losses was made as palatable as possible for the public.

At l664 HCU, Dishforth, in January 1944, Stanley Fletcher and his crew returned from a cross-country training flight, landing at about 2100 hours. Fletcher returned to his billet, a Nissen hut used by two crews, both of which had been on the same exercise that evening. The other crew hadn't returned. Fletcher went to bed. Some hours later he found Ken, the Cockney flight engineer from the other crew, sitting on his bunk, "his face white and very strained." The reason soon became apparent. Ken's navigator had erred. Instead of flying across England, the sprog crew had travelled to La Pallice in occupied France, where the *Scharnhorst* and *Gneisenau* were docked. A veritable forest of flak batteries greeted the solitary Halifax. Miraculously, it slipped through the defences. The crew found their way back to England, their aircraft peppered by flak. The navigator was later sent back to Canada, Fletcher relates, as an *instructor*!

Casualties at many advanced training units were as bad as, or sometimes even worse than, those on operational squadrons – the unavoidable result of inexperienced crews operating elderly, overworked aircraft, most of which should have been scrapped. Bomb-aimer George Sweanor recalls one course losing ten out of fourteen crews. Jack McIntosh of Calgary, a 419 Squadron pilot, attended eleven funerals in two weeks at OTU. Steve Puskas flew Whitley Vs at OTU, elderly twin-engined bombers that had long since retired from ops. Their serviceability was always in doubt. On a training exercise in B-Baker, Puskas experienced a fire caused by a glycol leak. He successfully force-landed the burning Whitley at a USAAF base where a small detachment of RAF ground staff was stationed. After repairing the Whitley, the ground crew presented Puskas with a list of technical faults that should be repaired as soon as he got the aircraft back to base. Dutifully

Puskas handed the list over to an overworked and understaffed flight sergeant at his OTU. Later the same day he saw B-Baker take off again on another exercise. It vanished and was never heard of again. Shortly afterwards, two Whitleys blew up in flight, killing everyone on board.

At his OTU, Glenn Bassett, an air gunner from Lucky Lake, Saskatchewan, crewed up with a New Zealand pilot named Patterson. On May 10, 1943, Patterson went up for a session of "circuits and bumps" (take-offs and landings). Bassett didn't accompany him but an RAF wireless operator did. The aircraft, another of the ancient Whitleys, flew into the ground for reasons never explained. Patterson's back was broken but he survived. The wireless operator wasn't so lucky; he died instantly. Several days later the remaining members of the crew decided to go to Birmingham to pay their respects to the wireless operator's family. What the airmen didn't know was that the authorities had been unforgivably slow about informing the next of kin of the wireless operator's death. The airmen arrived at the house at the same time as the telegraph boy with his dreaded message. They became reluctant witnesses of the heart-rending little drama that was played out in so many wartime homes. Bassett recalls the family bravely insisting on the airmen coming into the house and having tea and relating all they knew of the accident.

Another gunner, Doug Penny from Abernethy, Saskatchewan, was due to go on a fighter affiliation exercise at OTU in company with several other gunners. He missed the flight because he was picking up a new bicycle. It was just as well. The aircraft, an old Halifax II, broke up in the air while performing the standard corkscrew manoeuvres. All aboard were killed.

On July 17, 1943, Roger Coulombe of Montmagny, Quebec, took off from East Moor (1679 HCU) on his first solo flight in a Lancaster: "I had already done one take-off and landing solo and I was taking off for another 'circuit-and-bump.'" During the take-off run the port tire – worn thin from countless take-offs and landings – blew out. Fortunately, Coulombe had attained flying speed and was able to pull the aircraft off the runway. "Flying Control ordered me to do a belly landing," Coulombe recalls. He didn't agree. It seemed to him that the best course of action would be to land the aircraft on one wheel. But Station Standing Orders ordained that a heavy bomber could not be landed wheels-down with a flat tire.

From the control tower came repeated requests for Coulombe to acknowledge the instructions. "I elected to ignore them," he says. "I chose a runway with a cross-wind coming from the right since I knew the aircraft would swing to the left as soon as the wheel with the burst tire touched the ground; but the natural tendency of the aircraft to turn into wind would give me some help in keeping the aircraft straight." Coulombe calculated that if he opened up his port engines and throttled the starboard engines right back he could keep the left wing up until the speed had slackened off. "I ordered my entire crew to assume crash positions and I proceeded to land, approaching with my wheels down." This caused pandemonium in the control tower; Coulombe could hear the orders from flying control officers "actually being screamed," instructing him to go around and land with his wheels retracted. He noticed ambulances and fire trucks assembling at the end of the runway. But, as Coulombe recalls, "the awaited crash never materialized." Coulombe and his crew clambered out, unhurt.

The station commander demanded to know why his orders had been disobeyed. Coulombe replied that in order to concentrate on the tricky landing, he had turned his radio off. "After that episode," Coulombe writes, "the Standing Orders were changed, authorizing the landing of Lancasters on one wheel only in cases of burst tires."

Bill Johnson, an RAF engine fitter, spent sixteen months at Wombleton on 1666 and 1679 HCUs. He has vivid memories of standing beside runways and watching the superannuated aircraft taking off: "The old, well worn planes needed every yard of the runway to lift off; their worn-out Merlins, although sounding just as sweet as ever, didn't have the power any more. I've seen both Halifaxes and Lancasters as far as three miles away and still only about two hundred feet off the ground." Johnson remembers being instructed never to fill the fuel tanks to the top but to put in just enough for the next trip. Weight-saving was vital with such weary aircraft. He saw a Lancaster at the end of the runway running up prior to take-off. Johnson noticed white smoke coming from the port inner engine; he realized at once that it was caused by an internal glycol leak. "I ran on to the runway about a hundred yards in front of the plane just as the pilot opened up his engines and moved forward. I jumped up and down and waved my arms about – and in general put myself in danger from the props – but I either wasn't seen or the pilot thought I was mad and he continued with his take-off." About one hundred feet off the ground the port inner cut out. The Lancaster thumped back to earth, exploding a few moments later, although the crew managed to scramble out in time.

One night Johnson was on duty, waiting for a Halifax to return to base. He saw it come into the circuit and go around a couple of times, then disappear. It never landed. "Later the next day, a farmer rang the airfield to let it be known that he was very displeased with the wheel marks across his field," Johnson writes. An investigation indicated that a Halifax had indeed made the marks. Was it the Halifax that Johnson had seen briefly? It seemed likely, but what happened to the aircraft? No one ever found out, although the most likely explanation is that it went out to sea, some twenty-five miles to the east, and crashed there, just another unexplained training accident, one of hundreds.

With few exceptions, bomber crews were extraordinarily tight-knit groups, their members' lives enmeshed on the ground just as they were in the air. Seven strangers became united in a common endeavour; countless close friendships born on some windy British airfield have lasted close to half a century. Every man sensed that he was a vital component in a complex organism. He experienced an intensely satisfying sense of belonging, taking genuine pleasure in performing a demanding job with efficiency and despatch. The pilot was always the captain – or "skipper" – even if his crew outranked him. It was one of the absurdities of the system that a sergeant could be in command of an aircraft full of officers, men whom Service law required him to salute and address as "Sir" on the ground. Once inside their aircraft, the vast majority of operational aircrew ignored rank. But the inequities could still chafe. Officers drew more pay than NCOs (which was why, most airmen told themselves, the miserly authorities restricted their numbers), lived in more congenial quarters, wore more appealing uniforms, and were far more likely to be decorated.

If an all-NCO crew was fortunate enough to survive the first half-dozen ops, the skipper and the navigator were usually offered commissions. Some refused them, saying that all the members of their crews should be commissioned or none at all. J. Douglas Harvey, a pilot with 408 Squadron, suggested as much. His CO was incredulous and said it was impossible: "'Do you really think,' he asked me, 'that air gunners and flight engineers should be officers?' 'Why not?' I replied, 'they do the same job that I do.'"[20] Coincidentally, another pilot on the same station, Linton, also refused a commission, and for the same reason. He was Sergeant Roger Coulombe of 426 Squadron, who had pulled off the successful one-wheel landing at East Moor. One night a heavy snowstorm hit Linton. Harvey writes:

> The aircraft from both squadrons had been marshalled in a line leading to the end of the runway. The CO of my squadron was the first in line for take-off; Roger Coulombe's Lancaster was next, and mine was third. All the aircrews, together with the ground crews, were busy with sticks and brooms trying to get the snow off wings and fuselages. It was a losing battle since the wet snow clung to everything, and it was difficult to see in the dark. We slipped and skidded high on the wings but accomplished little. Finally, we all gathered at the end of the runway for a confab. Time was running out. Either we started taking off in a few minutes or we would be late over the target and sitting ducks. My CO turned to Roger and said, "I'll pull out of line and you move on to the runway. If you make it we'll all follow." Roger glared at him. "You are in the number one position. You take off. If you make it, we'll all follow."[21]

Whereupon, Harvey relates, the CO decided that conditions were impossible after all. He scrubbed the operation. Such incidents only reinforced the belief among NCOs that they were considered expendable, when they were considered at all.

The skipper was responsible for making an efficient crew out of seven individuals. The best skippers insisted that their crews practise emergency procedures – dinghy and escape drills – again and again until every man knew precisely what to do and when. But a man's ability to fly was no guarantee that he possessed the indefinable quality that made him a leader, an individual who naturally commanded the respect of others. It was all too easy to be a "good guy" and ease up on the emergency drills and inter-com procedures. Such skippers' crews might have been happier in the Service but they seldom lasted long on ops. A relentless form of Darwinism was constantly at work, weeding out the lazy and the ill-disciplined. To survive a tour a crew needed all the skill and teamwork that a group of young men in their early twenties – sometimes late teens – could muster.

The habitability of the average wartime airfield usually depended upon how long the place had been in existence. Pre-war fields (or "aerodromes" as they were then known) boasted solid brick buildings in reasonable proximity to one another, plus well-planned roads and paths. Some 6 Group squadrons were lucky and found themselves at such bases – much to the chagrin of the former occupants. When two RAF squadrons had to vacate the permanent station at Linton-on-Ouse to make room for the Cana-dians of 408 and 426 Squadrons, there was a good deal of bad feeling: "Their bitterness about the transfer was heightened by the knowledge that it was caused by a political decision to give the most comfortable pre-war North Yorkshire bases to the newly formed Canadian 6 Group."[22] In fact, the majority of 6 Group personnel occupied bases that had been built since the outbreak of war. Cheerless, windswept, they seemed to have been chosen for their distance from any decent pubs, their tendency to remain damp and muddy even in dry weather, and their ability to attract ground mist at inconvenient times. Accommodations were to be found in Nissen huts with stoves, sanitary facilities in Nissen huts without stoves. Nissen huts were everywhere, dozens of them, looking like indecently large tin cans half buried in the mud. In addition, there were Orlit, Maycrete, Quonset, Seco, and other equally utilitarian and unlovely buildings that became offices, crew rooms, medical quarters, operations and briefing rooms, and all the other "departments" necessary in a bomber base. Cinder paths and wooden duckboards connected every-thing. A concrete perimeter track encircled the field; the aircraft used it to taxi to and from the dispersals scattered in the farthest corners of the field. On bomber bases, the fuel storage areas, the bomb dumps, and the firing butts were to be found as far away from the accommodations as possible. Three runways criss-crossed the field: the main runway some six thousand feet long and two shorter strips each about forty-five hundred feet in length. And dominating the scene was the inevitable water tower, perched on spindly steel legs like some Wellsian monster from another planet.

For the sprog crews fresh from HCU, the first glimpse of their operational station was always to be remembered. Here was where all the training and the new-found skills would be put to the test. Here was where the war was being fought in earnest, where the airmen found out whether they had the stuff to do the job. It was common knowledge that the odds weren't good, at least until the latter part of 1944. Overall casualty figures were, however, a closely guarded secret throughout the war; Portal seemed to hope that the unsavoury subject might go away if no one spoke about it. On Christmas Eve 1942, he wrote to Air Marshal A.G.R. Garrod, the RAF Air Member for Training: "I am extremely anxious that statistical information relating to the chances of survival of air crews in the various types of operational employment should be confined to the smallest possible number of people . . . on the other hand, it is undesirable to issue general instructions on safe-guarding this information since it would be dangerous to spread the knowledge that the subject is regarded as being of great secrecy."[23]

Calgary's Ken Shedden, a navigator, arrived at Skipton-on-Swale, Yorkshire, to join 433 Squadron. Four complete aircrews turned up that evening late in 1943. No one was expecting them. The Mess had closed for the night. So had Stores. After some searching, the newcomers found an unoccupied Quonset hut. It contained bunks but no sheets or blankets. Worse, there was no fuel for the solitary stove. Ever resourceful, the airmen tore up the linoleum floor, stuffed the pieces into the stove, and put a match to them. Finding fuel for the voracious stoves was a problem on every base; many a Nissen or Quonset hut became structurally unsound because of the amount of wood liberated from roof trusses and partitions to provide heat in the damp, chilly English winter.

Gallows humour flourished on operational stations, new arrivals being natural targets. Air gunner Glenn Bassett journeyed with a group of RCAF personnel from 1659 HCU, Topcliffe, to Middleton St. George to join 428 Squadron. On arrival, the airmen were told that there was no room for them; not to worry, though, they should make themselves as comfortable as possible in the easy chairs in the Sergeants' Mess; there was a big raid on that very night so there would undoubtedly be room for everyone by morning. So it turned out. Another airman who went to Middleton St. George to join 428 Squadron was Ernie Dickson of Toronto, a navigator. Upon arrival, he was informed that the squadron was called the "Ghost Squadron" because everyone who flew with it got killed.

John McQuiston, a pilot with 415 Squadron, was far from impressed by his first glimpse of his new base in mid-1944: "The Mess at East Moor was a T-shaped arrangement of three Nissen huts about a central hall. These were furnished as two ante-rooms and a dining room with a bar, an inhospitable hole in the wall off a narrow corridor." Later, McQuiston was taken on an introductory tour by an officious (and wingless) pilot officer, the station's effects officer:

As he threw open the door to a hut about half the size of a football field, he said, "This is our storage warehouse. As soon as a crew is posted missing we clean out the billets. This prevents any appropriation of property by unauthorized personnel. Everything is sorted out here. Letters and photographs are screened. Any pornographic material, condoms, etc., are removed. Eventually the belongings are returned to the next of kin. We at East Moor look after our own." He stood aside with a smile on his face. What did he expect, a round of applause? I looked at the rows of uniforms swaying in the breeze from the open door. What an introduction for a new crew about to begin operations! I mentally marked Pilot Officer Davies a prick of the first water and a ground gripper of the worst type.[24]

McQuiston soon became aware that he had been posted to "a sloppy squadron with a morale problem. In August a mid-air collision occurred during practice flying and all fourteen aircrew were killed. Unfortunately this total included nearly every section leader and the CO, Wing Commander McNeill . . ."[25] McNeill's aircraft collided with one flown by Squadron Leader Brian Wilmot. Until some weeks before, Wilmot's mid-upper gunner had been Flight Sergeant Bob Furneaux of St. Catharines, Ontario. But, flying with another crew, Furneaux had been shot down during a raid on Boulogne. He evaded the Germans aided by several "extraordinarily courageous citizens of France," and returned to England just too late to rejoin his crew. Only one was left, the rear gunner, Harvey Powell of Frankford, Ontario. Powell had missed the fatal flight by minutes, because he had completed his second tour of operations. McNeill himself had screened him that morning, adding that he was not to fly on the forthcoming training flight. Throughout his operational career, Powell had enjoyed extraordinary good fortune, breezing through all the fighters and flak, the weather and the mechanical troubles that beset so many thousands of his fellow aircrew. Powell began his operational career with the thousand-bomber raid in May 1942, occupying the front turret of a Wellington flown by Wing Commander "Moose" Fulton, CO of 419 Squadron. In all he completed fifty-eight ops – "without a scratch."

One of the first Canadian-trained flight engineers to go overseas was Ted Radford who joined 427 Squadron at Leeming, Yorkshire, in the fall of 1944. He remembers the NCOs' living conditions as abysmal and the food inadequate, necessitating much "lifting" of snacks from the Mess, a variety of edible items being stuffed inside battledress blouses for consumption later. Radford's quarters were damp and cold – "a poor place to return to after a raid." Heating was erratic; coal for the hut's stove was dumped on the grass outside, and one of the airmen's major tasks was to protect the precious fuel from the occupants of nearby huts. That winter, staying warm was a full-time occupation; the bathtub was always filled with coal – and "we stole blankets," Radford admits. "I had nearly a dozen on my bed." A sergeant, Radford was of the opinion that the NCO aircrew billets were the worst on the station, far inferior to those of the officers or the ground crews.

Harry Holland, a pilot from Biggar, Saskatchewan, served on the same squadron. He shares Radford's opinion of the NCOs' quarters, although he went on to be commissioned and to enjoy the privileges of the Officers' Mess. He feels the marked difference between the living conditions for officers and NCOs was totally unfair, since all aircrew took the same risks and accepted the same responsibilities. Roger Coulombe remembers the NCO living quarters at Linton as "appalling . . . a hateful place filled with rats!" The pests ran around, biting sleeping airmen and gobbling their rations: "I vividly remember a huge rat eating my chocolate bar one night a few inches from my face while I lay in my bunk trying to sleep! Several years after the war," he writes, "I still had frequent nightmares involving rats!"

Before a sprog skipper was permitted to take his crew on ops, he had to go on one or more "Second Dickey" trips. The term was an echo of the days when RAF heavy bombers had two pilots, the co-pilot being known as the Second Dickey. The idea was to show the fledgling skipper how an experienced crew performed under operational conditions.

Unfortunately, the Second Dickey ride turned out to be the last for all too many fledglings. Although no statistics were kept, it does seem that a disproportionately high percentage of them died on those introductory flights over enemy territory, leaving "headless" crews that were broken up or assigned to other skippers.

John Neal, a bomb-aimer from Verdun, Quebec, was posted to Croft to join 434 Squadron. His skipper went off on a Second Dickey trip. He didn't return. The same thing happened to Ed Moore of 426 Squadron: "On January 2, 1944, Lloyd Offer, our pilot, while flying Second Dickey with a very senior crew, failed to return from a Berlin trip. He was later listed as Presumed Dead." Ironically, this was the second Second Dickey trip for Offer; the first had been so uneventful that the CO decided he should have another introductory sortie.

The first op was a never-to-be-forgotten experience for any crew. Despite all the lectures, all the handbooks, all the well-meaning advice, no one was ever really prepared for the realities of a maximum effort raid. Every crew had flown together countless times during training; every man knew his job and had proved it on numberless exercises. But preparing for the first op, everything was suddenly different. Even the aircraft didn't feel the same. The controls, the switches, the gauges, the engines; in some peculiar way, they seemed to know that this was, at last, the real thing. The crew clambered aboard, their footsteps loud in the thin metal tube of the fuselage. They made their awkward way past the uncounted obstructions that were such a feature of every wartime airplane's interior. Designed expressly for the purpose of transporting high explosives and incendiaries, a bomber contained only minimal space for its crew; a man had just enough room to do his job and no more. The airmen stowed their parachute packs within easy grasp and connected intercom and oxygen, becoming, in a subtle yet practical way, integral components of the aircraft. The skipper strapped himself into his seat and began the familiar pre-flight ritual, in company with the flight engineer: ground/air switch, tanks, fuel booster pumps, tank selector cocks, pressure warning lights, throttles, pitch, and a hundred other systems and items of equipment. When the engines had been started, it was time to check the intercom to ensure that all members of the crew were in contact: the bomb-aimer surrounded by his switches in the nose, the navigator at his tiny metal table with his charts, his instruments and his inevitable pencils, all freshly sharpened, the wireless operator (many of whom were also trained as gunners) at his radios, and the air gunners in their turrets. The aircraft of that era were numbingly noisy and uncomfortable by today's standards. Their heating systems were inadequate; some members of the crew would be too cold, others too hot. The gunners wore electrically heated suits. Although they manned batteries of machine guns, the gunners were primarily watchers. In this war, it was usually wiser to avoid combat with the heavily armed fighters. Many of the best gunners never fired a shot in anger.

It was hard work flying a Lancaster or Halifax. Although they carried auto-pilots – known as "George" – most pilots of the period were suspicious of them and seldom turned them on. There were no power-assisted controls for the pilot; it took considerable muscle to wrestle the bombers in and out of evasive manoeuvres. Despite the chill, a pilot could be soaked with sweat after a few corkscrews to get away from a night fighter.

The sight of a city under attack was simply a totally new experience, like nothing you had ever seen before, a sort of lunatic fireworks display with the sound turned off and replaced by the monotonous thunder of the engines interspersed by the thuds of near misses and the clatter of bits of shrapnel hitting the metal skin of the aircraft. A kaleidoscope of darting, streaking lights, eruptions in the sky, like obscene sores that vanished instantly, leaving the stink of themselves to find a way through your oxygen mask, swaying columns of searchlights, glowing, wobbling flares, airplanes dying, being consumed by fire. Most neophytes regarded the sight in horror, convinced that no aircraft could fly through *that* unscathed. Shocks assailed you from every direction: a bomber tumbling out of the sky, fire eating through its thin metal flanks, a parachute seeming to skid by, a man suspended helplessly beneath its outspread canopy. Inevitably you felt a twinge of guilt at such moments, not because you were responsible for your fellow flyer's misfortune, but because every calamity suffered by one crew helped to tip the scales of chance a fraction in favour of the others. Everyone knew the basic truth about bombing casualties: no matter how many got shot down, the majority would get through.

Leslie McCaig went on his Second Dickey trip in May of 1943 with a twenty-four-op crew of 426 Squadron. He wrote in his diary: "I can't say that the feeling after supper is exactly one of extreme enthusiasm – rather that of accepting fate as it comes and hoping for the best." He found that the company of the other crew members helped to bolster his confidence: "Once I joined the crew I was no longer apprehensive. There is something decidedly comfortable about bomber work – with others willing to share your fate." Later he recalled his impressions of the target, Dortmund:

To our left one aircraft was blazing as the searchlights held it in a cone. It came down slowly and the crew should have baled out. To our right were about five cones, each having at least forty searchlights. Dead ahead the scene was a blaze of colour. Fires covered an extremely large area; colours blended into each other while certain sectors seemed sufficiently different as to possess life. They ran and sparkled as though trying to escape their fellows and knew no course to steer. The green markers of the Pathfinders were clearly visible. We dropped our load and turned sharply home. Light flak traced snaky patterns through the sky beneath us – colours and designs weirder than those from any mad scientist's lab.

On the way home, McCaig reflected on the experience of his first raid and it seemed "remote and unreal, like something I had dreamed and would never see again. It represented death and destruction in glorious colour much as Disney might illustrate music." Although he pondered on the terror inflicted on the people below, he had to admit to himself that his pity was somehow "remote . . . and it did not seem possible that flesh and blood should belong in that conflagration. But my sympathy was academic and short-lived; I was interested in myself and our aircraft – nothing else was of any importance."[26]

A raid on Dessau introduced Jim Emmerson, a 424 Squadron pilot, to the realities of ops: "The flak wasn't nearly as frightening as the fighter flares which dropped, lighting you up like a beacon. Occasionally a ball of fire erupted in the sky, indicating another plane going down . . . but I tried to convince myself it really wasn't. Almost as frightening as the fighter flares were the searchlights which eased toward you in long, lazy arcs. Then, just as you were certain they were going to lock on to you, they would swing away or even go out. Nerve-racking!"

Joe Widdis, a bomb-aimer with 429 Squadron, also found the searchlights unnerving. He remembers the worst moment of his tour when his aircraft was coned over Düsseldorf. The light inside the aircraft was so intense that "it felt as if you were being suffocated." There was seldom any escape for a bomber caught by the blue-tinged, radar-controlled master searchlight. As soon as it locked on to an aircraft, slave lights hurried to its aid; together, they formed the cone into which the flak batteries directed their fire. In Widdis's case, luck in the form of a twin-engined Mosquito played an unexpected part in the drama. While intense flak poured up into the cone, the Mosquito suddenly appeared. Its presence seemed to confuse the German gunners. Widdis's Halifax was able to slip away into the comforting darkness. Whether the Mosquito flew into the lights intentionally or by accident will probably never be known, for the bomber crew couldn't identify the aircraft's squadron identification letters. "It was a great deed and the pilot should have received a medal," Widdis comments. Unfortunately, the Canadians were unable even to write to the Mosquito pilot thanking him.

The Widdis crew was another that had a stressful introduction to ops, without even making it to the target. The armaments section of 429 Squadron had installed .50-inch Brownings in the bellies of their Halifaxes to defend them against night fighters attacking from below. Shortly after take-off, the mid-upper gunner on Widdis's crew slipped out of the dorsal turret to check on the ventral gun. He spent a few moments in the belly of the bomber, then hoisted himself back into the mid-upper turret. As he did so a grinding, ripping roar stunned the crew. The propellers of another Halifax had torn into Widdis's aircraft, striking it in the lower section of the fuselage where, a moment earlier, the mid-upper gunner had been crouched beside the Browning. The skipper, Jim Atkins, jettisoned the bombs into the North Sea, then coaxed the mangled Halifax back to Leeming. He landed safely. But if he expected praise for his performance, he was to be disappointed. The squadron CO roundly criticized him for not avoiding the collision in the first place!

The first op for Jim Moffat, a mid-upper gunner with 427 Squadron, was a raid on Mannheim in September 1943. Reflecting on the experience afterwards, Moffat found that it had a strangely unreal quality in his memory. He had a spectacular view of the proceedings from his vantage point atop the fuselage of his Halifax. As the aircraft neared the target, flak lacerated the night sky all around him. Far below, the ground "twinkled as if diamonds had been scattered"; the "diamonds" were incendiaries that had just landed; quickly they turned orange as the fires took hold. Moments later, Moffat's aircraft lost an engine – mechanical trouble sometimes struck at the most inconvenient of times. The heavily laden Halifax began to lose height. George Laird, the skipper, discussed the situation with the rest of the crew. Abandon the sortie or press on? They voted to keep going. By the time their bombs hurtled earthward, the Halifax was down to ten thousand feet, considerably below the Stirlings – usually the unfortunate low men on the aerial totem pole. In this case, however, the gunners concentrated on the higher-flying aircraft; the flak streamed past Moffat's three-engined Halifax. After a tense low-level trip back to England, Laird landed successfully at Boscombe Down on Salisbury Plain.

Ken Shedden, the navigator who had helped to tear up a linoleum floor for fuel at Skipton-on-Swale, also had an eventful introduction to operational flying. On the night of January 21, 1944, his crew went to Magdeburg, a raid which cost Bomber Command 15.6 per cent of the Halifaxes taking part. Shedden flew in a Halifax but he and his crew returned unscathed. Six nights later, however, they went to Berlin and weren't so lucky. A fighter attacked their Halifax over the target. Its accurate fire killed the rear gunner and damaged the port wing, ripping the dinghy out of its compartment. Still attached to the aircraft by its line and having automatically inflated, the dinghy kept thumping against the fuselage side, a bulbous burden which remained firmly fastened as the skipper, Jack Mitchell, went on to bomb the target. Eventually the dinghy broke away, but the fighter's attack had hit the Hally's fuel tanks, permitting the precious fuel to leak out. The flight engineer said they wouldn't make it back to England. Nevertheless, the crew set course for home. And hoped.

During the interminable trip, the flight engineer juggled the tanks, trying to use every drop of precious gasoline. But near the English coast he reported only a few gallons left, insufficient to attempt a landing at an airfield no matter how close it might be to the coast. Mitchell ordered the crew to bale out: better to jump while there was power left to control the aircraft. But was it still over water? No one could be sure. Below, all that could be seen was a carpet of cloud.

In the Halifax's nose compartment, they had trouble opening the emergency exit hatch. When at last it came free, Shedden was the first to jump – only to find himself firmly wedged in the narrow aperture, his legs dangling helplessly in the frigid slipstream. Shedden recalls that the wireless operator solved that problem in short order by jumping on him. Shedden popped out of the Halifax like a cork from a bottle.

His parachute opened with a loud bang. Dangling beneath his canopy, he stared anxiously into the darkness below. What was down there? Land or sea? Down he went, through murky cloud, until at last he could see something below . . . a great area of grey. His spirits slumped. Hell, it was the sea, no question about it.

There was a ship, large as life! Shedden tried to manoeuvre his parachute to edge him closer to the vessel, praying that the crew would see him and pick him up without delay. The North Sea was a lousy place in which to take a dip in January.

Then, to Shedden's astonishment and relief, the "sea" miraculously became a ploughed field and the "ship" assumed the unmistakable shape of a farmhouse. How the gloom had deceived him! Beautiful solid ground below! He prepared himself for the landing. Thud! He was down, safe and sound in the ploughed field about a hundred yards from the house. Disentangling himself from his harness, he trudged along the muddy furrows and knocked on the front door of the farmhouse. A middle-aged man answered. Shedden asked if he might use the telephone. The man responded by slamming the door in the Canadian's face. Perplexed because he was accustomed to friendly treatment by British civilians, Shedden knocked again. This time a girl answered. Shedden repeated his request. And was admitted. Apologizing, the girl explained that her father had taken Shedden for a German – "because of your funny accent."

The other survivors of the crew baled out successfully. A few days later, they were ordered to become the burial party at the funeral of their rear gunner, his body having been found in the remains of the Halifax near Thirsk, Yorkshire. Under the circumstances, it was not a good idea. After their eventful op, the airmen were still suffering from various degrees of shock. The day of the funeral saw continuous rain. The crew had to carry their dead comrade's coffin over muddy, slippery wooden duckboards. It was hard to maintain a foothold. Or to keep a straight face. More than once they came close to dropping the coffin. Laughter kept bubbling up within all of them – and the solemnity of the occasion only made it that much harder to control the chuckles. By the end of the service they were all helpless with mirth in spite of their genuine feelings for their dead crew-mate.

Shedden's Halifax was another of the countless casualties which never became part of the official tally of bomber losses. It crashed on British soil and its loss was thus categorized as an "accident."

Some airmen's first ops ended even before they left their airfields. At Croft, County Durham, 427 Squadron was still flying

Wellingtons in April 1943 when George Wilson of Ottawa, a bomb-aimer, and his crew set off on their first op. Given the green light, the pilot poured on the power and the Wellington began to roll. Like most aircraft of the period, the Wimpy tended to swing violently during take-off because of the torque of the engines at full power. A full load of bombs and fuel only exacerbated the problem. It took skill and experience to get a fully loaded Wimpy aloft. On this occasion a strong cross-wind made the pilot's job that much harder. Picking up speed, the bomber began to swing. The pilot corrected. Too much! Again a rapid correction. Now the big machine was locked in a frightening zig-zag at full power, rushing from side to side of the runway. Worse, it suddenly ran off the solid surface and careered across the grass, engines bellowing. The pilot had two choices: cut the power or attempt to take off from the grass. He tried to take off. He almost made it. But in the darkness a wingtip hit a small hut. Skidding, the bomber partially ground-looped and crashed into the fence surrounding the station's bomb dump.

The impact knocked Wilson out for a few seconds; it couldn't have been much longer. When he came to, he found himself sitting in a pool of blazing fuel. Remarkably, he had the presence of mind not to breathe in. But how could he escape? He couldn't move! The Wimpy's structure had wrapped itself about him, trapping him. Through the flames he caught sight of an aluminum structural member. If he could grasp it he might be able to haul himself out of the blaze. The aluminum was already burning. He had no choice. He reached out, his fingers closing on the red-hot metal. Still holding his breath, he heaved. He had to do it. *Had* to. But he couldn't budge himself. He saw his hands burning away before him. His lungs were bursting. In a moment he would have to suck in the fiery air...

Help arrived. And not an instant too soon. The form of Harry Anderson, the crew's navigator, materialized through the flames and smoke. Without hesitation, Anderson reached into the inferno and grasped Wilson, dragging him bodily out of the wreckage.

Wilson's injuries were desperate. He remained in the famous Ward III at East Grinstead Hospital for many months, one of Sir Archibald McIndoe's "guinea pigs." After undergoing scores of operations to reconstruct his face and hands, he was released. By then the war was over. Wilson was a casualty of operational flying who didn't complete a single sortie. The gallant Anderson suffered serious burns to his arms. But he received no official recognition of his brave action.

The Canadian crews had to learn the tricks of their dangerous trade quickly. They were about to participate in the first of Bomber Command's major battles.

3

THE BLOODY RUHR

"One trip over the Ruhr in 1942/43 was equivalent to one hundred against other targets."

Lucien Thomas, DFM, air gunner, 405 Squadron

The Ruhr River rises in Westphalia and flows westward past Essen and Mulheim to join the Rhine at Duisburg. The river lends its name to one of the most heavily industrialized areas in the world. Embracing some seventeen hundred square miles, it is perched on top of a vast anthracite basin that has spawned immense coal and steel industries. From Duisburg in the west to Dortmund in the east, the Ruhr is a huddle of cities and towns linked by a maze of railways, roads, and canals, a megalopolis that is home to five million citizens – with a name that can still strike a chill in the heart of the most stalwart veteran of Bomber Command. The

Ruhr meant Krupp and Thyssen, flak and searchlight batteries by the dozen, endless rows of factories spewing out a permanent carpet of haze, a brownish layer of muck hanging in the air over the huddled cities, a murderous target that the Germans could be counted on to defend with all their skill and courage. No one took Ruhr trips lightly. Bill Swetman, who became one of the most highly regarded 6 Group squadron commanders, was a veteran of some three years of raids on the Ruhr; he says candidly: "The mere mention of the place always put the fear of God in me. There were so many searchlights, it seemed impossible to get through them without being picked up. The worst target was Essen. You had to fly right across the whole Ruhr to get to it." In his early forays on the Ruhr, Swetman remembers the flak being particularly dangerous because of the mediocre ceiling of the Merlin-powered Wellingtons he flew with 405 Squadron. Later the German night fighters would become the most feared adversaries over the region.

For Bomber Command's planners, the Ruhr was the archetypical strategic bombing target, the heart of German heavy industry, the arsenal that supplied the armed forces with artillery, shells, tanks, and all the other paraphernalia of war. Thousands of plants. Millions of homes. It didn't really matter which the bombs hit. Destruction of factories was the goal, but destruction of the factory worker or his home achieved the same end. In spite of all the hypocritical propaganda of the time, the truth was that, when the Battle of Ruhr began in the spring of 1943, area-bombing had been Bomber Command's principal method of attack at night for more than a year.

The Ruhr was the first major battle of Bomber Command's war. After a year at the helm, Harris felt his force had attained sufficient strength and technical prowess to deliver the shattering blows that Churchill had been promised for so long. And what more appropriate target than the Ruhr?

It might be said that Harris had been training for the job of AOC-in-C Bomber Command all his adult life. He was one of the singular characters of World War II, a man blessed with the extraordinary gift of being able to lead by personality. He seldom left his HQ at High Wycombe near London, rarely came face to face with any of his long-suffering aircrews, yet he managed to implant his personality upon the entire Bomber Command organization. Even more remarkable is the degree of loyalty he engendered. His airmen would do anything for him. And in return he never spared them.

Arthur Travers Harris, "Bert" to his friends, "Butch" to his crews, and "Bomber" to the general public, was born in 1892, the son of a member of the Indian Civil Service. Harris Senior wanted his son to go into the Army. Arthur didn't. So he sailed for Rhodesia with five pounds in his pocket. He was sixteen. Harris loved Rhodesia. In the next few years he worked at a variety of odd jobs including farming and gold-mining. When war broke out in 1914 he was twenty-two. He joined the First Rhodesia Regiment and fought in the tough German South-West African War, a campaign renowned for its punishing route marches across vast stretches of the continent. The experience cured Harris of any fondness he might have had for physical exercise. Thereafter he never walked if he could ride.

In 1915, Harris made his way to England to join the RFC, perhaps influenced by the fact that airmen went into battle sitting down. By early 1916 he was flying the Vickers FB5 "Gunbus," a pusher biplane that looked outdated even in those pre-Somme days. After some months in France, he was posted back to England to serve with a Home Defence unit. Harris served both in England and in France for the rest of the war, rising to the rank of major.

Harris had intended to return to his beloved Rhodesia after the war. By now, however, he had a wife and a young family to support. And when the air force offered him a permanent commission, he accepted it. His first assignment in the peacetime RAF was both a triumph and a bitter disappointment. Sent to India to command 31 Squadron, he was delighted by the way his small force of war-weary Bristol Fighters and DH9As proved capable of keeping order among the troublesome tribesmen of the North-West Frontier. The airmen regularly handled in a few hours actions that used to take battalions of troops weeks or even months. A light bomb here, a burst of machine gun fire there; the tribesmen soon got the message. It was an impressive display of air power in action. Harris could hardly have been blamed for expecting the support and thanks of the Army. Instead, he found himself embroiled in constant arguments, usually about money. The Army controlled the budget and hated the idea of spending any of it on such frivolities as spares to keep the old aircraft operating. Incredibly, some flew without tires. The aircraft traversed the savagely inhospitable terrain powered by single-ignition engines at a time when up-to-date dual-ignition engines were available from the Disposal Board in England for a few pounds.

Harris next went to Mesopotamia (now Iraq), where he became involved in more highly successful aerial police work. Again he found the Army controlling the funds. More harsh words. More patching of ancient aircraft. The generals' attitude astounded Harris. They all thought in terms of the Boer War. When Harris attended the Army Staff College in Camberley in the late Twenties, he learned that since 1918 the Army had reduced its artillery and machine gun strength to pre-1914 levels and had abolished the Tank Corps. But the cavalry thrived. Harris was presented with a "magnificent first-class hunter" which was his for as long as he stayed at the College; he records in his autobiography that "when one horse was killed in the hunting field, it was immediately replaced by another, equally good."[1] The College ran a stable of some two hundred hand-picked hunters at a time when RAF aircraft on active service had to take to the air *sans* tires. Harris observed sadly that the only way for an officer to progress at the College was for him to be utterly orthodox, studiously ignoring every lesson taught by the war and all the technological improvements since.

His acerbic tongue and acid wit did not win him many friends at Camberley, although at least one Army officer thought highly of him: a cocky little fellow by the name of Bernard Law Montgomery.

During the remaining years of peace, Harris went from command to command, always direct, often rude, a man to whom efficiency was of infinitely more importance than anyone's sensibilities. He commanded a flying boat squadron for some months, an experience he found mildly amusing, regarding the aircraft as "almost entirely useless but splendid yachts for the upkeep of which someone other than myself had to pay."[2] Soon he became deputy director of plans. He had been recognized as a man of ideas with the energy and ability to carry them out. In 1937, with the international situation deteriorating almost daily, Harris found himself promoted to AOC 4 Group, Bomber Command. He immediately ran into trouble in his efforts to obtain a training ground on which his bomber crews might practise their craft. He favoured an area known as Abbotsbury. Local bird-lovers objected. The bombing would interfere with the swans' egg-laying, they said. "In actual fact," Harris later wrote, "once the site was given to us and we started bombing, the swans laid more eggs than they had ever done before. The reason was that they soon learned to regard the aircraft and the practice bombs as harmless things which served . . . to keep unwanted human beings away from their nests."[3]

Next he sailed for America to purchase suitable aircraft for the war lurking just around the corner. He selected the North American NA-26, later to become world-famous as the Harvard, and a modified version of the Lockheed 14 airliner that would go into battle as the sturdy Hudson. He had no sooner returned from the United States than he had to go to the Middle East to take up the appointment of AOC Palestine and Transjordan. In the summer of 1939, accompanied by his second wife, Jill, and suffering from an ulcer, he returned to England in time to hear Chamberlain announce that a state of war existed between England and Germany. He sounded to Harris ". . . about as stirring as a school-master confirming the fact that mumps had broken out in his prep school."[4]

On September 11, 1939, Harris took command of 5 Group Bomber Command. His Group's eight squadrons were equipped with the twin-engined Hampden. A sleek, rather rakish-looking machine, the Hampden proved to be a disappointment in action. It was a pleasant aircraft to fly, but the manufacturers seemed to have gone to some lengths to make it as difficult as possible for the individual crew members to move around during flight, hardly an ideal state of affairs for an operational bomber. In addition, the armament was woefully inadequate, consisting of a fixed .303 machine gun in the nose operated by the pilot (who was presumably expected to throw his aircraft around like a fighter to bring the weapon to bear), plus three hand-held Vickers guns in defensive positions admidships. Harris's displeasure with the

Hampdens knew no bounds when the Germans shot down five out of eleven of his aircraft during a daylight raid on German shipping. Harris demanded additional guns and better mountings. When he failed to obtain the mountings through official channels, he contacted a metal-working firm and had them made locally.

Harris remained in command of 5 Group for fourteen months, long enough to see his squadrons begin the process of exchanging their disappointing Hampdens for equally disappointing Manchesters. Basically a sound design, the twin-engined Manchester had the misfortune to be powered by one of Rolls-Royce's few failures, the massive twenty-four-cylinder Vulture, a power plant that probably served the Germans better than the British. Possessing an alarming tendency to burst into flames at inconvenient moments, the Vultures never delivered their rated power. Manchesters couldn't stay in the air on one engine if their tanks were more than half full. To complete a tour of operations on Manchesters was to possess the sort of luck that won the Irish Sweepstakes. Jack Bushby, an air gunner who flew in Manchesters in 1942, recalls: "The Rolls-Royce Vulture was a mighty engine which could be considered as equivalent to two Kestrels set at an angle to each other in an 'X' configuration, and with a paper and slide-rule theoretical output of two thousand horsepower. In fact, it never attained its paper promise and on the way developed other serious snags. Thus the whole machine was underpowered. The odd thing seemed to be that the airframe and equipment also acquired strange and obscure faults . . . the Manchester crews of 5 Group were well aware before the first months of 1942 were out that they had a 'Stinker'."[5] Thankful airmen watched without regret as the last Manchesters took off for the OTUs, to be replaced on most squadrons by the superlative Lancaster, essentially the same airframe with four Merlins replacing the treacherous Vultures.

After a year as deputy chief of the Air Staff at the Air Ministry, Harris moved to the post that will always be linked with his name, AOC-in-C Bomber Command. It was one of those appointments that seems to have been ordained by destiny. It is impossible to think of any man better suited either by training or temperament for the job.

If Harris was glad to have Bomber Command, it may be said

that Bomber Command was overjoyed to have Harris. After two and a half years of war, the much-vaunted bomber squadrons of the RAF were at a low ebb, the crews all too conscious of their shortcomings. They had done their utmost. But the job was too big for them and their equipment. Increasing numbers of them were being killed on every operation. The truth was, the Germans had become more skilled at defending their cities than Bomber Command had become at attacking them. The fate of Bomber Command was in the balance. Although Coastal Command had already taken over many bombers, the RN wanted the rest converted to maritime duties to hunt for the U-Boats which were decimating Allied shipping. Many senior officers supported the sailors.

When Harris took over Bomber Command on February 22, 1942, he was shattered to find that he had fewer than four hundred bombers and crews ready for operations. It was incredible. The force was little larger than it had been when Britain went to war two and a half years before. The factories couldn't be blamed; they had been turning out bombers in huge numbers. But production had barely kept pace with losses – losses in action and accidents and losses to the RN and to other RAF Commands. Everyone wanted bombers, it seemed, but no one was using them for the purpose for which they had been built. The only encouraging fact was that the four hundred bombers of 1942 could deliver a much larger bomb load than the four hundred of 1939. The big, four-engined Stirlings, Halifaxes, and Lancasters were at last equipping a significant number of squadrons. What's more, the scientists – the "boffins" – were coming up with ways to help Bomber Command's airmen to find and hit their targets at night. A few aircraft had already been fitted with Gee. Other electronic navigation aids would soon follow.

It might not have been immediately apparent, but the timing of Harris's appointment was fortuitous. He took over at a period when many of the most important technical challenges of night bombing had been solved, although it would take months for most of the new equipment, techniques, and aircraft to get to the squadrons.

Harris calculated that he needed a force *ten* times the size of Bomber Command to win the war. But such an air armada would gobble up vast amounts of money. Was it realistic to expect the War Cabinet to gamble the nation's wealth – what was left of it – on a weapon that so far had been such a dismal disappointment? Many of Churchill's advisers sided with the RN. Use the big bombers to win the Battle of the Atlantic before worrying about anything else, they said.

It was a cogent argument. The war could easily be lost in the Atlantic. This first-things-first attitude went against the Harris grain. No, Britain had to *attack*, again and again, shattering the enemy's ability to wage war. No matter that the first couple of years hadn't seen any remarkable achievements from Bomber Command. The *potential* of the bombers was what mattered.

Despite his gruffness, his caustic tongue, and his steely gaze, Harris possessed a sure instinct for the dramatic. He realized that his force was at a crossroads. Either it would go on to infinitely greater glory or it would be whittled away to nothing by the sailors and the politicians, robbing Britain of her only means of taking the war to the enemy. Rhetoric wouldn't do the job. The way, Harris reasoned, was to mount a smashing, headline-making raid that would capture everyone's imagination.

Thus was born the idea of the thousand-bomber raid.

It was unprecedented. Not even the Germans had ever managed to put up more than a few hundred bombers on a single operation. The whole world would sit up and take notice. Everyone would be talking about it. No one would dare dismember Bomber Command.

But the difficulties were daunting, one transcending all others. How was a force of four hundred to become a force of one thousand? Harris knew how. He asked Coastal Command to come in on the raid, using the bombers which had originally been supplied by Bomber Command. To his delight, the response was an immediate yes. Harris then turned to his training organization, to the operational training and conversion units. By using tour-expired instructors and a handful of crews in the last stages of their training, Harris could just reach the magic figure of one thousand. It *had* to be a thousand. Intuitively, Harris knew that nine hundred and fifty just wouldn't do.

He first chose Hamburg as the target for his massive force; it was Germany's second-largest city and a major centre of U-Boat construction. If the weather didn't cooperate, the bombers would go to Cologne. He plunged into the complex organization of the operation with all the drive and enthusiasm of which he was capable, sensing that this might well be a "do-or-die" operation. If it failed, there was no telling what might happen to Bomber Command.

At this point, the Admiralty nearly scuttled the whole plan. No Coastal Command aircraft were to be used, the RN decreed. Harris was furious: how typical of the sailors to "borrow" squadron after squadron of bombers, then refuse to let them be used on a single Bomber Command operation! But in retrospect it is hard to blame the admirals. They knew perfectly well that Harris was planning an immense air show designed to get the government recommitted to heavy bombing, a policy which the RN opposed. Besides, Harris was gambling with aircraft desperately needed over the Atlantic.

A quarter of his force had vanished but, characteristically, Harris refused to give up. Squadrons were ordered to round up every available aircrew "bod": bring them back from leave if necessary; rope in senior officers to make up crews. The balance would come from the training units; Harris would dig even deeper into his precious manpower reserves. He was literally gambling his entire force on a single operation.

On May 26 the orders were issued. Then cancelled. The weather deteriorated. It remained bad for three days with rain, thunder, and heavy clouds. But on May 30, Harris decided that the raid would take place that night. Met informed him that Hamburg would be cloud-covered; very well, then, the target would be Cologne.

The huge operation pioneered some of the tactics that would become standard practice later in the war. Harris concentrated his bombers in a stream like a tightly packed school of fish. His aim was to get them through the target area in a mere ninety minutes, swamping the defences with sheer numbers. The fervent hope was that so many fires would be started simultaneously that the firefighters wouldn't be able to cope. Neither would the flak and fighters. In theory at least, the tactic would result in minimal casualties among the bombers. At briefing, the aircrews cheered when they heard that a thousand bombers would be operating, but were aghast when they pictured the massed bombers, imagining dozens of collisions. Not to worry, the briefing officers assured them, there would be only one or two collisions. The statisticians had worked it all out. The crews shrugged dubiously but, as always, clambered aboard their aircraft and took off.

Harris's gamble paid off. Spectacularly. The first thousand-bomber raid in history claimed headlines around the world. It provided the Allies with a boost in morale when it was most needed, when news from the rest of the war fronts ranged from dismal to catastrophic. Interestingly, the slide-rule experts were remarkably accurate in their prediction of the collision risk. Only one occurred. Flak and fighters accounted for thirty-nine more bombers. It all added up to a loss rate of 3.9 per cent. An acceptable rate, in Harris's view. He had feared that as many as a hundred bombers might be lost in the clear, moonlit conditions.

The raid did wonders for Harris's reputation among his airmen. At last, they realized, they had a leader with the drive and imagination to get the job done. They coined the nickname "Butch" in ironic tribute to his determination to bomb Germany out of the war. A curious affection sprang up. The aircrews knew that Harris would probably kill most of them, yet they would do anything, fly anywhere, bomb any target for him. It was an extraordinary loyalty, for few of the airmen ever saw their commander-in-chief. He rarely visited any of his squadrons, always maintaining that his presence was required at High Wycombe. Inevitably he is compared to Field Marshal Haig. Both were dour, distant figures, apparently never troubled by self-doubt, convinced that *their* approach was totally, utterly correct. Both men bore an awful burden of responsibility, sending thousands of men into battle day after day. Why, then, was Harris loved by the vast majority of his men and Haig loathed by the vast majority of his? The answer seems to be simply that Harris's men regarded him as a "winner," a commander able to get the job done, whereas most of the troops in World War I considered Haig an incompetent "Blimp" without imagination or ability.

It says much for the toughness of Harris's constitution that, despite his ulcer and the stress of his command, he took not one day's leave throughout the war. He lived and breathed Bomber Command. The prime minister's country home, Chequers, was only a few miles away from High Wycombe. Harris spent many an evening there. Until late in 1943, the PM was always eager to hear of Bomber Command's latest accomplishments; thereafter, the impending invasion of Europe became the focus of his attention. There is no evidence to suggest that the two men ever became close friends; possibly they were too similar in temperament, too opinionated, too intolerant of others. But in one important respect they differed. Churchill, the complete politician, always succeeded in phrasing his pronouncements as if half a dozen historians were peering over his shoulder, pointing out how *that* particular comment might look ten years after the war or how this one could conceivably become an embarrassment. Such thoughts never seemed to trouble Harris. His passionate faith in strategic bombing and in his young airmen led him to make one rash promise after another, fatally undermining his credibility in the latter stages of the war.

Such was the man who led Bomber Command when it began its assault on the Ruhr.[6]

In January 1943, Churchill, Roosevelt, and the Combined Chiefs of Staff (CCS) had met at Casablanca to plan Allied strategy. They had decided that the principal task was the defeat of Germany and Italy; when that was accomplished, all resources would be directed toward Japan. Both the Americans and British knew that an invasion of the European mainland had to come. They disagreed on the timing. The Americans wanted to do it as rapidly as possible, perhaps in 1943, with an enormous force that would confront and defeat the Germans on the battlefield. The British urged patience; they had a great deal of respect for the fighting qualities of the *Wehrmacht* and for the strategic and tactical abilities of its commanders. They favoured a number of incursions at various points in "Fortress Europe" with the main blow to be decided upon at a later date. The Allies arrived at a compromise. After complete victory in North Africa, they would invade Sicily. Meanwhile, in Britain, a huge invasion force would be built up in preparation for the invasion of France in 1944.[7] As part of the build-up, the "Casablanca Directive" decreed that the Combined Bomber Offensive would be mounted against Germany's war economy and the morale of its civilian population.[8] The air forces that would carry out these orders were RAF Bomber Command and 8th United States Army Air Force. For Harris, the Directive represented an important precedent: it was the first time that the CCS and not the Air Ministry had dictated bombing policy. The change reflected the new Anglo-American chain of command at the most senior levels.[9]

"Your primary objective will be the progressive destruction and dislocation of the German military, industrial and economic system, and the undermining of the morale of the German people to a point where their capacity for armed resistance is fatally weakened." Thus the Directive delineated the responsibilities of Harris and General Ira Eaker, the commander of the 8th USAAF. Their task was the destruction of the enemy's U-Boat construction program, followed by the aircraft industry, transportation system, oil plants, and other war industries; in addition, the Directive called for attacks on various military and political targets, including the Bay of Biscay U-Boat bases, Berlin, northern Italy, and the German Navy. Moreover, the Directive called for daylight raids, designed to inflict the maximum number of casualties on the German fighter force, as well as for tactical support for the invasion that would take place in 1944.[10]

The Casablanca Directive was a direct challenge to Harris's avowed belief that Bomber Command alone could win the war or, at the very least, batter Germany to such an extent that the invasion would be little more than a mopping-up operation.[11] It must have galled him to realize that the war leaders no longer believed that his bombers could do the job alone.

No doubt the CCS saw the two bombing forces as working together as a team: the Americans bombing by day, the British by night. The phrase "round-the-clock bombing" impressed everyone. Unfortunately, it seldom meant anything. The Casablanca Directive was a policy statement, not a detailed order. The two "Bomber Barons," Harris and Eaker, were given so much latitude that they operated almost independently, each dedicated to his own brand of strategic bombing, each determined to prove the efficacy of his particular approach.[12] On the one hand, the "selective" bombing favoured by Eaker, on the other, the "general" bombing practised by Harris; the former by day, the latter by night. Both men's professional reputations were at stake. Eaker believed in the existence of "linchpin" industries in the German war economy, industries whose destruction would cause the entire military/industrial complex to collapse. It was better, in Eaker's opinion, to cause a "high degree of destruction in a few really essential industries than to cause a small degree of destruction in many industries." Eaker saw six priority targets: the aircraft, ball bearing, oil, synthetic rubber, and military vehicle industries, and the U-Boat construction yards. The entire American bombing effort was based on huge, self-defending formations of bombers using precision bombing techniques to hit such targets. It was, of course, precisely the same concept with which the RAF had entered the war with such confidence.[13]

Convinced that the Americans would suffer prohibitive losses, Harris did his best to bring them into the night-time area-bombing campaign. He pointed out that if there were certain industries on which the entire German war effort depended, then the enemy would take the necessary steps to disperse or relocate them. To Harris, it was far better to lay waste to an entire urban/industrial area than to aim at specific targets; area-bombing promised the destruction of all military and industrial objectives within a given city. Besides, he argued, too much emphasis on a few targets was unwise because of the limitations of weather and the seasons; in addition, there was the ever-present danger of the enemy being able to discern patterns in Allied attacks and prepare accordingly.[14] The Americans didn't agree. They were determined to make daylight precision bombing succeed.

Although the Casablanca Directive did little to reinforce Harris's belief that he could win the war by area-bombing, it did grant him the freedom to pursue his policy. Harris soon proved himself a master at using the Directive's loopholes to justify his actions. In his memoirs he writes that he was "to proceed with the general 'disorganization' of German industry, giving priority to certain aspects of it such as U-Boat building, aircraft production, oil production, transportation and so forth, which gave me a very wide range of choice and allowed me to attack pretty well any German industrial city of 100,000 inhabitants and above."[15] Harris justified his actions by interpreting the Directive's preamble to read: "... the primary objective of *Bomber Command* will be the progressive destruction and dislocation of the German military, industrial and economic system *aimed at undermining* the morale of the German people to a point where their capacity for armed resistance is fatally weakened" (emphasis added). Adroitly, Harris reserved general bombing for Bomber Command and made morale the "supreme object."[16]

Early in the war, Bomber Command's bombs had been notorious for their inefficiency and unreliability, with high percentages of "duds" that failed to explode and a generally poor ratio of bomb weight to explosive content. By the time of the Battle of the Ruhr, however, the situation had improved. The first of the so-called "Light Case" bombs had been introduced, a 4,000-pound mild steel tube into which molten RDX explosive was poured. The "cookie" would become a major weapon in Bomber Command's arsenal, a bomb noted for its tremendous blast. Bigger and more powerful cookies would appear later in the war. They were ideal weapons for area-bombing, the perfect partners for the incendiaries, four-pound models usually, packed into containers which broke open when dropped. A phosphorus-filled thirty-pound incendiary was also employed: "its use had a marked effect on the morale of the enemy," Harris commented in his memoirs.[17] German reports bear this out, although they tended to call all incendiaries "phosphorus bombs," which they weren't. About 10 per cent of incendiaries were of the "X" type, containing small explosive charges, designed to discourage and disrupt rescue work. With the same goal in mind, many high explosive bombs embodied time-delay fuses set for an hour or two or up to a week. Bombs were sometimes as dangerous for the aircrews as for the people below. Disturbing reports from crews indicated that some aircraft had been lost during operations because their bomb loads had exploded shortly after release. Investigators soon came to the conclusion that, under certain circumstances, 500-pound bombs released from the rear centre station of Lancasters could collide with 2,000- or 4,000-pound "Heavy Case" bombs released from the forward bomb stations. After travelling two or three hundred feet, the lighter bombs could become "armed" and explode if they touched, often setting off the heavy bomb by "sympathetic detonation."[18]

Another technical innovation of great significance in this

Making do: Oxen help drag a Fleet Finch trainer out of the mud at 17 EFTS, Stanley, N.S. The vast majority of 6 Group pilots took their first flying lessons on Finches and Tiger Moths. (DND/PMR 84-977)

Student pilot error: Aircrew inexperience resulted in the destruction of scores of aircraft throughout the history of the BCATP. This unusual accident, involving two Ansons, took place at 19 SFTS, Vulcan, Alta., February 23, 1944. (DND/RE 23061-11)

Pressure time: At the RCAF Medical Investigation Centre, Toronto, in June 1942, recruits are tested on their ability to withstand drops in air pressure, an essential attribute for aircrew candidates. (Nicholas Morant/DND/NAC/PA 140655)

Classroom time: At 19 EFTS, Virden, Manitoba, wireless operator students gain experience in the classroom overseen by a scale model Tiger Moth. (Nicholas Morant/DND/NAC/PA 140653)

Hally: The Handley Page Halifax was 6 Group's first four-engined bomber. In its early versions, such as the Mark II illustrated, flown by 405 Squadron, it was unsatisfactory; Harris wanted production switched to Lancasters, so did its aircrews. (DND/PL 10457)

Wimpies: The twin-engined Vickers Wellington equipped six 6 Group squadrons early in 1943 but were soon replaced by four-engined Halifaxes and Lancasters. Pictured are Wellingtons of 426 Squadron at Dishforth, Yorkshire. (DND/PL 15382)

Improved Hally: The Hercules-powered Halifax variants were successful and equipped most of 6 Group's squadrons in 1944 and early 1945. Thereafter, the Lancaster predominated. Above, a Halifax from 420 Squadron over Le Havre, September 1944. (DND/PL 32846)

The superlative Lanc: A Lancaster of 424 Squadron shows off its sleek lines for the photographer. By the end of the war in Europe, the Lancaster had become 6 Group's principal equipment. (DND/PL 44204)

Preparing the weapons: At Linton-on-Ouse, Yorkshire, armourers remove bombs from the dump in preparation for an operation (top left). At nearby Tholthorpe, the trolleys (top right) are readied for the job of transporting the hundreds of bombs to the dispersals. A few miles away at Croft, County Durham, home of 431 and 434 Squadrons, armourer F/S Tom Elsworthy (centre) inserts the "pistol," the vital link between the fuse and the explosive. LAC Robert Pinsonneault (bottom) secures the detonator on a delayed-action bomb. Next, he attaches the bomb's fin (opposite top left) to stabilize it in flight. Finally (opposite centre), the bombs are loaded into a Lancaster's capacious bomb bay as "Black Mike" McEwen, AOC of 6 Group, centre, looks on approvingly. (DND/UK11739, UK20970, UK15530, UK15531, UK15532, UK21117)

Kitting up: Aircrew of 408 Squadron (above) don flying gear prior to an operation.
(DND/UK 16235)

Briefing: At Croft, County Durham, crews of 431 and 434 Squadrons are briefed for a raid on Essen. The two senior officers seated in the aisle are Group Captain R.S. Turnbull and Wing Commander A.L. Blackburn.
(DND/UK 16239)

A welcome "cuppa": RAF flight engineers of 434 Squadron enjoy a hot drink on their return from a raid on Essen, October 1944. At left, taking a cup from Section Officer Marjorie Long, is P/O Norman James who tempted providence by failing to take his lucky penknife on an op – but only once. (DND/UK 16261)

Safe return: Skipper F/O Jim Allan (right) and rear gunner Sgt. Don Veri (left) emerge from their 419 Squadron Lancaster after a harrowing op on Stuttgart, during which they fought off two German fighters. (DND/UK 13194)

Battle damage: Crew members of a 408 Squadron Lancaster II examine the serious damage inflicted by an Me 410 night fighter during a raid on railway yards, spring 1944. Left to right: F/S J.H. Walker, Sgt. Fred Ward, and Sgt. Ken Adams. (DND/UK 11782)

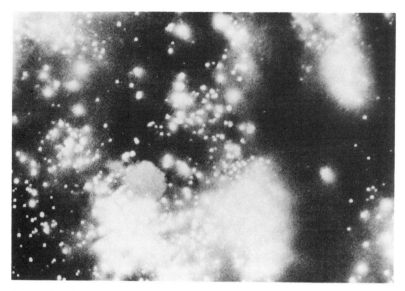

City on fire: An airman's view of Dresden during the firestorm raid of February 13/14, 1945, which killed an estimated 135,000 people. The Canadian Bomber Group sent 67 aircraft on the raid; all returned safely. (UK/PMR88-036)

"Thoroughly plastered": The enthusiastic assessment of 6 Group aircrews after a daylight raid on Volkel airfield in southern Holland on September 3, 1944 seems to have been justified. More than a hundred aircraft of the Canadian Bomber Group took part in the attack, leaving the airfield pitted with bomb craters. (UK/PL32218)

Emissary: Harold "Gus" Edwards was Canada's top airman in Europe and chief negotiator during 6 Group's formative months. He incurred the wrath of Harris, head of RAF Bomber Command, and of Lord Mowbray, who owned the mansion that Edwards selected as 6 Group HQ. (DND/PL8761)

First leader: George Eric Brookes was 6 Group's AOC through its most difficult days, from January 1, 1943 to late February 1944. (DND/PL142657)

Ace: Clifford M. "Black Mike" McEwen took over command of 6 Group from Brookes. A hero of World War I, McEwen downed 28 enemy aircraft on the Italian front. (DND/PL24444)

Hold on to your hats: McEwen and Harris nearly lose their headgear in the slipstream of the Canadian Lancasters taking off from Middleton St. George for Canada shortly after the German collapse, May 1945. (DND/UK21881) period was "Oboe," a radar device installed in the Mosquitoes of the Path Finder Force. Given the perpetual carpet of industrial haze hovering over the Ruhr, it's doubtful that Bomber Command could have waged the battle successfully without Oboe. Each set worked in conjunction with two radar stations in England transmitting radar pulses at five hundred repetitions per second. A transponder in the Mosquito received the signals, "boosted" them, and sent them back to the transmitting stations. The first station, the "Cat," directed the Mosquito along an arc, a section of an imaginary circle at the centre of which was the station. The circumference was so great, however, that in fact the aircraft flew along a straight north-south line over the Ruhr, following a preset path to the target. If it deviated, a series of dots (for westward deviations) and dashes (for eastward deviations) advised the crew of their error.

The second station, the "Mouse," was located one hundred miles from the "Cat"; its job was to measure the aircraft's progress along the arc by calculating the time elapsing between the original transmissions and the reception of the amplified pulses. Both ground speed and altitude were fixed. When the Mosquito reached the target, the Mouse sent a signal. It was, of course, infinitely more complex than it sounded. Much skill was needed by both pilot and navigator; for the last ten miles before reaching the release point, the pilot had to fly a perfectly straight and level course. Fortunately the Mosquito was able to mark from 28,000 feet, high enough to avoid most of the flak and fighters over the targets.

The Cat and Mouse stations sent their radar pulses at a tangent to the earth's curvature; thus the higher the aircraft could fly, the greater the range. At 28,000 feet, the range of Oboe was 270 miles. In 1943, only the Mosquito could attain such altitudes and operate as an Oboe marker.[19] It is noteworthy that during the Battle of the Ruhr, the Mosquitoes flew 282 sorties and lost only two aircraft.[20] (Small wonder, then, that some airmen put forth the suggestion that the squadrons of heavy bombers be replaced by "swarms" of Mosquitoes, each of which could carry some four thousand pounds of bombs, about as much as the B-17 Flying Fortress.)

Although it was a masterly device representing a major technical advance, Oboe had its limitations. It possessed a relatively short range; it was easily jammed and it tended to pick up interference from the bombers' other radar devices. The latter problem led to the development of Oboe Mark II, in October 1943, and, a few months later, Mark III. A serious snag was the inability of each pair of stations to direct more than one aircraft at a time. Since each Oboe run to the target took a full ten minutes, two stations could handle only six aircraft in the course of one hour. The TIs dropped by the Mosquitoes burned for only six minutes, thus there were four-minute gaps between aircraft. If one was shot down – fortunately a rare occurrence – or if Oboe malfunctioned – not quite such a rare occurrence – the gap grew wider. One solution was multi-channel signalling, which involved sending pulses on several frequencies simultaneously. Another obvious solution was to build more ground stations. Until July 1943 (when the Ruhr campaign ended), there were only two pairs of stations in existence. A third pair was added that month. By December 1943, fourteen pairs of Oboe stations were in operation. The web of electronic wizardry was spreading. And, anticipating the invasion of the Continent, the boffins had been busy developing mobile Oboe stations; the first of these would be shipped to France shortly after D-Day, enabling Bomber Command to mark targets deep within Germany.[21]

Oboe worked best in clear weather when ground marking could be employed, a fairly rare state of affairs during the Ruhr battle. The device's "occasional failures" underlined the fact that it was not accurate enough for precision bombing. It was an area-bombing tool and an excellent one. During the Ruhr battle the margin of bombing error was between six hundred yards and a mile, impressive for area-bombing but not good enough for precision attacks. Indeed, except for the famous "Dams" raid in mid-May, there were no attempts at precision bombing during this period. With good reason, Webster and Frankland, authors of *The Strategic Air Offensive Against Germany, 1939-1945*, concluded that a precision bombing campaign would have been a waste of effort.[22]

The Battle of the Ruhr began on the night of March 5/6, 1943. A force of 442 Bomber Command aircraft headed into the hornets' nest of flak and searchlights that was the Ruhr, a stream of bombers flying in close, even unnerving, proximity to one another. There was no attempt to fly in formation; each crew was responsible for navigating its own way to the target and back. Seventy-eight of the bombers came from 6 Group: twenty Halifaxes of 408 and 419 Squadrons and fifty-eight Wellingtons from 420, 424, 425, 426, 427, and 428 Squadrons. One did not get airborne. Nine never reached Essen. For a variety of reasons, mostly technical, eight of the Canadian bombers had to turn back en route. One experienced a turret failure and dropped its bombs on an airfield at Leeuwarden, Holland. Technical problems abounded that night. In all, fifty-six bombers, some 13 per cent of the force, became "early returns," an unusually high percentage. It was one of the few occasions during the battle when 6 Group's early-return rate would be lower than that of the force as a whole.

Ground haze obscured the target. It was typical Ruhr weather. On this occasion, however, the poor visibility had little effect on the bombing. Oboe had guided the Mosquitoes unerringly to the centre of Essen. At 2100 hours precisely, they dropped their red TIs. More Pathfinder aircraft, the "backers-up," kept replenishing the markers; for the next forty minutes the area to be bombed remained clearly visible to the Main Force bomb-aimers crouched over their sights in the clamorous, confined noses of their aircraft. Two-thirds of their loads were incendiaries, one-third high explosive. Three waves of bombers flew over Essen, first Halifaxes, then Wellingtons and Stirlings, and finally Lancasters. Of 362 crews claiming to have bombed the primary target (83 per cent of the total force), 153 bombed within three miles of the aiming point. It was area-bombing of a high order – thanks to Oboe.

Crews of the Canadian Bomber Group rated the Pathfinder marking as "accurate and concentrated." They saw many fires and explosions "with smoke rising to 15,000 feet." One massive explosion left a "huge orange cloud hanging in the sky for some minutes." One Canadian pilot observed a sheet of flame soaring upward to about a thousand feet; it lit up his cockpit, he said. The glow of the fires was visible 150 miles away, returning 6 Group crews declared; they rated the attack the best of recent months. Other Bomber Command crews agreed, citing "substantial fires" with many "spectacular explosions." Most of the damage appeared to be in the centre of Essen; subsequent reports claimed that 160 acres of the city had been destroyed, and in a further 450 acres "at least three-quarters of the buildings had been demolished or damaged by high explosive or gutted by fire." The principal target was the Krupp armaments complex which suffered destruction or damage to thirteen main buildings and fifty-three individual shops, mostly the result of fire. Explosions and fire demolished 3,018 houses and damaged 2,166 in the city. More than 450 people died.

The raid – which Bomber Command called "a triumph" – cost fourteen bombers (3.2 per cent of the force), by no means a heavy loss considering the results achieved. Three of the missing aircraft came from 6 Group.[23]

Pilot Officer George Pierre Cornelius Vandekerckhove of Winnipeg was nearing the target when flak scored direct hits on his 427 Squadron Wellington, inflicting serious damage. The resolute Vandekerckhove was not deterred, however. He kept his ailing aircraft headed for the target and dropped his bombs before turning for home. Unfortunately, the crew's troubles were far from over. A Ju 88 night fighter suddenly loomed out of the darkness, firing its formidable arsenal of cannon and machine guns. The Wellington's rear gunner, Sergeant J.J. McLean, returned the fighter's fire with his four Brownings, scoring hits. Damaged, the twin-engined fighter vanished in the gloom.

The Wellington limped across the North Sea. Close to the English coast, the starboard engine burst into flames. Moments later, the propeller on that side fell off. In spite of all these difficulties, Vandekerckhove managed to put the crippled Wellington down safely on British soil. He received a well-deserved DFC.[24]

Thus ended the first foray in the Battle of the Ruhr. The airmen of 6 Group, and, indeed, of Bomber Command as a whole, had every reason to feel pleased with the results. Oboe had demonstrated its worth, providing Harris's force with the sort of accuracy that had once been little more than a pipe dream. If only Oboe had the range, it would be the means to wreck Germany's industrial might from end to end.

*   *   *

After raids on Nuremberg and Munich (operations in which 6 Group suffered no losses) there followed a disappointing attack against Stuttgart on March 11/12. Most of the bombing fell on decoy fires set by the Germans just outside the city. The Canadian Group lost five aircraft that night, one from 408 Squadron and four from 405 Squadron, which had just joined 6 Group after duty with Coastal Command. It was a disastrous introduction for the newcomers. Although 405 suffered severely, one of the squadron's air gunners made his presence felt among the German night fighters over Stuttgart. A single-engined Me 109 attacked the Halifax flown by Nat Daggett. His rear gunner, an American in the RCAF named Lucien Thomas, promptly shot it down. It spun earthward, passing through cloud, exploding when it hit the ground.

The Canadian Bomber Group returned to Essen on March 12/13, contributing ninety-six aircraft to the force of 457 bombers: twenty-four Halifaxes from 405, 408, and 419 Squadrons, and seventy-two Wellingtons from 420, 424, 425, 426, 427, and 428 Squadrons.

The operation might be described as a qualified success. Relatively clear weather permitted the use of ground marking, accurately placed by the Pathfinder Mosquitoes. As far as the crews were concerned, the "concentration of fire and explosions around the markers looked very satisfactory" and they saw "good and very destructive concentrations of bombs at the centre of the target." After reconnaissance photographs were taken, it was announced that "another great blow had been struck at the heart of Essen."

The Krupp plants were once again the focus of the attack. Some crews claimed that the works received "30 per cent more damage on this night than on the earlier successful raid of 5/6 March." In fact, the bombing on this occasion was less accurate. A substantial proportion of the bombs missed the area so carefully marked by the Oboe Mosquitoes, landing in the city's northwest suburbs and destroying some five hundred homes and killing several hundred civilians. About one-third of the bombs fell outside the city, some on nearby Bottrop.[25]

Bomber Command suffered a higher rate of casualties than on the earlier sortie; the vigour of the defences undoubtedly contributed to the scattered bombing. A bomber crew under attack could seldom drop its bombs accurately. Conscious of the problem, Bomber Command's Operational Research Section did its best to persuade crews not to take any evasive action over hotly defended targets. This from 6 Group HQ during the Battle of the Ruhr:

> Evasive action for the avoidance of flak is meaningless, especially when a high concentration of aircraft is achieved. The collision risk is seriously increased. Attempts to avoid flak bursting ahead are just as likely to lead to a hit from other bursts off the original track. Violent evasive action makes it impossible for gunners either to see or to hit attacking fighters. Heavy bombers cannot "out-manoeuvre" properly handled fighters. Finally, evasive action in the target area makes accurate bombing impossible and necessitates, therefore, repeated attacks; these in turn lead to an overall higher total of casualties in achieving a given object.[26]

It was one thing churning out these dicta from cosy offices, quite another to obey them in bouncing, vibrating aircraft in imminent danger of being blown to bits. HQ might as well have told the airmen not to flinch if someone threw bricks at them. Operational crews continued to do their best to evade flak and fighters.

The Essen raid cost twenty-three aircraft, 5 per cent of the total. Again 6 Group lost three bombers. One, a Wellington of 425 Squadron, BK340, was making its way back to England when, over Holland, a Ju 88 climbed out of the darkness below and raked it with cannon and machine gun fire. The combat didn't last long; combats rarely did. The skipper, Gilles Lamontagne, had no time to take evasive action. In moments, fierce fires had broken out in the cockpit and bomb-aimer's position. While Lamontagne struggled to maintain control, the other crew members fought the flames. They couldn't complete the task. The fighter struck again, setting off another blaze in the fuselage. Now the crew had used up all the fluid in the extinguishers. The bomb-aimer succeeded in beating out the flames with his hands. But the fighter bore in yet again. More flames roared through the fabric-covered Wellington. The situation was hopeless. Lamontagne ordered the crew to bale out. He remained at the controls, trying to keep the crippled bomber on an even keel while the others jumped. But escaping proved difficult. The fire had distorted the escape hatch. It had to be smashed open with an axe while the precious moments slipped away and the flames ate at the bomber's vitals. Astonishingly, all five members of the crew succeeded in baling out, although sergeants Jean Aumond and Rolly Goulet were badly injured, Aumond eventually losing his legs. The aircraft crashed near Spaabruck, Holland. The navigator, Bud Brown, and the bomb-aimer, Vince Gauthier, were uninjured. Lamontagne managed to evade capture for a couple of days, but soon the Gestapo found him. He spent the rest of the war as a prisoner.

Of the ninety-six 6 Group crews detailed for the sortie, ninety-three took off and seventy-three claimed to have bombed the primary target. The Canadian crews were generally ebullient about the raid, reporting "well concentrated" markers and fires that "sprang up and appeared to merge into one blazing mass." They said they could see the glow from Essen when they were well out over the North Sea. However, they acknowledged that the German defences had been greatly increased since the previous raid; they reported many encounters with enemy fighters.[27]

During this period, the CO of 427 Squadron was an RAF officer, Wing Commander Dudley Burnside. A popular and highly regarded CO who habitually puffed on a large, Sherlock Holmes-type pipe, Burnside made it a practice to fly on all the toughest ops. The Essen op proved to be particularly demanding for him and his crew. Close to the target, flak hit his Wellington, instantly killing Rod Heather, the navigator, and tearing one foot off Geoff Keen, the wireless operator. The gunfire also damaged the Wellington's aileron controls and pierced the windscreen de-icing fluid tank, sending the chemical liquid splashing over the bomb-aimer, Pilot Officer Rex Hayhurst. The front section of the bomber instantly became filled with "suffocating fumes." The oxygen system had failed, so Burnside was obliged to descend to ten thousand feet. Despite these problems, he pushed on to the target, bombed it, and obtained a photograph of the hits. But moments later, the Wellington was coned by searchlights – and only the skipper's experience and skill enabled him to slip out of the deadly trap of blinding light. Relieved, the surviving crew members looked forward to getting home. But they had no navigator.

Despite his appalling injuries, Geoff Keen assisted in navigating the aircraft, dragging himself on his mangled leg to the dead navigator's table between attempts to repair his damaged radio equipment. Meanwhile, the Germans kept trying to shoot the Wellington down. Over the Dutch coast, Burnside evaded two night fighter attacks, with the assistance of the rear gunner, Dave Ross, who maintained a steady flow of information over the intercom, describing the situation from his vantage point, calling for evasive manoeuvres as they became necessary. Robbed of their prey, the fighters disappeared into the night.

Burnside put the Wimpy down safely at Stradishall, and the four surviving members of the crew were decorated for their "very fine display of courage and determination."[28] Burnside received a bar to his DFC; Ross and Hayhurst were awarded DFCs. And the redoubtable Keen, who already wore the coveted ribbon of the DFM, was now the recipient of the Conspicuous Gallantry Medal. Many thought he should have received the Victoria Cross, and in fact such was the original recommendation from Burnside, endorsed by Brookes and Harris himself. But higher authority decided otherwise.

For two weeks, poor weather kept Bomber Command away from the Ruhr. For the aircrews, such breaks in ops were simultaneously a relief and a frustration. It was good to know that one would probably be alive to enjoy breakfast in the morning; not so good to reflect on how many trips were still to be flown to complete one's tour. Aircrews led strange lives, residing in reasonably comfortable, civilized surroundings, with plenty of free time when they weren't required to fly. But the war was always close at hand. An airman could be strolling among shoppers in a Yorkshire village in the morning, and then, a few hours later, fighting for his life over a flak-filled target. Some married airmen even managed to set up homes close to their airfields, renting accommodation and living there with their wives. But such domestic arrangements were acceptable to only a few COs. Most insisted on airmen living on the station.

*   *   *

On the night of March 26/27, 455 Bomber Command aircraft attacked Duisburg. Twenty-five per cent of the force was provided by 6 Group: thirty Halifaxes from 405, 408, and 419 Squadrons and eighty-six Wellingtons from 420, 424, 425, 426, 427, and 428 Squadrons. For the first time, the Canadian Bomber Group had despatched more than a hundred bombers on an operation. But the raid failed – and its failure reflected the dependence of the bomber force on Oboe. The first of the two Oboe Mosquitoes to be lost in the Battle of the Ruhr went missing that night, ditching in the North Sea. The rest of the Mosquitoes equipped with the precious device returned early with various problems. Clouds blanketed the target area. It was a "widely scattered raid" according to reports. The results: fifteen homes destroyed and seventy more damaged. Eleven people died and thirty-six were injured.

Failures seemed to dominate the night. Even the German night fighter crews were largely unsuccessful. Only six Allied aircraft were lost, little more than 1 per cent of the total. Two of the missing aircraft were 6 Group bombers. Sergeant E. Hall and his crew from 426 Squadron radioed to base that they were running low on fuel. They were told what course to steer. Soon afterwards a message was received indicating that the crew was baling out. No trace was ever found of any of them.

The other missing 6 Group aircraft belonged to 429 Squadron. Its fate was not ascertained until after the war when the rear gunner, Sergeant J.M. Murray, was interrogated on release from POW camp. Murray said his Wellington left East Moor, Yorkshire, at 2100 hours, in very poor weather with rain and low cloud. Arriving early over the target, the Wellington encountered very heavy predicted (radar-controlled) flak and was hit several times. Homeward-bound over Holland, the aircraft became unmanageable; the skipper ordered his crew to bale out. Murray, still in his turret, heard the wireless operator say that he couldn't bale out because he had been hurt and his parachute harness had been damaged by flak. Moments later, the intercom went silent. To add to his discomfiture, Murray found his turret jammed; he couldn't rotate it manually in order to get out. He had no choice but to remain with the doomed aircraft. He was still crouching in his turret, waiting, when the Wellington hit the ground, knocking him unconscious. He awoke a few moments later to find the aircraft in flames. Fortuitously, the impact of the crash had ripped the doors off the turret. Murray crawled out unhurt. The Germans soon captured him, telling him that the rest of the crew was dead. In fact, however, Murray later received a letter from the bomb-aimer who had evaded capture and had made it back to Britain. He reported that the other members of the crew had been killed and were buried in Holland.[29]

The Canadian Group's aircrews had encountered poor weather over Duisburg with ten/tenths cloud. They were of the opinion that the bombs had fallen over a wide area of the Ruhr. The Pathfinders' marking was rated as "very scattered," due, of course, to the absence of the Oboe Mosquitoes. Some markers were seen to fall up to thirty miles apart. Nevertheless, one crew noted "three violent explosions in quick succession" and an "exceptionally big fire which turned the clouds above into a vivid red."

Of the 114 aircraft from 6 Group that took off on the evening of March 26, twelve returned early, just over 10 per cent.[30] The early return rate would be a source of increasing anxiety in 6 Group for many months to come.

Harris couldn't confine his attacks to the Ruhr. It was essential to keep the enemy guessing where the next blow would fall. On March 28/29, he sent 323 bombers to St-Nazaire. The Canadian Bomber Group contributed 106, about a third of the force: fifteen Halifaxes from 405, 408, and 419 Squadrons and ninety-three Wellingtons from 420, 424, 425, 426, 427, and 428 Squadrons. Once again, however, 6 Group had to record an early return rate of over 10 per cent.

The St-Nazaire operation succeeded because of accurate mark-ing by the Oboe Mosquitoes. Crews reported that the bombs fell mainly in the dock area. It was a night of excellent visibility: "the whole of the town stood out clearly." Fires blazed "over great areas"; "one violent explosion occurred at the south end of the docks." The next morning, reconnaissance aircraft observed smoke columns rising to fifteen thousand feet over the U-Boat pens.

This operation was 6 Group's largest and most successful raid against the U-Boat pens, although subsequent investigation indi-cated that it had done far more damage to the French town than to the submarine facilities. Losses were light, only two aircraft, less than 1 per cent of the force. One of the lost bombers was a Halifax from 419 Squadron, commanded by Sergeant R.F. Beckett. He and his crew were killed.[31]

On the night of March 29/30, an attack on Berlin cost two of the twenty-three 6 Group aircraft involved. The next night saw seventy-five 6 Group aircraft, all Wellingtons, join eighty-two RAF aircraft to attack Bochum. The raid failed because of poor coordination between the Pathfinders and the Main Force. Only minor damage was caused in Bochum but twelve Wellingtons failed to return, 8 per cent of the force. The Canadian Group lost six aircraft and crews.

Harris gave his crews little time to rest between sorties. They set off for St-Nazaire again and Lorient on April 2/3 (no 6 Group losses) then successfully attacked on Essen on April 3/4. Again, there were no 6 Group losses, although twenty-one bombers from RAF groups, 6 per cent of the force, failed to return.

It was an intensely active period for 6 Group. Most airmen were feeling the strain. Mac Reilley of Montreal, a bomb-aimer with 405 Squadron, recalls that period well: "From what I saw, there was no future, no way I could survive," he declares with refreshing candour. "At a party I told one of our ground crew that our time was about up, that we had been around 405 too long and would soon be gone." Shortly after that conversation, Reilley and his crew were shot down and taken prisoner. He remembers that in the last few weeks of his operational tour, he had found take-offs and landings particularly frightening – "whereas at the start of my squadron career I used to lie in the bomb-aimer's position and delight in the ups and downs, at the end I huddled in the rest position in complete terror." Earlier in his tour with 405, Reilley's aircraft was coned by searchlights over Cologne. Flak burst all around. "I was in absolute terror and became an instant believer, murmuring, 'God, get me out of this!' We literally fell out of the sky in a violent plunge towards earth. It was not until a POW reunion in Toronto years later that I found out what happened. The pilot and flight engineer had agreed that if we ever got coned, the F/E would cut the throttles. They were not too certain that they could get the engines going again and pull out but they thought it could be done. The only trouble was, they forgot to tell the rest of us." Reilley remembers the plunge as a horrifying experience; in retrospect, however, the actions of the pilot and engineer were warmly applauded: "They had a theory, applied it and brought it off. It sure lost the searchlights in a hurry."

Many young airmen took the view that it was as well to consider themselves already dead; that way, perhaps, they would no longer worry about dying. Reilley remembers a young airman cleaning latrines in the Sergeants' Mess at Topcliffe: "Evidently he had been busted down to AC2 [Aircraftman second class] for a case of so-called LMF [Lack of Moral Fibre]. Be it noted that I heard no one condemn him; he was the subject of some sympathy and, yes, some admiration. He had enough guts to do what most of us would dearly have loved to do, namely, quit while we were still alive."

Denis Jennings, an RAF flight engineer who flew thirty-two ops with 427 Squadron, remembers wishing he had the courage to quit flying. He admits to being constantly scared during ops; frequently he would "let off steam" by yelling at the top of his voice; since he always made sure his intercom mike was switched off, none of his crew was any the wiser. In one period, Jennings flew five ops in eight days and he found himself *hoping* to be shot down, to get the inevitable over and done with, to put an end to the unbearable tension. But like so many others, Jennings kept his fears to himself and carried on. The strain of operational flying manifested itself in odd ways. Jennings recalls a flight engineer on 427 Squadron who was convinced that he had a pet dog that followed him everywhere. Eventually the man was stripped of his rank and assigned to duty as an M/T driver, but Jennings is still of the opinion that the man was a psychological case, not a malingerer.

From the collective experiences of hundreds of bomber crews, it became possible to predict how the average aircrew would react to the stresses and strains of an operational tour. The first two or three sorties were such totally bewildering new experiences that airmen tended to become spectators as much as participants, absorbing one fantastic impression after another: the flak that really did seem thick enough to walk on, the searchlights that criss-crossed the sky with such terrifying deliberation, the fighters that came pouncing out of the darkness, the bombers that blew up, smearing the darkness with flame and scattering burning fragments as if participating in some nightmare fireworks display. Stan Boustead, a wireless operator with 429 Squadron, remembers being horrified by his first glimpse of flak over Bochum. It seemed to him to be "an impassable barrier."

Every sortie consisted of hours of tension, unrelieved until the aircraft squealed to a halt at its dispersal; all the way home there had been the nagging fear that one of those shadows to the rear might be an intruder following the bomber stream; and in the last few moments of the trip, there was always the possibility of another bomber blundering into one's flight path on final approach. Dangers came in all shapes and sizes on ops. If a crew was fortunate enough to survive the first half-dozen ops – and at this period of the war, one in two didn't – they could begin to appreciate the magnitude of the task they had undertaken. How could they possibly keep coming back from *that*? It was a point at which most crews' morale sagged. The task ahead seemed impossible. Curiously, a somewhat illogical feeling of confidence came next. The first few trips were done. The enemy had done his best and had failed. It was hard not to feel that one had the measure of the job. But with most crews the feeling was short-lived. As they chalked up more sorties, they came to realize how lucky they had been to survive so long and how tough it was going to be to complete their tour. By the time a crew had done fifteen to twenty ops, the morale curve had sagged to its lowest level. Oddly enough, as sortie succeeded sortie, the members of the average crew began again to believe that they might just make it after all. By this time the crew was highly experienced; they could "read" the night sky and sense its dangers; they could readily distinguish the Pathfinders' markers from those set off by the Germans in their non-stop efforts to confuse the attackers. (For some reason, the Germans never managed to match precisely the colours used in Bomber Command's flares, the reds being particularly noticeable. But only crews who had seen them all many times could spot the difference.) The members of the crew worked together as a highly efficient team, each man knowing exactly what was expected of him and when. In other words, they had become complete professionals.

And now the end of the tour was in sight. They felt as if they could reach out and grasp it. All the old fears came back to haunt them. How had they managed to get this far? How could they expect their luck to hold any longer? Every man knew he was a statistical aberration, already dead, wounded, or a prisoner, according to the odds. Nerves tautened to breaking point as the time came for the last few trips. Every crew hoped for a "milk run" for the last op. But it seldom worked out that way. Indeed, one of the saddest aspects of operational flying at this dangerous time was the number of crews who set off on their last trips and didn't come back. Walter Miller, a pilot with 433 Squadron, recalls a night when three end-of-tour crews took off from Leeming. None returned. Norman Bullock, a 419 Squadron flight engineer, was originally a member of Bob Millar's crew; but after twenty-three ops, Millar became ill and his crew was broken up. Later he returned to the squadron and, with a new crew, undertook the balance of his tour. He didn't come back from his last op. Bruce Betcher, an American pilot with 419 Squadron, recalls: "We wrote ourselves off. We never expected to finish a tour . . . Bomber Command was losing 5 per cent a raid, Halifax II squadrons, 7 per cent . . . It took the courage of a steer ascending the slaughterhouse ramp to climb aboard seven thousand pounds of bombs and two thousand gallons of high octane fuel and fly eight hundred miles into Germany . . ." Phil Weedon was a pilot with the same squadron early in 1943: "The closer one got to finishing a tour of ops, the pressure seemed to build," he remembers.

During March, the AOC-in-C, RCAF Overseas, "Gus" Edwards, visited 6 Group. In his subsequent report to Ottawa, he declared himself "very pleased" with what he had found. He talked of a general feeling of pride in the Group and was confident that all personnel were "out to make this the best Group" in Bomber Command. Edwards admitted that he had spent "many a sleepless night" fretting over Canadianization and the problems inherent in setting up a new bomber group, but now he was happy to report how "groundless these fears were." He felt that the Group was "proof that we were right" about Canadianization.

Impressed by the work of the ground crews, Edwards made a

point of insisting that senior squadron officers pay particular attention to praising them for their efforts. As for the aircrews, he felt that they were generally "well satisfied" with their aircraft. Halifax crews were happier and more confident since the recent modifications to improve the bomber's performance, principally the removal of the front turret, the installation of more powerful engines, new radiators, a remedy for its engine "breathing" difficulties, and attempts to cure the old problem of rudder overbalance, although this extremely dangerous shortcoming in the design would not be eliminated until the development of a completely new fin and rudder assembly. It is interesting to note that Edwards found 6 Group's Wellington crews reluctant to give up their faithful Wimpies until they could convert to Lancasters; they had no wish to fly Halifaxes. (This antipathy to the Halifax would virtually disappear with the introduction of the Hercules-powered Mark III version late in 1943. Many 6 Group pilots claimed to prefer it to the Lancaster in both its Merlin- and Hercules-powered versions.)

The rising toll of casualties could not be ignored. Edwards claimed that it was all due to the increased tempo of operations[32]; but why were 6 Group's losses consistently higher than those of other groups? Inexperience? Lack of training? The problem would be with 6 Group for many months to come; it would be the biggest worry of the senior officers at Allerton Hall.

Meanwhile, operations continued. After loss-free raids on St-Nazaire, Lorient, and Essen, on April 4/5, 6 Group participated in a disappointing attack on Kiel, contributing 129 of the 577 aircraft detailed: twenty-three Halifaxes from 405, 408, and 419 Squadrons and 106 Wellingtons from 420, 424, 425, 426, 427, 428, and 429 Squadrons. Again, approximately 10 per cent of 6 Group's bombers returned early. The crews that reached the target encountered "thick cloud and strong winds" that made accurate marking impossible. Decoy fires appear to have been particularly effective on this occasion, for only a few bombs fell in the town. Most of them landed on residential areas, killing twenty-six people.

Bomber Command lost twelve aircraft, 2.1 per cent of the total. Four were from 6 Group: Halifaxes from 405 and 408 Squadrons and Wellingtons from 426 and 428 Squadrons.

Crews reported extremely dense clouds over the target, so dense, in fact, that even the searchlights could not penetrate them. It was hardly surprising that the airmen had difficulty in assessing the results of the raid. Those crews who ventured beneath the cloud saw "many great fires"; some crews saw "two tremendous explosions" in the course of the attack.

The pyrotechnics could be deceptive. The Pathfinders' target markers proved unequal to the task and were rapidly swallowed by the thick cloud over Kiel. The dense clag obscured the green TIs and the white sky marker flares hid the greens. Although definitely not a success, the Kiel operation had some significance as the Group's most ambitious effort during the Battle of the Ruhr and as the second occasion on which more than one hundred 6 Group aircraft were in action. Of 129 crews detailed, 128 took off and 108 claimed to have bombed the primary target.[33]

The raid marked the debut of 429 Squadron in 6 Group's ranks. The unit had recently been transferred from 4 Group and was based at East Moor, Yorkshire, equipped with Wellington Xs.

The Germans defended Kiel energetically. Crews reported many encounters with fighters and "active" ground defences. They claimed several fighters damaged, with "some probably destroyed." One such encounter involved Sergeant M. Chepil and his crew from 428 Squadron. After bombing Kiel, they turned for home and were immediately attacked from the port quarter by a single-engined Me 109 which opened fire at a range of three to four hundred yards. As the bomber dived steeply to port, the rear gunner, Pilot Officer E.J. Andrews, returned the fire. The fighter burst into flames, falling away into the darkness. Chepil claimed the fighter as destroyed.[34]

Of four missing 6 Group bombers, three were never heard of again. However, Flying Officer D.L. Kennedy's Wellington from 426 Squadron ditched in the North Sea after a notably eventful trip. The trouble began five minutes before reaching the target. Flak hit the Wimpy, causing considerable damage. The rear gunner, Sergeant C.N. Beaton, found his turret inoperable; he was trapped inside the claustrophobic metal and Perspex cage. The bomb-aimer, Pilot Officer Dallas Laskey, went to work on the stubborn turret and eventually freed Beaton. Meanwhile, Kennedy had jettisoned the bombs and had turned for home. In the nose the crew noticed a "light was burning under the fuselage." They assumed it was caused by a short circuit; however, they couldn't put it out. Unfortunately, the fire attracted the attention of a Ju 88 night fighter which came to investigate – and promptly opened fire.

Kennedy managed to evade the Ju 88, but only after the fighter severely damaged the Wellington's hydraulics; the undercarriage dropped from its compartment in the engine nacelles and the bomb doors fell open, all adding substantially to the drag. In spite of the damage, Kennedy almost succeeded in getting back to his base at Dishforth. But the fuel ran out five minutes from the English coast. Kennedy put the Wellington down on the water; it broke up on impact. Laskey and the wireless operator, Sergeant L.L. Anderson, swam to the capsized dinghy and succeeded in scrambling aboard. A destroyer rescued them a few hours later. Kennedy and the other members of the crew weren't so fortunate. The young skipper's body eventually washed ashore; the navigator, Pilot Officer D.M. Walley, and the rear gunner, Beaton, were never found. Laskey received the DFC and Anderson the DFM for "great courage and fortitude."[35]

Vile weather was responsible for the poor results of a raid on Duisburg on April 8/9. Thick cloud and icing conditions made the trip to the target nightmarish. Again 6 Group recorded a distressingly high early return rate: twenty of the seventy-five Canadian aircraft turned back for a variety of reasons. In addition, the Group lost four aircraft to the enemy defences. That night saw the remarkable return to base of a Wellington of 428 Squadron with Sergeant Leonard Williamson in the pilot's seat. Flak had dealt the aircraft a catastrophic blow over the target, completely destroying the rear turret and killing the gunner. Most of the fabric covering the tail and what remained of the rear fuselage was torn or burnt away. Incredibly, Williamson managed to retain control of the crippled bomber and fly it back to England; he landed safely at West Malling in Kent.

Frankfurt (two lost), Stuttgart (eight lost), Mannheim (four lost); the bombers of 6 Group were flying whenever conditions permitted – and often when conditions didn't, as many ex-airmen remember. Then, on April 16/17, Harris mounted a double raid, simultaneous attacks on two targets, Pilsen in Czechoslovakia and Mannheim in the Ruhr. The idea was to split the German night fighter defences. Harris sent Lancasters and Halifaxes to Pilsen, and Wellingtons, Stirlings, and a small number of Halifaxes to Mannheim.

A force of 327 bombers attacked Pilsen; twenty-eight were Halifaxes from 408 and 419 Squadrons of 6 Group. (405 Squadron didn't participate in the sortie; it had been stood down from operations pending its transfer to the Pathfinders of 8 Group.) The target was the Skoda armaments complex, the importance of which had grown considerably since the successful attacks on Essen in March; its tank and gun production was now vital to the Germans. The operation involved a flight of eighteen hundred miles, twelve hundred of them over hostile territory. Bomber Command chose to wait for a full moon for this sortie; Oboe could not function this far from the Cat and Mouse stations; distance forced the attackers to use the tactics of an earlier period in the air war.

The raid was a disappointment. The hope was that individual crews would use the moonlight to identify their aiming points; Pathfinder marking was intended only as a general guide. It didn't work. Not a single bomb hit Skoda. But, in one of the more grotesque incidents of the war, bomb-aimers mistakenly identified an insane asylum as their aiming point, obliterating the place and its unfortunate occupants, in addition to about two hundred German soldiers whose barracks happened to be close by.

The raid cost Bomber Command dearly. Thirty-six aircraft didn't return, 11 per cent of the total. Four of the missing bombers came from the same squadron in 6 Group: 408. Of the twenty-eight 6 Group aircraft detailed for the sortie to Pilsen, twenty-seven took off, twenty-two claimed to have bombed the primary target, and, undoubtedly to the relief of the Group's senior officers, only one bomber returned early.

The Canadian Group's crews provided the explanation for the failure of the raid. It was all a matter of timing, they said. The Pathfinders had arrived late. Many Main Force aircraft bombed without waiting for the markers. Others followed suit. The Group's ORB reveals that the attack had been centred on a "small town some miles to the southwest" of Pilsen, where crews saw large fires and some explosions, a far cry from the newspaper accounts of the raid that talked of the Skoda plant being "enveloped in smoke, with vivid flashes from the bursting of bombs and explosions among buildings."[36]

The Mannheim part of the operation was more successful. Situated across the river from Ludwigshafen, Mannheim was an important centre of munitions production in the Third Reich. The force comprised 271 bombers, including ninety-one Wellingtons from 420, 424, 425, 426, 427, 428, and 429 Squadrons of 6 Group.

Weather and visibility were excellent. Crews could see the river and marshalling yards clearly, although Mannheim itself was soon obscured by smoke from numerous fires burning in the centre of the city and to the south and north of Ludwigshafen. The fires took a "very strong hold," the crews reported; columns of smoke rose to ten thousand feet. Even the river took on a reddish hue. Searchlights and flak were active and accurate but no fighters put in an appearance.

Bomber Command destroyed 130 buildings and damaged an estimated 3,000 more. Forty-one industrial concerns either "stopped or reduced production." In addition, 130 people were killed, 269 injured, and some 7,000 "dehoused", in the callous terminology of the period.

But it was a costly night for the attackers. The Mannheim raid resulted in the loss of eighteen bombers, 6.6 per cent of the force. In all, then, fifty-four bombers failed to return, the heaviest loss of the war for Bomber Command to that date. Five bombers from the Canadian Group went down over Mannheim, making a total of nine for the combined operations; it was the worst single night for 6 Group during the Battle of the Ruhr. Of ninety-one Wellingtons detailed, ninety took off, sixty-five claimed to have bombed the primary target, two bombed an alternative target – and nineteen, 20 per cent of the total, returned early.[37]

Meanwhile there was no let-up in operations. It was Stettin on April 20/21 with the loss of one 6 Group aircraft, and Duisburg again on the 26/27th with the loss of four more. While the Battle of the Ruhr raged, 6 Group was still active in Gardening. On April 28/29, Bomber Command sent a sizable force of 207 bombers to mine an area stretching from the French coast to the Baltic, the aim being to hinder the flow of German reinforcements and supplies to the Eastern Front. The force included nineteen Halifaxes from 408 and 419 Squadrons and eighteen Wellingtons from 426, 427, 428, and 429 Squadrons.

In spite of intense flak and much low cloud, the operation was successful. The force laid more mines than on any other Gardening operation during the war: 593 in all. But it was a costly night, with twenty-two aircraft lost. Three were 6 Group aircraft: a Halifax of 419 Squadron and two Wellingtons of 428 Squadron. Of the thirty-seven bombers detailed, twenty-five laid their mines as briefed. But, once again, the early-return report made worrisome reading, with seven aircraft, 18.9 per cent of the force, returning to their bases without having dropped their mines.

The Canadian Group had been ordered to mine a narrow strait approximately two hundred yards wide near the coast of Norway. The crews had never been to that area before and had little information about flak and searchlights. They rapidly learned that the enemy had plenty of both. Flight Sergeant S. Pennington from 426 Squadron ran into heavy and accurate fire from a flak ship. His aircraft took several hits but his rear gunner, Sergeant J.D. Watts, fired back at the vessel with such accuracy that the flak ship's guns fell silent. Watts later received the DFM for his courage under fire.[38]

It was a time of constant comings and goings among the squadrons of the Canadian Group. Soon after the Group's formation, 429 Squadron was transferred from 4 Group (although it remained at its base, East Moor). In March, the first Canadian bomber squadron overseas, 405, had joined 6 Group, but the unit remained only six weeks, moving in April to the Path Finder Force. Then in May, 432 Squadron came into being at Skipton-on-Swale, flying Wellingtons. The Canadian Bomber Group had at last acquired ten squadrons. But not for long. Three squadrons, 420, 424, and 425, received orders to stand down in preparation for a move to the Middle East. Now the Group was actually smaller than it had been in January. In June, 434 Squadron was formed at Tholthorpe; in July, 431 Squadron moved over from 4 Group and traded its Wellingtons for Halifaxes. In September, long after the Ruhr campaign, 433 Squadron became a reality at Skipton-on-Swale. Two months later, 420, 424, and 425 returned from the Middle East, bringing 6 Group's strength up to thirteen squadrons.

The constant movement of units during 6 Group's early days did nothing for its stability or cohesion. Or performance.

On June 10, 1943, the Combined Chiefs of Staff issued their "Pointblank" Directive. It named the *Luftwaffe* and the German aircraft industry as the "intermediate objective," their destruction being essential preconditions for successful Anglo-American tactical and strategic bombing.[39] Although it was supposed to be a blueprint for a highly effective round-the-clock bombing assault, Pointblank served only to perpetuate the difference between American and British policies. Harris's successes in the Ruhr led the Chiefs to allow him to continue his general bombing campaign – in the daylight attacks favoured by the Americans. Nothing had changed. Harris and Eaker could still run their own shows more or less as they pleased.[40]

By mid-1943, 6 Group had acquired a sorry reputation in Bomber Command. Most airmen regarded it as a "chop group," its losses consistently higher than those of the other groups. It was the same story where early returns were concerned. The Canadian Group kept recording the highest percentages of aircraft abandoning their sorties before reaching their targets. Reasons varied from mechanical troubles to gastric problems among the crews. To top off the dismal results, 6 Group regularly had the lowest percentage of aircraft ready for operations. No doubt many senior staff at Bomber Command sighed and shook their heads. Didn't they say this would happen? The Canadians should never have been allowed to set up their own group. They simply weren't ready; they didn't have the depth of organization, the experience, or the right types of senior officers to command a unit of such size and importance. All of which was essentially true. Equally true was the fact that Canadian airmen were dying because 6 Group was a hastily assembled force thrust into battle before its time, its newer squadrons brought into being by robbing the older units of their most experienced crews. As spring turned to summer, Edwards's concern about 6 Group's casualties became acute. In January, February, and March, 6 Group's losses had been considered acceptable: 2.9, 1.8, and 2.6 per cent, respectively, of the forces involved. But in April, May, and June, the losses jumped to 5.1, 6.8, and 7.1 per cent, rapidly approaching and exceeding critical levels.[41] Bomber Command considered that a casualty rate of 5 per cent "for three consecutive months would reduce a group's effectiveness to a dangerously low level and 7 per cent for the same period would produce a state of outright ineffectiveness."[42]

The Operational Research Section (ORS) at High Wycombe decided the matter was serious enough to justify an investigation, and immediately set out to compare the loss rates of 6 and 4 Groups, since the two groups operated much the same types of aircraft and flew from bases in Yorkshire and nearby.

After the comparatively low losses of January and February, the report observed, 6 Group's casualty rate grew "both absolutely and in comparison" to that of 4 Group. And it continued to rise. On German operations, the pattern was erratic. In February, 6 Group's Halifax losses were actually lower than 4 Group's. From March to June, the Canadians' losses crept higher. The gap kept widening. While Wellington losses in 6 Group were lower than 4 Group's from February to April, they had been "distinctly higher" in May and June. Why? One reason may well have been the transfer of 405 Squadron to the PFF, followed in short order by the transfer to the Middle East of 420, 424, and 425 Squadrons. They took with them many of the Group's most experienced crews. In most cases, comparatively inexperienced personnel had replaced them.

German night fighters had a "higher tendency" to attack 6 Group's aircraft, the report stated. The ORS eliminated 6 Group's tactical systems as the culprit, since 6 and 4 Groups usually bombed "from similar heights" and flew "in the same stage of the attack." Curiously, the ORS report found that, although German night fighters made contact with 6 Group aircraft more frequently than with 4 Group's bombers, they were generally more successful against the latter.

Luftwaffe night fighter crews were always on the lookout for bombers that flew undeviating paths. Few experienced pilots flew that way; they were constantly weaving gently to give their gunners a good view in every direction; many repeatedly varied their altitudes to reduce the risk of being hit by predicted flak. Such tactics sent a signal to the German pilots: We are an experienced crew and we are not going to be caught napping. The statistics revealed how vulnerable sprog crews were; they flew at higher risk simply because they hadn't yet learned some of the basics of survival in a notably dangerous occupation.

On Gardening operations and sorties against French targets, 6 Group's losses were "low and not significantly higher" than those of 4 Group, the report found. Indeed, during January, 6 Group's Wellingtons had suffered fewer casualties than had 4 Group's, even though the Canadians were more active. The ORS did not deal with the French attacks in detail because the raids against the U-Boat pens took place before the sharp increase in losses; however, the subsequent casualty rates indicated that the operational training provided by these milk runs was not sufficient.

Predictably, the ORS report found that 6 Group had an "appreciably higher proportion" of crews who turned back without bombing the target. The Group's early return rate had begun to climb in March for Halifax crews and in May for those flying Wellingtons, the same months the casualty rates began to rise. The reasons for early returns varied but, according to the report, the most common were icing problems, gun and turret failures, and malfunctioning oxygen systems. Engine troubles were experienced about equally by 4 and 6 Groups.

The ORS report recommended further study of several factors, namely, 6 Group's higher Halifax losses on German operations, its growing rate of Wellington losses, its high rate of contact with enemy night fighters, and its training programs for both aircrew and ground staff. It's curious that the authors of the report did not compare the *stability* of the two groups, which unquestionably affected performance. 4 Group was long-established and experienced very few organizational changes during the period under review; on the other hand, 6 Group was new and, adding to the inevitable problems of a fledgling group, it found itself in a constant state of flux, with squadrons coming and going and units moving from airfield to airfield.[43]

For Edwards, the lack of what he called a "logical reason" for 6 Group's persistently high casualty rate made the problem "all the more distressing." At any rate, Edwards assured RCAF HQ in Ottawa, the situation would be examined "from every angle" to find a solution. He even suggested that perhaps the Group should "stand down for a while" – a suggestion that no one in Ottawa seemed to take very seriously.[44]

On the night of May 12/13, Bomber Command attacked Duisburg for the fourth time in the Battle. A force of 572 Lancasters, Halifaxes, Stirlings, Wellingtons, and Mosquitoes took off. The Canadian Bomber Group contributed twenty Halifaxes from 408 and 419 Squadrons and forty-one Wellingtons from 426, 428, and 429 Squadrons. Forty of the 6 Group crews claimed to have bombed the primary target, two bombed alternative targets and ten returned early. After "near perfect" marking by the Pathfinders, the Main Force's bombing was "particularly well concentrated." Eighty per cent of the red TIs fell within two miles of the aiming point, and of 483 crews who claimed to have attacked the primary target, 410 dropped their bombs within three miles of the aiming point. The excellent results proved the efficacy of Oboe ground marking. The city took a fearful pounding. Forty-eight acres, including most of the old town and suburbs, were devastated. Also badly hit were the town centre and port areas. In all, the raid destroyed 1,596 buildings and killed 273 people; 21 barges and 13 vessels sank, totalling 18,921 tons. A further 41,000 tons of shipping were damaged. After the raid, Bomber Command rated the destruction as so intense that no further raids on the city were considered necessary during the Battle.

The Canadian Bomber Group's crews reported clear, cloudless weather, although the ever-present industrial haze and smoke blotted out many ground details. Many crews saw "unusually heavy explosions." One report talked of a particularly large eruption that "threw reddish-orange flames and black smoke high into the cloudless sky." Searchlights were "very active," according to returning crews, but flak seemed lighter than usual. Nevertheless, it was a costly night for Bomber Command, with thirty-four bombers, 5.9 per cent of the force, failing to return. Eight of the lost bombers came from 6 Group.[45] One was the Wellington flown by Sergeant I.R.A. Runciman of 426 Squadron. Shortly after bombing, the aircraft staggered, hit by flak. The Second Dickey was killed. The Wimpy itself was badly damaged. Flak had severed the main fuel connections to both engines and had smashed the control cables and rods of the elevator and rudder. Six-foot holes had been ripped out of both sides of the fuselage. The navigator, Flight Lieutenant G. Miller, used linen maps to repair the broken petrol lines, enabling Runciman to restart the port engine. The resourceful Miller then proceeded to splice the elevator controls with wire. Runciman kept the limping bomber airborne long enough to reach the Dutch coast, where the surviving members of the crew baled out successfully. Miller received the DFC.[46]

Little more than a month later, on the night of June 21/22, seventy-two bombers from 6 Group were part of a force of 705 Bomber Command aircraft attacking Krefeld. It was to be another major blow in the Battle of the Ruhr. The Canadians sent forty-four Halifaxes from 408, 419, and 427 Squadrons and twenty-eight Wellingtons from 429 and 432 Squadrons. Fifty-seven of the 6 Group aircraft claimed to have bombed the primary target and seven returned early – another figure of close to 10 per cent to worry Brookes and his staff at Allerton Hall. A total of 619 bombers released their bombs on "almost perfect" ground marking. The results were dramatic. A large area of the city rapidly became a mass of flames which "raged out of control for several hours." Fire destroyed most of the city centre and an estimated 47 per cent of the built-up area. The fire wrecked or demolished more than five thousand homes. About seventy-two thousand citizens of the city found themselves without accommodation. Twenty thousand were immediately billeted "upon families in the suburbs," thirty thousand "moved in with relatives or friends," and twenty thousand "were evacuated to other towns." Thus did the civilian population of Germany feel the impact of total war. Casualties numbered 1,056 killed and 4,550 injured. Returning crews reported "good concentrations of fire" with smoke rising to ten thousand feet; one described the city as "one solid mass of fires, glowing red and giving off great clouds of thick smoke."

Like all major Ruhr cities, Krefeld was well armed with searchlight and flak batteries. Thus, crews were surprised when they found the defences "only moderately active." Perhaps Harris had caught the Germans off guard by mounting the attack in the moon period. But if the flak and searchlight batteries were slow to react, the night fighters weren't. Many 6 Group crews encountered the *Luftwaffe* that night. Eight Canadian bombers went down, out of a total loss of forty-four, 6.2 per cent of the force.[47] The combats weren't all one-sided. On their way to Krefeld, the crew of a 419 Squadron Halifax, BB323, spotted an Fw 190 about to attack. The rear gunner, Pilot Officer R. Harling, called for a corkscrew to port. Harling opened fire when the fighter was about six hundred yards away. It caught fire and dived into the ground, burning "for some time after."[48]

It was a particularly bad night for 408 and 429 Squadrons, which lost three Halifaxes and four Wellingtons respectively. One of 429 Squadron's Wellingtons, commanded by Flight Sergeant E.A. Eames, was attacked by a fighter en route to the target. As the rear gunner called for evasive action, cannon shells sliced through the fuselage, setting it on fire. The bomb-aimer called out that he had been hit and the navigator reported a fire aft of the cabin which rapidly spread to fill the fuselage from the tail to the main spar. Eames, noticing the first red TIs over the target, turned in an attempt to bomb. But another burst of gunfire hit the starboard engine. Eames quickly feathered it and jettisoned the 4,000-pound cookie. He ordered the crew to bale out as the fighter fired again, hitting the port engine and wing. Flames streamed from punctured tanks. The bomber was now a mass of searing, wind-beaten fire. Sergeant W.H. Wright, the wireless operator/ air gunner, helped Eames fasten his parachute pack on his harness, then he baled out. The blazing Wimpy whipped into a spiral dive – and, with a roar, the port wing exploded and ripped away. The force of the blast pitched the injured navigator and Eames into the nose. Another explosion flung them clear of the doomed bomber. They and Sergeant Wright survived.[49]

The night saw the loss of Texan Flight Lieutenant Sidney Murrell. The recipient of 6 Group's first DFC, Murrell had transferred to the PFF and was serving with 405 Squadron. He and his crew died.

On the night of July 13/14, Bomber Command set out on the final operation of the Battle of the Ruhr. The target was Aachen. In excellent visibility, a force of 374 Lancasters, Halifaxes, Stirlings, Wellingtons, and Mosquitoes attacked the industrial centre. The Canadian Group's contribution comprised sixty-nine bombers: forty-eight Halifaxes from 408, 419, 427, and 428 Squadrons, plus twenty-one Wellingtons from 429 and 432 Squadrons. Fifty-five of the 6 Group crews claimed to have bombed the primary target. Seven aircraft returned early, another 10 per cent tally for 6 Group's unimpressive record.

A brisker-than-predicted tail wind resulted in the first waves of Main Force bombers arriving ahead of the Pathfinders. In this instance, however, conditions were so clear that the absence of TIs had little effect on the accuracy of the bombing. Crews reported that "large areas of Aachen appeared to burst into flames at once." The weather deteriorated after the Pathfinders released their TIs. Cloud obscured the TIs, but crews saw fires that "merged into a good mass" and several large explosions.

Although crews rated Aachen's ground defences as light, *Luftwaffe* fighters made the operation costly. In all, twenty aircraft, 5.3 per cent of the force, were lost, including seven bombers from the Canadian Group.[50] It was a loss that only confirmed many airmen's opinion that service in 6 Group was to be avoided in any way possible. The Halifax V commanded by Flight Lieutenant D.S. Morgan of 428 Squadron ran into trouble near the Dutch coast. A *Luftwaffe* fighter "took us completely by surprise," Morgan later reported. The enemy's fire wrecked the intercom and elevator controls. Morgan prevented the aircraft from stalling by "kicking on [the] rudder." Verbally and with the aid of the call light, he ordered the crew to abandon aircraft. As Morgan escaped through the nose hatch, someone called. Morgan assumed that the voice belonged to the bomb-aimer "who had probably gone back to see the gunners." To his relief, Morgan later heard that the bomb-aimer had survived and had evaded capture.[51]

The last raid in the Battle of the Ruhr had dealt Aachen a crippling blow, wrecking nearly three thousand buildings, including 16,828 apartments. Citizens were shocked to find that the town theatre, *Rathaus*, cathedral, main post office, police headquarters, local prison, army food depot, two infantry barracks, and eight factories producing rubber, wagons, and aero-engines had been severely damaged. Civilian casualties totalled 294 dead and 745 injured, and close to thirty thousand people were believed to have fled the town.

The Battle of the Ruhr was the first major bombing campaign involving 6 Group. It was a testing time for the Canadians, a period of high casualties and constant organizational and administrative changes. For Bomber Command as a whole, the Ruhr campaign was considered an "impressive victory."[52] It marked the first time Bomber Command had mounted a truly effective "series of consistent and pulverizing blows" on the enemy, with "failures much rarer than the successes."[53] At last, Bomber Command had delivered the sort of blows that the airmen had long been promising; and, according to Harris, this was "only the beginning."[54] More than thirty thousand German civilians had been killed during the campaign.[55] Nazi Propaganda Minister Joseph Goebbels wrote that such heavy civilian casualties would inevitably affect morale. He considered the Ruhr's flak and fighter defences inadequate. Glumly rating the damage to Essen as "ghastly," he was of the opinion that the city might have to be "written off." If it could be repaired, he calculated, the job would take a dozen years. The Nazis sent a hundred thousand workers to the Ruhr to help with repair work, and they brought more flak guns and fighters in from other theatres of war. In such ways did the bombing war relieve pressure on the Soviets and the Allied armies in the Middle East.[56]

When Hitler learned of the casualties and damage, he ordered immediate retaliation against Britain. He succeeded only in helping to cripple German efforts to defend the *Reich*. His biggest mistake was to insist on the development of the so-called "vengeance" weapons, the V-1 and the V-2; although these missiles caused much damage and many casualties, they consumed a disproportionate amount of manpower and resources that might otherwise have been used to bolster the *Luftwaffe*'s strength.[57]

The success of the Oboe Mosquitoes galvanized the *Luftwaffe*'s chief, Göring, into creating *Jagdgruppen* 25 and 50. These fighter squadrons flew "specially modified" interceptors for the express purpose of hunting and destroying the agile, speedy Mosquitoes.

The units failed to score a single victory and were disbanded late in 1943.[58]

Although many of Bomber Command's raids on Ruhr targets had been highly successful, losses proved serious, at times close to "insupportable."[59] Throughout the battle, the vast majority of aircrew continued to do their duty, despite the awful strain of intensive operational flying and the poor prospects of survival. Bomber Command mounted 18,506 sorties and lost 872 aircraft, 4.7 per cent of the force.[60] The Canadian Group mounted 2,649 sorties and suffered 145 losses, 5.4 per cent of the force. Thus, on paper at least, the Battle wiped out 6 Group. Every German raid cost the Group an average of four aircraft and crews. French targets and Gardening operations cost an average of one aircraft for every two ops.

The percentage of 6 Group crews claiming to have attacked the primary targets rose steadily in the months from March to June (79.2, 82.9, 86.1, and 87.9 per cent respectively). The tonnage of bombs dropped by the Group ranged from 1,475 tons in March to 1,027 in April, from 739 in May to 1,886 in June, the variations being due to the comings and goings of the Group's squadrons. Of particular concern to Brookes and his staff was the ominously steady rise in losses: twenty-nine in March, forty-one in April, thirty-five in May, and thirty-six in June, representing 2.6, 5.1, 6.8, and 7.1 per cent of the forces involved, heavy losses indeed for a new group and, with one exception, considerably higher than the losses for Bomber Command as a whole over the same period.[61]

It always nettled Harris that Bomber Command's achievements caused such little excitement at home. "What shouts of victory would arise if a Commando wrecked the entire Renault operation in a night, with the loss of seven men!" he wrote,

> What credible assumptions of an early end to the war would follow upon the destruction of a third of Cologne in an hour and a half by some swiftly moving mechanized force which, with but 200 casualties, withdrew and was ready to repeat the operation 24 hours later! What acclaim would greet the virtual destruction of Rostock and the Heinkel main and subsidiary

factories by a Naval bombardment! All this, and far more, has been achieved by Bomber Command, yet there are many who still avert their gaze, pass by on the other side, and question whether the thirty squadrons of night bombers make any worthwhile contribution to the war.[62]

The Group's flying accident rate was yet another cause for concern at Allerton Hall in those early days, although it began to decline as the squadrons acquired experience and became better established in their new bases. In March, the rate was 29.1 accidents per thousand hours; in succeeding months, it fell to 27.9, 24.9, and 22.3 accidents per thousand hours. The Group's record of serviceability over the same period was hardly enviable at 59.8, 63.1, 60.8, and 63.2 per cent, but it would improve.[63]

The Canadian Group had acquitted itself reasonably well in the Battle of the Ruhr, although its losses, its poor early-return and serviceability record, and its higher than average tally of flying accidents did little to encourage its aircrews and ground staff. The wonder is that morale among the operational squadrons remained as high as it did.

Day by day, 6 Group was finding its feet, learning to operate in a no-holds-barred air war. It had to learn rapidly. Bomber Command and 6 Group were about to embark on another major battle.

4

THE BATTLE OF HAMBURG

"I had taken three other pilot friends to
Scotland on leave to stay with my aunt. All three
were killed; my aunt was so broken up."

Jack McIntosh, DFC, pilot, 419 Squadron

The raw nerves and confusion were bad enough. But, since take-off, they had become wrapped up in the certainty that something was wrong, seriously, dangerously wrong. Alarmed, the German night fighter pilots cursed. Their radar operators kept calling out targets. But, hell, they were targets that simply didn't exist! According to the radar screen, the sky was full of bombers, all flying uncommonly slowly. But no shapes materialized out of the darkness. No slipstream joggled the fighters. The signal vanished, to be replaced a moment later by another, equally false.

The controllers on the ground sounded baffled, almost panicky.

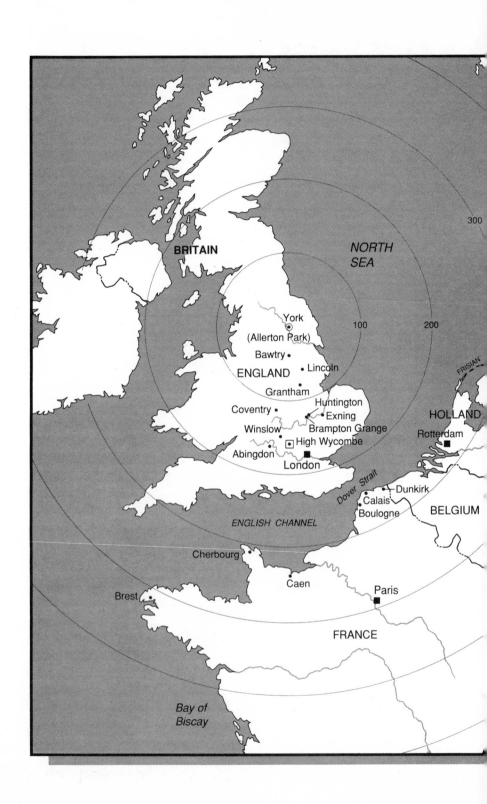

NORWAY

SWEDEN

600

DENMARK

BALTIC
SEA

Peenemünde

400 Kiel •   500
Lübeck •   Rostock
      • Hamburg

700   800   900

Ruhr

■
Berlin

River

Gelsenkirchen
• Dortmund   GERMANY
Essen
Cologne   • Dresden

Rhine
River   • Prague

• Frankfurt
• Mannheim   • Nuremberg

Munich •

**DISTANCES FROM YORK, ENG.,
TO EUROPEAN CENTRES**

⊙ 6 Group Headquarters

▣ Bomber Command Headquarters

0   100   200 miles
Scale

Technical problems, they kept muttering. A massive attacking force ... but no one seemed to know its precise location. They'd have things sorted out in a moment. They hoped.

Luftwaffe veteran Wilhelm Johnen later wrote: "It was obvious no one knew exactly where the enemy was or what his objective would be. An early recognition of the direction was essential so that the night fighters could be introduced into the bomber stream. But the radio reports kept contradicting themselves. Now the enemy was over Amsterdam and then suddenly west of Brussels, and a moment later they were reported far out to sea in Map Square 25. What was to be done?"[1]

Nothing could be done. The German defences had been outmanoeuvred – and by the simplest of devices: several million strips of coarse black paper each 27 cm long and 2 cm wide, backed on one side by aluminum foil. The bombers had started dropping the strips near the German coast, creating a veritable snowstorm of echoes on the German radar screens.[2] To alarmed operators, it looked as if countless thousands of aircraft were approaching – but from what direction or at what height no one could say.

It was the night of July 24/25, 1943. Despite the evidence of the wide-eyed radar operators' sets, the force attacking Hamburg did not consist of thousands, but of less than eight hundred bombers. And despite the ferocious defences set up to protect Germany's major port city, only twelve bombers were shot down, a mere 1.5 per cent of the force. Not until the morning, and the discovery of millions of metal strips that festooned the countryside like out-of-season Christmas decorations, did the Germans understand what had happened.

Harris had for some time been planning a devastating series of attacks on Hamburg. His avowed intention was to destroy the city. How long could Germany continue to wage war with its cities being wiped off the map one by one? But the question might just as well have been asked: How long could Bomber Command continue to take the sort of excruciating losses that it suffered in the Battle of the Ruhr? It says much for the courage and morale of Bomber Command's airmen, the efficiency of the training organization, and the productivity of the British aircraft industry, that Harris could embark on his campaign against Hamburg so soon after his series of attacks on the Ruhr.

Two months earlier, on May 27, 1943, Harris had issued his Operations Order No. 173: "The importance of HAMBURG, the second largest city in Germany with a population of one and a half millions, is well known and needs no further emphasis. The total destruction of this city would achieve immeasurable results in reducing the industrial capacity of the enemy's war machine. This, together with the effect on German morale, which would be felt throughout the country, would play a very important part in shortening and winning the war."

The intention, Harris declared in his unequivocal style, was to "destroy Hamburg." He estimated that it would take ten thousand tons of bombs to do the job, delivered in a series of attacks so intensive that the city's defences would not have time to recover from one before the next struck home.[3]

It was a priority target. Germany's major port and its second largest city, Hamburg was the centre of U-Boat construction. This fact alone justified the most strenuous efforts by Bomber Command. But Hamburg offered more plum targets: oil refineries and an enticing selection of factories and chemical plants. Indeed, Hamburg was the perfect military/industrial target. In May of 1942, Harris had intended to send his laboriously assembled force of one thousand bombers to the city. But weather conditions had necessitated a last-minute switch to Cologne. Since then, Bomber Command had raided Hamburg close to a hundred times, but none of the attacks could be classified as "devastating." Harris meant to correct that state of affairs. His code name for the operation was suitably ominous: *Gomorrah*.[4]

Coincidentally, the government at last gave Harris permission to introduce the device that would so bewilder the German fighter pilots as well as the radar operators of the Kammhuber Line, Germany's first line of defence against Allied bombers. The device's code name was "Window." The concept of "blinding" the enemy radar by filling the screens with countless echoes had been around for some time. Early in 1942, the tireless boffins in England had come up with the idea and had conducted tests with excellent results. But in Britain, as elsewhere, the nation's leaders regarded with extreme caution any idea that appeared to offer significant technological advances. For example, the introduction of new types of sea mines was held up for years, the politicians pointing out that Britain was even more vulnerable to sea-mining than was Germany; since it was certain that any worthwhile idea would eventually get into the hands of the enemy and be used against Britain, Britain might, in the end, suffer more from its own invention than Germany.

While this cautious approach infuriated many people, it was far from irrational. When the anti-radar strips first appeared, Allied fortunes had hit rock bottom. Russia was still reeling from the German assault, its defeat by no means an impossibility. And if Russia fell, wouldn't the *Luftwaffe* immediately resume its assault on Britain? And wouldn't the Germans be able to use their version of the device to devastating effect?[5] And wouldn't it also neutralize much of the Navy's efforts against the U-Boats?[6] It's interesting to note that much the same sort of agonizing was going on in Germany. The *Luftwaffe* had experimented with an anti-radar device known as *Düppel*. It alarmed Germany's leaders as much as the aluminized strips alarmed the British hierarchy. General Wolfgang Martini, the head of the *Luftwaffe*'s signals organization, warned that if it was used against Germany it would mean the "end of the German air defence system."[7] Aghast, Göring issued one of his many ill-conceived orders: No one, under pain of death, must talk of the existence of *Düppel* – and all research, even on countermeasures, must cease forthwith.[8]

In Britain, Harris had been impatient to make use of Window. He knew that Germany's Kammhuber Line, stretching from northern Denmark to the Swiss border, was totally dependent upon radar. *Freya* and *Würzburg* sets tracked incoming bombers; radar guided the searchlight and flak batteries. The thought of being able to render the elaborate system impotent was almost intoxicating. But he had to wait. In his memoirs he wrote: "It would have been idiotic to drop metallised paper over Germany in August of 1940, but in 1942 I was certain that the time had come to take such risks, which did not seem to be very serious, for the sake of the offensive. During the summer of 1942 I continually pressed for the development and, where possible, immediate use of equipment and measures to jam and interfere with the enemy's radar and radio transmissions. But the authorities considered that we were still too vulnerable to air attack . . ."[9]

In mid-1943, the politicians at last agreed: the time had come to put the new device to the test. In the last twelve months, the whole complexion of the war had changed. The position of the Axis powers had deteriorated to such an extent that they couldn't make much use of *Düppel* against Britain; besides, the latest radar equipment installed in the RAF's night fighters could "outsmart" it. On July 15, Portal gave Harris permission to use Window.[10]

The aircrews heard about it at briefing late on the afternoon of July 24. They perked up when told that Window would confound the enemy defences and reduce casualties, although it was a mixed blessing for the crew members who would have to dump the packets of strips down flare chutes. Some squadrons selected flight engineers for the job; in other units, wireless operators or air gunners handled it. Whatever their trade, the crewmen reckoned it would be hard work trussed up in flying gear with oxygen and intercom connections hindering their movements. They were right. Unaccustomed to handling the bundles, some airmen found the strips blowing back up the flare chutes and filling their aircraft.[11] One man even sported a black eye on his return from Hamburg; a whole bundle of Window had come hurtling back into the aircraft and had hit him full in the face.[12] (Soon all Bomber Command aircraft would have special chutes to facilitate the deployment of Window.)

Bomber Command sent 791 aircraft to attack Hamburg on the night of July 24/25. Slightly less than 10 per cent of the force, seventy-two bombers, came from 6 Group: fifty-one Halifaxes from 408, 419, 427, and 428 Squadrons and twenty-one Wellingtons from 429 and 432 Squadrons. Six of the Canadian aircraft returned early (along with forty from the RAF Groups). The force followed a northern route crossing the Baltic, the Pathfinders leading the way.[13]

As they neared the target, the Pathfinder navigators peered into the flickering screens of their recently installed H2S sets. The H2S-equipped aircraft were instantly identifiable; an odd bulge spoiled their underside lines midway between the wings and tail unit. At this stage of the war, relatively few of Harris's bombers carried the equipment, although it had been used on about one-third of the raids during the Battle of the Ruhr.[14] Self-contained and thus independent of any transmitting stations on the ground, H2S sent a directional beam of high energy directly earthward, the beam rotating with its antenna approximately once per second. The aircraft's antenna picked up reflections from these beams; they appeared on a cathode ray tube with a radial scanning line from its centre to its circumference rotating in phase with the antenna. Each signal received registered as a bright spot on the screen; thus areas with good reflectivity, such as coastlines, urban areas, forests, and lakes appeared strongly, creating the necessary contrast to "paint a picture" of the terrain below.[15] It sounded simple, but it wasn't. Operators found they needed skill and practice to interpret H2S accurately; the screen produced a "flickering, often indeterminate picture."[16] Furthermore, at this early stage in its development, the equipment had an appalling record of serviceability; indeed, at the time of the Hamburg raids, if a set remained serviceable for an entire sortie, navigators were known to make delighted entries in their logs along the lines of: "H2S actually worked!" Hamburg was a good test for the device. With the sharply defined coastline to the northwest and the estuary of the Elbe providing a virtual signpost to the city, it possessed all the right characteristics.[17]

On this attack, the Pathfinders were to mark the target by the "Newhaven" method, a combination of H2S and visual target identification. Conditions were excellent with good visibility, except for slight haze.

At two minutes after one in the morning, the citizens of Hamburg saw the eerie lights of the Pathfinders' TIs. The attack had begun. From the air, it was obvious that the markers were "a little scattered." The "backers-up" and "recenterers" came in and did their best to get the marking back to the middle of the aiming point. In this they were only partially successful. Less than half the aircraft dropped their bombs inside the three-mile radius of the city centre. As anticipated, the Main Force bombers began to "creep back" as they bombed, although much of this may have been caused by the fact that their new Mark XIV bombsights had no terminal velocity setting for bombs as light as the standard four-pound incendiary, which were used in large numbers that night. In this case, absolute accuracy mattered less than usual.

Hamburg was a huge target. As long as a bomb fell within the city limits, it would probably hit something of importance. On the night of July 24/25, the northwestern and central areas of the city suffered badly. Bombs or fire destroyed or damaged the main telephone exchange, the zoo, the central police station, the *Niko-laikirche*, and the *Rathaus*. About fifteen hundred people died.[18] "Coal and coke supplies stored for the winter in many houses caught fire and could only be extinguished weeks later. Essential services were severely damaged. . ."[19]

The Canadian Group's Wellingtons attacked in the fourth wave of bombers starting at 0126; the Halifaxes formed part of the next wave which began dropping its bombs at 0134 hours.

Returning 6 Group crews were enthusiastic. In spite of the "intense pall of smoke" from countless fires, crews identified the target and talked of the "heavy concentration" of bombs, of thick black smoke rising to a height of four miles, and of "many violent explosions." Reports declared ebulliently: "This was an excellent attack with a high degree of concentration. The target area was left a mass of raging fires . . . The defences, which were strong in the initial stages of the attack, became very wild toward the end."

Window had performed brilliantly. The Canadian Group's crews had reason to feel particularly grateful to the device. Not one of their number had been lost. Crews saw searchlights "wandering all over the sky" as they "groped blindly" for the bombers. Sometimes "thirty or forty beams would build up to form a cone – on nothing." The flak batteries, robbed of their radar control, reverted to the box barrages of an earlier era, firing "vast quantities of shells" without hitting anything. Window had reduced the German radar stations to "hopeless confusion." British "Y" Service operators heard the Germans exclaim: "The enemy are reproducing themselves!"[20]

Flight Lieutenant G.F. Pentony of 429 Squadron later wrote: "The Master searchlights and all the others were waving aimlessly about the sky like a man trying to swat a flying ant in a swarm . . . The crew hoped to do as many trips as possible in the next few weeks so they would finish their tour before the enemy found a solution."

Unable to obtain any help from the ground, most German night fighter pilots turned off their radar sets and relied on their eyesight. They succeeded in spotting many bombers silhouetted against the bright fires burning in the city below. They shot down at least half a dozen, plus several more en route for home. Flak got the rest.

Although none of 6 Group's aircraft was lost, two Halifaxes from 419 Squadron encountered German night fighters. Near the German coast JD270 was flying at 19,000 feet when the rear gunner, Sergeant A.D.H. Garland, saw a Ju 88 "with a large white light in the nose." For a few moments, the fighter flew 300 yards to port and level with the bomber. Then it turned to attack. Garland "opened fire at 250 yards and continued" to blaze away until the fighter dived away to port. The Ju 88 did not fire a shot.[21]

Halifax DT548 was at 20,000 feet when the rear gunner, Sergeant J.N. Pilon, saw a single-engined Me 109 above. Pilon rotated his turret, "but before he could call out evasive action, the fighter opened fire." Two bursts passed below the rear turret. In return, Pilon gave the German fighter a "long accurate burst." It immediately broke off the attack and "rolled off to starboard seemingly out of control. It was seen to go down in a fast spiral dive and was lost to view 15,000 feet below." The crew claimed the fighter as probably damaged.[22]

Thus ended the first operation in the Battle of Hamburg. It was by any reckoning an excellent raid with amazingly low casualties. The city was still burning when the bombers left, the fires in the districts of Altona, Hoheluft, and Eimsbuttel out of control for hours. When the all-clear finally sounded soon after three o'clock, one thousand citizens were still trapped in an air raid shelter in the Bismarckstrasse surrounded by roaring fires. They later escaped. In Hagenbeck Park, lions, tigers, elephants, and bears wandered, dazed and frightened, having survived the bombs that killed most of the inhabitants of the zoo. Shortly after four in the morning, the city declared a "Major Catastrophe." Fires still blazed when, at last, the pale light of dawn crept over the stricken city. A miasma-like pall of smoke rose to some fifteen thousand feet, hanging motionless in the still air. Survivors looked up at it and shook their heads in wonder that they had come through the ordeal. Now they began the awful task of digging out their dead and injured and getting the city back to some semblance of normality. But in the early afternoon their work was interrupted.

Heads were raised in disbelief. No, it couldn't be. But it was. Another air raid alarm! This time the Americans attacked in their heavily armed Flying Fortresses. They concentrated on the docks, but the dense smoke still rising from the fires started by Bomber Command made accurate bombing difficult. Then, when darkness returned, six RAF Mosquitoes screamed across the city, sending the ragged-nerved citizens running for the shelters to the sound of more explosions and gunfire.

Hamburg had taken a terrible beating. But the city's ordeal had only just begun.

The success of Window exceeded Harris's expectations. If only he had been allowed to use it during the Battle of the Ruhr, how many airmen's lives would have been spared? How much greater would have been the damage inflicted upon the enemy? Impatient to test the device again, he immediately ordered a maximum effort attack on one of the most formidable of Ruhr targets, Essen. Twenty-four hours had elapsed since his bombers had set off for Hamburg. A force of 705 took off for Essen; 66 were 6 Group aircraft. Window again demonstrated its effectiveness; however, it was clear that the Germans had already begun to recover from the shock of its introduction and that the radar operators were learning to "read" the differences between the echoes created by Window and those created by actual aircraft. The crews reckoned it wouldn't be long before Jerry came up with countermeasures.

Twenty-six bombers didn't return from the Essen op. Two were 6 Group aircraft. At 3.7 per cent of the force, it was by no means a catastrophic loss, certainly not by Ruhr standards. But it indicated that the Germans were finding out how to cope and were experimenting with new ideas, all too conscious that the rigid tactics of the Kammhuber Line no longer sufficed.

The Essen raid was a singular success, with particularly heavy damage being inflicted on the Krupp plants in the eastern sector of the city. It is said that when Gustav Krupp saw what the bombers had done to his factories, he suffered a stroke from which he never recovered.

As the crews flew home from Essen, U.S. Eighth Air Force crews were clambering out of their beds to be briefed for yet another raid on Hamburg, an effective attack that caused extensive damage in the yards of Blohm & Voss, the principal builder of U-Boats. The city's already-strained utilities suffered an almost fatal blow when the Neuhof power station took several direct hits. The Army had to be called in to maintain order and to help clear paths through the rubble-strewn streets.

Bomber Command's aircrews had the night of July 26 off; Harris's practice was to rest his Main Force crews for twenty-four hours after they had operated on two consecutive nights. Nevertheless, he despatched six Mosquitoes to Hamburg to keep the defences – and the citizens – on edge.

On the 27th he ordered another maximum effort on Hamburg. It was to be a virtual carbon copy of the highly successful raid on July 24/25. Only the course was slightly modified, apparently in the hope of convincing the Germans that the target was Kiel or possibly Lübeck.

Nearly eight hundred aircraft took off in the late evening of July 27 after a perfect summer's day. 6 Group contributed eighty-one: sixty-two Halifaxes from 408, 419, 427, and 428 Squadrons and nineteen Wellingtons from 429 and 432 Squadrons. Nine returned early, 11.1 per cent of the Canadian force, another worryingly high figure for the staff at Allerton Park to ponder.

The bombers encountered cloud as they crossed the North Sea, but the skies cleared near the German coast where the crews began dropping Window. They could see Hamburg clearly in the distance; fires still burned, orange glows spawning great columns of black smoke rising vertically into the night sky. Again the Pathfinders marked by H2S, their electronic transmissions piercing the smoke and dust that rose to some twenty thousand feet and hung threateningly over the battered city.

It had been uncommonly hot and dry in Hamburg that summer. Less than 1.7 inches of rain fell in July. At 1800 hours on July 27, the temperature stood at thirty degrees Celsius, with the humidity reading barely 30 per cent. The air, utterly still, clung like a stifling shroud. Sweating, puffing, the citizens stayed at their open windows and doors until the bombers were overhead. Then they hurried to the shelters, familiar havens after several nights and days of raids.

The first markers went down a few minutes before one in the

morning, July 28. The bombs followed. In the next little while, the high explosives and incendiaries would work in awful concert with the climatic conditions to create a rapacious monster of a fire that erased an entire section of the city and added a new word to the lexicon of war: "firestorm." The blaze took hold at once; crews reported huge billows of smoke rising as high as twenty-four thousand feet. One airman described the scene below as "a sheet of flame." An Australian gunner found his turret coated with soot.[23] Al Avant, a Canadian pilot on his first tour with 115 Squadron, recalls: "You had to see the place to believe it. The whole city seemed to be burning." Most skippers ordered their gunners not to look down; the intensity of the blaze would spoil their night vision. For Harry Holland of 427 Squadron, the Hamburg firestorm raid was his introduction to operational conditions. Flying as Second Dickey to Pilot Officer Rodwell, an RAF pilot, he had a grandstand view of the burning city and remembers it as a sight beyond belief: "It was incredible. The place was a great mass of flame. Halfway home we could still see the smoke rising from Hamburg." Holland recalls too the "aimless waving" of the searchlight beams and the ineffective flak over the city.

Although this raid had such horrific consequences, it should be understood that it was in every way a standard area-bombing operation. High explosive bombs and incendiaries fell on Hamburg in approximately equal tonnages, as they did on most targets.[24] The mixture had been developed empirically; it had been found that the small four-pound incendiaries were effective at starting fires in roofs while the larger thirty-pound incendiaries were heavy enough to smash through roofs and start fires within buildings. The job of the high explosive bombs was to blow out windows, doors, and walls to help spread the fires, at the same time wrecking roads and destroying water mains and power facilities, disrupting the work of firemen and rescue workers. In the popular imagination, air raids tended to be series of giant explosions, but in fact fire was the principal means of destruction on area-bombing operations.

That night in Hamburg, the intensely concentrated bombing had set in motion a horrific phenomenon. First, scores of fires in the Hammerbrook District merged into one huge conflagration, a process probably aided by the presence of a large lumberyard in the centre of the area. Roaring, bellowing, the vast fire was quickly out of control. It consumed oxygen in gargantuan quantities. Hungry for more, it pulled in air from all around, in many cases from buildings already burning. Sparks, cinders, chunks of burning wood went spinning through the air, sucked in by the fire's voracious appetite, immediately setting more buildings alight, spreading the blaze, adding to the pyre. Soon the fire's need for oxygen became frantic. What had started as a relatively gentle movement of air rapidly gathered strength. In minutes, winds became gales, then hurricanes, as the flames dragged in ever-increasing volumes of air. Gobbling the precious oxygen, the furnace desperately reached out for more, then even more, creating a kind of chimney which kept sucking in increasing volumes of oxygen with a force born of desperation. Howling, screaming, the winds became a maelstrom that dragged trees out of the ground, tore roofs off houses, plucked people from the streets, flinging them all into the holocaust. No one will ever know precisely how many people the hellish vortex swept into the blaze to be incinerated in a second; some people managed to lie down behind walls while the winds roared over them. In all too many cases, they never moved again; baked where they lay, their bodies soon melted into the asphalt. Occupants of shelters died by the thousand, victims of carbon monoxide poisoning. Many fell dead as they tried in vain to escape, their bodies roasting on steps or in doorways. Trees, buildings, even people, suddenly burst into flames in the superheated, tinder-dry atmosphere.

To make matters worse, most of Hamburg's fire-fighting equipment was at that time engaged in the western part of the city, working to extinguish fires that had been burning for days. Even though equipment was hurriedly moved to the affected area, the firemen couldn't get near the biggest fire any of them had ever seen; the heat was far too intense. Besides, they had nothing capable of making an impression on this monstrosity of a blaze. They could do little but wait for the firestorm to burn itself out. It took more than three hours, the flames fanned and spread by ferocious winds that sounded "like the devil howling," according to survivors.

The heat soared to an incredible eight hundred degrees Celsius, only falling slowly as the fire began to subside, having consumed everything within reach. A four-square-mile area of the city had ceased to exist. Some forty thousand people had died; about sixteen thousand apartment units had been destroyed. More than a million people, two-thirds of the population, fled the city. The peacetime predictions of the airmen were coming true. Bombing was eliminating a major city. Karl Otto Kaufmann, *Gauleiter* of Hamburg, was "forced to close down all normal life in his city" so that all available resources could be harnessed for the living, the injured, the trapped, the lost. There was food to be found, medical treatment to be organized, fires still to be extinguished. Kaufmann faced a monstrous task, made tougher by the possibility of widespread looting and the very real danger of some fearful epidemic sweeping the shattered city.[25]

The bomb-aimers in the last waves of bombers hardly knew where to drop their bombs. Many crews said they could feel the heat billowing up from the city that writhed below them like some vast creature in torment. The stink of smoke was sharp in their oxygen masks. When the last bombs had fallen, the airmen turned for home. Although they thought the defences stronger than on July 24/25, they said they "appeared to lack punch and accuracy." Flak was erratic, as were the searchlights. The CO of 419 Squadron, Wing Commander M.M. Fleming, felt that "the greatest danger was the risk of collision with other aircraft over the target." He had had four near misses during his run over the city. One 6 Group aircraft had been hit by incendiaries dropped from above, but the crew managed to bring the bomber back to base.[26]

Mobile flak batteries had supplemented Hamburg's defences. The guns put up a spirited but not notably accurate barrage up to an altitude of eighteen thousand feet. Above that level, the night fighters held sway; for the first time they had priority over the anti-aircraft guns. Already recovering from the shock of Window, the Germans were experimenting with new tactics. On the night of the firestorm they introduced the concept of a "running commentary" (*laufende Reportage*). Operations officers gathered information on the bombers' direction, speed, and height from ground observers' and pilots' reports and passed it on to any fighters on their frequencies. It was a somewhat rough-and-ready system but it proved far more flexible than Kammhuber's rigid setup, although it enjoyed only modest success on this occasion. Under the code name *Zame Sau* ("Tame Boar"), the system would become Germany's main line of night defence in the brutal months ahead, with fighters joining the bomber streams en route to the target and home.[27]

Over Hamburg, the Germans also introduced another concept, the so-called *Wilde Sau* ("Wild Boar") fighters of Major Hans-Joachim Herrmann, a former bomber pilot, a Knight's Cross winner who had flown a remarkable total of over three hundred operational sorties. Herrmann's idea was an extension of an earlier system, "Illuminated Night Fighting" (*Helle Nachtjagd*), using single-engined fighters, Me 109s and Fw 190s, flying over the flak and seeking out the bombers by the glare of searchlights, fires, and flares. Herrmann had first proposed his system in January. It had been fiercely opposed but, early in July, over Cologne, a dozen of Herrmann's pilots attacked bombers above the flak's supposed maximum altitude of twenty thousand feet. Communications had failed and the flak commanders did not know of the fighters' presence. In spite of the need to dodge their own flak, the fighters shot down twelve bombers. Herrmann received immediate approval to form a Wild Boar squadron.

Herrmann needed airmen with experience in instrument flying; thus, dozens of ex-bomber and ex-transport personnel were soon clambering into the confined cockpits of high-powered single-engined aircraft and attempting to learn how to be fighter pilots in a few hours. Some did astonishingly well. Captain Friedrich-Karl Müller became the "Wild Boar Ace of Aces" with twenty-three kills in fifty-two sorties. Thus, while the painstakingly organized Kammhuber Line collapsed in a welter of Window, the freelance fighters under Herrmann operated without the assistance of radar, except, of course, for the early-warning *Freya* which was impervious to the metallic strips. Herrmann's fighters scored many successes during the period of the Battle of Hamburg and later, but the concept possessed several shortcomings. The single-engined Messerschmitts and Focke-Wulfs lacked the endurance of the twin-engined Ju 88, Me 110, and other night fighters and had never been designed for nocturnal operations. Flying accidents wrote off dozens of Herrmann's aircraft and pilots, many of whom found themselves unable to cope with the sudden transition from good-natured Ju 52s to spirited fighters. Moreover, the lack of cooperation between flak and fighters proved to be a serious shortcoming. Again and again Herrmann's pilots found the anti-aircraft batteries blazing away to whatever height they thought necessary. Inter-Service cooperation seems to have been a problem in Germany as in every other nation. But perhaps the most serious shortcoming of the Wild Boar concept was that none of the ground controllers knew when or where the fighters would operate. Echoes would appear on radar screens, but the controllers didn't know whether they came from enemy bombers or Herrmann's fighters. The limited range of the single-engined fighters made it imperative that they found their targets quickly. But the British kept shortening their raids, pushing their streams of bombers through the target areas as rapidly as possible. As the bombing war intensified, the RAF devoted increasing efforts to confuse the Germans as to the targets for any given night. So-called "spoof" raids became an inevitable adjunct to any maximum effort. The work of the fighter controllers was also made more difficult by the broadcasting of false orders by German-speaking RAF operators – and the jamming of fighter frequencies by Bomber Command wireless operators who transmitted the din of their aircraft engines on the fighters' frequencies.[28]

Bomber Command's losses on the night of the firestorm were seventeen aircraft, 2.2 per cent of the force, higher than on July 24/25, but still gratifyingly lower than what had become the accepted norm for raids on Hamburg. The Canadian Group lost two, a Wellington from 429 Squadron and a Halifax from 408 Squadron. The 429 Squadron loss involved the CO, a Canadian in the RAF, Wing Commander Jimmy Piddington. He and two of his crew, the bomb-aimer, Paul Renton, and the navigator, Ron Farquhar, were killed. One of the two survivors, the RAF rear gunner, Reg Scarth, recalls that the crew was operating a brand-new Wellington "which was developing too much power." He says the skipper couldn't throttle back sufficiently because of over-heating problems – and "we found ourselves anything up to two minutes ahead of the wave and consequently a sitting duck for the German radar." An Me 110 night fighter shot the Wimpy down. Scarth remembers Piddington as "a very popular and well-liked officer. He was quiet, he had a sense of humour and he earned the respect of both his crew and the squadron."

The flight engineer of the missing 408 Squadron Halifax, Flying Officer J.H. Borley, recalls what happened as the aircraft crossed the Kiel Canal: "It was rather hazy and a fighter made a frontal attack from below and set No. 2 starboard fuel tank on fire. I reported the fire to the pilot and before I had finished speaking another fighter came in from astern . . ." This second fighter wrecked the rear and mid-upper turrets and the tail controls. Borley found his intercom out of action. He checked on the wing fire, handed the skipper, Flight Lieutenant C.C. Stovel, his parachute, then turned to look down the fuselage and ". . . the next thing I remember was swinging in my chute with parts of the aircraft floating around me." The crew's wireless operator, Pilot Officer G.J. Richardson, remembered Stovel ordering the crew to bale out: ". . . he told me over the intercom he was coming next . . . but he never did get out; why, I don't know as when my chute opened the aircraft was still flying straight and level . . ." Richardson, Borley, and the navigator, Flying Officer Bemister, survived to become POWs. Stovel and four others (including a Second Dickey) perished.

Bomber Command dropped 2,326 tons of bombs that night. The last bomber to unload over Hamburg was a 427 Squadron Halifax commanded by Sergeant R.L. Henry. Coincidentally, Henry's had been the last bomber to land back at base after the Hamburg raid on July 24/25. (A month later, Henry would die with three ground crew when the Oxford aircraft he was flying hit a hill in England.)[29]

Harris was determined to give the still-smouldering city of Hamburg no respite. Uncounted numbers of her citizens, dead and alive, remained buried in rubble. Troops and emergency workers laboured to remove corpses – many little more than ash – and clear the city's streets. Smoke rose from scores of fires still smouldering beneath mountains of wreckage. The sickening odour of burning flesh hung over every corner of the blackened ruins. Those who had survived so far went about with a hunted look in their eyes. When would the *Terrorflieger* return? Just before midnight on July 29 they had their answer. Another major force was approaching from the northwest: 777 bombers, including 76 from 6 Group (83 took off and 7 returned early). Again the marking was by H2S, with the northern and northeastern sectors the prime targets since they had so far escaped the worst of the bombing. But the Pathfinders missed the aiming point by at least two miles; subsequently, the Main Force bombing crept back another four miles. The residential areas of Barmbek, Wandsbek, Uhlenhorst, and Winterhude suffered the most. A shelter in a department store in Wandsbek collapsed and close to four hundred people died. Well over two thousand tons of bombs fell, setting off more fires, though no firestorm.

Returning crews remarked that the ground defences had made a "considerable recovery" buttressed by "unusually large reinforcements" of searchlights that extended for forty miles across the target area. They remarked that the effectiveness of Window had already declined. Fighters claimed most of the twenty-eight Bomber Command aircraft (3.6 per cent of the force) that failed to return that morning. Two of the missing bombers were from 6 Group.[30] One, a Halifax from 428 Squadron, was commanded by Sergeant D.H. Bates. The sole survivor, the bomb-aimer, Warrant Officer P. Demcoe, remembered the starboard outer engine "running away." The crew couldn't feather it; moments later it burst into flames. Bates told the crew he had no control. A moment later the aircraft went into a spin. Demcoe was knocked unconscious as he escaped through the emergency exit. He came to "falling through the air – my parachute had come off the snaps and was above my head. I reached up, found the ripcord and pulled it."[31]

The other 6 Group loss was a Wellington flown by the CO of 432 Squadron, Wing Commander H.W. Kerby. The crew's navigator, Warrant Officer J.H. Smith, later reported that the bomber had been coned by "a large number" of searchlights, although he saw little flak. Kerby kept corkscrewing energetically, doing his best to escape the lights. But an Me 109, one of Herrmann's Wild Boars, appeared from the starboard side. Both aircraft opened fire. Smith thought Kerby had been hit although he managed to give the order to abandon aircraft. By now the Wellington had plunged in "a long dive." Smith put his parachute on but couldn't reach the exit, the centrifugal force pinning him against the aircraft's roof. A moment later he found himself tumbling freely, the aircraft having broken up around him. His parachute opened at about one thousand feet and he landed safely, if heavily, to be taken prisoner, the only survivor. Kerby was the second squadron commander to die in the Battle.[32]

Several 6 Group aircraft encountered German fighters. Pilot Officer Vandekerckhove of 427 Squadron, who in March had fought his way through a series of difficulties over the Ruhr, was turning away from the target when "forty or fifty" searchlights coned his Halifax. Simultaneously both gunners saw an Fw 190 at 150 yards "on the port beam up." The fighter turned in to attack and opened fire. Vandekerckhove's gunners replied. Neither aircraft hit the other. The fighter then proceeded to fly a parallel course to the Halifax's at about five hundred yards. By this time the bomber was clear of the searchlights – and was immediately attacked by a Ju 88 from the rear. Again both aircraft opened fire and again the Halifax was almost unscathed. The fighter, on the other hand, went into a spin and vanished from view. The Halifax's rear gunner, Sergeant J.J. McLean, received credit for one fighter probably destroyed.[33]

Harris was impatient to deliver the *coup de grâce*, the final blow that would eradicate Hamburg from the German industrial scene. And once Hamburg had gone, Harris planned to move on to Berlin and other cities, destroying them one by one until Germany could no longer continue to fight. At last the enemy – and a lot of Allies – would find out what accurate, concentrated bombing could accomplish. Bomber Command would cut the industrial and urban heart out of Germany. But the weather deteriorated. Harris had to wait.

Reconnaissance photographs revealed that, in spite of the unquestioned success of the raids to date, some areas of Hamburg had suffered relatively little damage. Bomber Command's planners set to work to finish the job. They decided to use two aiming points on the next raid, one in the north of the city for the first wave of bombers, a second in the south for the last two waves. They reasoned that if any creepback developed in the early part of the raid it would tend to edge the attack in the direction of the second aiming point. For the first time in this campaign, the bombers would cross the city from south to north, then turn sharply northwest midway between Hamburg and Kiel on their way home.

The weather prevented the planned attack on the thirtieth; instead, a small force went to Remscheid in the Ruhr, a raid that cost two 6 Group aircraft. Again, on August 1, the weather was unsuitable for a raid on Hamburg. Impatient, Harris vowed to finish off the city the next day. Not for the last time he would place his crews' lives at risk by taking a calculated gamble on the weather developing the way he wanted.

At briefing, the 763 crews detailed for the raid heard that marking was to be by the Newhaven method – with emergency "Wanganui" (blind sky-marking) should weather conditions necessitate the switch. The more experienced aircrew frowned uneasily. Conditions looked far from ideal. At station after station, the Met officers got up and assured the crews that things appeared to be improving . . . although it had to be admitted there was a *possibility* of some troublesome cumulus developing near the target. It sounded to most crews as if this was going to be one of those days that would see all the multitudinous preparations for an op, only to have everything cancelled at the last minute. The signal would come through any time, they assured each other. But the minutes kept ticking by. No signal. No improvement in the weather. With resigned shrugs, the airmen struggled into their gear, collected their parachutes and rations, and clambered aboard the vans that took them out to the dispersals.

A green Verey light soared, sparking, into the dank air. The op was on.

The clouds were a gigantic wall, a barrier that stretched across the North Sea, cumulo-nimbus, great rolling, boiling masses of it up to twenty-five thousand feet, an aerial hell's kitchen of icing and turbulence that could tear a fully loaded bomber apart.

It was a frighteningly beautiful world: vast mountains of cloud and enormous chasms, calm, clear valleys between the clouds that promised a way through the clag but which invariably ended in violence. To fly through the stuff was to feel enormous, iron-clad fists pummeling the aircraft, to hear the structure groaning and crying out in agony, and to wonder how long the poor old thing could remain in one piece. Nearly two hundred bombers turned back, 25.1 per cent of the force, a phenomenally high figure. But 6 Group topped it. No less than forty-two 6 Group bombers returned to base because of the conditions, 57.5 per cent of the Canadian force.[34]

Simply staying aloft in such weather was a full-time job, and a difficult one at that; to attempt to bomb a heavily defended city in such conditions seemed hopeless. The storm area extended for some eighty miles, a heaving ocean of rain and lightning, ice and hail. In the understated way of official reports, many Canadian crews commented on the "very difficult weather" with "heavy icing" and "severe electrical storms," and on their aircraft being "rocked by violent winds." Lightning was a particularly severe problem. After picking up ice and losing several hundred feet of altitude, Sergeant M.M. Humphreys of 408 Squadron experienced a "direct hit" by lightning which stopped all four engines and the aircraft's instruments.[35] In the midst of violent turbulence, Sergeant J.S. Sobin of 419 Squadron fought to maintain control of his Halifax. The target was only a few minutes away – but would the aircraft hold together long enough? He asked for a vote from the crew: keep going or turn back while they still could? They voted to press on. But a moment later ice began to form on the aircraft's wings, its dull sheen illuminated fleetingly by streaks of lightning that lacerated the sky ahead. Sobin told the crew that he was going to jettison the bombs and turn for home. At that moment, a blinding flash seemed to envelop the aircraft. The four engines stopped and the entire electrical system failed. The wireless operator, Sergeant J.W. Farrow, later reported: ". . . the receiver appeared to have blown up . . . I am quite confident that it was lightning that struck us." The bomber rolled over on its back and plunged earthward, starting to break up. Farrow saw a huge hole appear in the fuselage on the starboard side. Sobin told him "by signs" to follow the bomb-aimer and navigator who had already baled out. Farrow jumped. Sobin, the flight engineer, and the two gunners died when the Halifax crashed. The others survived to become POWs.[36]

That resolute airman from 427 Squadron, Pilot Officer Vandekerckhove, had overcome formidable problems with searchlights and fighters during the previous attack on Hamburg as well as over the Ruhr earlier in the year. Now he had engine trouble and, to compound his difficulties, he encountered icing. Despite all his efforts, the ice-burdened Halifax sank to a mere four thousand feet over the Kiel Canal. The crew discussed the problem among themselves. All agreed that they would rather attempt the long trip home across the North Sea than abandon the aircraft and almost certainly become POWs. They made it home.

The raid itself failed miserably. Little more than half the force managed to get through to the Hamburg area. The unspeakable conditions made it impossible for the Pathfinders to mark the target. The Main Force crews, buffeted by the storm, often unable to see more than a few hundred yards in front of their aircraft, could do little but release the bombs they had brought so far and with such difficulty and hope for the best. Most fell outside the city; towns and villages up to one hundred miles away reported raids. The town of Elmshorn, a dozen miles from Hamburg, suffered a considerable number of bombs, due, it is thought, to lightning having started a fire which the crews took for a blaze in the city of Hamburg. More than 250 houses were destroyed in Elmshorn – probably more damage than was inflicted upon Hamburg that disastrous night.

The ill-starred operation cost Bomber Command thirty aircraft, 4.1 per cent of the attacking force. Four were 6 Group bombers: Sergeant J. S. Sobin's Halifax from 419 Squadron, Pilot Officer D.R. McDonald's Wellington from 432 Squadron, and two Halifaxes from 428 Squadron commanded by Sergeant M. Chepil and Pilot Officer V.T. Sylvester. Coincidentally, two sprog pilots, flying officers Len Rogers and Harvey Funkhouser, had recently arrived at Middleton St. George to join 428 Squadron. They were friends from Port Colborne, Ontario, and both were assigned to fly with experienced crews that night to do their Second Dickey familiarization trips. They flew with Chepil and Sylvester. Neither returned.[37]

Flight Sergeant H.L. Pattison of the same squadron, 428, encountered a pair of Herrmann's fighters as he neared Hamburg. It was his first op with his own crew and he had battled his way through the storm to the city. Visibility improved momentarily as he approached the target. Pattison's rear gunner, Sergeant Glenn Bassett, could see fires still burning from earlier raids: "... the closer we got to the target the drier my throat got ... I just looked, hardly able to believe my own eyes." Then Bassett spotted the fighters, both Me 109s, one high on the starboard quarter, the other on the port side. The starboard fighter sported a light in its nose. It was a familiar ploy: one fighter would draw the attention of a bomber's gunners while the second would come in to attack. Bassett wasn't falling for it. Ordering a corkscrew to port, Bassett lined up on the second fighter. Sure enough, it turned to attack. Its fire went wide. Moments later both fighters had disappeared in the clag. Pattison went on to drop his bombs. Shortly after turning for home, Bassett called from the rear turret to say that a Ju 88 was dead astern: "Corkscrew, skipper, go!" As the heavy bomber snapped into a diving turn, Bassett opened fire. The Ju 88 vanished from view and the Halifax plunged into cloud, bumping, thumping its way through the turbulence and then home.

Thus ended the last raid in the Battle of Hamburg, a disappointment to Harris, a disaster for many of the crews who participated in it. Although his concern for the young airmen of Bomber Command was undoubtedly sincere, Harris had taken a calculated risk with their lives when he bet they would be able to beat the storm that was brewing that night. He lost. They lost. In his memoirs, Harris dismissed the raid: "A further heavy attack was made on the night of August 2nd-3rd, but weather proved unexpectedly bad, with thick icing clouds over the target. No real concentration of attack was achieved and we lost a number of aircraft because of the appalling weather."[38] No explanations, no excuses. Harris ran true to form, no matter what the circumstances.

The Battle of Hamburg was "an outstanding Allied victory" despite the failure of the August 2/3 raid. The Canadian Group had performed well. It had mounted 306 sorties, and 203 aircraft had bombed the primary target, 76 per cent, a figure depressed by the fact that only twenty-six out of seventy-three aircraft got through to bomb Hamburg on the night of August 2/3. The campaign against Hamburg had cost the Canadians eight bombers, 2.6 per cent of the force, an acceptable loss rate – and one that would seem trivial in light of the losses to come.[39]

Harris's prestige among Allied commanders would never be higher. He had proved his point: area bombing *could* win the war by knocking out the enemy's cities one by one. It's not hard to imagine him peering over his glasses, icily gazing at the blackboard while he chalked a line through "Hamburg." One down. Half a dozen or so to go. In a few nights and days of intensive aerial operations, Europe's largest port and Germany's second largest city had suffered a catastrophe. Five hundred public buildings destroyed. More than two thousand commercial enterprises wrecked. Half the residences in the city eliminated; most of the rest damaged. Some 45,000 people dead. Nearly a million made homeless. Four big shipbuilding yards heavily damaged. Dock installations a shambles. Approximately 180,000 tons of shipping sunk in the harbour.[40] General of the Air Force Erhard Milch, state secretary at the German Air Ministry, wailed: "If we get just five or six more attacks like these on Hamburg, the German people will just lay down their tools, however great their willpower ... What the home front is suffering now cannot be suffered much longer." Albert Speer, Hitler's armaments minister, wrote that the Hamburg disaster put the "fear of God" in him; like Milch, he believed that the same treatment meted out to half a dozen more cities would put an end to the war. Goebbels termed the firestorm a catastrophe that "staggers the imagination"; the city had been "destroyed in a manner unparalleled in history." He saw the problems of food, shelter, and evacuation as "almost impossible" to solve. Worried about an immediate collapse of civilian morale, the Nazis sent truckloads of SS troops to patrol the streets of the shattered city and to put a speedy stop to defeatist talk.[41]

Harris was pleased by the raids' successes. But in the weeks to come he would also be disappointed. Somehow life managed to continue in what was left of Hamburg. People subsisted and struggled to repair their homes and tend to their wounds. The astounding thing was how rapidly they brought their city back to life. By the end of the year, Hamburg had "regained eighty per cent of its former productivity" and the rest of the German war machine was able to produce what Hamburg no longer could.[42] The German, British, Russian – and in more recent times, the Korean and Vietnamese – peoples have demonstrated that determined citizens can withstand the worst that non-nuclear bombing can deliver. The sages of the Thirties were wrong; the working-class districts didn't panic, didn't run wild in the streets, demanding immediate surrender. Perhaps the factor that all the proponents of area-bombing kept forgetting is the stubborn pride that causes people of every nation to display astonishing endurance and quite magnificent courage when *their* city and *their* homes come under attack.

A few days after the last raid of the Battle of Hamburg, in the mid-summer heat and humidity of Ontario, a brand-new bomber rolled out of a hangar at Malton (now Toronto International Airport). It was the *Ruhr Express*, the first Canadian-built Lancaster X. A year earlier, a Lancaster had been taken off the Avro production line in England and flown to Canada where National Steel Car (later Victory Aircraft) had been awarded a contract to build the type under licence. Originally, the intention had been to build Stirlings, an idea hastily abandoned when the inadequacies of that type became apparent. The Lancaster production line took form rapidly as engineers pored over the acres of blueprints that kept arriving from Britain. Many modifications were necessary because of the use of Packard-built Merlins and various items of North American electrical equipment.

August 6, 1943, was the date chosen for the first Canadian Lanc to be christened by Mrs. C.G. Power, wife of the minister of national defence for air. It was to be a major media event. The popular belief was that, after the ceremony, the aircraft would immediately take off to do battle with the enemy. An advertisement in the Toronto *Globe and Mail* declared confidently that the so-called "battleship of the air" was heading east and "in a week or two it will be in action over Germany."[43] In fact, the Lancaster, KB700, was scarcely ready for the air, let alone the fray. The ceremonies went ahead anyway, with the stentorian tones of Lorne Greene providing a blow-by-blow commentary for the country-wide radio audience. C.D. Howe, minister of munitions and supply, declared that the Lancaster was "the greatest weapon of destruction that Canada has produced in this war." While the crowds watched – and while twenty thousand workers at three

Montreal aircraft plants were on strike for better pay ("We will not be intimidated by the dictatorial threats of Messrs Howe and Mitchell"[44]) – the crew clambered aboard. On this special occasion it was augmented by Bambi, a French poodle puppy owned by Flight Sergeant R.K. Burgar, the mid-upper gunner. In command was Squadron Leader Reg Lane from Victoria, British Columbia, whose brilliant wartime record may on this occasion have been overshadowed by his photogenic good looks. This was, after all, a public relations exercise, a showing-off of Canada's best, a demonstration of Canada's new-found status as an industrial power capable of producing the most sophisticated weapons of the time.

With the applause and good wishes of the assembled crowd still ringing in their ears, the crew rapidly discovered that none of the Lancaster's engine instruments was working. But they decided to push on anyway, Lane recalls, "in view of all the publicity." Although many an onlooker imagined the airmen speeding away to Europe soon to face enemy fighters and flak, the Lancaster got no further than Dorval, Quebec. There it was hastily pushed into a hangar where workers immediately swarmed over it, installing instruments and other equipment, and, in effect, completing the big aircraft. It remained at Dorval more than a month. On an air test an engine failed. A replacement had to be sent, surreptitiously, one suspects, from Malton. Early in September, the aircraft was at last ready for the flight across the Atlantic. A Ferry Command pilot joined the crew. The trip went well except for several days' delay at Gander because of poor weather. Then it was Prestwick and finally London and a ceremonial greeting from High Commissioner Vincent Massey, accompanied by an army of reporters. Canada's first Lancaster had arrived in the war zone and, declared the *Globe and Mail*, none of the crew liked her name, *Ruhr Express*; they would have preferred *Bambi*.[45]

At about this time, the ORS at High Wycombe was putting the finishing touches to another report on the performance of the Canadian Bomber Group. It must have come as no surprise to anyone in the Group to be told that its airmen lacked experience and needed more operational training. The diligent statisticians revealed that the Group's Halifax casualties tended to be uniformly high until the crews' twentieth op, after which the losses dropped by more than 50 per cent. Also significant was the high casualties among Wellington squadrons, largely, it appeared, because of the proportion of sprog crews among their ranks.[46]

The reputation of 6 Group as a chop group showed no signs of diminishing. To the common complaints of its high casualties, its poor serviceability, its unsatisfactory location, were added rumours that Bomber Command discriminated against the Canadians by reserving the newest and best aircraft for RAF groups and allotting what was left to 6 Group. "Canadian squadrons were the last to be equipped with the fabled Lancaster bombers – Canadian-built Lancasters, please note. And the francophone squadron with which I served ... was the last of the 'colonial' squadrons to be re-equipped with that excellent aircraft," writes Jean Pouliot, a veteran of 425 Squadron.[47]

But the available evidence doesn't support such complaints. As new Canadian squadrons were posted to 4 Group in the months before 6 Group was formed, it was inevitable that they would be equipped with Halifaxes, at least as a temporary measure. The Directorate of Repair and Maintenance was set up to handle only Halifaxes in northern England. In addition, Lancaster production was limited, and it was essential that the segment of Halifax production that could not be switched to Lancasters be used to its fullest extent. The unacceptable alternative was a reduction in the strength of the air offensive against Germany.

Harris refused to practise reverse discrimination in favour of the Canadians. He felt that, since it was the newest group in Bomber Command, 6 Group could not expect to obtain Lancasters ahead of longer-established and more experienced RAF units – many of which had operated inadequate aircraft since the beginning of the war. Harris blamed the Canadian government for the current state of affairs. In spite of warnings, they had persisted with Canadianization, fully aware of the consequences. In his opinion, they had no reason to complain.[48] Nevertheless, in this period, three 6 Group squadrons, 408, 426, and 432, were re-equipped with the Hercules-powered version of the Lancaster, an excellent aircraft, its only shortcoming being a higher fuel consumption than its Merlin-powered counterpart.

For Power and Edwards, the equipment question was undeniably tricky. They were responsible for the lives and welfare of RCAF personnel overseas. Had they not pressed as forcibly as they could for the best equipment available, they might have been accused of shirking their duty. It was an undeniable fact that aircrew operating Halifaxes, Wellingtons, and Stirlings suffered the highest casualties; their morale tended to be correspondingly lower. It's hardly surprising, therefore, that the Canadians wanted Lancasters as rapidly as possible.[49]

Although it was not actually part of the Battle of Hamburg, the famous raid on Peenemünde on August 17/18, 1943, may be considered in the same context since it came so soon after the assault on the port city. It was a period when Harris's crews – and Harris himself – were enjoying a period of extraordinary confidence. At last Jerry was *really* feeling the impact of Bomber Command. At last most of the squadrons had the right aircraft, the right bombs, the right navigational tools. The days of fumbling and making do were over. From now on it would be a matter of bigger and better raids until the Germans threw in the towel.

The Peenemünde op afforded Harris another opportunity to demonstrate the capabilities of his force. Intelligence reports had been filtering through to London for some time about the top-secret experimental work going on at the remote peninsula on Germany's Baltic coast. Eventually it became clear that the enemy had a sizable establishment there, scientists, engineers, and production staff, busy creating a whole series of alarming new rocket weapons. The place had to be destroyed without delay. Bomber Command got the job.

Three areas of Peenemünde were to be attacked: the experimental site, the workshops, and the living quarters. The Air Ministry wanted Bomber Command to wipe out the lot, the people as well as the paraphernalia. But this was no run-of-the-mill target. It might be described as a target that had to be hit with the force of an area-bombing operation but with the precision of the Dams raid of the previous May.

"Offset" marking and "time-and-distance" runs would be

important techniques in the Peenumünde operation. The former was developed because crews often found target markers obscured by smoke from fires or smoke screens. 5 Group pioneered the technique of placing markers some distance from the targets under attack; bomb-aimers simply added a pre-arranged over-shoot factor to bring the bombs down on the aiming point. The time-and-distance method used a prominent geographical feature, a promontory, perhaps, or a lake; crews flew directly overhead at a certain speed, height, and direction, dropping their bombs after the correct amount of time had elapsed. Harris himself had commanded 5 Group in the early part of the war. Now its leader was the autocratic and opinionated Air Vice-Marshal the Honourable Ralph Cochrane, the bitter rival of the equally auto-cratic and opinionated Donald Bennett, AOC 8 Group, the Path-finders. Cochrane wanted his group to handle the Peenemünde operation alone; it was just the sort of pinpoint job his crews had been trained for. Harris said no; if it failed, the element of surprise would be lost and the Germans would bring in untold numbers of flak batteries and searchlights and put God only knows how many fighter units on permanent readiness. Any second attempt would be suicidal. The job had to be done the first time and that meant the use of a major force. Bennett selected the Master Bomber for the raid, a highly experienced bomber pilot, the CO of 83 Path-finder Squadron, Group Captain John Searby. His deputies were Canadian Wing Commander Johnny Fauquier, CO of 405 Squad-ron (formerly of 6 Group), and Wing Commander John White, a flight commander of 156 Squadron.

The raid came at a time when everyone, including the enemy, knew that Harris would soon embark on an intense bombing campaign against Berlin. The planners of the Peenemünde raid used that fact to their advantage. If the enemy was expecting raids on Berlin, he would get them, but in reality they would be spoof raids taking place principally to divert the enemy's attention from the next target, Peenemünde. In the week preceding the Peene-münde operation, Mosquitoes attacked the German capital on three occasions, each time taking a route over Denmark and pass-ing near Peenemünde.[50] Thus the speedy bombers became a famil-iar nocturnal irritation. The hope was that when Bomber Command sent a force to attack the secret research establishment, the Germans would think it was yet another bomber stream heading for Berlin.

As ever, the weather was critical. Harris knew that the raid had to take place in clear moonlight if the individual targets were to be correctly identified and hit. It made the raid infinitely more hazardous for the aircrews, but the risk had to be accepted. The moon period began in the second week of August, but conditions were disappointing for several days. If the weather was good in the target area it was poor over the bombers' bases, and vice versa. Not until the morning of August 17 did Met have good news. Everything pointed to excellent weather that night both in northern Germany and over Britain.

The route was straightforward: out across the North Sea, crossing the Danish coast near Esbjerg, then angling in a southeasterly direction to the target. The return trip would follow much the same track. In all, the bombers would fly about 1,250 miles; the trip would take between seven and eight hours. During the day the mechanics and armourers checked the aircraft and loaded them with fuel and bombs – almost exclusively high explosive to minimize the smoke that might spoil the bomb-aimers' view of the target; on this raid incendiaries would constitute only a tiny fraction of the bombers' loads.

In Yorkshire and Durham, the squadrons of 6 Group were well rested, not having flown operationally since a relatively uneventful op on Milan on the twelfth. At Linton-on-Ouse, Squadron Leader Bill Swetman had just arrived to start his second tour of operations as a flight commander with 426 Squadron. Much impressed by the Lancaster IIs with which the unit had recently been equipped, he commented: "A great improvement over the old Merlin-powered Halifaxes." He found his name on the Battle Order for that night. It would be the first time he – and indeed the whole unit – flew the new aircraft on an op. On the same airfield, another 6 Group squadron, 408, had just moved into newly constructed quarters. The accommodations were found to be infested by insects. The CO sent the squadron on leave.[51]

The aircrews who filed into their briefing rooms that afternoon commented on the number of Service Police all over the place. Why so much security? What was so special about this op? The answer they received during the briefings probably satisfied most

of them; the raid, declared the intelligence officers, would demol-
ish a secret plant the Germans had built to make advanced radar
equipment designed to interfere with the RAF's bombing raids.
The cover story had been carefully worked out at Bomber Command; it not only gave the airmen a personal reason for pressing
home the attack with maximum enthusiasm, but ensured that any
who were captured would be genuinely ignorant of what was
really going on at Peenemünde. The authorities worked diligently
and intelligently to prevent any hint of the Germans' experiments
reaching the British public in advance of the weapons themselves.
Some briefing officers developed their own variations on the
theme for the benefit of the crews; one described how a particularly large meeting of Germany's top scientists was taking place
that very night at Peenemünde. By blowing them all to bits, the
bomber crews would shorten the war by months, perhaps years.

But one feature of the raid dismayed the aircrews: the bombing
was to take place from modest altitudes *in bright moonlight.* To
anyone who had flown more than half a dozen sorties, this raid
seemed to promise the chop for a lot of crews. This impression
became fortified with the news that the target was so important
that, if it wasn't completely destroyed the first time, the bombers
would have to keep going back until the job was done, regardless
of casualties. After the briefing, Sergeant K.W. Rowe of 434
Squadron recalls: "There wasn't the usual babble and horseplay
and I remember coming out on to the airfield, right into the rural
surroundings and sunshine and I thought, 'This can't be happening to us on such a lovely day.'"[52]

The force that took off that summer evening consisted of 324
Lancasters, 218 Halifaxes, and 54 Stirlings. The Canadian Group
supplied 62 bombers, of which three returned early. Over the
North Sea, the last glimmers of daylight faded away; but instead
of being plunged into the comforting blackness they knew so well,
the crews found themselves bathed in a curiously metallic light
from the moon. The lovely evening had given way to a spectacularly clear night. The Danish coast could be seen in perfect detail.
In every aircraft skippers instructed their gunners to keep their
eyes peeled for fighters; there would be no hiding in clouds
tonight.

As the bombers approached the target, the Germans activated

their smoke-screens. But no flak. No searchlights. Obviously they didn't want to draw attention to the target until it was absolutely necessary. Peenemünde lay below, the whole complex of workshops, offices, and accommodations clearly visible in the moonlight.

Just after midnight, the Pathfinders' markers went down over Peenemünde. Already there was a problem. The Pathfinder navigators had erred because the tiny island of Ruden hadn't registered on their H2S sets. The markers went down two miles south of the aiming point. The Visual Markers who came next helped to correct the error, but many of the Main Force aircraft had already started to bomb on the first markers. Bill Swetman had arrived early due to the unexpectedly sprightly performance of his Lancaster II. "It was the best bomber the RAF had," he recalls. "I couldn't believe how quickly it climbed with a full load on board. I had a great trip all the way to the target – then I had to orbit for twenty minutes over Peenemünde until it came my turn to bomb."

The 6 Group aircraft flew in the third and last wave of bombers. Their target was the experimental works. The first wave of Stirlings, Halifaxes, and Lancasters had bombed the housing estate; the second, Lancasters only, had bombed the production works. The Canadian Group's aircraft were joined by more than a hundred Lancasters of 5 Group plus eighteen Pathfinders.

Peenemünde's defences were extraordinarily slow to react, perhaps because of orders to hold their fire until they received permission from a suitably elevated authority; the secrecy which enshrouded every aspect of life at the establishment worked on this night to the advantage of the attackers.

Most of the first wave of bombers were on their way home before the flak opened up. The crews in the later waves found themselves in the thick of intense gunfire. Particularly worrisome was the light flak which the bombers usually never saw. On this occasion, many aircraft bombed from as low as four thousand feet; they became perfect targets for the 20 mm guns. Although the aircrews seemed to be pressing home their attacks with all the gallantry and determination that could be expected of them, the raid was not going as well as had been hoped. The fault lay in the Pathfinders' marking. Compounding the original navigational error, unexpectedly strong breezes kept taking the descending markers and blowing them towards the sea. The Master Bomber, Searby, detected the trend and maintained a steady flow of instructions to the crews to make the necessary corrections. Searby had a busy night over Peenemünde.

Meanwhile, more than a hundred Mosquitoes were attacking Berlin, solely for the purpose of diverting the *Luftwaffe*'s attention from Peenemünde. The ruse succeeded. The German controllers ordered all available fighters to the capital. Only when the aircraft had used up much of their fuel in fruitless chases after the nimble Mossies did the controllers realize that they had been outwitted. The fighter crews could see the distant glow of the fires burning at Peenemünde – although few if any of them had the slightest idea of the work being carried out at the place. No doubt there were umpteen puzzled shakings of leather-helmeted heads. What the devil were the *Tommis* doing up *there*? Was it another spoof? Many of the fighters had to land and refuel before they could head north for the hundred-mile trip to Peenemünde.

Over the target, the second wave of bombers saw some fighters, but it was the third wave, 5 and 6 Groups', which encountered the majority. Moreover, they had to contend with great clouds of smoke, both from fires and from the Germans' smoke-screen equipment. So confusing did the Pathfinder crews find the conditions that some of their markers fell nearly two miles off target. Searby, gallantly continuing to risk his neck in repeated low-level orbits of the target area, did not immediately notice the inaccurate markers. However, his deputy, White, marked the target accurately, and the majority of bombs fell in the right areas.[53]

The contribution of the Master Bomber and his deputy was of inestimable value over Peenemünde. The Main Force crews held these exceptionally brave airmen in the highest esteem. Sergeant P. S. Crees of 434 Squadron, commented: "The fact that someone was there, telling us what to do, was a great morale booster. Normally, you felt that it was an individual effort that you were making but, now, you felt as though you were part of a combined force and everything was more organized. I don't know how he managed to stay so calm..."[54]

Another 6 Group airman, Flying Officer J. A. Westland of 419 Squadron, recalls that by the time he bombed, the target was totally obscured: "I don't think anyone except the first crews over the target really saw the ground as the area quickly became an obscured mass of great billows of smoke and flames. My bombing picture showed no ground detail at all – it was almost as if we had taken a picture of the inside of a locomotive funnel. Those damned fires must *still* be burning."[55]

But conditions could hardly have been better for the fighters. They arrived just as the last waves of bombers were leaving the target area, labouring as they climbed to cruising altitude for the trip home. Silhouetted against bright flames on the ground and bathed in brilliant moonlight, the bombers were perfect targets. The fighters waded in, cannons and machine guns blazing.

"All over the sky, RAF planes were going down in flaming infernos," wrote Pilot Officer R.W. Charman, a navigator and one of only two survivors of a 427 Squadron Halifax. "I had barely given Frank [Frank Brady, the skipper] a course for home, when Jimmy Fletcher, the tail gunner, broke in with evasive action. A Junkers 88 was bearing down on our tail. We went down in a dive, trying to avoid the fighter. Then the aircraft quivered, like in killing poultry you strike the brain with a knife and the feathers release – that is the way the aircraft felt. A horrible smell of gunpowder enveloped the aircraft and the wireless operator lay beside me dying, with his entrails exposed. . ."[56]

Keith Rowe, an RAF flight engineer and a member of Sergeant G.M. Johnston's crew of 434 Squadron, reported: "Doug Labell, the rear gunner, was very good – a tough, husky French-Canadian who seemed to be absolutely impervious to cold; he had cut all the Perspex out of his turret to improve visibility. He also had good eyesight – a bit of a 'cat's eye.' He was very emphatic in his 'Dive port!' and we took really violent evasive action – a very steep dive to port but, almost instantaneously, I saw tracer – whitish-orange, I think – going into our port wing-tip . . . Both wings were burning fiercely within seconds . . ."[57]

Another 434 Squadron Halifax went down under the onslaught of a fighter. Peter Crees, the flight engineer, remembers: "You could see its outline quite clearly because it was so bright. I was sure it was a twin fin and ruddered aircraft which I assume was an Me 110. He was on fire between his starboard engine and the fuselage, quite a furious fire. We lost him after that . . . Then, when we were pulling ourselves together and summing up the damage, another lot of cannon shells came in without any warning at all. The first lot passed beneath us, but . . . the next lot got us. It must have been a very long burst, the first shells hitting the rear turret, killing the gunner." From the astrodome, Crees saw the fighter's shells working their way along the fuselage, "the tracer entering the fuselage with a little burst of sparks; I watched it reach the mid-upper turret, killing the gunner there as well, I think. . . ." Crees was the only survivor from the crew.[58]

Bomber Command lost forty aircraft that night, 6.7 per cent of the force. But 6 Group losses were proportionately even higher: twelve aircraft or 19.3 per cent of the sixty-two which took off. Cochrane's 5 Group, which attacked alongside 6 Group in the last wave, also suffered heavily, with seventeen of its 109 bombers being lost, 14.5 per cent of its number.

Three 6 Group squadrons, 419, 428, and 424, each lost three aircraft; 426 lost two and 427 one. Bill Swetman returned safely to Linton-on-Ouse, Yorkshire, to learn that his CO, Wing Commander Leslie Crooks, had been shot down and killed over Peenemünde. Swetman was immediately promoted to the rank of wing commander and took over the squadron. He was twenty-three.

Did the results at Peenemünde justify the cost? There is little doubt that the raid delayed the V-weapon attacks on London and other cities. But for precisely how long is a matter of conjecture. Estimates vary from between two to six months.[59] Harris had again gambled with his force; this time he had been reasonably successful, largely because of the torpor of the local flak commanders and the late arrival of the fighters, thanks to the Mosquitoes which diverted them to Berlin. Had it not been for those two factors, Bomber Command might well have suffered a slaughter comparable to – or even more horrific than – the Nuremberg disaster of the following March.

Perhaps Flying Officer F.T. Judah of 419 Squadron summed up the Peenemünde operation best when he added this succinct comment in his log book: "Hot."[60]

5

THE "COLONIAL" BOYS

**"These fellows were a very long way from home
doing a dangerous job and a lump comes to my throat
when I think of them."**

David van Vlymen, LAC, RAF

Jim Lovelace, a Cape Bretonner, was among the first Canadian-trained wireless operator/air gunners to go to Britain. He arrived in January 1941 to an impressive welcome. No sooner had the airmen put their baggage down than they were whisked away on a tour of Hampton Court Palace, a dazzling edifice that Cardinal Wolsey had built for himself in 1515. Later the Canadians travelled to Windsor Castle where, to their amazement, they met the two *princesses*, Elizabeth and Margaret! And before the afternoon was over, they had received an invitation to have tea with none other than the *Queen* herself! It was all quite overwhelming.

England was turning out to be far more hospitable and interesting than any of them had dared hope. Lovelace hardly had time to feel homesick for Nova Scotia.

It couldn't last. It didn't. Within a few days Lovelace was posted to Upper Heyford for operational training. But when he got to the place, no one seemed to have heard of him. So for a few days he strolled about the airfield examining the Hampden bombers and their totally unfamiliar equipment. The presence of Sergeant James Cameron Lovelace, RCAF, was clearly of little significance to anyone at RAF Upper Heyford.

But it was a different story in the local pub. To its patrons the Canadian airman was a curiosity, an exotic figure from a far-off land of adventure that still had real live *Indians*! Lovelace felt right at home in the pub. He went there every evening until closing time when, reluctantly, he returned to the station.

Another posting soon arrived for Sergeant Lovelace. This time his presence was required at Cranwell, the RAF Staff College in Lincolnshire, for what was termed "vocabulary, technical, and procedures training." At Cranwell, Lovelace encountered many of the Canadian WOP/AGs with whom he had trained. The RAF had billeted them in a dismal barrack block, each room containing thirty-two iron bunks and a single stove.

Before long, the Canadians were ordered to go outside and fall in on the parade ground. Chilly winter rain poured down. A self-important little flight sergeant appeared. He bellowed something at the assembled Canadians. Something threatening, by the sound of it. But no one was sure because no one could understand him. What did he want? Why was he hollering? Everyone shrugged; they didn't know. At last the "chiefie" snorted into silence. The Canadians glanced at one another and trudged back to their billet through the deluge. No doubt it would all be explained in good time.

Within minutes, the incomprehensible flight sergeant was back, as splenetic as ever. He took one look at the floor – now thoroughly begrimed by the Canadians' muddy footwear – and his face took on a bright pink hue. Voice throbbing with outrage, he at last made himself understood. Bloody *Canadians* . . . savages . . . and, worse, *colonials* . . . brought up in bloomin' log cabins. He ordered them all to scrub the billet, and to wax and polish the

floor. The Canadians ignored him. When a succession of disciplinary corporals arrived, the Canadians simply laughed at them.

"After a week," Lovelace recalls, "a youthful, one-armed flight
lieutenant took over the parade while the flight sergeant strutted
around like a peacock ... Those of us who knew the air began
humming to the strains of *Figaro! Figaro!* as he strutted..."

When the Canadians were taken on a route march, it was a
disaster; the neat lines soon broke up into small groups that
drifted away on their own. What was the point of the marches
anyway? the Canadians asked. Weren't they supposed to be here
for technical training? Later, at yet another parade, the flight
sergeant appeared with a covey of corporals. All bore the tense
expressions of men determined to have their way. One of the
corporals objected to the smile on the face of a man in the front
rank, a good-natured fellow from Timagami, Ontario. The corporal thought he was being laughed at. This led him to make a
serious error of judgement. He grabbed the man from Timagami,
who, still smiling, delivered a single, highly effective punch. The
corporal lost interest in the proceedings, and the Canadians
strolled back to their barracks where "we threw every single stick
of furniture out the door of the barracks at the edge of our parade
square and set fire to the lot! That incident got us some fame, far
and wide, as 'The Canadian Revolt at Cranwell,'" Lovelace
recalls.

When an air vice-marshal arrived from the Air Ministry, he
called for a parade. He referred to the Canadians as "mutinous
colonials." Wagging an authoritative finger, he declared that the
British had had years of training in "that sort of situation" and
they knew how to handle mutineers.

"That did it!" Lovelace says. "We all broke off and went inside.
We had our own meeting and appointed two of our number to go
AWOL to London and send some senior officer up to settle the
issue." Lovelace himself was one of the emissaries; he returned to
Cranwell a couple of days later with an RCAF squadron leader
despatched personally by Canadian High Commissioner Vincent
Massey. Shortly afterwards it was agreed that the Canadians were
to have their own organization, commanded by Canadians rather
than the RAF. Over the next few weeks, the airmen were posted (as
rapidly as possible, it has to be assumed) to OTUs, thence to

operational squadrons. Lovelace was one of the few who survived the war.

Although the Cranwell Mutiny was an event of little importance in the annals of World War II, it had a lasting impact on relations between the RCAF and the RAF. It created a Canadian "image" in the minds of the British. The image has persisted, intensified by various historians' descriptions of Canadian airmen as "brash and quarrelsome" on the one hand, and "happy-go-lucky men, great gamblers and very fond of and successful with the girls" on the other.[1] Such historians like to depict Canadian aircrew as operating almost totally without discipline, ignoring orders, taking short-cuts, a sort of Wild West posse of the air. What is the truth of the matter?

Canadians behaved outrageously. Canadians behaved well. Canadians were crude. Canadians were gentlemen. It all depended on the individual. At one end of the scale were the airmen who revelled in being the "wild men" of British legend,[2] challenging authority at every turn, doing their best to reinforce their reputations with suitably impudent behaviour wherever they went. At the other end was the majority, those Canadians who simply got on with the job and never looked for trouble. But they sometimes found it because, in the main, they tended to be self-reliant individuals, seldom intimidated by rank or reputation. If conditions were sub-standard, they complained, vociferously. If an order was stupid, they questioned it. If there was a better way of doing something, they saw no reason not to try it.

The vast majority of Canadians objected to being referred to as "colonials."[3] This bewildered most Britons. They thought Canadians *were* colonials. When informed in no uncertain terms that Canada was not a colony but a Dominion, the Brits tended to shrug. What difference did it make? Colony or Dominion, it was all the same, wasn't it? Interestingly, this uncertainty extended to high places. In February 1943, just after 6 Group became operational, Air Marshal Sir Bertine E. Sutton of the Air Ministry found it necessary to explain to his colleagues that: "Canada is a Dominion and as such is no less entitled to a separate and autonomous Air Force than is the United Kingdom . . ."[4]

*   *   *

Many Canadians going overseas seemed to have unrealistic expectations of the welcome, and the life, that awaited them. The RCAF Public Relations staff did its best to prepare them, providing pamphlets that explained the differences between England and Canada, pointing out that incessant complaints about wartime inconveniences would only cause bad feelings. Attempts to change the English because their ways were different would not be appreciated. And, one pamphlet cautioned, it would be unwise to ridicule regional accents; in England, the *Canadians* were the foreigners with the odd accents. Gamely, the PR staff set out to prepare the airmen for the conditions that awaited them: the consistently awful English weather, an almost total lack of central heating (a 426 Squadron pilot, Leslie McCaig, noted in his diary: "I don't believe the English ever knew anything about heating, even in peacetime"), and the strict rationing of food (the Canadians were instructed to take their ration cards and gifts of foodstuffs to any British family with whom they stayed).

Curiously enough, it was considered necessary to tell the Canadian airmen to avoid thinking of wartime service as some sort of holiday. Furthermore, stressed the experts, they should not assume a "Crusade to Save Britain" mentality.[5] It is clear that many Canadians failed to heed the advice. The censoring of mail revealed how countless airmen expected to be welcomed as heroes in England. There was surprise and some resentment when their reception turned out to be cool and, occasionally, downright inhospitable. A significant percentage of airmen's letters in the first years of the war indicated an "active and growing dislike of the Englishman though seldom of the Scot." Some Canadians wrote home advising friends not to enlist, but if they did, to avoid overseas service.[6] Predictably, thousands of young men had set off on the greatest adventure of their lives only to find that it was far less fun than they had anticipated. The British were turning out to be human beings, often irritable, often rude, more often simply disinterested. And they had some *weird* ideas about Canadians. A former engine mechanic with 405 Squadron, Lucide Rioux of Fredericton, New Brunswick, remembers a group of airmen from the unit visiting a local tavern. To the dismay of the Canadians, "the few civilians quickly and quietly vacated the place as we entered." The airmen soon found out why. The locals had been told that "Canadians were quite uncivilized and all carried concealed knives which they would not hesitate to use."

The rough-and-ready wartime accommodations did little to endear life in Britain to Canadian airmen. In one letter home, a Canadian airman called RAF Yatesbury the "damdest dirtyest hole this side of hell," with no lights in the latrines and toilets awash in two inches of water. He added: "The guys that serve out the food have dirty hands and filthy overalls on." Sometimes such criticism was justified, often it wasn't. Yatesbury, a training establishment, had been bombed shortly before the letter was written; much damage had been done to some of the facilities, including the laundry.[7]

Although the Canadians unquestionably caused many of their own difficulties, the essential problem was the inability of the British and Canadians to understand one another – a not unfamiliar failing of the human species. And, inevitably, there were those who gleefully exacerbated the situation. In Canada, some citizens even went to the trouble of saving letters from unhappy Canadian airmen overseas and sending them to American newspapers for publication, for goodness knows what purpose.[8] The wonder is that any of the newspapers' readers were naive enough to be surprised that every serviceman overseas was not totally enchanted with his lot.

In 6 Group, morale sagged badly during the first year of operations. For George Brookes and his staff at Allerton Park it was a matter of intense concern. Was the slump in morale caused by high casualties? Was the constant movement of units contributing to a general sense of uncertainty? One wonders whether they ever considered another factor: the lack of operational experience of many of the Group's senior officers. Throughout history it has been demonstrated that men will willingly go anywhere or do anything for leaders who are prepared to share the same risks. Ralph Green, a squadron leader and a flight commander with 424 Squadron, declares unequivocally: "The other squadron on our base had a CO who was afraid to fly, and who went on only the shortest and easiest ops. The morale of that squadron was poor and their losses higher than ours." On all squadrons, the state of morale depended to an enormous extent on the CO. He had to "combine the best qualities of the technician, the fighter, and the leader,"[9] a tall order for young men who were, in the main, untrained for the job. When Bill Swetman took over command of 426 Squadron in the late summer of 1943, he was twenty-three years old. A year earlier he had been a sergeant pilot. He declares that the rapid promotion he enjoyed had little to do with any latent executive talents; it was simply that he had managed to survive longer than most of his contemporaries. Swetman may have had doubts about his administrative abilities, but he was a skilled bomber pilot, having already completed a tour of operations. As such he immediately earned the respect of his crews.

Canadians often complained about the standoffish British, but sometimes they were the guilty parties. LAC Bill Johnson, an RAF engine fitter, encountered more than a little hostility when posted to the HCU at Wombleton, Yorkshire, where most Canadian heavy bomber crews undertook the final stage of their flying training. In the billet to which he had been assigned, Johnson heard someone remark, "We don't want no goddam Limeys in here." Johnson found the Canadians a mystery: "I really did get depressed and couldn't understand these lads at all." Even when established in the billet, he suffered from the attentions of practical jokers – "childish things like moving my kit, sweeping rubbish under my bed, knocking my bed as they walked past as I was trying to get some sleep, kicking the table as I was trying to write a letter..." But eventually, in the inexplicable way of human relationships, Johnson found that the Canadian roommates who had irritated him the most became his closest friends. He recalls: "The friendships grew until there was a real bond between us, and I now rate the period I was with them as the greatest of my life, and when the time came for me to move on over a year later, the handshakes and goodbyes were sincere; it was a sad day for me."

When Gus Edwards arrived in Britain in 1941, the conduct of RCAF personnel at HQ Overseas horrified him: "The discipline of the place is lousy," he asserted. He considered the airmen's deportment disgraceful. "They come over here with little idea of discipline, no idea as to how an officer or NCO should behave." Edwards blamed Ottawa for sending poor quality personnel overseas, as a result of which "the name of the RCAF stinks in the nostrils of the RAF."[10]

Many rank-and-file RAF airmen would have disagreed with Edwards. They envied Canadians. They envied them their pay and their better quality uniforms. And they envied their freedom of action: if they didn't like an order they simply rang up their high commissioner and complained,[11] unthinkable behaviour for the average British serviceman, even if he had *had* a high commissioner.

In March 1943, Brookes despatched a "rocket" to 6 Group's stations and squadrons about "the marked deterioration in the general smartness and turnout" of officers. The brass at Castle Dismal didn't like the way personnel were saluting one another with a mere "flick of the hand."[12] In fact, on most operational stations no one saluted anyone lower than a group captain. Engine mechanic Lucide Rioux recalls a pilot officer becoming upset because Rioux and another ground crewman didn't salute him. The squadron CO, Wing Commander Johnny Fauquier, happened to be nearby; he drew the offended pilot officer's attention to the three rings on his sleeve and pointed out that no one ever saluted *him*! An ex-WAAF, Felicia Locke, tells of an incident at Dishforth involving two WAAF recruits who approached a pair of young Canadian aircrew officers, and: "Up came the arms of the WAAFs in a smart salute. The two officers stopped dead in their tracks. One said, 'Gee, thanks!'" It was, says Felicia, "probably the first and only time they were saluted."

The report from HQ claimed that officers tended to walk "in a slovenly manner, with hands in pockets." Furthermore, it went on, officers had been seen wearing grubby uniforms with incorrect insignia; and many of them had removed the stiffening wire from their service dress caps to give them "the thirty-op look" – and then, heaven forbid, had worn the caps at a "rakish" angle.[13] Although the directive may have resulted in some improvement, chances are it was short-lived. Throughout the war, the Canadians' operational squadrons were casual about dress and deportment, which probably generated most of the myths about the Canadians' lack of discipline. The fact is, when it came to matters of operational efficiency, discipline tended to be stricter on the average 6 Group squadron than on its RAF counterpart. Indeed, towards the end of the war, when 6 Group's casualties had become among the lowest in Bomber Command, some second-tour aircrew expressed a preference for RAF squadrons so that they might avoid the stricter discipline on Canadian units. Alex McFall, an RAF flight engineer who flew with 433 and 405 Squadrons, recalls that daily life on the Canadian units tended to be "free and easy, but our captain (Flying Officer Tom Ellison) was a strict disciplinarian while we were flying which, as far as I was concerned, was as it should be."

This assessment is supported by an ex-WAAF intelligence officer, Edith Kup, who had been transferred to 405 Squadron after serving with Fighter Command at Debden: "I found 405 rather brash at first, but soon got to know them and appreciate them. Generally speaking, they were undisciplined, except in the air . . . madcaps of the first water and anything could and did happen. However . . . it didn't take long to understand them and we became very involved with their fate. I think, because we knew exactly what the crews had to face and they knew they could trust us to keep confidences sacrosanct, we were treated as sisters and mothers, the ones to talk to when perhaps they wouldn't have confided in another man."

British servicemen and women were constantly fascinated by the Canadians' gambling and by their casual attitude to money. Eddy Collyer, an RAF flight engineer who flew a tour with 425 Squadron, remembers a Canadian pilot named Vincent who "was always ready for a game of craps" and carried his dice everywhere, often playing at dispersal before taking off on sorties. "After a particularly good game and a night in York with some of his crew, Vincent hired a battered old taxi to return to camp the next morning," Collyer relates. The taxi driver demanded "a grossly inflated fare." Vincent refused to pay it, saying it was more than the cab was worth. "After a very heated argument, Vincent ended up buying the taxi and putting the driver on the bus back to York." Collyer adds, "Sadly, Vince and his crew were lost on a trip to Hamburg on 28th July, 1944, on what was to be the completion of their tour." An LAC fitter with the RAF, David van Vlymen, spent some weeks among the Canadian bomber squadrons during the winter of 1943/44, replacing the suspect "arrow-head" fins and rudders of the older Halifaxes with the rectangular type. "To

us," he writes, "the Canadians and their stations were wonderful
... it was the first time I had seen craps played legally by *all* ranks
and for *money*! One pilot ... threw a bundle of bills on his bed
before donning his jacket to go to the Mess. I said to him, 'You're
not going to play with all that money, are you?' He replied, 'Why
not? I might not be here to enjoy it much longer.'" Jack Summers,
an RAF radar mechanic, remembers a "huge" game of dice in the
Sergeants' Mess at Leeming, at the end of which one sergeant
"scooped the entire amount of money staked, amounting to £790.
Next day he went to the races at Stockton and lost the lot."

As the Canadians became better acquainted with the grim realities of wartime living in the United Kingdom, they developed a
genuine admiration for the fortitude of the British: "... the spirit
of these Limeys is remarkable," commented one officer. "It is the
greatest thing I have ever seen." The people of London came in for
particularly keen admiration from many Canadians who found
them "well worth fighting for" because they were "the real
stuff."[14] The airmen of 6 Group often found themselves invited to
enjoy the hospitality of British homes. (In the majority of cases
the Canadians seemed to have remembered the advice of the PR
pamphlets to take ration cards and gifts of food.) Billeting also
helped foster good relations between Canadians and the British.
When Canadians lived in the towns and villages near 6 Group's
airfields, they quickly got to know the civilians and mutual affection usually developed. In order to provide extra food for the
perpetually hungry airmen of the local RCAF base, a Mrs. Mudd
of Tholthorpe regularly served them game obtained by poaching.
When she was caught, the Canadians took up a collection to pay
her fines.[15] Lucien Thomas, an American-born air gunner with
405 Squadron, recounts that he became a popular member of the
Mess because "I owned a twelve-gauge shotgun and generally
shot four to six pheasants every day. This came to an abrupt halt
... when I was rudely apprehended by the Magistrate of York
who informed me that I was shooting his birds! The Magistrate
was furious until he saw the air gunner's wings and the USA flashes
on my sleeve. He then became quite civilized and remarked: 'I see
you're a flyer. That makes a difference. I also note you are an

American. I've never met one before. But please leave my birds alone because we are going to have a shoot and I will personally invite you' . . . I might add that he did extend an invitation to me," Thomas says. Edith Kup remembers that local townspeople "kept virtually open house for the boys . . . the Canadians were accepted and liked by the surrounding populace, just the same as the British squadrons were." Interestingly, she recalls that when 405 was first based at Pocklington, Yorkshire, the locals "complained to us about the noise of take-offs and landings after midnight." In all seriousness, the villagers requested that flying be restricted to hours that wouldn't interfere with their sleep.

Joe Hartshorn, an American-born pilot with 419 Squadron, has fond memories of the civilians of Britain. When he first arrived, he was approached by an organization dedicated to introducing Commonwealth servicemen to families in various parts of the country. Hartshorn and another American with the RCAF, Ogden Gorman, went to stay with the well-to-do family of a judge near Oxford – only to discover that the family had requested two *Australians.* In spite of the confusion, the airmen were welcomed warmly. Acts of kindness by civilians can be recounted by every Canadian ex-serviceman. Jim Moffat, a 427 Squadron air gunner, remembers how an Epsom policeman gave him and a fellow crew member a night's lodgings when they arrived in the town late at night and couldn't find accommodation in a hotel. In the morning, the policeman (whose wife had been killed in an air raid) cooked breakfast for the Canadians before they left. Donald Smith from Toronto, a pilot with 425 Squadron, also speaks warmly of the civilians: "All were most friendly and understanding. If the positions had been reversed I doubt that we would have been so tolerant."

Probably the most important social aspect of the RCAF presence overseas was the "interaction" between the Canadians and the civilian womenfolk. Generally speaking, English women liked the Canadians *almost* as much as they liked the Americans, possibly because they were *almost* as exotic and *almost* as well paid.[16] Inevitably, countless liaisons took place. The airmen were away from their wives and sweethearts for years on end; for aircrew, the tedium of service life was aggravated by the stress of operational flying and the very real possibility of an early and probably unpleasant death. Local women, too, were deprived of their men-folk. In her memoirs, Jean Ellis, a Red Cross welfare officer, wrote that servicemen should not be condemned for seeking comfort on the nearest available shoulder. There was "considerable criticism of philandering Canadian servicemen and undoubtedly many broken hearts and broken homes have resulted from their wander-ings. But anyone who saw the awful tension under which they lived is not likely to judge them harshly."[17]

Many thousands of marriages resulted from wartime liaisons. By the end of 1946, close to forty-five thousand war brides had moved to Canada. About 18 per cent of them had married air-men. Official policy dictated that RCAF ground personnel had to have six months' service before they could marry, but oddly enough, this restriction did not apply to those serving overseas. Spur-of-the-moment marriages were not encouraged, however. The Canadian authorities insisted that the prospective bride produce a certificate attesting to her good character; the bride-groom had to sign a form declaring that he was, as yet, unmar-ried.[18]

The Canadians ranked second only to the Americans as patrons of Britain's oldest profession. In the cities clustered around the bases of 6 Group, prostitutes raised their prices when the Canadi-ans took up residence – and, according to some reports, reduced the time spent with each "client." At the same time, the incidence of venereal disease increased dramatically. In 1943, the infection rate for 6 Group's aircrew was almost double that of Bomber Command's aircrew as a whole.[19]

There is little doubt that some aircrew contracted VD deliber-ately in order to get out of operational flying for a while – and a few openly admitted to nurses that, once cured, they would soon return with another "dose." Harris was of the opinion that such aircrew should be treated as malingerers and should be compelled to start their operational tours over again after treatment. The Air Staff didn't agree.[20]

"We were fighting two wars with equal intensity," says ex-405 Squadron air gunner Lucien Thomas; "one was against the Brit-ish . . . the other against Germany." J.K. Chapman of 415 Squadron remembers that English administrative officers "regarded us as untutored and uncivilized savages from the colonies and looked down their noses at us." In many a Sergeants' Mess, young aircrew NCOs clashed with the permanent staff NCOs who had earned their stripes by long and faithful service. They felt the youngsters had been "jumped up" through the ranks.[21] At some units, feelings ran so high that special Aircrew Messes had to be created. Jim Emmerson, a pilot with 424 Squadron, remembers "quiet hostility" from RAF staff personnel at the Long Marston OTU; the "residents" regarded the RCAF airmen as noisy, rude transients.

In contrast, it is difficult to imagine how relations between aircrew of the RAF and RCAF could have been improved. An RAF wireless operator/air gunner, Les Dring, was invited to become part of the Canadian crew of William B. Patrick in mid-1943. Later they joined 427 Squadron at Leeming, Yorkshire. Early in their tour, Dring contracted mumps ("of all things") and had to go into hospital. During his incarceration, the crew did two ops with a spare wireless operator. Finally released from hospital, Dring returned to Leeming and resumed his tour with the crew. But eventually there came the time when the rest of the crew had completed their tour and Dring still had two trips to do. Without hesitation, the skipper and crew volunteered to do two extra ops so that Dring might complete his tour with his own crew. Dring comments: "What can I say about my skipper . . . and also my full crew of Canadians who volunteered to put their lives on the line on my behalf." Dring remembers his skipper saying to him, "We all started together and I'm seeing to it that we all finish together." Dring considers the eleven months he spent with Patrick's crew the best time of his five years in the RAF; the crew, he says, "made me feel as if I was a Canadian."

Many RAF flight engineers served with 6 Group. One was Stanley Fletcher who flew in the 420 Squadron crew led by Flying Officer Harold Damgaard. He remembers their extraordinary generosity: "My crew found my home address and, without telling me, sent my family a parcel for Christmas. Each gave a portion of his own parcel from Canada, things like oranges and bananas. I saw my first orange since 1939!" Fletcher adds: "The Damgaard crew could do no wrong in our house. My mother and sisters thought the world of them." Alex McFall, also an RAF flight engineer, flew fifty-five ops with the same Canadian crew. He recalls being "a little dubious" when first posted to 6 Group because he had had virtually no contact with Canadians; but he became "integrated very quickly." Like Stanley Fletcher, he was deeply impressed by the generosity of his fellow crew members: "Sweet Caporal cigarettes and Life Saver sweets were given to us in profusion as I think all the relations of the crew in Canada were sending gifts galore . . . and we [McFall and the RAF wireless operator, Bob Henderson] were not omitted when things were shared." Eddy Collyer of 425 Squadron has similar memories: "We shared the dangers and the difficulties, the good and the bad times, the parcels of goodies from Canada . . . but most of all the comradeship." Dudley Burnside, an RAF wing commander, was CO of 427 Squadron in 6 Group's early days; he thought highly of the Canadians under his command: "Despite very heavy casualties the squadron spirit was such that there was incredibly high morale amongst all ranks right from the start of our night bombing operations . . . I cannot speak too highly of the extraordinary courage and endurance of the air and ground crews I was privileged to command . . . The initial inexperience of the Canadians was quickly overtaken by their remarkable fortitude in battle despite appalling losses, particularly during the Battle of the Ruhr." An RAF Pilot Officer, R.B. Haywood, DFC, who served on 424 and 432 Squadrons, wrote: "I shall always consider myself fortunate to have been attached to the RCAF Group. I joined 6 Group in January 1943 and saw it advance from its first operation until it became recognized as the best Group in Bomber Command. In that time, I learnt to admire my Canadian colleagues not only for their skill and daring but also for the fine and friendly spirit which prevailed on the squadrons."

Such close bonds among aircrew were the norm on operational squadrons. Nationality meant nothing. Chapman writes: "The English aircrews called us 'Ruddy Colonials.' But we didn't mind that and in turn called them 'Bloody Limeys.'"[22] Familiarity bred mutual regard. Amid the stark realities of life and death on operational squadrons, the differences that generated such irritation and anger at other times and in other places rapidly assumed their proper proportions. The Canadian and British airmen found that their common bonds were infinitely more important than their differences.

6

THE BIG CITY

"Berlin was the hottest, most heavily defended
city in Fortress Europe."

Russell McKay, pilot, 420 Squadron

High on Harris's list of undesirables were the bureaucrats at the
Ministry of Economic Warfare. Panacea merchants, he called
them. Behind their snug Whitehall desks, surrounded by their
maps and charts, they spent their days convincing each other that
Germany was a sort of industrial house of cards that would collapse if only they could find just where to hit it. They kept trying.
The famous Dams raid was one of their more recent efforts. Knock
this target out and the whole Ruhr area will be paralyzed, they had
claimed. But in fact, the enemy's war effort seemed to have

suffered remarkably little from the breaching of the Eder and Möhne dams – which cost almost half the Lancasters participating. Harris had had little regard for the denizens of the MEW before the Dams raid, none at all after it. As the war progressed, he became increasingly scornful whenever the subject of "panacea" targets came up.[1] It's curious, then, that he should have been so sure that if he could destroy Berlin he would win the war. Obviously the total destruction of the city would have been a shattering blow to German morale. But would it have meant the inevitable collapse of the war effort? It's questionable in the extreme.

After the triumph of Hamburg and the highly successful Peenemünde attack, Harris must have felt like a boxer who has his opponent on the ropes, tottering, reeling, incapable of taking much more. One last enormous wallop would do the trick. Harris wrote to Churchill: "I feel certain that Germany must collapse before this programme which is more than half completed already, has proceeded much further. We have not got far to go. We must get the USAAF to wade in in greater force. If they will only get going according to plan and avoid such disastrous diversions as Ploesti, and getting 'nearer' to Germany from the plains of Lombardy (which are further than 9/10ths of Germany than is Norfolk), we can get through with it very quickly." Following which he made his famous – or infamous – statement: "We can wreck Berlin from end to end if the USAAF will come in on it. It will cost between us 400–500 aircraft. It will cost Germany the war."[2] A few weeks later he was telling his immediate superior, Portal, that he expected to have bombed the Germans into a state of near-surrender by April 1944.

It was typical Harris. Assertive. Assured. And ill-advised. His words would come back to haunt him after the winter of 1943/44, although he would always be able to counter that the outcome would have been different if the Americans *had* come in in a big way. But the Americans didn't see Berlin as Harris did. To them it was just one of many targets. To Harris it was the *ultimate* target, a prize worth any sacrifice by his crews. Over the next few months he would send his bombers to the German capital again and again. The Battle of Berlin would cost both sides dearly – and the squadrons of 6 Group would suffer along with the other units of Bomber Command. Although Harris's force was far more efficient than it had been a year or even six months before, so was its nemesis, the German night fighter force. The battle to come would test both attackers and defenders to the limit.

The Battle of Berlin was Harris's own battle; he waged it in open defiance of the instructions of the Combined Chiefs. Why didn't Portal take him to task? Why indeed? The Americans kept asking for British support in destroying the German aircraft industry, as agreed at Casablanca; but Harris was too busy fighting the war his way, throwing in his entire force night after night, waging a private campaign against Berlin, utterly convinced that he was right and everyone else was wrong.

How could Harris get away with it? The answer lies in the ambiguities of the Casablanca Directive and in the reputation of Harris himself. We can be reasonably certain that a lesser man would soon have found himself fired or "retired for health reasons." The conclusion is inescapable that Harris was too popular to fire. And, apparently, too popular even to discipline in any meaningful way. He ranked with Montgomery as one of the few British commanders who had shown themselves capable of hurting the Nazis. The public adored him; so, inexplicably, did the majority of his long-suffering crews.

Portal's attempts to persuade Harris to obey orders seem in retrospect rather pathetic; Portal comes across as the weaker of the two characters, unable to control his subordinate. Their correspondence says a lot about the two men. Portal was constantly *suggesting* this or that rather than issuing the direct and unequivocal orders that might reasonably be expected from a senior officer to a junior under his command. Harris's responses were masterpieces. Again and again he *seemed* to be on the point of agreeing wholeheartedly with Portal, but then there was always some qualification, usually something to do with weather or equipment. Invariably Harris ended up doing just what he wanted to do. It cannot be said, however, that he was evasive about his intentions for Berlin. He raised more than a few eyebrows when he informed the Air Ministry that the demolition of Berlin would require forty thousand tons of bombs. It was a stupendous tonnage, far greater than had been dropped on any target to date – five times the weight of bombs so far unloaded on Hamburg. But Portal and others at the Air Ministry must have rationalized that, although it sounded outrageous, if Harris could do to Berlin what he did to Hamburg, they would have no complaints.

The battle was on.

The city had a population of four million and was situated on a plain of sandy, glacial outwash sliced diagonally by a depression along which flowed the River Spree. It was a city with a lengthy history; a village back in the 1200s before it merged with another village, Koelln, and became a town of some local importance. It assumed even greater prominence two hundred years later when the Hohenzollern family, rulers of the province of Brandenburg, made it their official home. The city suffered badly during the Thirty Years' War. Napoleon's army occupied it from 1806 to 1809. Then came the glory days: first, capital of Prussia, then, in 1871, capital of Germany itself. The city's modern form dates back to 1920 when it acquired several previously independent towns and rural communities, creating an enormous metropolis occupying more than three hundred square miles – more than eight hundred square miles if the sprawling suburban area was included.

This was Berlin, the target that loomed so large in Harris's thoughts. The second largest city in Europe. The third largest in the world. A major industrial area. Iron and steel. Chemicals. Machine tools. Engines. Electrical equipment. Tanks. Guns. Aircraft. The capital of the Third Reich.

A plum target. But the very devil of a place to hit. Lying deep inside the Third Reich not far from the Polish border, it was neatly positioned about as far from the bomber airfields in Britain as it was possible for a German target to be. And to bomb the city, an aircraft had to run a gauntlet of some eleven *thousand* flak guns, highly efficient 88 mm weapons, and more than three thousand searchlights, vigorously aided and abetted by hundreds of night fighters from airfields all over Germany. No wonder the crews called it the "Big City," plus a variety of other choice epithets. Any sortie to Berlin was an ordeal, a long and dangerous slog across hundreds of miles of enemy territory, with destruction by flak or fighter a very real possibility at any moment along the way. Moreover, the city was singularly isolated; a bomber stream heading for Berlin was unlikely to be headed anywhere else; only on rare occasions did the planners at High Wycombe succeed in deceiving the German fighter controllers about their intentions.

In those days of relatively slow aircraft, Berlin's location made it an autumn and winter target. There simply weren't enough hours of darkness in the spring and summer nights for the bombers to take off, fly to Berlin and back and land before daylight. Darkness was vital for Harris's bombers, ensuring that the majority of them would be able to slip through the defences to unload their bombs.

Although Bomber Command's aircraft had the cover of darkness, they had no protection from the winter weather, which could always be relied upon to be unpleasant but which seemed particularly vile in the winter of 1943/44. Throughout the Berlin campaign, the elements would prove to be just as implacable an enemy as the Germans.

The Big City presented another problem. It was just too vast to provide the sort of identifiable H2S "echoes" that the navigators of Bomber Command needed. The immense urban sprawl completely filled the screens, to the dismay of the navigators crouched in the vibrating, bouncing fuselages of their aircraft. In its own way, the size of Berlin was just as effective a counter to radar as was Window. The operators of those early H2S sets needed *features* – coastlines, islands, lakes – in order to determine their precise position. Berlin had lakes, but the Germans worked diligently to disguise them. They positioned great wooden floats on the water and in some cases attempted to alter the shapes of the shorelines to confuse the airmen.

For some months, Bomber Command had been improving its night-bombing tactics. The Pathfinders used three methods to mark targets. The first, known as Newhaven, was employed on those rare nights when conditions were ideal; it consisted of dropping markers that fell to the ground and outlined the area to be bombed by the Main Force. The second, "Paramatta," was ground-marking by H2S employing the 250-pound TIs when visibility was poor. The third, Wanganui, employed light parachute flares for sky-marking, with the Main Force aiming at the flares as they slowly descended. Sometimes these techniques worked perfectly. All too often, however, the winds suddenly became stronger than predicted by Met. Or they switched direction while the bombers were halfway to their target. Or heavy clouds moved in over an area that was supposed to be clear. With maddening frequency, the capricious weather prevented the sort of *concentrated* bombing that was so vital against an enormous target like Berlin.

Although the Battle of Berlin is usually considered to have opened with the raid on November 18/19, 1943, Harris mounted three attacks in late August and early September which he probably intended as the beginning of his campaign against the German capital. But the three raids cost Bomber Command more than a hundred bombers, a foretaste of the dreadful casualties to come. Thus, it seems likely that Harris decided to postpone his campaign against the German capital until his force was equipped principally with Lancasters and the new Hercules-powered Halifaxes then about to enter squadron service. The Battle of Berlin was the toughest, most costly conflict in Bomber Command's history. Lasting until late March 1944, it tested the aircrews as did no other campaign. Interestingly, the operational tour of a 6 Group pilot, Roger Coulombe of 426 Squadron, coincided almost exactly with the span of the Battle of Berlin. His first op was the first raid of the Battle; he flew on twelve more, although one trip had to be aborted. Known on the squadron as "The Berlin Kid," Coulombe later received an award for having dropped more bombs on the German capital than any other pilot. Astonishingly, he and his crew came through the conflict unscathed.

The opening blow in the Battle took place on the night of August 23/24. A force of 727 aircraft arrived over the German capital a few minutes before midnight. The Master Bomber was a Canadian, the formidable Johnny Fauquier of 405 Squadron, who had been one of Searby's deputies at Peenemünde. The Canadian Group detailed seventy-six aircraft and crews for the raid but only sixty-eight took off. Eleven returned early. Two failed to find the target. Thus, about a third of the Canadian crews detailed didn't reach the target. It was a disappointing beginning for 6 Group's involvement in the Battle.

Despite enthusiastic entries in the 6 Group ORB – "Excellent attack with the centre of Berlin extensively damaged" – the truth is, the raid failed. The Pathfinders couldn't locate the centre of Berlin by means of H2S; they dropped their markers on an area in the south of the city. Fauquier tried energetically (and colourfully) to direct the errant crews. Despite his efforts, the Main Force bombed inaccurately with a large proportion of their bombs landing in open country – although those bombs which did hit the centre of Berlin caused a good deal of damage, destroying government buildings and sinking twenty ships in the canals. It was a costly raid for Bomber Command. Fifty-six bombers didn't return, 7.9 per cent of the force – the highest loss to that date. Five 6 Group aircraft were numbered among the casualties.

Returning crews reported how night fighters had attacked them over the target area, with the searchlights apparently striving to assist the fighters more than the anti-aircraft guns. In the past, the fighters usually left the immediate target areas to the flak. On this night, however, the flak and fighters worked together, the guns keeping their fire limited to about twenty thousand feet; above that level, the fighters held sway.

Again on August 31/September 1, Harris's bombers took fearful punishment from Berlin's defences. Of the 622 aircraft despatched, forty-seven were shot down, 7.6 per cent of the force. Harris might have been prepared to accept such losses if he believed he was seriously damaging the German capital. But he wasn't and he knew it. Again the Pathfinders failed to mark the centre of the city and the Main Force's bombing became badly scattered, probably due in part to the vigorous flak barrages and determined attacks by fighters. On that night, the *Luftwaffe* introduced a pyrotechnical innovation. Flying high above the bombers, fighters dropped flares to illuminate their prey and to indicate the routes in and out of the target area. The sky above Berlin, already a kaleidoscope of Pathfinders' markers, searchlights, darting tracer, and flashing bursts of flak, now had another stratum of weird, otherworldly illumination. For the bomber crews huddled in their vulnerable, heavily laden aircraft, the flares had the same unnerving effect as the searchlights, robbing them of the comforting mantle of darkness. Fortunately, the fighter flares were just as vulnerable to high winds as the Pathfinders' markers. On this night most were soon blown out of the immediate area.

The Canadian Group lost seven of the fifty-eight aircraft which took off; eight had returned early. Among the missing was a Halifax of 427 Squadron commanded by that fine pilot, George Vandekerckhove. He and his crew died on the last op of their highly eventful tour.

The third and last raid of this "introductory" campaign took place on September 3/4. A relatively small force of only 316 bombers, all Lancasters, set off for the German capital. The contribution of 6 Group was negligible, just three aircraft (including Coulombe's of 426 Squadron); all returned safely. But the Main Force again took grievous losses: twenty-two Lancasters, close to 7 per cent of the force. Once more Berlin had demonstrated the strength and determination of its defences. And again, results came nowhere near to justifying the losses; most of the bombs landed in residential areas, although several factories took hits, according to city records.

Despite heavy casualties and unexceptional results, Harris made plans to attack the German capital again on the night of September 8/9. Poor weather forced him to cancel the operation. The following night saw little improvement. Then the new moon period prevented any long-range operations for almost two weeks. It was just as well; the three raids on Berlin had cost Harris 125 of his four-engined bombers and had achieved little. It was time for a pause to consider new tactics.

Bomber Command mounted several major operations in September, October, and the early part of November, in which 6 Group took part. Two raids on Kassel in October cost seventeen 6 Group aircraft and crews. The first, on the night of October 3/4, started badly with inaccurate Pathfinder marking – although, more or less by accident, a good deal of damage was done to military facilities on the outskirts of the city. En route to the target, a Halifax V of 427 Squadron, with Flight Lieutenant George Laird in command, suffered a devastating attack by a night fighter. "Jerry raked us from nose to tail underneath with cannon and machine gun and a fire broke out in the bomb bay," Laird later reported. To the mid-upper gunner, Pilot Officer Jim Moffat, the attack "sounded like frozen peas hitting a tin roof." He later found nine German bullets in his ammunition cans. The attack had killed two of the crew, the rear gunner and the wireless operator, and had seriously injured the flight engineer, Sergeant Bill Cardy, in one arm and an eye. The bomb-aimer, Sergeant Joe Corbally, couldn't jettison the bombs; fortunately, however, the fighter's attack had severed a cable holding the 4,000-pound cookie. It fell away, breaking through the closed bomb doors. Laird turned for home. Despite numerous holes in the fuselage, the aircraft handled reasonably well and Laird flew it back to Leeming, Yorkshire. During the trip the incapacitated Cardy kept drifting in and out of consciousness; when able, he insisted on checking with Corbally who had taken over as flight engineer, advising him on the operation of the tanks and other aircraft systems.

Over his airfield, Laird found that he couldn't lower his undercarriage because of hydraulic damage. From the control tower came the order to bale out. Laird refused, knowing that a jump would probably kill Cardy; even if his parachute opened properly, the wounded man might well die before he was found in the darkness. Fortunately, Cardy became conscious while Laird was circling Leeming and was able to "direct axe and back-saw operations which finally locked down both wheels," Laird said.[3] He brought the battered, perforated Halifax in to a perfect landing. He received a DFC; Cardy the CGM.

The second of the two Kassel operations, on the night of October 22/23, resulted in a firestorm which, though not as large as that in Hamburg two months before, caused an immense amount of damage in the city, killing more than five thousand people and injuring close to four thousand. "Incendiaries took hold and Kassel left blazing," reported the 6 Group ORB.

During October, the *Ruhr Express*, the first Canadian-built Lancaster, arrived at Gransden Lodge, home of 405 Squadron, formerly part of 6 Group and now the only Canadian Pathfinder unit. Coincidentally, Reg Lane had also recently arrived at Gransden Lodge, having been appointed CO of the squadron. Lane had seriously jeopardized his prospects of enjoying old age by volunteering for a third tour of operations, his second on Pathfinders (in which casualties averaged *twice* those on Main Force squadrons). The much-publicized Lancaster was still a headache for the ground crews, with the Packard-Merlins suffering all the technical problems so common when one company assumes the manufacture of another's product; in this case, the difficulties were exacerbated by the fact that Packard had to replace many of the British parts with those made in North America.

The month saw the release of yet another report from the ORS at High Wycombe. The high loss rate of 6 Group squadrons was again the subject. The report considered the Group's tactics in some detail, particularly the Canadian pilots' tendency to "push" their Halifaxes to maximum altitudes over the target. The report noted that 6 Group's Halifax loss rate had been consistently high over the average crew's first twenty sorties, whereas 4 Group's Halifax loss rate gradually declined as each crew accumulated more experience. The report suggested that the Canadians were slower to benefit from experience, not, it should be added, because of any mental torpor, but because of the constant organizational changes taking place within 6 Group. It should have surprised no one when the ORS concluded that this factor was crucial in the Canadians' loss rate. Only 419 Squadron had enjoyed organizational stability since January 1; this 6 Group squadron's loss rate was lower that those of two RAF squadrons of 4 Group, 51 and 77, both of which had become operational in January 1943.

The ORS report was undoubtedly correct in its conclusions. To date, the majority of 6 Group's squadrons had not been able to establish the *esprit de corps* so vital in promoting the good morale which led to operational efficiency. Senior staff and specialist officers had been preoccupied with administrative and organizational problems to the detriment of operational training. In addition, the fact couldn't be escaped that most of these officers were themselves inexperienced. The ORS suggested informing Brookes that the Group's problems were basically "teething troubles."[4]

An RCAF report revealed that the Canadian Group had suffered startlingly higher casualties than had 4 Group during the period January 1 to September 30, 1943: almost 10 per cent higher for Wellingtons and 25 per cent higher for Halifaxes. Two 6 Group squadrons, 431 and 434, were noted as having particularly serious loss rates (an average of 11.5 per cent from August 1 to October 25). Both were based at Tholthorpe, a "highly dispersed, non-permanent station." In addition to organizational instability, the RCAF report cited maintenance problems and the Yorkshire/Durham locations as important factors in the Group's worrisome loss rate. In many cases, RCAF ground crews were unfamiliar with some of the bombers' equipment. However, added the investigators, the airmen were quick to learn and would benefit from further training. The Group's location was also of significance, the report admitted; it meant that its aircraft had to fly greater distances to Germany; moreover, especially in the fall, they had to take off earlier than other groups, leaving less time for maintenance and preparation. In spite of all this, the report rated 6 Group's loss rate as reasonable, considering the circumstances.[5]

The main Battle of Berlin began during the evening of November 18, 1943. A force of 440 Lancasters, including twenty-three from 6 Group, and four Mosquitoes arrived over the city. The first bombs fell at four minutes to nine. The raid lasted a remarkably brief sixteen minutes. The Lancasters flew through the target area at a rate of twenty-seven per minute. (A year and a half earlier the thousand-bomber raid crews had been astounded when told that they would be attacking Cologne at a rate of twelve bombers per minute.)

None of the crews saw Berlin through the thick cloud that carpeted the city. And, as if to give the airmen a taste of what was to come in this merciless campaign, the winds proved to be far stronger than predicted. The bomber stream became scattered. Technical troubles added to the mess. Most of the H2S sets malfunctioned. Only one aircraft on the raid, a Mosquito, had been equipped with the new Mark III H2S on which so many hopes were pinned; but that set became unserviceable en route to the target. The Mosquito's skipper obeyed orders and returned to base. Meanwhile, over the target, one of the Pathfinder aircraft dropped a yellow TI in error, confusing the Main Force bomb-aimers who had been instructed to bomb green TIs only. "Markers scattered," stated the 6 Group report after the raid. Results were inconsequential.

There was in fact only one good thing to be said about the raid: Bomber Command's losses were relatively low: nine Lancasters, 2 per cent of the force. All of 6 Group's aircraft returned safely to base. Although the flak was fierce, few fighters made an appearance. The weary crews thankfully trudged off to bed, wondering how long it would be before Butch made them go back to that hornets' nest of flak and fighters.

The Canadian Group participated in another unsuccessful raid the following evening; the target wasn't Berlin, however, but Leverkusen. Sixty-six 6 Group aircraft set off. Eight returned early. Over the target, the bombers encountered ten-tenths cloud. Equipment failures resulted in an almost total lack of marking by the Pathfinders. The bombers had little choice but to drop their bombs on estimated positions. It was like 1941 all over again. The crews did their best. But, according to city records, only *one* bomb landed in Leverkusen; the rest were scattered about the surrounding countryside. Again, the only positive thing to be said about the raid was that it cost relatively few Bomber Command lives; four Halifaxes and one Stirling didn't come home, 1.9 per cent of the force. But three of the missing aircraft were from 6 Group, representing a 5 per cent loss for the Canadians.

During the afternoon of November 22, the crews in dozens of briefing rooms heard the target for that night: Berlin again. The crews sighed, stomachs lurching at the news. The Big Bloody City again. How many wouldn't make it back this time? What would go wrong? Bad weather, equipment failure, human failure? Or all three? Nothing had been going right recently.

But on this raid everything worked.

A total of 764 aircraft set out. One hundred and ten of the bombers were provided by 6 Group, although eleven returned early for various reasons, an early return rate of 10 per cent compared with a rate of 8.9 per cent for the force as a whole. Again a thick layer of cumulus cloud obscured the route all the way from the Dutch coast. Icing conditions added to the bombers' difficulties as they neared the target. But the Pathfinders' marking was exemplary – and so was the bombing of the Main Force. Although no one knew it at the time, this was to be the most effective of all the raids mounted against the German capital. For Berliners, it was a shattering blow: more than three thousand industrial buildings and homes were wrecked and some two thousand citizens killed. Fifty thousand troops had to be diverted from their normal duties and sent into the city to help with the clean-up work. With spectacular efficiency, Bomber Command had achieved its goal of concentrating its bombing, overwhelming fire and rescue services and laying waste to an entire section of the city.

The weather had been ideal for such an attack: clear over the airfields in Britain, yet cloudy enough en route and over the target to provide cover for the bombers. On this occasion, the attackers went over the target area at the unheard-of rate of thirty-four aircraft per minute, an even higher degree of concentration than that of four nights earlier. But it wasn't achieved by simply ordering the bombers to fly closer together.

For many months, Bomber Command's major efforts had been characterized by waves of bombers at different altitudes, the altitudes being dictated by the ceilings of the various aircraft on the operation. At that period there were three types of heavy bombers serving with Bomber Command: the Short Stirling, the Handley Page Halifax II and V, and the Avro Lancaster. The Stirling was the first of the heavies to see service. Although more manoeuvrable than its ungainly appearance suggested, the Stirling had a dismal ceiling of between twelve thousand and fifteen thousand feet. The Merlin-powered Halifaxes, which equipped many of 6 Group's squadrons as well as those of 4 Group, could fly a little higher, but not much. Thus both types were perilously vulnerable to flak – and suffered countless problems resulting from poor workmanship in the factories. Harris kept up an angry barrage of complaints about the types and their makers: "There should be a wholesale sacking of the incompetents who have turned out approximately 50 per cent rogue aircraft from S. & H., Belfast, and Austin's," he had written to Archibald Sinclair a few months earlier. "Much the same applies to the Halifax issue . . . In Russia it would long ago have been arranged with a gun, and to that extent I am a fervid Communist."[6] But Harris had no complaints about the Lancasters; they could cruise at twenty thousand feet or more, well above the Stirlings and Halifaxes. Inevitably, because the defences tended to concentrate on the lowest-flying aircraft, they suffered the lowest losses when all three types were involved on an operation. Many former Lancaster crewmen recall feeling intensely sorry for the Stirling and Halifax crews – yet secretly relieved when they heard that they would be coming along on a given night. Indeed, some Lancaster crews were known to *cheer* on such occasions! On the Berlin raid of November 22/23, the losses were typically apportioned: 2.3 per cent for the Lancasters, 4.2 per cent for the Halifaxes, and an alarming 10 per cent for the Stirlings. One can understand Harris's anxiety to equip all his squadrons with Lancasters – and the keenness of the crews to be so equipped.

On this highly successful raid, Harris abandoned the wave approach. The Stirlings, Halifaxes, and Lancasters attacked en masse. Clearly the lower-flying aircraft ran an even greater than normal risk of being hit by "friendly" bombs and suffering the inevitable attention from the defences. But the planners at High Wycombe apparently felt that the benefits of the method out-weighed the disadvantages. Whether the Stirling and Halifax crews felt the same way is arguable. In any event, it was to be the last time the inadequate Stirlings would be used on German targets. When Harris withdrew them, he immediately lost ten front-line squadrons. (Some of the Stirling units went to Transport Command and saw service as glider tugs in the invasion of Normandy the following spring, others were used for sea-mining. Most of the Stirling squadrons stood down, awaiting conversion to Lancasters. In many cases, they had a long wait; the factories had their hands full making good the dreadful losses of the Berlin campaign.)

"Appears to have been a concentrated attack," stated 6 Group's ORB of the November 22/23 raid. "Skymarkers well placed. A number of large explosions." The Group lost four aircraft, a modest price for the outstanding results achieved. In spite of the concentration of bombers, there were no collisions and no known losses from falling bombs. But a crew of 408 Squadron had an unnerving experience on their way home from the target. Energetically corkscrewing to evade enemy fighters, the skipper, Flying Officer W.B. Stewart, found himself in a high-speed stall. The Lancaster snapped into a spin to starboard and plummeted some five thousand feet before Stewart managed to recover – only to have the bomber whirl into a spin to port. Pinned by centrifugal force, the crew could do nothing but wait for the inevitable impact. They were lucky. When the aircraft had plunged to some five thousand feet, Stewart regained control; he had little choice but to continue the homeward journey at that dangerous height, an ideal target for light flak. Miraculously the Lancaster escaped. It headed out across the North Sea. But after its violent convolutions, the aircraft flew erratically, steadily losing height all the way to England, crossing the coastline at a mere twenty-five hundred feet. Stewart ordered the crew to prepare to abandon the aircraft; moments later he decided it might just be possible to coax the battered Lanc safely back to terra firma. This he did; and an intensely relieved crew chalked up another op.

The much-publicized *Ruhr Express* took off on this raid with Flight Sergeant Harold Floren of Weyburn, Saskatchewan, in command. The aircraft carried two passengers: a reporter and a photographer, whose job it was to record the historic event. But over the coast, the Packard-Merlins began to lose power. Floren dumped the light bombs. Despite the efforts of the crew, the altimeter kept unwinding, steadily, dangerously. Sixty miles from Berlin, Floren had no choice. He jettisoned the 4,000-pound cookie and turned back. Over the German-Dutch border, the troublesome Lancaster was down to four thousand, her engines sputtering and wheezing. Fortunately, the clouds provided a hiding place for the aircraft, and Floren was able to get her home – where Reg Lane had to undergo the ordeal of a faked debriefing for the crew so that Public Relations – and the Canadian public – wouldn't be disappointed.[7]

Poor visibility the next day prevented detailed photography of the raid's results. But Harris and his staff were fairly sure that a major blow had been struck. Typically, Harris ordered another attack for the following night, November 23/24, this time with a force consisting almost entirely of Lancasters, 365 of them, plus ten Halifaxes and the customary cluster of Mosquitoes: 383 aircraft in all. The Canadian Group's contribution was modest on this occasion: only twenty-six aircraft of which nineteen got away and three returned early.

Harris's decision to go back to Berlin that night caused pandemonium on the stations. The aircrews had had only a few hours' sleep; the ground crews were still working on their aircraft, repairing minor damage and carrying out normal maintenance. Many wouldn't be ready in time – no matter how stridently the COs, the flight commanders, and the chiefies demanded the impossible. Some stations could ready only a few of their aircraft in time for take-off on the twenty-third. Determined to repeat the success of the previous night, Harris issued virtually the same operational orders, with the same take-off time, the same route, the same zero hour. Even the same section of the city came under attack. And, except for a smaller load of bombs being dropped, the results were remarkably similar. The raids differed in one important respect, however. The bad weather which kept many of the German fighters grounded the previous night had improved. Strong forces of *Luftwaffe* aircraft arrived over Berlin within a few minutes of the bombers. Evidently the fighters were given priority, for the bomber crews rated the flak as relatively light. Twenty bombers were shot down, 5.2 per cent of the force. 6 Group lost one aircraft, a Lancaster II of 408 Squadron. Another Lancaster, LL629 of 426 Squadron, was damaged by flak and crashed at Malton, Yorkshire. The skipper, Pilot Officer D.R. DeBloome, was injured. Two members of the crew died in the crash, three more were injured, and one was unhurt.

The raid was another severe blow to the Berliners, coming as it did a mere twenty-four hours after the most damaging raid of the war to date; many fires from the first raid still raged when the second raid began. But it was also extremely hard on the aircrews and their aircraft. Twelve per cent of the attacking force, forty-six aircraft, returned early, in most cases dumping their bomb loads in the North Sea before turning for home. After the raid, six Lancasters crashed in Britain. Both phenomena were indicative of the effects of fatigue on determination and on flying ability. No doubt some of the crews who turned back might have kept going if they had been feeling "on top line," in the jargon of the day. No doubt some felt that Harris was asking too much of them. And no doubt more than one exhausted pilot made a fatal error when trying to land his aircraft in deteriorating weather, his judgement blunted by sheer weariness.

Two nights later, on November 25/26, a sortie to Frankfurt cost 6 Group six aircraft. Eighty-eight had taken off, part of a force of 262. In all, Bomber Command lost twelve bombers, 4.6 per cent of the force. Cloud covered the target and the "markers were few and scattered," noted 6 Group's ORB.

On the night of November 26/27, the Bomber Command planners tried new tactics. An attack on Berlin would be combined with a raid on Stuttgart in an effort to confuse the German controllers. Thirty-nine 6 Group bombers took off to attack Berlin; fifty-six set out to bomb Stuttgart. Four aircraft from each force returned early, representing 10 per cent and 7 per cent respectively. In all, 450 aircraft attacked Berlin and 178 attacked Stuttgart. The two forces flew the same route, almost reaching Frankfurt before diverging. On this occasion the diversionary tactics worked; the night fighter controllers seemed uncertain which city was the prime target; they lost precious minutes while they made up their minds. But much of the advantage went for nought over Berlin, for the Pathfinders dropped their markers several miles from the aiming point. Most of the bombs fell in the suburbs, and although they did a good deal of damage, the raid was not as successful as either of the two earlier attacks.

"FIRST TORONTO-BUILT LANCASTER STARS IN SORTIE ON GERMAN CAPITAL," chortled the Toronto *Telegram* proudly.[8] The *Ruhr Express* had at last completed a sortie – although most of the Canadian public must have been puzzled. Hadn't they been told that the renowned aircraft had been in the thick of things since it took off from Malton the previous August?

The November 26/27 Berlin raid was costly for Bomber Command with twenty-eight Lancasters lost, 6.2 per cent of the force. Fourteen more Lancasters crashed back in England for various reasons. 6 Group lost two Lancasters, one from 426 Squadron, the other from 408 Squadron, flown by the CO, Wing Commander A.C. Mair, who had been with the unit less than four weeks. Peter Dennis, skipper of a 432 Squadron Lancaster, and his rear gunner, Joe Quesnel, both won DFMs for this sortie. A trio of Me 210s attacked their aircraft three times over the target area and caused serious damage. During the attacks, Quesnel found that his turret was out of action; nevertheless he "coolly directed his pilot's combat manoeuvres and the attackers were evaded," in the words of the official history. A Lancaster of 408 Squadron commanded by Flight Sergeant R. Lloyd had engine trouble before reaching the target; the starboard outer failed and the heavily loaded bomber lost height. Nevertheless the crew bombed their target from eighteen thousand feet – whereupon the recalcitrant engine came back to life. Delighted, Lloyd climbed back to the altitude of the stream, only to find that the intercom to the mid-upper turret had failed. Moments later, flak hit the aircraft, wounding the mid-upper gunner in the foot, after which a Ju 88 night fighter attacked, damaging the mid-upper turret and the starboard inner engine, which the crew feathered. Fortunately the fighter disappeared into the darkness and Lloyd managed to get his battered bomber across the North Sea; he headed for Fiskerton, Lincolnshire – and when he arrived, the starboard outer that had given trouble en route to Berlin promptly expired. With two engines out on one side, the Lanc became impossible to control, sliding into a shallow spiral dive. Lloyd ordered his crew to bale out, quickly countermanding the order when the escape hatch couldn't be opened. Calls of "Darky" and "Mayday" generated no responses. Finally Lloyd put the Lancaster down in a sewage disposal farm near Lincoln, the crew surviving.[9]

The raid on Stuttgart undoubtedly achieved its objective of drawing most of the fighters away from Berlin; it's surprising that the bombers' losses weren't higher. Only six Halifaxes, 3.4 per cent of the force, became casualties. One of those Halifaxes came from 419 Squadron of 6 Group with Flight Sergeant S.E. Clarke in command. Group records claimed that the raid "appears to be highly successful. Markers and bombing well concentrated and two definite areas of fires." But Bomber Command dismissed the op as a failure with scattered bombing that caused little damage. Pilot Officer H.W. Mitchell of 429 Squadron lost an engine of his Halifax about one hundred miles before Stuttgart; nevertheless he pressed on and bombed the target, later nursing the ailing bomber back to base. Mitchell received the DFC; Lloyd of 408 Squadron, who appears to have contended with an even greater onslaught of problems, received no recognition.

The failure to recognize Lloyd's courage and determination may have been unjust but it was not uncommon. An officer was five to ten times more likely to win a DFC than was an NCO to win the DFM; this inequity seems to have been inherited from the British. The result was that airmen held the DFM in much higher regard than the DFC; many felt it was equivalent to the DSO.

Lucien Thomas, who flew with 405 Squadron in the early days of
6 Group, received the DFM for shooting down a Ju 88 en route to
Duisburg in the summer of 1942 and two more over the Ruhr in
1943. He recalls a warrant officer on the squadron being awarded
the DFC – and complaining bitterly because he had earned the
medal as a flight sergeant and felt he should have been awarded
the DFM which he considered far superior.

The whole system of awards was highly contentious and the
subject of endless discussions, which occasionally became heated
arguments. Many crews felt that "gongs" were often awarded for
the wrong reasons. For example, en route to attack the synthetic
oil plant at Wanne-Eickel, a 415 Squadron Halifax was hit by flak
that seriously wounded the navigator, Flying Officer C.J. Prawdzik, and damaged the nose and mid-upper turret. But the aircraft
was still flyable so the skipper, John McAllister, pushed on to the
target. On the way home, the bomb-aimer, Bud Moynes, took
over the navigator's duties and successfully directed McAllister to
an emergency airfield where he landed safely, although the Halifax was a write-off. Sadly, the wounded navigator, Prawdzik, later
died of his injuries. McAllister and Moynes both received the
DFC. A former 415 Squadron pilot, John McQuiston, writes:
"McAllister was suitably modest and maintained they were only
doing their job and in a sense this was true. A pilot had to make
many difficult and lonely decisions in the course of a tour and
Mac decided to press on. The die was cast and each member of the
crew had to rise to the occasion. Prawdzik's death dampened
much of the sense of celebration. Whether or not they were just
doing their jobs, McAllister and Moynes deserved their awards
and their exploit was typical of the type that won decorations:
aircraft shot up; crew member wounded; press on to the target and
return to a crash landing." But, McQuiston adds,

there was a general gripe on the number of decorations
awarded; some felt anyone who completed a tour of operations
in a service that suffered fifty per cent casualties deserved some
special recognition. A crew could perform perfectly, rising to
every occasion and, because of its skill and application, could
very well complete its tour without incident. There was no
mechanism designed to identify and reward such a consummate

performance. Sometimes an award came through after the crew had left the squadron but, almost always, it was only the pilot who was decorated. On the other hand, we could have below-average crews who tended to wander all over the night skies of Germany, beyond the protection of the bomber stream. These stragglers were prime targets for flak and fighters, and so they were attacked, damaged and often destroyed. But some survived, limped home with engines out, crew members dead or wounded. They came back, not because they were proficient or brave, but simply because they didn't want to die. These were the people who were decorated! Gallantry medals were highly prized and much coveted, but the method of deciding who should be decorated with what medal left much to be desired and was the cause of considerable bitterness among the aircrew.

McQuiston is of the opinion that, on a per capita basis, the Canadians lagged far behind the RAF in the number of decorations awarded to aircrew. Allan Caine of Toronto, a 420 Squadron pilot, agrees that medals were often awarded for the wrong reason – and *not* awarded to many who deserved recognition. His aircraft was damaged over the Ruhr, yet he managed to get back to base, whereupon the two port engines cut out. The Halifax started to roll over, but Caine succeeded in controlling it to make a crash landing with no fatalities. "In my mind, it was pure luck," is his comment. "For this and other endeavours, I was awarded the DFC. I feel that every member of the crew should have received the same award for their courage and support during this difficult time." There is little doubt that many airmen craved medals and deliberately sought them, usually at the risk of their own lives and those of fellow aircrew. Although Canadian and British servicemen scoffed at the American practice of awarding medals for relatively minor accomplishments, it probably did (and does) a good job for morale.

To follow up on the two-pronged attack on Berlin and Stuttgart on November 26/27, Harris again sent a maximum force to Berlin on December 2/3. He ordered the aircraft to fly an almost perfectly straight route across the North Sea into Holland, then on to

Berlin. In all, 458 aircraft took off: 425 Lancasters, fifteen Halifaxes, and eighteen Mosquitoes. Fog had formed late in the day in the area of 6 Group's airfields, grounding about two hundred aircraft. Only thirty-five of the Group's aircraft participated in the operation; of these, eight, or 22 per cent, turned back. 6 Group's early-return rate was still a cause for intense concern at Castle Dismal. On this night, nearly 10 per cent of the entire force turned back, principally because of the icing conditions encountered en route.

It proved to be another costly trip for Bomber Command, with forty aircraft lost, 8.7 per cent of the force; atypically, however, 6 Group suffered less than the average, losing only two.

The clouds diminished as the bombers neared Berlin, giving way to thin stratus over the target. "Target well lit by markers, and attack fairly concentrated," was the sanguine 6 Group report on the sortie. Bomber Command didn't agree, citing inaccurate wind forecasting that resulted in the Pathfinders' flares being scattered. The bombs fell all over southern Berlin. Night fighter activity undoubtedly contributed to the scattered bombing. The fighters dropped flares that created weird avenues of light and shadow along which the bombers had to fly, prime targets for the eager *Luftwaffe* pilots. Their successes were registered by great blossomings of fire that tumbled, blazing, spinning, into the destruction below.

It was a hectic night for Roger Coulombe, the "Berlin Kid" of 426 Squadron. He found his Lancaster coned by a gigantic battery of searchlights – "sixty to seventy," he reckons. For five nerve-grinding minutes, "from 2024 to 2029 hours," the solitary Lancaster, DS707, P-Peter, became the centre of attention of Berlin's defences as it twisted and turned, like an aerial acrobat in the glare of the spotlights. For the crew, it was a heart-stopping experience.

"I felt *discovered . . . isolated . . . denuded*," Coulombe recalls. In a desperate attempt to evade the lights he dived until his Lancaster reached 450 mph, about 100 mph above the permissible diving speed, "while being completely blinded by the glare of the powerful searchlights. It was like looking right into the sun! Pulling the Lancaster out of the dive at that speed was a most difficult job!" Coulombe had to jam both feet against the instrument panel and heave on the control column with all his strength. "In spite of the danger of plunging right into the ground, I am certain that diving at that high speed saved our lives that night."

While Coulombe's Lancaster was still coned, a Ju 88 night fighter made several attacks. Coulombe's mid-upper gunner, Sergeant Stan McKenzie, had spotted the Ju 88 on the port quarter at four hundred yards. Coulombe immediately corkscrewed towards the night fighter, which broke off its attack; no shots had been exchanged. A moment later the fighter attacked from the starboard side. Again Coulombe hurled his heavy Lancaster into a corkscrew manoeuvre. And again the fighter broke off without firing. Now the twin-engined fighter attacked once more from the starboard side. Arms aching, Coulombe slammed the controls to the right, tipping the bomber over and plunging, then hauling it upward again at full power. It was exhausting. But effective. The German night fighter pilot couldn't hold the bomber in his sights long enough to fire a single shot. He kept trying. On the fifth attempt the fighter came within two hundred yards on the port quarter; Coulombe corkscrewed yet again – and at sixty yards' range McKenzie opened fire and saw hits on the German aircraft. "Tracer appeared to enter the belly of the enemy aircraft; sparks and tracer were seen to ricochet off the fighter which dived steeply and was lost to view," he later reported.

"There was also an Me 109," Coulombe relates. "He was dropping flares on our starboard side level with us, no further away than about three hundred yards. An Fw 190 flew for a few seconds in formation with me on port wingtip. I could see the face of the pilot so clearly that I could have recognized him had I met him on the ground the next day." Incredibly, Coulombe succeeded in slipping away from the target area. His Lancaster had suffered a bad battering with the port inner engine and radio out of action and damage to the port tire, the port outer fuel tank, and the aircraft's hydraulic system. The crew had escaped injury, however. Coulombe set course for home on the three remaining engines. But the starboard outer "just stopped running between the target and England . . . I had to feather the propeller on that engine in order to reduce drag." Now, limping along on only two engines, the Lancaster set out across the North Sea. The crew began to unwind. What a hell of a trip! Thank God they were at last nearing home. The starboard inner engine began to lose power. "I could not get more than 1,700 rpm," Coulombe recalls. He needed 2,400 rpm to maintain height. Close to the English coast he sent out a Mayday call "and immediately one airfield near the coast illuminated its runways for us." It was an American B-17 base and Coulombe put the Lancaster down there, landing on one wheel as successfully as he had at 1679 Conversion Unit some months before. The faithful Lancaster was critically damaged; a cannon shell had smashed through the main spar. When Coulombe went out to look at the aircraft in the morning, "the starboard wing had completely collapsed with its tip touching the ground." The Americans volunteered to fly Coulombe and his crew back to Linton-on-Ouse in a B-17, but the weather was too foggy. They made the journey by train. Later that month Coulombe received the DFC for his actions over Berlin.

Another 6 Group crew had an unusual encounter in the night sky over Germany. Flying Officer C.V. Wales of 432 Squadron was the skipper of Lancaster II, DS251; on the way home from Berlin, he received a report from the rear gunner, Sergeant Dickinson, of an unidentified four-engined aircraft flying behind and slightly below the Lanc. Dickinson ordered Wales to corkscrew – just as the mysterious aircraft opened up "with cannon and machine gun fire from a range of about six hundred yards." The Lancaster took hits which broke the hydraulic pressure line and wrecked the mid-upper turret. Soon afterwards, the other aircraft vanished into the night, its identity still a mystery. But Wales's problems were not yet over. A searchlight beam caught the Lanc and a fighter came near, dropping flares. Wales managed to evade the light and succeeded in getting his badly damaged aircraft back to base at East Moor, running off the runway and ending up in a field, battered but unhurt. (Wales and his crew would go missing on a Berlin raid in January but most of them would survive to become POWs.[10])

Casualties were mounting. Depressingly few crews completed their tours. Most airmen never thought much beyond the next op or the next leave. What was the point? Your fate was in Dame Fortune's shaky grasp. It helped to fly with a crew of professionals who worked as a team and took nothing for granted; but the vital asset was luck. Luck played such an enormous part in operational airmen's lives that to most of them it assumed a kind of form; it was a presence that flew with the crew and looked after them. But it got upset when strangers such as Second Dickeys, squadron commanders, and AOCs came along; at all times it had to be humoured with charms and rituals. And woe betide the man who grew uncaring!

Norman James, a flight engineer with 434 Squadron, carried a jackknife, a memento of his boyhood days. On one op he left it behind. Clearly a mistake. The trip turned out to be the roughest the crew had encountered. The warning had been issued. James immediately started carrying the knife again and completed his tour in good order. Bob Marshall, a gunner with 428 Squadron, remembers how the squadron padre made a point of seeing every aircraft off on ops, handing out gum and candy to the crew. Marshall's crew had just taken off on the last trip of their tour when in some alarm the rear gunner reported that the padre had somehow missed their aircraft. "A few hours later we were in trouble," Marshall writes. However, although badly shot-up, the aircraft brought the crew home. Jim Emmerson, a 424 Squadron pilot, recalls that his crew's wireless operator, Doug Whillans, made a point of carrying a rag doll stuffed into the top of his flying boot. Her name was Lilli Marlene and she became an important member of the crew. When she was accidentally left in the aircraft one day, Whillans and the rear gunner, Chuck Helsdon, trudged a couple of miles across the airfield to retrieve her. Gilles Lamontagne, a 425 Squadron pilot, never went on an op without his small leprechaun doll. It didn't prevent his being shot down in March of 1943, but perhaps it contributed to his survival and that of every member of the crew.

Charms looked after you when the flak and cannon fire came near. George Sweanor, a bomb-aimer with 419 Squadron, recalls going aft to sit beside the skipper after he dropped the bombs. A few minutes later, the flight engineer requested his assistance in changing over fuel tanks. Sweanor did as he was asked. When he returned to the jump seat beside the pilot, a frigid wind hissed through the fuselage, entering via a jagged hole in the Perspex. A chunk of flak had done the damage – and from the hole's position it was easy to see that it would have struck Sweanor in the side of the head if he had remained in the jump seat.[11] Doug Scanlan, a bomb-aimer with 415 Squadron, remembers flak hitting his aircraft over the Ruhr. A fragment came ripping through the floor, passing neatly between Scanlan's arm and body, finally smacking into a structural member just above his head. He still wears the piece of flak on his watch chain. Ed Moore was a navigator in the 426 Squadron crew of Jack Hollingsworth. The crew developed an unusually strong attachment to the identification letter "K" and only flew aircraft so identified, even when the squadron's equipment changed: "Our crew was assigned K-Kitty starting with Lancaster IIs through Halifax IIIs and VIIs," he says. So firmly established was the belief that the crew would go missing if they flew an aircraft with another letter, that, late in their tour, Hollingsworth succeeded in getting the CO to take them off an operation when K-Kitty was temporarily unserviceable. Lucien Thomas, a 405 Squadron air gunner, recalls another gunner on his unit who had adorned his turret with brassières. But on arriving at the aircraft one day, he discovered, to his horror, that someone had stolen the bras. "He flagged down a crew truck. The WAAF driver listened patiently and then did a striptease and handed him her bra." Thomas adds: "I would like to say that this generated a romance. Sadly this was not the case. The guy got the chop."

Rituals assumed vast importance. Al Avant who commanded 429 Squadron in mid-1944 had a mid-upper gunner who would never board the aircraft until he had patted the propeller blades, imploring them to keep going. Les Dring, an RAF wireless operator/air gunner with Pat Patrick's crew of 427 Squadron, remembers a pre-take-off ritual that was always faithfully observed. After stowing their gear aboard the aircraft, the crew got out and the navigator, George Clayton, handed Sweet Caporal cigarettes to everyone. After the smoke, the crew relieved themselves on the tailwheel, then re-entered the aircraft in a sequence that never varied: first, the skipper; then the bomb-aimer, Jim Robinson; the flight engineer, Bruce Smith; Clayton; Dring; the mid-upper gunner, John Weibe; and finally the rear gunner, Billy Smith. Just before take-off, Weibe always handed chewing gum to everyone.

Doug Penny, an air gunner with 432 Squadron, always left his bed unmade when he went off on an operational sortie: an untidy but important symbol of his belief that he would get back to make it later. If the bed happened to be made when he left, he would unmake it. Harry Holland, a 427 Squadron pilot, was uneasy about having anyone take photographs of the crew or of their aircraft just before an op – although he later discovered that some-one had snapped him and the crew on their way to the aircraft, without adverse effect.

Most stations had one or more "chop girls." WDs, WAAFs, or civilians, these unfortunates acquired their reputation by dating airmen who "got the chop," "went for a Burton," "bought the farm," or whatever euphemism was favoured in that squadron at that time. Some skippers issued strict orders to their crews not to consort with them, threatening instant expulsion from the crew as the penalty for disobedience. Others shrugged off such stories. Glenn Bassett of 428 Squadron remembers a chop girl at Middle-ton St. George. Unafraid, a friend of his dated her and subse-quently married her. Their union has lasted well over forty years!

On the night of December 3/4, Harris sent 527 bombers to Leip-zig. 6 Group contributed ninety-seven – of which nineteen, 19.5 per cent, returned early, undoubtedly causing more grey hairs at Allerton Hall. This was one of the rare occasions on which the German controllers erred when they took Berlin to be the target. The bombers, 307 Lancasters and 220 Halifaxes, flew straight for the German capital, turning toward Leipzig at the last moment. It was a successful raid, causing damage to many industrial areas, including the former World Fair site in which war production facilities had been located. Twenty-four bombers were lost, 4.6 per cent of the force. 6 Group lost seven aircraft.

Poor weather and a full moon gave the aircrews a chance to catch up on their rest and the ground crews time to complete the service work on the aircraft. The respite lasted until the middle of December. Then, on December 16/17, Harris mounted another major effort against the German capital, sending 483 Lancasters and ten Mosquitoes. 6 Group provided forty of their number, of which four returned early.

The raid had to be categorized as moderately successful, but it was also costly. As on so many previous occasions, the aircrews saw nothing of the city through the dense clouds. Fortunately, the Pathfinder sky-marking was accurate and the majority of bombs fell on Berlin, although most of the damage appears to have been inflicted on residential rather than industrial areas. The tenacious Roger Coulombe of 426 Squadron encountered trouble again that night: "On the way to the target, just north of Hannover, we were attacked by a Ju 88 – and again we lost the port outer engine. We flew to Berlin just the same, on three engines but having to sacrifice height and speed. Fortunately, we were on the first bombing wave, so when we arrived over Berlin, the raid had just finished." Exhibiting characteristic *élan*, Coulombe completed his bomb run, dropped his bombs, and returned to base at Linton-on-Ouse, to discover that, in addition to the loss of the port outer, the aircraft had lost its rear entrance door, part of a cowling over a starboard engine, and the wing-covering over the dinghy compartment, the dinghy itself having disappeared somewhere over the Big City. "Nobody had seen the Ju 88 attacking and it was only after I saw its tracers that I quickly initiated evasive action by corkscrewing the aircraft . . . and diving into the clouds," writes Coulombe.

Twenty-five Lancasters, 5.2 per cent of the force, didn't get back from the operation. Even those who returned faced unexpected problems when they arrived over Britain. The weather had deteriorated during their absence. Now many of the bases were fogged in. Nature was again to prove a more dangerous enemy than the *Luftwaffe*. Attempting to land, an appalling total of *twenty-nine* more Lancasters crashed (plus one Stirling returning from a Gardening trip), a serious loss never reported to the public because it was categorized as non-operational.

The operation cost 6 Group four aircraft.

The Canadian Group did not participate in the Berlin raid of December 23/24; however, on the evening of December 29, the Group despatched 129 bombers to the German capital, part of a force of 712 aircraft. The official 6 Group records declared: "Target covered with ten-tenths cloud. Bright red glow visible on cloud and several explosions were seen." But the bombing did not achieve the concentration that Harris so desperately needed. Again, houses seem to have been the main victims; by now, it was estimated, as much as 25 per cent of Berlin's accommodations were uninhabitable.

On this, the last operation of 1943, fifteen of 6 Group's bombers returned early, 11.6 per cent of those despatched. Bomber Command lost twenty aircraft, a mere 2.8 per cent of the force. By Berlin standards, the force had escaped almost unscathed. But five of those missing aircraft came from 6 Group. Thus the Canadians' losses, at 3.8 per cent of the aircraft despatched, were again substantially higher than those of Bomber Command as a whole. A Halifax of 434 Squadron commanded by Pilot Officer R.A. Pratt had a passenger, a Second Dickey, Sergeant Stinson, who was gaining operational experience before taking his own crew on ops. A night fighter attacked the Halifax, killing the flight engineer, Sergeant A. Bostock, and wounding Pratt. Stinson promptly took over and bombed the target, later bringing the aircraft back safely.[12]

As the book on the first year's operations was closed, Brookes and his staff at Allerton Hall could look back with a certain amount of satisfaction – and some disappointment – on what had been accomplished. The Group had flown 7,233 sorties and had dropped 12,630 tons of bombs. Losses amounted to 341 aircraft, a grim and barely sustainable 4.7 per cent average.[13] The Group's losses and its dismal early return rate combined to give it an unenviable reputation in Bomber Command. Avoid 6 Group at all costs, was the advice of the wiseacres. Poor location. Poor maintenance. Poor organization. Poor show. The Canadian Group now stood at thirteen squadrons, 420, 424, and 425 having returned from the Middle East in November. The last of the twin-engined Wellingtons had gone. Although the Wimpy crews had not received the Lancasters they wanted, they got a version of the Halifax so improved that many crews rated it superior to the Lanc. The Mark III Halifax, powered by Hercules XVI radial engines each delivering an impressive 1,650 horsepower, possessed a far better performance than earlier versions. It had a completely redesigned fin and rudder, rectangular in form, that at last put paid to the aircraft's evil reputation as a killer that would snap into an uncontrollable spin at the slightest provocation. "My personal preference went to the Halifax," remarks Bill Gerard, a pilot who flew both Lancasters and Halifaxes with 426 Squadron,

"even though it doesn't have the same image as the Lancaster."
"When we got the Mark III Halifax, we knew we had the best there
was," comments Joe Widdis, a former bomb-aimer with 429
Squadron. He feels the Halifax was stronger than the Lanc, provided more crew comfort, a better fuel system, and a livelier
performance. Many ex-aircrew point out that it was easier to
escape from a Halifax than from a Lancaster. "From the aircrew's
point of view, the Halifax III was more of a pleasure to fly and to
fly *in* than the Lancaster," declares Wilbur "Wib" Pierce who flew
both types with 433 Squadron.

A few days before Christmas a Lancaster, KB700, landed at
Middleton St. George. It was the *Ruhr Express* with Flight Sergeant J.A. Parker in the pilot's seat. The best-known aircraft in
the RCAF was taking up residence with 419 Squadron because of
the difficulty of providing spares at Gransden Lodge where all the
Lancasters on charge were British-built. Both squadrons at
Middleton, 419 and 428, were shortly to be re-equipped with
Canadian-built Lancaster Xs, and would be fully provided with
spares. The *Ruhr Express* would have an eventful year.

By now 6 Group was regularly able to "put up" well over one
hundred aircraft, all four-engined bombers. Within a month or
two, the figure would rise to 150. But the Canadian Group's
efficiency was still in question – and Headquarter's displeasure
with the relevant figures invariably reverberated down the chain of
command to the youthful officers who led the flights and squadrons. It was up to them to make sure that the ground crews didn't
get away with inferior maintenance work and that the aircrews
were imbued with the sort of "press-on" spirit that made an early
return virtually unthinkable. But how was this to be accomplished? No one could tell them. Most led by example. Bill Swetman, who had taken over 426 Squadron after the Peenemünde
raid, recalls that he was always "acutely conscious" of the necessity of setting the right example. He admits that he sometimes
pressed on when, on reflection, it would have been more prudent
to have turned back. On one occasion, en route to the target but
having not yet reached the enemy coast, Swetman's rear gunner
reported his turret unserviceable. Swetman decided to keep going,
even though the bomber's most important defensive position was
out of action. "We were lucky," he admits. "We weren't attacked."

Later, Swetman, who had completed more than fifty ops in two complete tours with only one early return, went to Allerton Hall, 6 Group's HQ, and helped to develop a list of reasons that could be accepted by all squadrons for early returns. The idea was to take the onus off individual skippers. To his surprise, when the list was issued, there was a good deal of resentment among the pilots; they felt that they were being robbed of their "right" to make on-the-spot decisions.

Russell McKay of 420 Squadron had to abandon a sortie because of the failure of his aircraft's oxygen system. He says that when he returned to base he was met at the dispersal by a group of officers including the CO, the engineering staff officer, and ground crew representatives. "They swarmed over the aircraft checking out oxygen equipment. Luckily for me, our reasons for early return were sound." McKay adds:

One of our squadron crews returned early without a bona fide reason. The pilot was labelled "lack of moral fibre" and sent to a detention camp for disciplinary action. He told me that the bugler blasted them from bed at 6 a.m. The inmates ran to the parade square for an hour of continual physical exercise and ran to breakfast ... did drill with packs on their backs 'till noon hour, more drill and obstacle course routines in the afternoon ... Ran to the evening meal. Two hours more pack drill in the evening before bed. This physical exercise was repeated every day for six weeks. He returned to the squadron a trim 160 pounds with a loss of sixty pounds from his old weight. He told me, no way would he return early from any op – shortly afterward the same skipper was awarded the DFC on a flight to the Ruhr.[14]

During 6 Group's first year of operations, it became glaringly obvious that its aircraft maintenance was generally inferior to that of the RAF bomber groups. This in turn led to lower percentages of aircraft taking off on operations and, inevitably, higher early-return rates. The Canadians were finding out how difficult it was to push a complex organization into being rapidly, breaking up existing units to create new ones and filling the ranks with inexperienced technical staff. The situation would not improve until the new year. But what of the aircrews themselves? Did they have a tendency to turn back more readily than their confrères in the RAF groups? Possibly. And one of the reasons was unquestionably leadership. The RAF had developed a coterie of experienced officers, squadron leaders and up, who had been flying operationally since the earliest days of the war and who were able to guide fledgling flyers as they became operational. In its early days, 6 Group relied heavily upon the RAF for its squadron and flight leaders, replacing them with Canadians as they acquired the necessary experience. But at a higher level, 6 Group never really solved its personnel problems. From the start, every effort was made to give senior RCAF officers operational experience in 6 Group. Many of these men had been in the service since the Twenties, some having flown in the Great War. In recent years, they had spent much time in Canada with the BCATP, rising to senior rank and undoubtedly doing a sterling job. But in the main they knew very little about conditions in the current conflict. Such men were sent overseas and placed in charge of squadrons or bases, directing the day to day activities of operational aircrew. Harris was particularly opposed to the presence of such men in front-line squadrons. In his uninhibited way he wrote to Portal in January 1943, calling RCAF commanders "hangovers from a prehistoric past" who were totally inexperienced at best or incompetent at worst; he said he had heard that many airmen resented serving under officers whose careers consisted of " 'six months flying training and 25 years political intrigue.' "[15]

Many RCAF airmen felt the same way. Arthur Bishop of New Minas, Nova Scotia, joined 419 Squadron after completing a tour on Stirlings with the RAF. He is unequivocal in his criticism of many of 6 Group's senior officers: "My crew were all on their second tour and had little use for the Training Command officers on our station who lacked operational experience and were directing our fortunes." He cites the example of a base commander who appeared to be more concerned about dress codes than about ops. It was Bishop's first day on the station and he found his name on the Battle Order for that night: "All the aircraft were marshalled for take-off and we were about to get into the aircraft when the base commander drove by. He called me to his vehicle and dressed me down for wearing a split cap, stating that Station Standing

Orders required us to wear flat caps on operations." Bishop, who had not had time to read the standing orders, declares: "If I had known what I know now I would have had charges laid against this officer for 'lending aid and comfort to the enemy.'" On a later occasion, Bishop recalls the same base commander standing before aircrew in the briefing room, censuring them for not always flying over the target long enough and steadily enough to ensure that their cameras took their full "travel" of pictures of the bombing. "His remark was, 'Hold the aircraft steady, that flak won't hurt you.' I stood up and stated flatly that after forty-five trips over the target I had it on good authority that flak *could* hurt you." Bishop's comments were not welcome, it would appear, for when he had completed his second tour, he, the skipper, was the only member of his crew not to be decorated.

"I was always bitter towards 6 Group for this kind of treatment," is Bishop's not unreasonable comment.

Roger Coulombe of 426 Squadron recalls that one night his aircraft was detailed to carry an 8,000-pound bomb plus five cans of incendiaries, a formidable load: "My flight commander was a squadron leader fresh from Canada where he had spent his time as a flying instructor and had only one raid to his credit. He called me into his office and, since I was only a sergeant pilot, he proceeded to instruct me how to take my Lancaster off the ground with such a heavy load! 'Make sure you gather plenty of speed before pulling your aircraft off the runway,' he told me. 'You don't say, old boy,' I responded. 'You know all about it!' I turned around and left his office, disgusted with so much nerve and arrogance."

Some senior officers displayed a lack of sensitivity that bordered on the incredible. Russell McKay of Forester's Falls, Ontario, remembers an incident in the spring of 1944: "One of the crews on operations, while taxiing on the perimeter track to the take-off point, unfortunately had one wheel off the paved track. The wheel sank in the mud and the fully-loaded Halifax could not be moved. The pilot, G. ('Johnny') Walker, an American, did his best to move the aircraft. It sank to the wing tip in the mud. Five other aircraft following were caught in the traffic jam and unable to take off." The following morning, McKay remembers, Walker was paraded before the station commander who had made a

German Iron Cross out of cardboard. This senior officer then "made a little speech saying how the skipper had scuttled the operation, and pinned the decoration on the pilot's chest. The assembled crews booed and hissed this officer. He was removed from the station the next day."[16]

Leslie McCaig of 426 Squadron recorded in his wartime diary that his CO, Bill Swetman, interviewed any crew turning back before reaching the target, a normal procedure. But on one occasion, Swetman was joined by the station commander who contributed such homilies as "one duff engine not always being a legitimate reason for turning back." McCaig commented: "I might say I did not take too kindly to the Groupy's interference; he has done no ops at all and can therefore have no appreciation of the difficulties of a long trip ... he is a young man for his rank and likes to use his authority. He's ... a man of vigorous physique who should be in a more active role ... but he should remember to be more diplomatic with operational crews."[17] Leslie McCaig was undoubtedly speaking for a large number of 6 Group's aircrews when he jotted down those words.

Harris lost no time in starting his 1944 campaign against the Big City. On New Year's Day, 421 Lancasters set off for Berlin (actually, because of take-off delays, the operation did not start until the early hours of January 2). The Canadian Group contributed thirty-one bombers, of which two turned back before reaching the target.

Again the bombers flew a direct route, but the homeward journey involved a broad sweep southward near Leipzig, over Belgium and the northern tip of France, crossing the Channel and passing over the English coastline near Hastings. It made the trip particularly long for the 6 Group squadrons, which had to fly over much of Britain to reach their bases in Yorkshire and Durham.

The raid was not notably successful. Despite the presence of thick cloud cover, *Luftwaffe* night fighters succeeded in shooting down several Pathfinder aircraft, resulting in poor sky-marking. Inevitably this led to scattered bombing, mainly in the southern sections of the city, including the Grunewald, a wooded area. It was a costly night for Bomber Command, with twenty-eight Lancasters lost, 6.7 per cent of the force. All 6 Group aircraft returned safely.

Snow fell during the night. A pale winter dawn revealed airfields blanketed with white. Runways and taxiways had vanished. Parked aircraft assumed odd forms as the snow built up against cabins and wing roots. Many a weary pilot or gunner peeped through the blackout curtains and turned over to go back to sleep. There'd be no flying today; they were sure of that. They were wrong. Orderlies soon shook them awake. Ops were on! Butch had ordered yet another assault on Berlin. Briefing 2000 hours, take-off midnight. And right now, grab a shovel and help to clear snow! Britain, the Canadians discovered, had virtually no mechanical equipment to tackle the infrequent snowfalls. On most airfields, every man and woman on the place had to get to work to clear the runways and taxiways in preparation for the raid that night. The Big City again. How many would be lost this time? The aircrews tried not to think about it.

The bombers again flew an almost direct route to Berlin, with only a minor variation, involving a turn just beyond Bremen that sent the stream northeast with a subsequent turn to the south, taking advantage of a strong northwest wind. As they flew over Berlin, the bombers would turn east, rejoining the inbound track close to the Dutch coast. The weather was less than promising with heavy, ice-laden cloud up to some thirty thousand feet, creating an enormous barrier before the clearer conditions around Berlin.

Consecutive nights' operations invariably meant a progressive reduction in the numbers of bombers available. Thus, on January 2, Bomber Command could field only 383 aircraft, compared with 421 the night before. Again the *Luftwaffe* fighter pilots concentrated on the Pathfinder aircraft. Ten went down to their guns. The loss of the Pathfinder aircraft doomed the raid, producing scattered and ineffective bombing by the Main Force. Twenty-eight 6 Group aircraft took off. Four returned early. Three were lost.

Jim McIntosh, a pilot of 432 Squadron, experienced technical problems just before take-off. His Lancaster's rear turret was out of action. Repairs took thirty-seven minutes. But by "giving the kite the works going out and by taking one short-cut" he was able to make up all but two minutes of the lost time. As so often happened, operational troubles came in batches. Twenty minutes before reaching the target, McIntosh found his airspeed indicator unserviceable. Then the altimeter gave up the ghost. "I continued climbing," McIntosh reported, "and bombed from at least twenty-three thousand feet." He had no sooner turned for home than the rear gunner, Sergeant Bandle, yelled, "Fighter!" McIntosh felt cannon shells slamming into the Lancaster's fuselage and tail unit. The bomber tipped into a vertical dive – just as the gunners succeeded in disposing of the fighter.

McIntosh had his feet on the instrument panel, one arm locked around the control column while he worked the elevator trim. But the bomber continued to plummet, hurtling through layer after layer of cloud, seemingly bent on smashing itself to smithereens on German soil. He managed to coax the Lanc out of its dive at about ten thousand feet. The crew reported in, shaken but unhurt. The Lancaster was still flying but it had suffered serious damage. The rear turret that had caused the delay back at East Moor was again inoperative. So was the mid-upper turret, its hydraulics having been shot away. The flight engineer reported that the gauges for the starboard outer engine were out of action. From the bomb-aimer came the news that the bomb doors had fallen open. He and the flight engineer tried in vain to close the drag-producing doors manually. On the positive side of the ledger, the radio still worked, and the navigator was able to provide an approximate course for home despite having most of his instruments and charts scattered about the fuselage during the terrifying dive. McIntosh found his compasses useless, his rudder controls jammed, and he "could get very little response from the elevators. It required both arms around the control column to hold height." Having noticed fighter flares in the vicinity, McIntosh decided to remain in the cloud tops despite the icing conditions. "We had been losing a lot of fuel from the starboard inner tank but by the nav's calculations we should [have been] able to make a base in the U.K."

Over the sea, McIntosh slowly descended through the clouds, collecting a frightening amount of ice in the process. Fortunately, it melted as the aircraft encountered drier air beneath the cloud. "The aircraft was now becoming very sluggish and only with difficulty was I able to hold any height. . ." He instructed the crew to throw out guns and other movable equipment and chop out any other weighty items that weren't vital. McIntosh put the worse-for-wear bomber down on the emergency strip at Woodbridge, Suffolk. The crew jumped out with alacrity. Their faithful aircraft was a complete write-off, with both starboard nacelles gone, no hydraulics, two large holes in the starboard wing, the dinghy half out of its compartment, the propellers, fuselage, and tail unit riddled, and the starboard tire blown off.

McIntosh received a DFC, only to be shot down two months later on another Berlin raid, although he and most of his crew survived to become POWs.[18]

A second 432 Squadron crew had an eventful night. When Pilot Officer T.B. Spink was still more than an hour from the target, a night fighter opened fire from ahead, a most unusual mode of attack at night. Spink corkscrewed to starboard then resumed course. The fighter attacked again. Once more Spink managed to evade the fighter. The crew apprised him of the damage suffered during the attacks: "The navigator reported his oxygen had been cut off ... The engineer reported a bullet through the instrument panel which damaged the oxygen regulator causing a leakage which he estimated would cause total loss of oxygen in approximately three quarters of an hour." From the bomb-aimer came the news that the electrical bomb release was unserviceable; the mid-upper and rear gunners said that several holes were visible in the rear of the fuselage and tail. "By this time the navigator estimated we were one hour from the target. Having arranged with the WAG to release our 4,000-pound bomb manually over the target and to collect all the oxygen bottles and bring them to the navigator, I decided to carry on and hope our oxygen supply would last until reaching the target."

The weather did nothing to help the crew; they flew through ten-tenths cloud "with static lightning flashing on the windscreen." The oxygen gave out five minutes before the target. Nonetheless, the crew continued at twenty thousand feet, dropping all their bombs except for the incendiaries, which would have had to have been released individually. Immediately after leaving the target, Spink descended to sixteen thousand feet and stayed at that altitude until reaching the coast – "although every member of the crew was severely affected by the lack of oxygen." The crew made it home, Spink receiving the DFC for his night's work.

A 6 Group squadron, 432, suffered the loss of an experienced skipper. Flight Lieutenant J.A. Allen was on the eighth trip of his second tour. Warrant Officer S.R. Sweetzir, a gunner with 408 Squadron, had a lucky escape from death. His Lancaster II completed a successful attack – and Sweetzir remembers Berlin as a "blazing hellhole: flak and rocket fire of all shapes and sizes." Half a minute after the Lancaster's bombs fell away, an Me 210 attacked from starboard, setting the wing on fire. The skipper gave the order to jump. A minute later the fire went out. The skipper cancelled the bale-out order. Then the fighter attacked again – and within moments the wing was burning once more. Sweetzir returned the fighter's fire and saw flames in the Messerschmitt's port engine. The skipper again ordered the crew to abandon the aircraft. Sweetzir didn't hear the order but he scrambled out of his turret anyway because burning oil had appeared on the floor beneath his feet. He squeezed through the narrow aperture, going forward to the door beside the tail. There he encountered the mid-upper gunner who, although he wore his parachute, was disinclined to jump. Sweetzir took hold of the man's harness and told him to hurry up. There wasn't much time, he yelled. He was right. The aircraft blew up. Sweetzir lost consciousness, coming to on the ground. His parachute had somehow opened without his assistance. The Germans captured him and he spent the rest of the war as a POW, the sole survivor of the crew.[19]

Weather conditions interfered with Harris's Berlin plans for the next few nights, no doubt to the relief of the weary aircrews and the overworked ground staff. Not until January 20/21 did Harris launch another attack on Berlin. It was a maximum effort, with 769 aircraft participating: 495 Lancasters, 264 Halifaxes, and ten Mosquitoes. Thirty-five were lost, 4.6 per cent of the force. The Canadian Group contributed 144 aircraft of which thirteen, 11.8 per cent, returned early and nine, 6.25 per cent, were shot down. The sacrifices of the aircrews seemed to have been largely in vain. Very little damage could be seen in the city. "Target shrouded in smoke," commented the official 6 Group record. "Marking plentiful ... Smoke rose to 18,000 feet." One of the nine 6 Group aircraft lost that night was Halifax LK739 of 428 Squadron commanded by Flight Sergeant Reaine. It was the crew's first op. Twenty minutes before reaching Berlin, flak hit their aircraft. They couldn't maintain altitude but they pushed on, still losing height. At the perilous altitude of 12,500 feet they at last dropped their bombs on Berlin. Relieved of its burden, the Halifax managed to climb to 19,000 feet. Reaine turned for home. But fuel streamed from No. 3 fuel tank; the flight engineer, Sergeant Fell, calculated the aircraft could stay in the air another five minutes.

Reaine had no choice. He ordered his crew to abandon aircraft. The navigator, the flight engineer, and the two gunners jumped from the front escape hatch. The bomb-aimer, Flying Officer Lavoie, had difficulties, catching his parachute on the hatch. The wireless operator, Sergeant Banner, tried to pull him back into the aircraft but couldn't manage it. Eventually Lavoie freed himself and fell away. Banner and Reaine followed. All the crew landed safely and, remarkably, all of them except the rear gunner, Sergeant Wynveen, evaded the enemy and got back to England by mid-1944. Wynveen was captured by the Germans and finished the war as a POW.[20]

Another Canadian crew had to bale out that night. The Halifax commanded by Flight Sergeant Johnson of 434 Squadron was hit twice by flak which damaged the rudder and controls, the oxygen system, and the ailerons. Nevertheless, Johnson got the ailing aircraft back to England; he and the crew baled out near Driffield, Yorkshire; all survived. Flight Sergeant Cozens of 427 Squadron ran out of fuel attempting to land his Halifax at Coltishall. He hit a tree and a house. He and three of the crew were killed, the others survived. Cozens had been married a month earlier. His loss did not count in the official tally since it occurred in England.

Near Berlin, a German night fighter intercepted a Lancaster II, LL628 of 426 Squadron. A burst of accurate fire set the bomber on fire. Trailing flame, it crashed at 2010 hours on January 20 two kilometres south of Liebenwalde. All the crew died. The skipper was Leslie McCaig who had earned a DFC only a few weeks earlier and who had kept such an informative diary of his career in the air force. He and his crew were buried in the local cemetery, their bodies later being moved to the Heerstrasse British Cemetery.

A raid on Magdeburg the following night, January 21/22, was a disaster for 6 Group. A total of more than six hundred bombers participated in this, the first major raid on the important rail centre. The Canadian Group contributed 114 bombers, thirteen of which returned early. Fourteen, 12.2 per cent of the Canadian force, didn't return.

The operation failed. High winds brought some of the H2S-equipped Main Force aircraft over the target ahead of the Pathfinders. Many bombed before zero hour. Adding to the confusion, the Germans set several extremely realistic decoy fires which attracted large numbers of bombers. Indeed, most of their bombs are believed to have fallen outside the city.

In all, this disappointing sortie cost Bomber Command *fifty-seven* aircraft, nearly 9 per cent of the force. Particularly hard hit were the Halifaxes, the force of 224 losing thirty-five, 15.6 per cent.

The German defences fought hard and well. Searchlights coned a Halifax V of 427 Squadron with Flight Sergeant A.R. Clibbery in command. A fighter attacked, shooting away the intercom system, the oxygen supply, and most of the instruments and starting a fire in the flight engineer's position. The mid-upper gunner, Sergeant R.E. Qualle, lost one gun and much of his canopy, yet managed to shoot the fighter down. Clibbery succeeded in completing his bomb run and bringing the bomber safely back to base at Leeming, Yorkshire.

Flying Officer J.B. Mill of 408 Squadron, was incredibly fortunate that night. A fighter attacked his Lancaster II while he was lining up on the target, immediately setting the two port engines on fire. After feathering the burning engines and jettisoning the bombs, Mill ordered the crew to bale out. "The stick seemed to tighten up and then the aircraft went into a spin and flew up after two complete circles," Mill later recounted. A moment later it exploded. "There was an ear-splitting noise and everything went black. I regained consciousness in an already-opened chute." The bomb-aimer, Pilot Officer W. Johnston, was equally lucky. Thrown into the nose compartment as the Lancaster went into a spin, he saw the Perspex cone blown to pieces by the explosion and fell out, unconscious. He woke up to find himself falling, the ground terrifyingly near. He opened his parachute just in time.[21]

The Second Dickey on a 408 Squadron Lancaster also enjoyed remarkable good fortune. Flight Lieutenant J.B. Dinning heard the flight engineer warn of a fighter approaching. An instant later,

the fighter raked us from stem to stern in the port side. No warning came from the gunners. The aircraft caught fire immediately. We spun and then it was corrected. The rear gunner was screaming for help; he was jammed in his turret. I put on the pilot's chute and then my own ... We spun violently and I was thrown up to the nose where I lay watching the bomb-aimer still trying to hang on and open the hatch. I couldn't get near to help him as the aircraft was spinning with four engines running wild. The next thing I knew I was about a thousand feet off the ground, then I landed. I figure the aircraft must have blown up at approximately nine thousand feet.[22]

It was during this period that the Germans introduced a new radar device, the SN-2, to their twin-engined night fighter units. The equipment worked on a frequency of ninety megacycles and was impervious to the effects of Window. The device facilitated the introduction of new night fighting tactics which would become standard practice for the balance of the war. Devised by Colonel Viktor von Lossberg, the Tame Boar technique called for night fighters to join the bomber stream and find individual targets among the hundreds of aircraft. H2S was the key. The blind-bombing device had been a significant advance for the bombers; now the night fighters interpreted H2S transmissions as proof that a major raid was in progress. It was an intelligent deduction; H2S was seldom employed on minor or diversionary raids. By this time, too, many *Luftwaffe* night fighters had been equipped with the upward-firing armament which the German crews called "Jazz music" (*schräge Musik*) cannons. First seen by Allied crews over Peenemünde, the weapons enabled their pilots to cruise unseen beneath potential victims and fire into their wings. No longer was it necessary for the fighter to attack in a climb, always a risky business because of the possibility of the fighter being damaged or destroyed if the bomber blew up, as many did.

Harris sent his bombers back to Berlin on the night of January

27/28. The force consisted of 515 Lancasters and fifteen Mosquitoes. The Canadian Group contributed forty-eight aircraft of which two returned early. Again the crews saw little of the ground below; the Canadians reported ten-tenths cloud: "Marking good at first, but scattered later." According to German reports the bombing was spread over a wide area with several towns outside Berlin being hit. However, "several explosions were noticed," the Official History declares, "while the glow was visible for 150 miles after leaving the target."

An Me 110 attacked a Lancaster of 408 Squadron, commanded by Warrant Officer J. Douglas Harvey at a range of six hundred yards. The fighter "appeared to be trying to position himself to fire rockets." Harvey's rear gunner opened fire at about three hundred yards. "He observed his tracer entering the enemy aircraft's starboard wing, hitting the engine and knocking off one of the rockets." A few moments later, the rear gunner again spotted the fighter and fired another accurate burst – with unusual results. "A large blue flash appeared in the cockpit, and every light came on." The illuminations notwithstanding, the German pilot pressed home another attack. He was an easy target for the Lancaster's gunners and was soon spinning earthward out of control "with flames completely enveloping the fuselage." A glow appearing through the cloud was assumed to be the fighter hitting the ground.[23]

The sortie cost Bomber Command thirty-three Lancasters, 6.4 per cent of the force. The Canadian Group lost eight, no less than 16.6 per cent of its aircraft. The Berlin campaign was decimating Bomber Command, but Harris didn't give up. And his crews didn't fail him, in spite of the apprehension that must have gnawed at them every time they set off for the Big City. They rarely saw the place through the semi-permanent cloud cover; the sky above was invariably a nightmare of exploding flak, of probing lights, of fiery death in every direction. The young airmen gaped at the aerial battleground above Berlin, wondering how anyone could get through alive. Every cubic foot seemed to be full of lethal lights and flashes.

Harris ordered another raid for the following night. This time the force was even larger: 677 aircraft, of which 6 Group contributed 124 bombers. Early returns totalled sixty-six, or nearly 10 per cent of the force; 6 Group's early returns were fourteen, or 11.2 per cent. On this occasion, however, 4 Group's figures were even worse: 22.3 per cent of their bombers turned back before reaching the target. The Battle of Berlin had become a fearful test of resolve for the crews of the Halifax IIs and Vs, the lowest-flying bombers in the stream now that the Stirlings had gone. Halifax losses were insupportable.

To be a member of an operational Halifax crew at this period was to be a condemned man. It should have surprised no one, then, that increasing numbers of the crews found their engines sounding odd or the controls feeling wrong en route to the target, leading them to the inescapable conclusion that they should turn back, without delay. But by now several of 6 Group's squadrons had received the new Hercules-powered Halifax IIIs. Scores of airmen heaved heartfelt sighs of relief when the last Mark IIs and Vs went off to the OTUs or the scrap heap. The new Hally's performance was a splendid boost for morale when it was most needed – although the Mark IIIs had their problems initially with many training accidents and high losses on their first ops. One of the reasons may have been the remarkably casual way in which some squadrons handed the new aircraft over to the crews. No one seemed to have given much thought to the provision of adequate training manuals. Denis Jennings, a flight engineer with 427 Squadron, recalls that when his unit received Halifax IIIs, the only technical information he received was a sheet of paper bearing a list of the correct oil and cylinder head temperatures. Its inadequacy became apparent when the Jennings crew took off on their first operation aboard the new aircraft. Everything seemed in good order at first, with everyone being impressed by the power of the Hercules engines. The Halifax climbed steeply. "It was a chilly night," Jennings recalls. As the bomber gained height, he noticed that the oil temperature was also soaring: "At between seven and eight thousand feet it started going off the clock." Jennings pointed out the problem to the skipper. After a brief discussion, they decided to dump the bombs and turn for home, the crew's first – and only – early return. On the way back to base, Jennings noticed the oil temperature readings returning to normal. But, with the bombs reposing on the bottom of the North Sea, there was no point in resuming the sortie. Back at base, Jennings found himself on the carpet, accused of aborting an op unnecessarily. A trip to the aircrew disciplinary centre at Sheffield seemed probable. "But luckily for me," Jennings says, "the next day a representative from Bristol visited the station to answer the crews' questions about the new engines – and he warned of this very condition. When the engines were cold, the oil circulated in the cooler without going through the honeycomb. When hot, a valve opened to allow the oil to pass through . . . but when climbing fast into a very cold layer of air, as it was that night, the valve tended to stick and would not allow the oil to pass through, so the oil just kept going round and round, the jacket getting hotter and hotter."

On January 28, the weather was poor for the journey to Berlin via Denmark; 6 Group crews reported severe icing conditions up to twenty thousand feet. But conditions improved over the target with areas of broken cloud permitting some ground marking, a rare luxury on Berlin ops.

The crews believed this to have been a raid of exceptional concentration. The 6 Group report talked of "huge fires" and "particularly violent explosions." The "jubilant crews" could see the results of their work all the way to the Baltic coast and talked to the intelligence officers about "the best yet," "the best of eight," "really wizard," "a first-class do." In fact, although the raid did some significant damage within Berlin, a large proportion of the bombs fell outside the city.

The raid cost forty-six bombers, 6.8 per cent of the force; six more crashed over England. The Halifaxes, although they constituted just 35 per cent of the force, represented 56 per cent of the losses. Particularly hard hit was 434 Squadron of 6 Group which lost four of its obsolete Mark Vs. In all, the Canadian Group's casualties amounted to nine aircraft, 7.2 per cent of its force. One of the Halifax Vs lost that night was commanded by Warrant Officer J.L. Wilkinson of 429 Squadron. Attacked by two fighters en route to the target, Wilkinson managed to evade and continued his trip. Then a third fighter pounced. The attack killed the rear gunner, Sergeant H. Clay, and wrecked the controls. Unable to handle the aircraft any longer, Wilkinson ordered the crew to bale out. He had to use the call light because the intercom was working only spasmodically. But at that precise moment, a violent explosion hurled the bomber on to its back. The overload fuel

tank in the bomb bay – a much-loathed necessity on long trips –
had blown up. "I was thrown out of my seat and the helmet was
torn off my head," Wilkinson later reported. He remembered
"going around and around" inside the aircraft. Then he passed
out, to wake up in the air. He barely had time to pull the rip-cord
of his parachute and landed with a badly sprained back.[24]

John Gray was in command of one of 433 Squadron's new
Halifax IIIs on his first operational sortie with his own crew.
Heavy flak caught the aircraft just as it crossed the enemy coast-
line; fuel poured out of No. 3 tank. It quickly became apparent to
Gray that if he went all the way to Berlin, the crew wouldn't have
enough fuel to make it back to the base at Skipton-on-Swale.
Nevertheless, Gray decided to continue and deliver his bombs.
And, as predicted, the fuel didn't hold out for the homeward
journey. The engines cut over the North Sea some fifteen miles off
Hartlepool. Gray did an excellent job of ditching the Halifax; all
the crew scrambled out and into the dinghy and were picked up by
Air/Sea Rescue. Gray was awarded an immediate DFC.[25]

Another 6 Group Halifax ditched that night, one of the old
Mark Vs still being flown by 431 Squadron based at Croft. Flight
Sergeant Corriveau was the skipper. A naval minesweeper
reached the scene about half an hour after the Halifax ditched,
but only Corriveau and three of his crew were rescued.[26]

The aircrews groaned, disbelieving, apprehensive, when on
January 30 the briefing room maps revealed the target as Berlin
yet again. Three Berlin trips in four nights! And this one in
moonlight! Almost every squadron had suffered serious losses in
the past few weeks. Ex-aircrew recall the all-too-frequent visits of
the padres and Service Police to aircrew huts to collect the belongings of those who didn't get back from the deadly Berlin raids.
Replacement crews arrived daily. Many vanished before anyone
got to know their names. They were the "Midnight Jones" crews:
the unfortunates who arrived on the squadron one day and were
told not to unpack because they were *on* that night – and were
dead by midnight.

A force of 534 aircraft – 440 Lancasters, eighty-two Halifaxes,
and twelve Mosquitoes – took off and flew a route that took them
north of Berlin, then angled in a south-easterly direction to the
city. To no one's surprise, the place was completely obscured by

thick cloud. 6 Group contributed forty-seven of the aircraft on the operation. Two returned early and one was lost. The Canadians were luckier than the RAF on this sortie; so were the Halifax crews – for the simple reason that Harris did not include the obsolescent Mark IIs and Vs in the Battle Order. Their losses had been too grievous of late. In all, Bomber Command lost thirty-three aircraft on the night of January 30/31: thirty-two Lancasters and one Halifax, 6.3 per cent of the force. "Markers well concentrated," claimed the 6 Group reports. "Four large explosions. Glow of fires on cloud." It was a well-concentrated attack and major fires broke out in the centre and southwestern sectors. There is little doubt that the city was reeling under the repeated attacks, its essential services breaking down constantly. But Berliners proved to be as resourceful and resilient as Londoners; in spite of the chaos, life went on. Moreover, although major sections of the city had been destroyed, enormous areas had suffered little or no damage. The planners at High Wycombe tried repeatedly to concentrate the bombing on those "virgin territories," all too conscious of the fact that dropping bombs on rubble accomplished little but the redistribution of bricks, and shattered buildings did not burn well no matter how many incendiaries fell on them.

In the course of fourteen raids, some twenty-four thousand tons of bombs had fallen on Berlin. Although the January 30/31 operation could be classified as successful, it did not achieve the degree of concentration necessary for the systematic eradication of a city of Berlin's size. Harris had still not succeeded in doing what he set out to do.

A moon period. A respite for the weary crews. A time to complete all the maintenance on the aircraft. A time to go on leave and forget about Berlin for a while. A time to take stock. To count the losses and lick the wounds. During the month of January alone, 6 Group had lost forty-eight aircraft and crews, the equivalent of two entire squadrons.[27] During the same month Bomber Command as a whole had lost more than *three hundred* four-engined bombers with more than two thousand aircrew, plus another forty or more aircraft to crashes in England.[28] Harris could withstand the losses in bombers; by now the factories were supplying the

Lancasters (including the Mark Xs constructed in Canada) and the new Halifaxes in impressive numbers. Replacement aircraft invariably arrived on the squadrons within twenty-four hours of losses being sustained.

But what of the aircrews? How long could they sustain losses that seldom fell below 6 per cent per sortie against Berlin? It did not require any great mathematical prowess to calculate one's chances of making it through the next half-a-dozen ops. The remarkable thing was how well the young crews stood up to the ordeal. Harris never seems to have been troubled by the thought that his crews might fail him. Morale might sag when a unit suffered particularly serious losses or when a highly regarded squadron or flight commander was lost. But in general it would bounce back rapidly. A good measure of morale among aircrews on a squadron was to be found in the records of early returns. As the Berlin campaign progressed, the numbers of early returns increased, but never enough to jeopardize operations. Most of the young men swallowed their fears and got on with the job. Many have harsh memories of the few who dumped bombs en route to their targets so that they might gain more altitude over the target. "Some," says Joe Widdis, a 429 Squadron bomb-aimer, "bragged about it afterwards."

There is no doubt that this was a tough time to be a member of a Bomber Command crew. Eddy Collyer, an RAF flight engineer, recalls no slump in morale in his unit, 425 Squadron, although ". . . in York we often met old pals from other squadrons who had aged physically in a matter of weeks . . . I think we were all aware that none of us might complete a tour." During the same awful period, the "Berlin Kid," Roger Coulombe of 426 Squadron, saw some crews before raids "with faces white as sheets and almost in a state of shock." Such crews seldom lasted long. Film and fiction have tended to portray the wartime flyer as a devil-may-care Lothario who laughed at danger and was never happier than when flying into action, the more hazardous the better. There were such individuals; they seemed to relish the challenges, apparently deriving enormous satisfaction from repeatedly cheating death. But they were a tiny minority. Most regarded ops realistically: they were hazardous and stressful journeys in the course of which some bombers would be lost. Ops were unpleasant; ops were dangerous; but ops were necessary. And the young men gritted their teeth and got on with the job. Bob Marshall, who came from the farming area of Dufferin County, Ontario, was a 428 Squadron mid-upper gunner, on his second tour of operations. He recalls "joking about being on borrowed time after twenty ops ... I think all of us felt that if you kept it up long enough, luck would run out. But," he adds, "for a reason that I have not yet seen explained, most of us, while relieved at surviving a tough trip, immediately looked forward to the next one. In a similar vein, almost all 'screened' personnel with one tour under their belts sooner or later were chomping at the bit to go on a second tour."

During the Battle of Berlin, depressingly few crews completed their tours. Fate seemed particularly cruel to those who had *almost* made it. Again and again, crews on their last or next to last trips would be numbered among the missing. Individual airmen recall periods of poor morale on some units, often manifested in subtle ways – the demeanour of the guard at the gate or the sad way the erks watched the aircrew climb aboard their aircraft. There were more obvious symptoms too: men with the infamous "operational twitch," men whose nerves were in sad shape, men who admitted openly that they had abandoned all hope of survival, men who should have been removed immediately from ops but who were kept flying because Berlin was far more important than a few youngsters' lives. Others can remember little sagging of morale even in this period of ferocious losses. In the final analysis, it all depended on a man's crew, because as the ops got tougher and as casualties increased, an airman's world became smaller, focused on the six men with whom he flew. If they were confident, efficient, effective, then in all probability he would be too. Most paid scant attention to the fortunes of other crews and had only passing contact with them.

Thus, although the commanders might talk at length about squadron morale, in fact it was the morale of individual crews that really counted. The fierce loyalty among crew members is fondly remembered by veterans half a century later. But there are some painful memories too. Robbie Armstrong was the wireless operator on two 428 Squadron crews – and the only survivor of both. His first crew, commanded by Flying Officer "Wolf" Woolverton, was lost on the sixth op, on February 19, 1944, over Leipzig.

Armstrong missed the trip because of illness. He then joined another crew led by Warrant Officer "Mac" Magill and flew with them until late July, by which time he had completed his tour of forty ops. On July 29, Magill's crew set off on their fortieth op, without Armstrong. They didn't return. Armstrong comments: "The miserable experience of losing two crews has remained with my family and myself ever since." Alex Nethery was a bomb-aimer with 427 Squadron and later 405 Squadron: "You had strong feelings about your squadron but even stronger feelings about your own crew." Yet in the pitiless air war, such loyalty could create its own problems. All too often crews would close ranks to hide the shortcomings of a popular but less than totally efficient man. No one will ever know how many crews were lost because loyalty won out over objectivity.

On February 13, Harris called for another assault on Berlin. But the weather forced him to scrub it. The same thing happened the following night. Not until the fifteenth did the elements cooperate. The crews were well rested, the aircraft fully serviced and repaired. A major force of 891 aircraft – 561 Lancasters, 314 Halifaxes, and 16 Mosquitoes – took off in the early evening, supported by more than a hundred engaged in diversionary and support operations. The Canadian Group put up 152 aircraft of which 10 returned early.

The bombers flew across the North Sea where the weather deteriorated. Russell McKay, pilot of a 420 Squadron Halifax, wrote: "I started to take on a heavy load of ice. The controls became sluggish...The ice broke off with a loud crashing." McKay remembers the phenomenon as "eerie."[29] The bomber stream traversed the mainland of Denmark before angling towards Berlin which, as usual, was obscured by cloud. The 6 Group airmen praised the accuracy of the Pathfinders' marking: "Markers plentiful and concentrated." Berlin suffered a good deal of damage, but many bombs fell outside the city. Bomber Command lost forty-three aircraft: twenty-six Lancasters and seventeen Halifaxes, 4.8 per cent of the force.

The raid cost 6 Group four aircraft, a mere 2.6 per cent of the bombers despatched. But two of the aircraft lost were skippered by highly experienced pilots: Squadron Leader A.V. Reilander of 424 Squadron and Squadron Leader F. Carter of 434 Squadron. A Halifax of 431 Squadron encountered a Ju 88 en route to the target. The German night fighter pilot was a good shot, for, with a single burst, he succeeded in damaging the Halifax's undercarriage, its rear turret, the intercom system, and the radio equipment, reducing the starboard fin and rudder to a tangle of metal and fabric, shooting away the starboard flap, and injuring the flight engineer. The skipper, Flight Sergeant A.W. Tinmouth, reported: "Crew cooperation perfect and everything went well, despite two occasions when it was necessary to corkscrew. Rear gunner was without oxygen and had no electrical power for over an hour." Tinmouth pushed on to the target and delivered his bombs, later bringing the battered Halifax safely back to base at Croft. He received the DFM.

For the 420 Squadron crew of Flying Officer Harold Damgaard it was their first op. They flew a brand new Halifax III, LW396. They had no sooner set course than the wireless operator, Lloyd Whale, reported that the radio was unserviceable; he could neither transmit nor receive. He said he would try to make repairs, but he didn't sound hopeful. Stanley Fletcher, the crew's RAF flight engineer, recalls: "More trouble. No. 3 engine, the starboard inner, had its cylinder head temperature way out of the safety range. Was it the engine? Or was it the gauge? I hoped it was the latter – we were having a lot of trouble with instruments at that time." His hopes were realized, for the Halifax continued to the target and descended from twenty-two thousand feet to the bombing height of nineteen thousand feet. Fletcher writes: "The ground below seemed to be one sheet of flame . . . parts of it white, almost incandescent . . . There was little flak and no sign of enemy night fighters." But shortly after leaving the target area, the rear gunner, Bernard Downey, called: "Ju 88 preparing to attack! Go port, go!" As Damgaard corkscrewed, both turrets opened fire. Then Downey called for a corkscrew to starboard. Again the machine guns blazed. "Go port, go!" came the command from the rear. After which a relieved voice announced: "Level up, skipper. One Ju 88 probable. It's on fire. We're both confirming it."

The Halifax continued its journey home, its interior reeking of cordite. Near the Ruhr, Fletcher saw a tiny light in the darkness below. "Suddenly there was a roaring sound," he declares, "like the sound of a fast express train passing by on our port wing tip and out into the vastness of space. Our bomber was tossed up and down like a leaf, the skipper struggling to keep control. It was just as if a giant hand was playing ball with us." Shaken, the crew wondered what had caused the sound. A missile? A shell from a gun? "There had been a rumour on the squadron that the Germans had some modified naval armament . . . travelling around the railway network. There were no searchlights, no lights that I could see."

Art Taylor, the navigator, asked Damgaard if he should set course for an RAF field in southern England since he had no idea of conditions at base and no way of finding out without the radio. "Keep on course for Tholthorpe," was the response. Near Flamborough Head, Fletcher recalls, he heard a "cultured English voice" in his headset instructing a Beaufighter squadron to return to base because of deteriorating weather: "Somehow the radio was picking up local traffic again." Fog had moved in over Tholthorpe and the squadron's aircraft had been diverted to other airfields but the Damgaard crew hadn't received the message. "I withdrew the mechanical uplocks for the undercarriage," Fletcher writes. "The bomb-aimer was doing second pilot so I jammed myself in the engineer's position. We descended for landing."

Damgaard had only the airfield's Drem lights to guide him. On the first approach, the lights vanished in the swirling fog. He tried again. The same thing happened. As Damgaard lined up for a third approach, Fletcher told him, "Skipper, it has to be this time. The gauges are on zero." Moments later, the Halifax touched down. But not on the runway. Damgaard, mistaking a railway fog light for a Drem, had landed on the York to Liverpool railway line. The impact tore the undercarriage off – "and the remains of the aircraft finished up in a grove of trees," Fletcher remembers. "I opened my eyes and I was lying under a hedge without any flying boots. My back hurt but no bones seemed to be broken." The wireless operator and rear gunner had been killed in the crash but the others survived and formed the nucleus of a new crew which completed a tour of operations. Fletcher was hospitalized for many months for his back injury, and, although he returned to the squadron, he flew no more operations.

Another 420 Squadron pilot, Russell McKay, who had earlier encountered icing over the North Sea, didn't return to Tholthorpe that night. He received a signal from base ordering him to land at Hethel, a USAAF field in East Anglia. Hethel proved to be a pleasant interlude in a grim period: "The contrast between Hethel and our base was like . . . day and night. The barracks were warm and comfortable. The bed was a bed with mattress and cover. One slept in comfort – like home. The most joyful difference was at the Mess. The food was excellent. . . ." So was the hospitality; McKay and his crew spent three "wonderful days" at Hethel. An American gunner gave McKay a section from his parachute: "It had saved his life when his bomber and another collided in the circuit on return from an operation. He was the only survivor of the two crews. It is a much-treasured souvenir of Hethel and the Americans. . . ." When McKay and his crew arrived back at Tholthorpe, they found that they had been reported missing; their belongings were already packed for shipment to their next of kin – a recurring problem for operational crews.[30]

Impatient to hit Berlin again as quickly as possible, Harris ordered operations for the nights of February 16, 17, and 18 but had to cancel them all because of bad weather. Late the following evening, however, a force of 832 bombers took off, many climbing through snow showers, straining to haul their great loads of bombs and fuel to cruising altitudes. But Harris chose not to hit Berlin on this occasion; the target was Leipzig, an important centre of aircraft production (and possibly its selection was a sop to the CCS who kept demanding Bomber Command's assistance in the destruction of the German fighter force). The raid turned out to be an unmitigated disaster for Bomber Command, largely because of the weather. Met had forecast a steady headwind. In fact, the bombers encountered a light wind from the north. The more experienced navigators detected the fact immediately and made the necessary adjustments to their calculations, but too many navigators didn't realize what was happening until much later. Inevitably, the bomber stream lost its cohesion, the aircraft becoming more and more dispersed as the long flight continued, creating ideal conditions for a Tame Boar interception by the German night fighters. They attacked in force, picking their targets at will, shooting down the fully loaded bombers one by one. Many of Harris's force blew up, illuminating the night sky for terrifying instants before vanishing, transformed to fragments of metal and flesh. Behind Perspex windows, young men scrutinized every quarter of the sky, peering until their eyes ached to catch a glimpse of a movement, a whirling propeller or a glint of metal, that might tell of an approaching fighter. Pilots maintained a steady left-right banking motion: hard on the stomach but the best way to give the gunners a good look in every direction. The slaughter continued all the way to the target. Although 6 Group records talk of the Pathfinders' marking being "concentrated" over Leipzig, in fact there was little that was concentrated about any aspect of the operation. Many crews arrived far too early because their navigators had failed to detect the wind change. Some didn't wait for the Pathfinders. They bombed before zero hour, using H2S, then headed home. When at last the Pathfinders did start marking, crews who had been circling in a state of high tension were eager to drop their bombs and get away from the heavy flak. Rushing in to get the job done, the aircraft encountered others doing the same thing. The hideous result was a rash of collisions over the target.

Glenn Bassett, an air gunner with 428 Squadron who flew on that raid, was a horrified witness to several collisions. "Our crew bombed on time and on target," he recalls, "and returned without incident to our base (Middleton St. George) but more disaster was in store. The Halifax in the landing 'funnel' ahead of us, piloted by a Canadian by the name of Black, with identification letter 'L-London,' got permission to land. All of a sudden another Halifax appeared in the funnel with wheels and flaps down, resulting in a collision between the two aircraft at an altitude of about one hundred feet. Before our eyes fourteen lives were snuffed out and two heavy bombers destroyed . . . Our pilot had to pull up quickly and put on maximum power to save us from the same fate." Bassett subsequently learned that the skipper of the second Halifax in the funnel had believed himself to be in the circuit for Croft, a satellite field a few miles southwest of Middleton St. George. When he heard the controller give "L-London" permission to land, he thought the message was directed at his aircraft. Such was the cost of having too many airfields packed too close to one another.

The official losses for the night did not include these two aircraft or the others wrecked on landing. It was just as well. The loss was awful enough: seventy-eight bombers, 9.6 per cent of the force, the worst casualties of the war to date for Bomber Command. Proportionately, 6 Group suffered even higher losses: eighteen of the 129 aircraft despatched, 13.9 per cent. Many bombers tottered back in such dreadful condition that they were immediately written off. A Halifax of 428 Squadron, commanded by Flying Officer W.V. Blake, suffered no fewer than eleven fighter attacks on the way to the target. Despite crippling damage to the aircraft, the young airmen continued their journey to Leipzig and dropped their bombs. Night fighters again singled out Blake's Halifax for attention on the trip home. Warrant Officer J.T. Houston, the rear gunner, had been wounded in the initial attack, but he stayed behind his guns and directed evasive action, using light signals because the intercom no longer functioned. Both Blake and Houston won the DFC. Much the same sort of story could be told by the crew of Flying Officer A.J. Byford of 419 Squadron: they were shot up before reaching the target but pushed on and delivered their bombs, only to be attacked again while homeward bound. The enemy's fire put the rear turret out of action. But the rear gunner, Sergeant N.C. Fraser, stayed at his post and supervised Byford's evasive manoeuvres. Byford was awarded a DFC and Fraser a DFM.

A 6 Group squadron, 427, lost an experienced skipper when the Halifax flown by Pilot Officer D.O. Olsvik went missing during the Leipzig sortie. The Olsvik aircraft had a Second Dickey on board, Flight Sergeant C.G. Burke. All aboard were killed.

The Leipzig disaster finally convinced Harris to withdraw the Halifax IIs and Vs from any attacks on German targets (he had already withdrawn them from Berlin raids). Their losses had been crippling – although on the Leipzig sortie more Mark IIIs had been lost than the older models. This was an anomaly, however; the new generation of Halifaxes would prove themselves worthy partners of the excellent Lancasters in the battles to come.

*   *   *

On February 29, a new commander took over control of 6 Group. He was forty-eight-year-old Air Vice-Marshal Clifford Mackay McEwen, popularly known as "Black Mike" because of his dark complexion. As a youngster in Griswold, Manitoba, McEwen had nursed ambitions to become a minister when he grew up. But World War I changed his life just as it changed so many others. McEwen joined the Western Universities Battalion. While waiting to be interviewed for a commission, he learned that one of the "elderly officers" who comprised the selection committee had the habit of positioning candidates beside a hot stove to see if the heat resulted in any "unsoldier-like" movements or complaints. McEwen went out and obtained narrow strips of asbestos which he fastened to his legs. Thus he was able to endure the interview in a suitably cool and collected manner. McEwen got his commission.

He volunteered for the RFC and began his training in the spring of 1917. By October of that year, he was a member of 28 Squadron's "C" Flight, commanded by the outstanding Canadian ace, Captain (later Major) W.G. Barker, VC. The unit moved to Italy in November and McEwen soon proved to be a superb pilot of the tricky but effective Sopwith Camel scout, scoring twenty-eight victories, winning the Military Cross and DFC and bar plus the Italian medals, *Medal Valori* and *Croce de Guerra*. He returned to Canada and was demobilized in 1919, later working for the Air Board of Canada on various forestry survey, aerial photography, and testing projects for the Dominion government. In 1924, he joined the newly formed Royal Canadian Air Force and spent several years as an instructor. When war came again in 1939, he found himself still involved in training, now with the BCATP. He had to wait until 1942 before he went overseas.

It is believed that McEwen was Harris's choice to replace George Brookes as AOC of the Canadian Group. McEwen was the sort of commander Harris liked, a man with extensive combat experience, a figure the aircrews would respect and admire. To some 6 Group airmen, McEwen was almost as illustrious a figure as Billy Bishop. But others had never heard of him. A former navigator with 431 Squadron, Richard Garrity of Pointe Claire, near Montreal, recalls that when McEwen was about to visit his station, "we had to be told who he was." But if the name McEwen was not immediately known by all his men, it soon would be. The new AOC lost no time in making his presence felt. In some ways his effect on 6 Group might be compared with Harris's on Bomber Command. Nothing was quite the same again after McEwen arrived at Allerton Park. He took a group that was still unsure of itself, still amateurish in some ways, still learning to cope with the awful realities of the air war, and made it tick. Acutely conscious of 6 Group's less than sterling performance to date, McEwen initiated rigorous training in all squadrons. Cross-countries. Bombing exercises. Fighter affiliation. Lectures. Drills. The crews didn't like it – neither did they like his edict about the wire stiffeners in officers' caps being left in place (most of the aircrew favoured the battered "thirty-op" look) – but they had no choice. McEwen's personality permeated the Group. Intensely proud of his service and his country, he was determined to make 6 Group the best in Bomber Command. He felt strongly that every man who flew on operations deserved a commission, not a popular idea with some traditionalists; but by the end of the war, he had gone a long way towards the realization of that goal.

While McEwen deserves much credit for the Group's improved performance, there's little doubt that he was fortunate to take over when he did, just as Harris was lucky to have assumed command of Bomber Command when he did. McEwen's predecessor, George Brookes, had to cope with all the nagging problems of a Group that was inexperienced, incomplete, and constantly in transition. McEwen, on the other hand, took over when the thorniest of the Group's technical and organizational problems were close to being solved. February 1944 was 6 Group's turning point; it would be an infinitely more effective formation in 1944 than it had been in 1943.

Although McEwen is remembered as an amiable, good-natured individual, he could be a stickler for discipline. Don Lamont of Port Elgin, Ontario, was a pilot with 428 Squadron when "Black Mike" visited Middleton St. George. McEwen entered the Mess at lunch hour. No one noticed; no one stood up. This irritated McEwen. Lamont recalled that the officers on the station were given "a rather severe lecture on deportment and protocol." In the main, however, McEwen was known for his rather courtly manner and his unfailing politeness to women and the clergy (he always rose when a padre entered his office). Despite his undoubted skill as a pilot, he had a reputation in his family of being an abysmal navigator, always getting lost when he took them for a Sunday drive. Among his airmen, he soon became a popular figure; they delighted in the fact that he went on occasional ops, despite orders to the contrary from Harris. (Rumours abounded that he was in the habit of wearing a sergeant's tunic when flying on ops to "disguise" himself if he was shot down and captured.) Such an attitude meant a lot; up to that time there had been too many senior 6 Group officers who seldom clambered aboard an aircraft. McEwen flew on at least seven ops officially, his name listed on the crew roster as "second pilot." He probably did as many again without any paperwork being completed.

Early in 1944, McEwen telephoned Bill Swetman, then CO of 426 Squadron, announcing that he intended to accompany him on the evening's sortie. He duly boarded the Lancaster just before take-off. Swetman recalls the intense buffeting on the outward journey, making him uncomfortably aware of the number of aircraft in the immediate vicinity, all loaded to capacity and beyond with high explosive, incendiaries, and fuel. The other aircraft couldn't be seen but they were no less dangerous for that. The buffeting became particularly severe over the Dutch coast. To Swetman's astonishment, the navigation lights of several aircraft suddenly came on. Evidently their skippers felt that the risks of collision had begun to outweigh those of being shot down. McEwen was so infuriated by the sight that he declared his intention of ringing up Harris in the morning and demanding that fighters accompany the bomber stream with orders to shoot down any such transgressors in the future. (Apparently he never made the call.) It was a night for fingernail-biting. The bomb run seemed to take forever. Swetman's Lancaster was one of the last to return to base at Linton-on-Ouse. "You could almost hear the sigh of relief when I called in, identifying the aircraft in which the AOC was flying," Swetman says. "But even then our troubles weren't over." During his approach to the airfield, Swetman had to dive to avoid another aircraft that suddenly loomed out of the darkness, narrowly missing his Lancaster. Even on the ground, Swetman had to swerve abruptly when another Lancaster came along the taxiway, travelling in the wrong direction. But at last they reached the dispersal. McEwen climbed out, followed by the other members of the crew. The ground staff clustered around the aircraft, grinning, extending hands to be shaken. Swetman's second tour of operations was over.

McEwen's takeover of 6 Group coincided with a remarkable shift in the Group's fortunes. The Canadians flew an astonishing total of ten operations without a single casualty: Stuttgart, Meulan-les-Meureaux, Trappes, Le Mans (twice), Amiens (twice), Frankfurt (twice), and Laon. It was unprecedented, a morale booster for every unit. During the same period the RAF groups suffered the loss of no less than 114 bombers.[31] 6 Group's early-return rate was still spotty, however; on some sorties it would be negligible, on others unacceptably high.

On March 24/25 came the last sortie to Berlin in this period – and it brought to an abrupt end 6 Group's respite from heavy casualties. As had happened so frequently in the past, the weather played a major role in the catastrophe. Indeed, almost up to take-off time, the target was in doubt. Berlin or Brunswick? It all depended on how conditions developed. The final decision was announced at briefing and no one welcomed it: Berlin again.

The mention of the Big City generated rumbles of apprehension among the airmen in the squadrons' briefing rooms, seated at their long tables, charts and note pads before them. Butch had stayed away from that area of Germany since the Leipzig shambles of more than a month earlier. Berlin trips were always costly. How many crews wouldn't be around by morning?

The route selected was similar to that taken on the mid-February raid: over Denmark and the Baltic, angling down in a south-easterly direction to Berlin, then heading homeward from a point southwest of the city. Diversionary operations would be a major part of the night's activities. A force of 147 aircraft from training units would venture into France in the hope of convincing the German controllers that the night's major raid was aimed at southern Germany. If most of the German fighters could be lured to that sector, casualties over Berlin would be dramatically reduced. In addition, a force of Mosquitoes would attack Kiel, another attempt to draw off the eager fighters. Thus, more than two hundred aircraft – which would have been considered a sizable force not many months earlier – were committed to the important task of diverting the Germans' attention from the intended target.

For the first time, two Master Bombers were to be employed, experienced senior officers who would supervise the operation and issue instructions to the Main Force as needed. The Master Bomber was a Canadian, Wing Commander Reg Lane, the CO of 405 Squadron, the pilot who had flown the *Ruhr Express* to Britain. A navigator, Wing Commander E.W. Anderson, was Lane's deputy, flying in a Mosquito.

The Canadian Group contributed 113 aircraft of which thirteen, 11.5 per cent, returned early. Bomber Command as a whole experienced a 6.5 per cent early-return rate on this operation.

Aircrew would long remember that night as The Night of the Big Winds. Once again the finest technology and the best brains of Bomber Command couldn't cope with the vagaries of nature. Met had promised winds of about twenty knots from 340 degrees for the first stage of the outward journey. But soon after take-off, the most skilled of the navigators realized that the winds were far stronger. Following procedure, selected navigators calculated the winds as they found them; wireless operators broadcast their findings back to England via coded messages. But when this system was devised, no one had heard of the jet stream – which is what the bombers encountered that night. Because of the codes employed, the maximum wind speed that could be transmitted was ninety-nine knots. In fact, winds well in excess of one hundred knots battered the bombers as they headed into Germany. Compounding the problem was the scepticism of the navigational staffs in England. Working on revised forecasts for transmission to all aircraft on the sortie, they were of the opinion that the airborne navigators were a bit off the mark; clearly there had been some serious miscalculations in the aircraft. Winds of *130 mph* and more simply weren't feasible! So Group staffs and Bomber Command staffs "massaged" the figures to the satisfaction of everyone in their comfortable offices, then rebroadcast them to the crews who were by then well out over the North Sea.

In tiny compartments crouched over shivering metal tables, the airborne navigators tried to make sense of it all. Inevitably some made better sense than others. And equally inevitably, the bomber stream lost whatever cohesion it had possessed, scores of aircraft attempting to fly the proper track in the face of the hurricane-force wind, others being carried far to the south.

Over the target, Reg Lane did his best to concentrate the attack. It was impossible. Aircraft swarmed in from all directions. Bombs fell everywhere except the aiming point. Although they did a certain amount of damage to some industries in Berlin, the bulk of the bomb loads landed on residential areas and in the country. Between one hundred and two hundred people were killed in the city and in the villages beyond. Ed Moore, a navigator with 426 Squadron, recalls how the ferocious winds at high altitudes drove the aircraft beyond the target, a fact, Moore notes, which became obvious

> ... when the Pathfinder flares went off behind us ... We turned around and dropped our bombs on target about twenty-five minutes late. Since the planned bombing run had been from the northwest, we were bucking a strong head wind and flying against the main stream of aircraft leaving the target area. We would be bucking high winds all the way home and thus would be short of fuel. Finally we would be travelling alone and would be vulnerable to fighters. Common sense should have dictated that the bombs be jettisoned and a course set for home. Nevertheless we all agreed with the skipper: "We've come this far; we'll drop the bombs in the right place."

Afterwards, Moore noted: "... people like myself with no H2S assistance relied on broadcast winds which were quoted at about 75 mph rather than 120 mph. That put you about fifty miles from where you thought you were at the end of each hour."

The homeward journey was a disaster. "The aircraft were scattered all over Germany," Reg Lane recalls. "You could map-read by the defences." Lane's navigator, Glen Elwood, joined him in the cockpit to see the horrific scene of bombers being shot down by the score, victims of the unprecedented winds that blew them away from the planned routes and over one heavily defended area after another. One of the aircraft lost that night was a Halifax III of 429 Squadron, flown by Stan Wick. It was the second op on which the Wick crew had flown the type; on the first, March 18/ 19, they were nearly shot down by a Halifax on the bomb run. "The rear gunner evidently mistook us for an enemy fighter," recalls Stan Boustead, the crew's RAF wireless operator. "We took two bursts but fortunately no one aboard was hit."

The crew was lucky on that occasion. But now, as they were making their way home from Berlin, their luck ran out. "At about 2245, I received a wireless message from HQ giving details of wind direction and speed . . . and I passed on the information to the navigator. He was talking to the bomb-aimer about the heading," recalls Boustead. "We were pointing directly towards heavy flak and searchlights, obviously Magdeburg. The navigator said we would track south of Magdeburg due to the heavy winds. I turned back to the wireless." At that instant flak smashed into the Halifax. To Bob Kift, the mid-upper gunner, it sounded as if someone was hitting the aircraft with a heavy hammer. The Halifax staggered, mortally wounded. Flames streamed back from the overload fuel tank amidships. Boustead heard the three or four thuds of direct hits plus the sound of tearing metal. He quickly switched back to intercom. The skipper, Wick, seemed remarkably sanguine about the situation, asking each crew member in turn for his opinion of damage. It rapidly became apparent that the situation was hopeless. Wick ordered the crew to bale out. Kift pulled off his helmet and felt the flames singeing his hair. When Boustead drew back the curtain of his compartment he saw flames "licking down the inside of the fuselage like the inside of an oil-fired burner." The reek of fuel filled the trembling fuselage. Clipping his parachute to his harness, Boustead saw Roy Clendinneng, the navigator, exit through the escape hatch in the floor. Boustead followed, but got stuck in the narrow aperture. He remembers how the bomb-aimer ". . . helped me out with his foot and I expected him to follow me but he never made it." Moments later the Halifax blew up. Stan Wick and three members of his crew died instantly. Only Boustead, Bob Kift, and Clendinneng survived to become POWs.

It was a grim night for Bomber Command with seventy-two aircraft lost in action (9.1 per cent) plus at least three more destroyed on their return to England. Proportionately, 6 Group's losses were even worse: thirteen Lancasters and Halifaxes, 11.5

per cent of the force. Particularly hard hit were 427 and 429 Squadrons, both based at Leeming, Yorkshire; each lost three aircraft and crews.

The loss rate improved sharply as the last week of March began. Just two aircraft failed to return from ops to Aulnoye, Courtrai, Essen, and Vaires. But then, on March 30/31, Harris sent his bombers on the most disastrous raid of all. The target wasn't Berlin, but the grisly losses suffered by the bombers seem to make the operation chillingly appropriate as the climax of the Battle. *Nuremberg.* Some ex-airmen still claim that the Germans had somehow obtained advance notice of Harris's intentions. Flying Officer Hughes of 408 Squadron was shot down during the raid; in prison camp, a wireless operator told him that he had been interrogated on March 30 at 1400 hours and had been informed by the German interrogator that the RAF would attack Nuremberg that night.

The Canadian Group contributed 118 aircraft to the force of 572 Lancasters, 214 Halifaxes, and nine Mosquitoes. The raid came at the beginning of a moon period, when Harris's squadrons were usually stood-down. But Met reports indicated unusually favourable conditions: protective cloud for the outward trip and clear conditions over the target. Harris ordered the operation *on.* Afterwards, he was reticent about his reasons for attacking Nuremberg that night; it seems likely that he saw it as his last opportunity to deliver a really pulverizing blow on his terms, for, after two years of virtual autonomy, Bomber Command would soon become another support arm for the impending invasion. No doubt Harris wanted to enter that phase of his wartime career amid the glory of a great victory, not still tasting the bitterness of the winter's defeats.

But it all went wrong. And, for the umpteenth time in Bomber Command's history, the weather was largely responsible – although many airmen and historians place at least as much blame on the almost straight-as-a-die route selected by Bomber Command. The cloud that had been promised to shield the bombers on their outward journey failed to materialize. A crystal-clear night greeted the airmen. At cruising altitude, every bomber painted gigantic trails in the sky, formed as steam from the engines' exhausts condensed in the frigid air. Normally invisible, the trails were all too apparent on this frightful night. Swarming in to the attack, the German night fighters had no trouble spotting the lumbering bombers. They picked them off with ease. It was a massacre. Lancasters and Halifaxes tumbled out of the sky at the rate of about one per minute, trailing flame, blowing up, disintegrating. Horrified, airmen watched the slaughter from their cabins and wondered when their turn would come. Many a navigator gave up logging sightings of shot-down bombers; it had become a full-time job. Bob Furneaux, a 425 Squadron air gunner, saw about a dozen aircraft shot down. Jim Moffat of Castleton, Ontario, a member of 427 Squadron, remembers counting twenty-two aircraft going down in as many minutes. Moffat had flown as mid-upper gunner on George Laird's crew during an eventful op against Kassel the previous October and had now transferred to the rear turret at Laird's request, the original rear gunner having been killed in the Kassel sortie. The move would have far-reaching consequences.

About eighty bombers fell during this stage of the journey. Then, to compound the attackers' problems, the weather deteriorated as they neared the target. The clouds that had been so desperately needed on the way to the target suddenly materialized *over* the target, obscuring it. This fact, combined with stronger-than-forecast winds, resulted in at least two Pathfinder aircraft mistaking nearby Schweinfurt for Nuremberg; more than a hundred Main Force aircraft bombed on their errant markers. Although Schweinfurt was itself a prime target, few bombs landed on the city. At Nuremberg the bombing was similarly scattered and ineffective.

Frank Hamilton, a pilot with 424 Squadron, remembers the Nuremberg op as the worst of his career – a "horror trip." An indication of the remarkably clear conditions was the fact that a night fighter attacked his Halifax head-on. The attack set one engine on fire. The trail of flame quickly drew the attention of other fighters. The fire could not be extinguished, so Hamilton gave the bale-out order. But at that moment, another fighter attack shot the burning engine completely out of the wing. It tumbled away taking the fire with it. To his surprise, Hamilton found the Halifax responded to the controls, despite the huge hole in the wing. He cancelled the bale-out order and managed to get the Halifax back to England at little better than stalling speed, landing at West Malling. Roger Coulombe, who had doggedly flown and fought his way through the entire Berlin campaign, went on the Nuremberg op and remembers it as "a hellish night."

Again Bomber Command suffered catastrophic losses: ninety-six bombers, according to official sources, 11.9 per cent of the force, the biggest loss of the war. And ever since that bleak day in the spring of 1944, there has been conjecture that actual losses were considerably higher. The Germans declared that more than a hundred bombers had crashed in the Third Reich. Some reports talk of as many as 150 being lost. The Canadian Group's losses were thirteen aircraft, representing almost exactly the same percentage loss as that sustained by Bomber Command as a whole.

There were several collisions. Jim Moffat of 427 Squadron, the rear gunner who had counted so many shot-down aircraft on the outbound trip, watched a solitary Halifax over the target. Suddenly, an Me 109 single-engined fighter dived down to attack. The pilot was either wounded or he miscalculated. His speedy fighter flew straight into the bomber, hitting it in the rear of the fuselage, tearing off the entire tail unit. Moffat saw the Halifax fall in a curious flat spin, its shattered tail end down and on the inside of the spin. It vanished from view. Moffat's aircraft bombed and turned for home, the crew relieved to get away from Nuremburg. But twenty minutes later, the navigator reported that he had made an error in his calculations. He ordered a forty-five degree turn to port. As the skipper banked to the new course, a Lancaster of 622 Squadron loomed out of the darkness. It happened too quickly for evasive action. No time to do anything. In an instant the two big aircraft had smashed into one another, crumpling, tearing, killing. In the tail turret, Moffat was at first unaware of the extent of the damage. He called the skipper, George Laird, but the intercom was dead. He looked about him. The rudder was on the right as it should be. But to the left ... nothing! The clouds seemed to be revolving about the aircraft. With a shock, Moffat realized that the bomber was in a flat spin, just like the one he had seen over the target.

He pulled himself out of the turret and tried to crawl forward. The aircraft was a total wreck. A huge hole gaped in one side. Moffat jumped through it to safety, the only survivor from the two crews. Afterwards he realized that if he had been flying in the mid-upper gunner's position, he would have died. In a curious twist of fate, the death of one gunner had resulted in the survival of another. Moffat spent the next six months evading the Germans with the inestimable help of many gallant civilians and Resistance fighters, steadily making his way westward, eventually meeting up with the Americans.

The Nuremberg raid was a ghastly and inglorious end to the campaign known as the Battle of Berlin. Did the Germans have foreknowledge of the raid? To many airmen, it seemed the only explanation for the tragedy. But when the facts are studied, it soon becomes apparent that it is just another of the countless myths that have flourished in the aftermath of the war. One of the most intriguing variations on the theme is the theory that British Intelligence deliberately leaked the information in order to convince the Germans of the reliability of a certain British double agent. Even in the unlikely event of an agent possessing such information, he or she wouldn't have had time to transmit it to Germany. Harris decided on a given target at his morning conference which took place at 0900 hours. He couldn't decide earlier because of the ever-changing weather. MI5's double agents had fixed timetables for radio transmissions to the *Abwehr* (German Military Intelligence); they were not permitted to transmit at other times. Thus, if the agent had the information, it might be days or weeks before it could be sent off. In addition, of course, such a ploy would have created a severe risk for the double agent. If the information had proved accurate, then the *Abwehr* would have demanded similar advance warnings of other ops. The result: a no-win situation. Refusal to provide information on raids would have compromised the agent's position; agreement would have meant needless aircrew casualties. By early 1944, MI5 knew from intercepting German messages that the *Abwehr* had the utmost faith in British double agents. Therefore, the ploy was totally unnecessary. Two key individuals stoutly denied ever being involved in such a ploy: Sir John Masterman, who ran the Twenty Committee that oversaw the work of double agents, and Sir Arthur Harris himself. It takes an incredible leap of the imagination to believe that Harris ever agreed to the use of his hard-pressed Bomber Command crews as a means of protecting MI5's double agents.[32]

So if the shadowy world of espionage did not contribute to the Nuremberg disaster, what went wrong? The answer is, almost everything. The plan itself was ill-conceived. Harris thought his bombers would fly deep into Germany under cloud cover. The clouds didn't appear until the bomber force – what was left of it – had reached Nuremberg. The hope presumably was that the *Luftwaffe* would fail to intercept the bomber stream. Yet the planners routed the bombers close to most of the night fighter bases in western Europe. Although the fighters were responsible for the majority of casualties that night, the clumsy handling of the situation by the fighter controllers is the surest evidence that they had no advance warning. Spoof raids mounted by 8 Group's Mosquitoes against Aachen, Cologne, and Kassel led to the despatch of most of the Wild Boar fighters to the Ruhr area. The entire First Fighter Division was kept in the Berlin area, and the Wild Boar fighters at Neuberg, near Nuremberg, did not even take off. Another night fighter group based near Stuttgart went searching for the bombers over much of Germany. If advance information had been at hand, the Me 110s could have stayed at their field, for the bombers flew directly over it. There seems to have been little coordination in the movement of the night fighters. The Germans chose to assemble their Tame Boar night fighters around radio beacons "Ida" (Aachen) and "Otto" (Frankfurt) in order to protect the latter city. If the controllers had waited another twenty minutes, most of the bombers would almost certainly have escaped, with the fighters left dogging their tracks. Forewarned, the Germans could have sent all their fighters to intercept the bomber stream and the casualties would have been even more grievous than they were.[33]

Harris was correct in estimating that the Battle of Berlin would cost as many as five hundred of his bombers and their crews. But he was wrong when he claimed that it would destroy Berlin from end to end and cost Germany the war. The city had proved to be too vast and too well protected; it refused to burn to a crisp as Hamburg had done and as Dresden would do nearly a year later. Harris simply didn't have the weapons to do the job or the technology to cope with the weather, the distance, and the tenacious defence of their capital by the Germans. The weather and the *Luftwaffe* night fighter force were the bombers' principal foes throughout the Battle. The Germans had recovered from the shock of Window. In fact, many Germans claim that the introduction of Window was a blessing in disguise because it forced the introduction of new ideas, making the night fighter arm far more flexible and effective than it had been the previous summer.

Bomber Command had lost virtually its entire strength during the Battle of Berlin; but the remarkably productive aircraft industry and the highly efficient training organization proved equal to the gargantuan task of supplying Lancasters and Halifaxes and fresh young crews to fly them. The skill and experience of the lost crews were infinitely harder to replace.

Roger Coulombe of 426 Squadron survived the Battle and completed his operational tour soon after the Nuremberg trip. He found himself involved in an odd little postscript to the disastrous campaign. A gentleman from Panama had offered Britain's King George VI a wrist watch to be given to the pilot who dropped the greatest tonnage of bombs on the German capital. The honour went to Coulombe. McEwen himself presented the watch at "a sort of investitute ceremony," as Coulombe describes it, adding that the "prize" was "nothing but a cheap Nevada watch ... worth about $20." He adds: "I am still wondering how the King of England could have accepted such a ridiculous gift. I am sure he never saw the watch, because he would have ordered the thing thrown away in the garbage!"

Somehow that inexpensive watch seems to be a curiously apposite symbol of the Battle of Berlin: so much effort, so much courage, so much blood ... for so little.

7

PREPARATION FOR INVASION

"The best moments were when one stepped from the bomber after running eight hours on adrenalin. Each step felt as if one were bouncing a foot high."

Bruce Betcher, DFC, pilot, 419 Squadron

"You will enter the continent of Europe and, in conjunction with the other Allied nations, undertake operations aimed at the heart of Germany and the destruction of her armed forces."[1] Thus, in January 1944, was U. S. General Dwight D. Eisenhower ordered to take over supreme command of the biggest amphibious operation in history, arguably the most important event of the entire war. The hard-pressed Soviets had been demanding the invasion for years; in response, the Americans had formulated plans to invade (Operation *Roundup*) as far back as 1942. But the British, heavily committed in North Africa, had rejected the idea. Churchill advocated an attack on "the soft underbelly" of Europe to knock Italy out of the war. The plan didn't impress the Russians; they saw Britain's suggestion as a ploy to permit the capitalist states to stand back in relative security while Russia and Germany tore each other to shreds. Early in 1943, the Soviets wiped out the German Sixth Army at Stalingrad. It was the turning point of the savage war on the Eastern Front. The Germans fell back. In Britain, the calls for a Second Front became more strident. This was the moment, declared the armchair strategists: the Soviets advancing in the East, the Allies coming from the West, the Nazis caught between, locked in a war on two fronts that they couldn't possibly win.

But getting the Allied armies across the Channel and making a successful landing was a daunting task. The Germans had long anticipated the invasion and had built The Atlantic Wall, a hodgepodge of fortifications ranging from elaborate and formidable concrete emplacements in some areas to rudimentary earthworks in others. The Germans had sizable forces in France, although it was widely believed in the Allied camp that most were second-rate, the units full of over-age and medically suspect men, including many recuperating in France after being wounded on the Eastern Front. As events unfolded, the efficiency and fighting spirit of these troops was one of the Allies' most unpleasant shocks.

Although the Allied leaders evinced the proper enthusiasm for the task ahead, many had grave misgivings. They knew only too well that the immense operation could turn out to be, in the words of Sir Alan Brooke, the Chief of the Imperial General Staff, "the most ghastly disaster of the whole war."[2] In addition, there is little doubt that the prime minister was haunted by memories of Gallipoli, that daring but catastrophic amphibious operation of 1915 with which his name was inextricably linked.

The numberless difficulties of invading Hitler's "Fortress Europe" spurred the Allied leaders to extraordinary efforts to ensure the success of Operation *Overlord*, as it became known. A key factor in the whole enterprise was total command of the air. Eisenhower dismayed the senior air commanders, both American and British, by insisting that all elements of Allied air power come under his command. Eisenhower was taking no chances. He demanded control of the air forces and he obtained it. Indeed, from the late winter of 1943/44, every aspect of the Allies' war operations in Europe became subservient to *Overlord*. And perhaps the most startling shift in responsibilities was demanded of RAF Bomber Command. Over Harris's strenuous objections, it took on a new role as a tactical air force undertaking *precision* attacks in support of the invasion, many by day.

Bomber Command had come full circle. After abandoning the concept of daylight precision bombing in the early months of the war and painstakingly equipping itself and training its crews for area-bombing by night, it was being called upon to wipe out marshalling yards, military camps, ammunition dumps, gun batteries, radar stations, and an assortment of other tactical targets. The accuracy of Bomber Command's bombing in support of the D-Day invasion build-up would be one of the surprises of that period of the war – and no one appears to have been more surprised than Harris himself. Like most mortals, Harris saw every situation in the context of his own ambitions. Although he wanted to win the war as much as the next man, he wanted to do it his way, by the strategic area-bombing of German cities.

Harris's staunch ally, Commanding General of the U.S. Strategic Air Forces in Europe, Carl Spaatz, was equally dedicated to bombing. But the two men couldn't agree on which targets should be hit, or how. In contrast to Harris's area approach, Spaatz opted for pinpoint bombing, removing key industries with surgical precision – the MEW approach – so that the enemy's war machine would grind to a halt, deprived of ball bearings, fuel, rubber, and other vital commodities. The two air forces seldom mounted the sort of round-the-clock combined aerial offensive that the Casablanca planners had envisioned. The British and Americans prosecuted the air war energetically – but individually. Eisenhower was right to obtain control of the enormous bombing forces; he knew that Harris and Spaatz regarded the long-awaited invasion as a somewhat tiresome side-show that interfered with the "real" war being waged by their bombers. Harris had written one of his typically cogent papers on the subject in January 1944. He declared that Bomber Command could best support the forthcoming invasion by continuing to do what it was already doing:

The effects of strategic bombing are cumulative. The more that productive resources are put out of action, the harder it is to maintain output in those that survive. It is easy to forget, however, that the process of rehabilitation if the offensive stops or weakens is similarly cumulative. To put it shortly, the bomber offensive is sound policy only if the rate of *destruction* is greater than the rate of *repair*. It is hard to estimate the extent to which Germany would recoup industrially in say six months' break in bombing. It would certainly be sufficient to enable her to take a very different view of her prospects on land, on sea and in the air. Indeed it is true to say that if the German army survives the present crisis in Russia (and if it fails to do this, *Overlord* will in any case be superfluous), the cessation of bombing even temporarily would make her military position far from hopeless. What the Russians have done and what we ourselves hope to do on land is fundamentally made possible only by the acute shortage of manpower and munitions which strategic bombing has produced, and by the preoccupation of nearly three-quarters of the enemy fighter force with the defence of Germany proper.

He concluded: "It is clear that the best and indeed the only efficient support which Bomber Command can give to *Overlord* is the intensification of attacks on suitable industrial centres in Germany as and when the opportunity offers. If we attempt to substitute for this process attacks on gun emplacements, beach defences, communications and ammunition dumps in occupied territory we shall commit the irremediable error of diverting our best weapon from the military function for which it has been equipped and trained to tasks which it cannot effectively carry out. Though this might give a specious appearance of supporting the Army, in reality it would be the gravest disservice we could do them. It would lead directly to disaster."[3]

It was Harris in full flight again, overstating his case with magnificent abandon, approaching this situation as he approached every situation, with a mind untroubled by any vestige of doubt. He was right and the others were wrong and that was all there was to it.

But Harris's credibility was already suspect in high places. His passionate polemic failed. On March 4, he received his orders.

Bomber Command was to mount a series of pre-invasion attacks on railway targets, activating the "Transportation Plan" that had been under discussion for months. It called for widespread damage to the railways around the proposed landing area, so the Germans would be unable to use them to bring up reinforcements or supplies. The first target was the marshalling yards at Trappes, southwest of Paris. The question that gnawed at the planners was whether Bomber Command could do the job without killing French and Belgian civilians in their thousands. Everyone agreed that some casualties were inevitable, given the fact that most of the railway targets were set in towns, villages, or suburbs, surrounded on all sides by rows of houses and shops, and that the airmen who would drop the bombs had been trained in area-bombing techniques. How accurate could they be?

On a clear late-winter night came the answer. The date was March 6/7, 1944. A force of 263 aircraft set off for Trappes on the first of the pre-invasion ops. Nearly half the aircraft, 124, were from 6 Group. Conditions were perfect. "In the bright moonlight the marshalling yards were clearly visible and we saw our bombs fall directly on the target," writes Dick Garrity, a 431 Squadron navigator who participated in the raid. The sortie was indeed a spectacular success with the tracks rapidly transformed into a tangled network of steel and most of the sheds and rolling stock wrecked or severely damaged. Practically no damage was done to the town. And not one 6 Group aircraft was lost on this operation despite the presence of four flak batteries in the vicinity. As far as Garrity's crew was concerned, the return to England was the worst part of the trip: "We were diverted south because of fog conditions at Croft," he recalls. "As we had dropped below the cloud base in preparation for landing, I was unable to get a Gee fix and a new course to our diversionary base. Finding ourselves low on fuel, we landed at Chipping Warden, an OTU." There, the orderly officer informed the crew that no accommodation was available for them. They had to bunk down in armchairs and on the floor. "In the morning," adds Garrity, "I learned from a very embarrassed orderly officer that standing orders from the CO prevented him from making quarters available to us, all because of a bad experience with an operational crew who had gotten royally drunk after a rough trip. We didn't get away until the next day, then had the misfortune to lose our starboard outer only five minutes after take-off. Determined not to return to Chipping Warden, we map-read our way back to base on three engines." It's little wonder that operational airmen sometimes crossed verbal swords with the complacent, comfortable denizens of training stations – a few of whom were downright hostile when aircraft fresh from battle had the temerity to drop in at inconvenient hours.

The next night the target was Le Mans. The Canadian Group provided about three quarters of the 304-bomber force that attacked the marshalling yards without loss. But, after the near-perfect raid on Trappes, nothing seemed to go well over Le Mans. The Pathfinders arrived twelve minutes behind schedule, and because of unexpectedly poor weather, their markers vanished in thick cloud. Denis Jennings, a 427 Squadron flight engineer, flew on that sortie and remembers the unit's CO, Wing Commander Turnbull, angrily greeting the crews on their return to Leeming with the news that the op was a failure and they would have to go back. They did, on March 13, following three days of poor weather. When the elements at last cooperated, the job could be done to everyone's satisfaction. "Good visibility," declared the 6 Group ORB, "bombing concentrated on well placed markers. Numerous fires." 6 Group had provided about half the force for the second attack on Le Mans. And again all its aircraft returned safely, although one Halifax of 4 Group didn't get back. Reports from the area indicate that the Maroc Station and two nearby factories received severe damage. A mid-under gunner on a 419 Squadron Halifax, Sergeant D. S. Weeks, saw his aircraft's load land squarely on railway buildings. Fifteen locomotives and eight hundred wagons were destroyed. Some light flak greeted the attackers but it scored no hits. Although most of the bombs landed on target, some went wide – and killed about one hundred civilians in the area. The deaths of French and Belgian civilians would become an increasingly severe problem in the weeks ahead. Churchill gloomily predicted that a hundred thousand might die before the campaign was over.

On the night of March 15/16, 6 Group sent fifty-four aircraft, part of a total force of 140, to the railway yards at Amiens. They did little damage. The following night saw fifty 6 Group aircraft return to Amiens in company with eighty bombers from RAF groups. This time the bombs landed on target, causing extensive damage and setting off several major fires. A huge explosion marked the site of a direct hit on an ammunition train. All 6 Group aircraft returned safely. On March 23/24, fifty-one 6 Group bombers journeyed to Laon, part of another force of medium size: 143 aircraft in all. The attack failed to destroy the railway yards. "Only the first wave saw the TIs," reported the 6 Group ORB. "Many crews had to orbit." The Master Bomber ordered the attack stopped after about half the aircraft had bombed; it was in danger of spreading to the residential areas surrounding the yards. Two Halifaxes from RAF groups were shot down, but there were no losses among 6 Group's aircraft.

Two nights later, seventy-three 6 Group aircraft joined more than a hundred bombers from RAF groups in an attack on Aulnoye, east of Cambrai. "Good weather. Excellent bombing. One very large explosion and several others," was the sanguine reckoning of 6 Group's crews. Several remarked on the violent eruptions, "some white, some orange, some deep red." In fact, however, the Pathfinders had failed to mark the railway yards accurately. All aircraft returned. The following night, March 26/27 saw an attack on the yards at Courtrai, Belgium, by 109 aircraft of which forty-seven came from 6 Group. "Several explosions. One good fire," was the operational report. But in fact the bombing was somewhat scattered with more damage being done in the town than in the railway yards. Again all aircraft returned safely.

On the night of March 29/30 came the last sortie in what may be described as the testing period of the Transportation Plan. The Canadian Group provided forty-nine of the eighty-four aircraft that attacked the railway yards at Vaires, near Paris, in bright moonlight. "Two huge explosions reported," stated the 6 Group ORB, "throwing flames up to six thousand feet and smoke to thirteen thousand feet." Two ammunition trains blew up, resulting in the death of more than a thousand German soldiers. One Halifax of 419 Squadron, commanded by Warrant Officer J.A. Greenidge, fell victim to the flak around Le Havre, the first casualty suffered by the Group in this series of raids on railway targets.

Although not every one of these attacks on railway yards had been successful, in most cases the fault was to be found in the accuracy of the Pathfinders' marking rather than that of the Main Force's bombing. In general, Bomber Command acquitted itself well in these attacks, which represented such a radical departure from its normal activities. After countless raids involving the biggest forces that could be assembled, flying as high as possible, the heavies were hitting the French and Belgian transportation systems with relatively small groups of bombers attacking at modest altitudes to ensure accuracy. Such tactics were possible thanks to generally light defences, although 6 Group's aircraft sometimes ran into strenuous opposition. On many of these operations, Master Bombers directed the proceedings, talking to the Main Force crews by radio, overseeing every aspect of the bombing. The benefits of having these skilled veteran airmen present throughout the operations can hardly be overstated. But it was dangerous work. Several Master Bombers lost their lives in the course of this series of operations, having tempted Providence once too often.

It was obvious to the Germans that the raids were part of the build-up to an invasion by Anglo-American forces. Far less obvious was precisely where the landings would take place. The Allies wanted the Germans to keep thinking in terms of the Pas de Calais, the area closest to the English coast. For that reason the air forces dropped at least as many tons of bombs on railway targets linked with Calais as on those connected with Normandy; and in the days leading up to D-Day the weight would actually shift *away* from Normandy.

For the crews, the transportation targets came as a welcome change from the brutally wearying and costly ops to Berlin and other targets deep within Germany. Besides, there was a sense of anticipation in every op, a feeling that one was contributing to a historic event that would help bring the war to an end.

But it was a frustrating time too. Mist and rain grounded 6 Group's bombers during the first days of April. Ops would be scheduled, then cancelled and rescheduled. On the night of April 9/10, however, the Group sent fifty-three bombers to join 186 RAF aircraft in an attack on the Lille-Délivrance freight yard. It was precisely the sort of raid that the planners had dreaded. Although the bombs did much damage to the railway facilities and destroyed more than two thousand freight cars, many fell in the town, demolishing or damaging some five thousand homes. Worse, the bombs killed a horrifying total of 456 French civilians. It's hardly surprising that Allied troops later encountered hostility among French and Belgian civilians in certain areas. On the same night, more than a hundred 6 Group aircraft accompanied 118 bombers from RAF groups in an attack on the railway yards at Villeneuve-St-Georges near Paris. Again, it was a case of considerable damage being done to the yards but too many French citizens becoming casualties: 93 killed and 167 injured. One RAF Lancaster was lost from these two sorties; all 6 Group aircraft returned safely.

There was little rest for the bomber crews when conditions were adequate. The following night, twenty-four 6 Group bombers set off for a return visit to the yards at Laon. "Crews unanimous that this raid was a success," was the chirpy report in the 6 Group ORB. Bomber Command was less enthusiastic, citing inaccurate marking that resulted in only a corner of the yards being hit. On the same night came the first in a series of "solo" operations in which all the Main Force bombers came from 6 Group. The target: the Merelbeke-Melle railway yards at Ghent, Belgium. The 122 RCAF Halifaxes dropped six hundred tons of bombs in about six minutes. With weather ranging "from clear to eight-tenths cloud," crews could see their bombs hitting the tracks. "Frequent explosions culminated in one violent upheaval lasting several seconds that threw flame and debris thousands of feet into the air, and columns of dense grey smoke even higher," declared the ORB with obvious satisfaction. But not all the bombs found the target. The raid caused the deaths of 428 Belgian civilians and injuries to some three hundred more. The defences were "negligible," according to the ORB. Why, then, did so many bombs go astray, killing and injuring hundreds of innocent Belgians? The answer is simple. Most of the targets were surrounded by built-up areas. It was all too easy to mistake, say, a post office for a railway repair yard in the glittering, confusing lights of markers. Civilians continued to die in these raids but the numbers were still "acceptable," at least to the planners, if not to the victims and their families.

On the night of April 19/20, a force of nearly two hundred aircraft flew to Paris to attack the railway yards at Noisy-le-Sec. The Canadian Group provided 137 aircraft. Unhappily, it was the same tragic story: severe damage to the target – indeed, the yards were not completely repaired until several years after the end of the war – but a sickeningly high death toll among French citizens: 464 killed and 370 injured. In addition, the bombing demolished 750 houses and damaged about two thousand more. Although a Master Bomber was in the area during the attack, he couldn't be heard because of jamming by the enemy. On this operation, the *Luftwaffe* appeared in some force and shot down four 6 Group Halifaxes. One was a 432 Squadron aircraft. The wireless operator, Sergeant S.D. Pett, had vivid memories of the incident: "I felt a thud, things went a bit hazy." Pett heard the voice of the skipper over the intercom but he couldn't make out what was being said. Suddenly a large hole appeared in the side of the fuselage opposite his position through which the target was visible. "I remember clipping my chute on, but after that I only remember floating down over the target area." The bomb load had exploded, blowing the aircraft to bits and hurling the lucky Pett clear. He was uninjured and became a POW, the sole survivor of his crew.[4]

On the twentieth, 6 Group despatched 154 Halifaxes to Lens, a few miles south of Lille, France; they were joined by fourteen Lancasters and seven Mosquitoes of the Pathfinders. The force encountered only light defences and, although the attack was late in starting and the marking somewhat scattered, the bombs fell on target and caused severe damage. One 6 Group Halifax was lost. Another Halifax, from 428 Squadron, was attacked by a night fighter and set on fire. The skipper, Flight Lieutenant C.G. Ford, ordered the crew to bale out. Within moments, three of the crew had escaped – but then the fire went out. Ford managed to get the Halifax back to England. He received the DFC.

On the same night (presumably with Eisenhower's permission) Bomber Command mounted an area-type attack on a much-visited target: Cologne. The force consisted of 357 Lancasters and twenty-two Mosquitoes. The Canadian Group provided twenty-two Lancasters, fifteen from 408 Squadron and nine from 426. One returned early. It was a successful attack concentrated principally in the northern sectors of the city. Ed Moore, a navigator with 426 Squadron, remembers the operation well:

426 Squadron was selected to go in early along with the Pathfinders. The idea was to split the German fighter and ground

forces. But why would anyone choose 426 which was not equipped with H2S? In this area, Gee was always subject to strong enemy interference; on this one trip we could expect no exception, neither did we get one. To make matters worse we had ten-tenths cloud cover and could not pick out the coast visually. I had the bomb-aimer drop the load and flare on dead reckoning based on a fuzzy Gee fix obtained quite a long time earlier. We were happy to see a number of flares dropped simultaneously over a small area. Whether the others were all dropped by 426 aircraft or by squadrons with more navigational equipment is open to question. Since we had passed over the target before the Pathfinders laid their target flares, we were not able to tell how close we had been.

Moore adds: "Afterwards I noticed with some amusement a remark by a well-known writer that the Allies had deliberately refrained from hitting the Cologne Cathedral despite the bombing of St. Paul's by the Germans."

During the raid, a Lancaster from 426 Squadron commanded by Flight Sergeant R.P. Sellen took hits from a number of "friendly" incendiaries dropped by higher-flying aircraft. The bombs tore holes in the wings and set one engine on fire; despite these problems, the crew completed the bomb run and returned safely to base.

Forty-eight hours later, on the night of April 22/23, Bomber Command set off on another area-bombing operation, this time against Düsseldorf. Nearly six hundred bombers took part, including 136 from 6 Group. According to the crews, the Pathfinders "had placed their markers perfectly." More than two thousand tons of bombs fell on the northern section of the city, demolishing or damaging in excess of two thousand houses and fifty-six industrial premises. Some nine hundred people died; six hundred more were injured. But German night fighters intercepted the bomber stream and shot down twenty-nine bombers, 4.9 per cent of the force. Eight of the lost aircraft came from 6 Group. "Markers concentrated and bombing good," noted the ORB.

Roger Coulombe, who had had his share of excitement over Berlin earlier in the year, was on his twenty-ninth op. His Lancaster

II was attacked twice by a Ju 88 night fighter. A cannon shell slammed through one of the fuel tanks in the starboard wing, then exploded, ripping chunks out of the leading edge and an engine cowling. "The fuel gauge went from 'Full' to 'Zero' within a few seconds," Coulombe writes. "The hole in the tank was enormous!" In spite of the damage, Coulombe characteristically pushed on and dropped his bombs on Düsseldorf. Near the target, another fighter intercepted a 429 Squadron Halifax commanded by Flight Lieutenant J. Atkins. Atkins lost one engine and found the Halifax almost impossible to control because of the damage inflicted by the fighter. Nevertheless, he continued to the target, bombed, and managed to get the limping aircraft back to base. He was awarded the DFC.

Another Halifax of the same unit was one of the Group's losses. The mid-upper gunner, Warrant Officer W.J. Miller, recalls: "Fighters began to appear in quite large numbers as we left the target area, at that time flying at about 23,000 feet; because of vapour trails, however, we dropped to 20,000 feet and had proceeded to the Dutch coast when a fighter attacking from the rear fired a burst from about six hundred yards and broke off immediately; the burst missed and we started evasive action. Within the space of a couple of minutes we were attacked suddenly from below and behind, the first enemy burst hitting the port side of the bomb bay, port inner and wing . . ." With the aircraft on fire, the two gunners jumped from the hatch amidships. Miller landed in the sea about a quarter-mile from shore near the town of Middelharnis. Kept afloat by his Mae West, he showed admirable presence of mind, using his parachute as a sail to bring him to shore.[5]

A navigator of 429 Squadron had a lucky escape. Warrant Officer H.A. Findlater reported that when his Halifax was hit during a fighter attack he pulled his helmet off and clipped his parachute pack to his harness. He and the wireless operator tugged the escape hatch open. "The aircraft then went into a very steep dive and I was held to the floor, unable to move. Looking toward the rear of the aircraft I saw a huge fire in the engineer's position and looking forward I saw the bomb-aimer pinned in the nose by the force of the dive. Then I passed out. I came to floating down in my parachute . . ."[6] When a Halifax of 433 Squadron took flak hits, the navigator, Flying Officer A.W. Norris, felt small pieces coming through the floor and peppering his legs: "The aircraft immediately went into a steep dive." On the floor of the nose compartment, Norris attempted to open the escape hatch in the floor. "From my position I could see that the mid-section of the aircraft was a blazing mass of flames. I hazily recollect someone pushing me away from the hatch and escaping through it. I fell through directly after him . . . I regained consciousness on the ground with the sounds of a burning aircraft about half a mile away." Norris adds: "The reason I passed out became apparent later when I recollected that my oxygen mask was yanked from my face as I fell to the floor."[7]

A wireless operator in a 433 Squadron Halifax, Sergeant T. N. Morris had an equally lucky escape. "When the kite was hit I got out of my seat and reached for my chute. I noticed that the rest position was ablaze. I have no recollection of what happened after this until I found myself on the ground." The aircraft apparently blew up and Morris was fortunate enough to be thrown clear without injury – as happened to a surprisingly large number of airmen.[8]

The Canadian Group participated in a highly destructive sortie against the marshalling yards at Laon the same night, April 22/23. Forty 6 Group aircraft joined 141 bombers from other groups. Conditions could hardly have been better; the crews lining up to bomb could see the yards clearly in the moonlight. But the moonlight also made things easy for the defenders. Flak and fighters shot down nine aircraft including one from 6 Group, a Halifax of 419 Squadron commanded by an American, Lieutenant C.A. Thomas. A night fighter intercepted the aircraft over the target, setting both port engines on fire. All the crew baled out with the exception of Sergeant V.A. Knox who is believed to have been killed when the fighter attacked. Another of the night's casualties was Wing Commander A.G.S. Cousens of 635 Squadron, the Master Bomber on the raid and a well-known Pathfinder pilot.

The capricious spring weather frequently made operational flying even more dangerous than normal. On April 24/25, 6 Group provided 137 bombers, part of a force of 637 aircraft that attacked Karlsruhe. The weather did its best to upset Bomber Command's plans with icing, static electricity and freezing rain on the way to the target. The bombers ploughed on, but a Halifax of 425 Squadron went down without the Germans' assistance. After being airborne for an hour, the crew found fuel leaking from the starboard outer engine. The skipper, Flying Officer J.W. L'Abbé, decided to continue to the target, then to fly home on three engines. But on approaching the target: "... we encountered the aircraft from the second wave coming head on to us as they had been briefed, so I decided to circle the target three times until they had all passed before going in to bomb." It's not hard to imagine the feelings of the crew as they orbited the heavily defended city. But they survived the ordeal, bombed and set off for home. L'Abbé feathered the problem engine and descended to twelve thousand feet. He promptly ran into icing that froze the trim tabs and caked the windows; the bomber began to shudder violently, and was soon unmanageable. He ordered the crew to abandon the aircraft. They escaped successfully, all being captured by the Germans on alighting.[9]

Flying Officer G. S. Coleman, the navigator of a 424 Squadron Halifax, was working at his desk when flak hit the aircraft; chunks ripped through his navigation table. The pilot ordered everyone to prepare to bale out. Coleman remembered handing the skipper his parachute; an instant later the aircraft exploded. Coleman regained his senses in mid-air, tumbling earthward. He just had time to pull his rip-cord before hitting the ground, breaking two ribs and spraining an ankle. He and the bomb-aimer, Sergeant May, were the only survivors.[10]

High winds in the target area had spoiled the Pathfinders' marking; bombs fell on the outskirts of the city and on several neighbouring communities. A Halifax of 425 Squadron commanded by Sergeant V. J. Lachille shot down a Ju 88 en route to the target; the successful gunners were Sergeants J.H. St. Yves and J.A. Croteau. Nineteen aircraft, including six from 6 Group, were lost on this disappointing and costly operation.

Harris continued to mount area-bombing attacks whenever he could wrest his bombers away from their tactical obligations. On the night of April 26/27, 117 of 6 Group's bombers joined 376 aircraft from RAF groups to attack Essen. It was a successful raid, according to 6 Group's ORB: "Good weather. Incendiaries started numerous fires which later merged into one large one. Several explosions." Crews reported columns of smoke rising three miles in the air. But they faced intense opposition. Russell McKay, a 420 Squadron pilot, has reason to recall the op vividly:

> The target opened up with a terrific barrage of heavy flak as the first wave approached to bomb . . . Suddenly, searchlights coned aircraft on either side, and in front of us. I quickly counted five aircraft coned. Dense ack-ack fire poured into the cones. In a matter of seconds, five bombers were blown out of the sky in balls of red flames. The huge white beams flicked across our wings. Two, three, five beams swung toward us, leaped at us, and held us. Desperately I pushed the control column full forward and hard rudder to port into the three closest beams; I pulled with all my strength to roll out of the dive and turn in the corkscrew manoeuvre. Miraculously, I found myself in cloud and the searchlights swept off to starboard.

Afterwards, McKay kept thinking about the operation and his lucky escape: "I had not seen cloud in the area until I dived." The next day, he says, he was "still sweating."[11] Interestingly, the raid bore out what Harris had said about the importance of maintaining the bombing pressure. Much of the damage done to the Krupp works in the great attacks of the Battle of the Ruhr the previous year had been repaired, according to crew reports. In this raid close to a hundred buildings received "extensive damage." Pilot Officer I.C. Gilchrist's 431 Squadron Halifax suffered a direct hit from flak and burst into flames. Gamely the crew fought the fire, eventually bringing it under control. Gilchrist flew the Halifax back to base at Croft, County Durham. One 6 Group aircraft was lost from this operation, plus six others from the rest of the force.

Villeneuve-St-Georges and Aulnoye were two more transportation targets attacked, on the 26/27th and 27/28th respectively, with good results. The Canadian Group suffered no losses. On the 27/28th, however, a force of 144 aircraft attacked the railway yards at Montzen, Belgium, and ran into ferocious opposition. Fifty-five 6 Group aircraft participated in the operation, and many of the Canadian crews were inexperienced, having just started their tours. Ten, a sobering 18 per cent of the 6 Group force, were lost, as well as five aircraft from other groups.

Pilot Officer J. L. Webb and his crew from 432 Squadron had a particularly harrowing time. Over the Belgian coast, flak hit Webb's Halifax and put the bomb doors out of action. Approaching the target, the crew worked frantically on the recalcitrant doors. At last they opened. Now Webb's crew could deliver the bombs. But their troubles were by no means over. Just as the load fell from the Halifax's bomb bay, an Me 110 night fighter emerged from the smoke and haze. Fighter and bomber opened fire simultaneously. It appeared that the Halifax got the better of the exchange; the Me 110 was last seen falling away to port with damage to one engine. Webb and his crew headed for home. On the way they encountered another fighter but they managed to evade it. The Germans seemed determined to destroy Webb's aircraft that night, for yet another fighter soon put in an appearance. But, oddly enough, it fired no shots and soon disappeared in the gloom. Twenty-three minutes later, still another fighter attacked. A cannon shell exploded in the Halifax's starboard outer engine. Webb feathered the engine and set off for home on the remaining three. "We obtained a W/T fix at the coast ... On the way we were trailed by another fighter, who left us only when we went into cloud at six thousand feet." Approaching to land, at about fifty feet "... and well down the runway, our starboard inner engine quit causing the starboard wing to drop and putting us on edge in a violent turn to starboard. The only thing left was to try an overshoot. We had quite a bit of difficulty in regaining sufficient height, but at six hundred feet finally got our starboard wing up and made another approach. This time everything went well and we landed safe and sound." Webb was awarded the DSO; his gunners, Sergeants D.H. Wright and W.J. Ziomko, received DFMs.[12]

Two crewmen of 6 Group aircraft had lucky escapes from death that night. Pilot Officer F. L. Perry was the mid-upper gunner on a Halifax of 431 Squadron. A fighter attacked as the Halifax approached the target. The port inner burst into flames; within moments the entire wing was on fire. Perry clipped his parachute pack on and went forward. The aircraft exploded. Perry later reported: "I woke up about two thousand feet from the ground, falling head first, pulled the cord and in a split second hit the ground."[13] Another gunner, Pilot Officer R.L. Small of 432

Squadron, lost consciousness when his Halifax went into a spin after being hit by flak. He awoke, tumbling through the darkness. He saw the handle of his parachute – fastened to his harness by only one hook – and managed to tug it. To his relief the chute opened and remained fastened to his harness. Small landed with only minor injury to his right arm and leg.[14] Numbered among the night's casualties was the Deputy Master Bomber, Squadron Leader E.M. Blenkinsopp, a Canadian with 405 Squadron. The Master Bomber, Wing Commander Reg Lane, CO of the squadron, recalls: "The operation was completed and I instructed Blenkinsopp to head home. Moments later I saw the flash of an aircraft blowing up. I realized at once it was Blenkinsopp's because the bright colours of his TIs came dripping out of the explosion. When I returned to base, I reported that he had been killed." Incredibly, however, Blenkinsopp survived the crash of his Lancaster. He was fortunate enough to join up with the Belgian Resistance. Then his luck ran out. The Germans caught him, and this gallant airman eventually died in the infamous Belsen concentration camp.

Also on the night of April 27/28, nineteen 6 Group bombers joined more than three hundred other Bomber Command aircraft in an attack on a distant target: Friedrichshafen on the shore of Lake Constance, a round trip of some fifteen hundred miles. (The city has a permanent place in the annals of aerial warfare. In November 1914, three Avro 504 biplanes of the RNAS took off from the French village of Belfort, flew rather more than a hundred miles to Friedrichshafen and dropped a dozen twenty-pound bombs on the Zeppelin hangars there, setting off fires among the inflammable airships. The daring raid is generally considered to be the first "major" strategic bombing operation in history.) With painful memories of the Nuremberg disaster fresh in his mind, Harris must have had grave misgivings about venturing so far south in moonlight. But the Air Ministry wanted Friedrichshafen hit because it contained several important plants making parts for tanks. Bomber Command planned a number of diversionary raids into the attack; these seemed to have served their purpose of confusing the controllers, at least temporarily. The bombers arrived at the target without encountering any fighters. They proceeded to inflict considerable damage. "A good carpet of incendiaries laid down," reported 6 Group's ORB. "Fires visible for two hundred miles." Crews saw smoke rising to eighteen thousand feet. But the night fighters arrived before the raid had been completed. In rapid succession they shot down eighteen Lancasters, 5.6 per cent of the force; however, no 6 Group aircraft were numbered among the casualties.

The month ended with a failure, an attack on the marshalling yards at Somain by 114 Halifaxes of 6 Group and twenty-nine Pathfinder aircraft. Excellent weather and negligible defences might have been expected to set the scene for a successful attack. Unfortunately, the initial Oboe marking was inaccurate. The Master Bomber instructed the Main Force to wait for more markers. But the 6 Group crews either ignored his directions or didn't hear them. Nearly all the Halifaxes bombed on the original markers and most of the load fell in open country.

Sea-mining, or Gardening, continued to be a major part of 6 Group's responsibilities. When an Australian, Wing Commander T.V. Stokes, sought the latest information on European sea-mining techniques for possible application in the Pacific, he chose to visit 6 Group, since he considered the Canadian Group "the most experienced and advanced" in Gardening.[15] Although it may never have dominated the headlines the way the major bombing raids did, over the course of the war the sea-mining campaign caused vast damage and endless problems for the German High Command. It has been claimed that Gardening sank more German ships than the RN. Possibly; but its biggest contribution to victory may well have been the fact that mine-sweeping duties occupied at least 40 per cent of German naval personnel on a full-time basis. The German sailors faced a formidable task. Bomber Command laid mines in vast numbers – more than twenty-two thousand in 1944 alone.

The early mines had to be dropped from between five hundred and one thousand feet, usually on timed runs from prominent landmarks. Although the bombers seldom encountered fighters, flak often proved to be a major hazard. Some aircraft flew into the sea because the aneroid altimeters then in use tended to deteriorate with age and provided incorrect readings. Gardening losses were at their highest early in 1942, reaching 3.3 per cent of sorties, with thirty-four mines laid per aircraft lost. Two years later, losses had dwindled to 1.3 per cent of aircraft despatched, with more than two hundred mines being laid per aircraft lost.[16]

The Canadian Bomber Group had become heavily involved in Gardening in mid-1943 when its Wellington squadrons were withdrawn from ops against German targets. The Wimpy may have become outdated for bombing Berlin and Hamburg but it proved to be ideally suited to the task of mining enemy waters. Soon 6 Group's Wellington squadrons became Bomber Command's acknowledged experts in sea-mining. Early in 1944, a new type of sea mine came on the scene. The aircrews liked it because it could be dropped from far greater, and safer, altitudes (up to twenty thousand feet) than could earlier types. Two 6 Group squadrons, 419 and 428, pioneered the use of these new mines. These two units became Pathfinders on several Gardening ops when 8 Group was unable to provide aircraft. Meanwhile, the introduction of H2S had made it a great deal easier to pinpoint dropping zones on the featureless sea. But Gardening could be hazardous. Bruce Betcher of 419 Squadron, an American who joined the RCAF while a student at the University of Minnesota in 1941, remembers a sortie in February 1944 when a dozen Halifaxes went to mine La Rochelle harbour. The weather, as was its wont, upset the airmen's plans. "We were briefed for a 60 mph wind from the north," he says. "We were still twenty minutes out when the flak started and we all flew over the target one at a time, giving the gunners a crack at each of us. The return leg took us over eight German fighter airfields." Betcher's aircraft was over cloud when the first glimmers of morning appeared. "The navigator said we were an hour from the French coast. We thought we would formate on other aircraft but when daylight came, we were all alone. We knew we were goners . . . however, we never saw another aircraft until we were over England. The wind was 110 mph, making our groundspeed about 130 mph!" Betcher believes he and his crew survived because the Germans couldn't send off their fighters in the powerful winds.

Throughout the latter part of the war, 6 Group always had a coterie of crews specially trained in sea-mining; Exercise *Pauper* was the name of their training program. It was one of the few non-horticultural names associated with Gardening – "Artichoke," for the area off the west coast of France, "Sweetpea," for the Baltic, and "Nectarine," for the Dutch coast, were more typical code names.

The crews dropped three principal types of mines: the Mark I-IV of 1,580 pounds, the Mark VI of 1,850 pounds, and the Mark VII of 1,000 pounds. All were of the non-contact type designed to lie on the bottom of the sea, to be activated by acoustic or magnetic waves, or by combinations of both. Battery-powered, they were rated as having a useful life of nine months, although some were known to explode up to three years after "planting."

There was a sense of anticipation in the air. No one could miss it. Gigantic military convoys thundered along every highway in Britain. Aircraft filled the sky every day that was fit for flying – and on many that weren't. Enormous stockpiles of trucks and tanks and supplies of all kinds kept appearing, the necessary *matériel* for the huge force that would soon brave the Atlantic Wall: twenty American divisions, fourteen British, three Canadian, one French, one Polish, an amalgam of combat veterans and those who had never heard a shot fired in anger. Wags claimed that the weight of all these mountains of invasion equipment was so Brobdingnagian that only the ubiquitous barrage balloons kept the British Isles from sinking into the sea.

Morale was generally high in the operational squadrons of 6 Group. But the intensity of the past few weeks, the constant round of briefings and preparations, the operations, and, all too frequently, the last-minute scrubs, took their toll. "There was a lot of frustration in those days," recalls Eddy Collyer of 425 Squadron. "We were often briefed at short notice with take-off being scheduled, then put back owing to weather, on again, postponed and finally scrubbed, all this time being spent out at or in the aircraft. Sometimes this would go on for days at a time, on stand-by, unable to settle down, with food being taken out to dispersal as we waited, with the 'scrub' always coming too late for a night out in York. It was at times like these that the CO, Joe Lecomte, would lay on a barrel of beer in the Mess and come in and help you drink it. What a character he was, one of the boys when it suited, but a leader who was respected by all his air and ground crews."

Unquestionably one of the finest squadron commanders in 6 Group, the burly good-natured Lecomte is fondly and gratefully remembered by many ex-aircrew. Jim Northrup, a former pilot, says: "415 Squadron had one of the most dynamic COs ever to run a squadron, Wing Commander Joe Lecomte DFC and Bar ... Anyone who had the good fortune to serve with this French-Canadian airman never forgot him. The training we received from him was outstanding and I have always thought I survived because of him." It was Lecomte whose breezy manner dismayed a telephone caller from Bomber Command HQ. "Joe here," exclaimed Lecomte when he picked up the phone. "Joe who?" the very British voice wanted to know. "Joe the CO, that's who," responded Lecomte.

The stress of intensive operations took its toll on some 6 Group airmen. Depression, sleeplessness, and shaky nerves were frequent reactions. In some cases, perceptive senior officers grounded men for a few days to give their nerves time to settle down. In other cases, the airmen themselves solved the problem. They refused to fly. Typical of such cases was a member of Steve Puskas's crew of 429 Squadron. They had started their tour early in 1944. Flying to Essen, Puskas ran into a succession of problems. First, the bomb doors wouldn't close after the bombs had gone. Then, en route for home, he encountered three night fighters, although he succeeded in evading them. Crossing the English coast, he was greeted by searchlights and a barrage from the anti-aircraft batteries, the result of faulty IFF (Identification Friend or Foe) equipment. It was a thankful crew who picked up the Leeming beam and landed, safe and sound in spite of the best efforts of the Germans and the gremlins.

The rear gunner, Wilf, was strangely silent, Puskas remembers. "We tried to involve him in our chatter, but to no avail."

The reason for Wilf's sudden taciturnity soon became apparent. He told Puskas that he was through with flying. He would never step into another airplane. Puskas felt sure that the gunner would change his mind after a few hours' sleep. He was wrong. The following morning Wilf told the station commander, Group Captain Bryant, the same thing. He refused to fly again. Nothing the group captain or anyone else could say would make him change his mind.

"Wilf must have done a lot of soul-searching to come up with this decision – and he displayed a lot of nerve to stick with it," Puskas comments.

The gunner was now a branded man. In a matter of hours he had been bustled off the station to undergo a series of scathing interviews, angry reminders that he had volunteered for aircrew duties and that he was reneging on his word. Then he was sent back to Canada and discharged from the RCAF, his file stamped LMF.

"I have always felt ashamed of what the 'organization' did to him," remarks Puskas. "They could have been more understanding and compassionate instead of sending him home LMF. Everyone has a breaking point and the limit varies with each individual."

LMF, Lack of Moral Fibre, was the much-hated term used by the RAF and RCAF throughout the war. It tended to be used far more frequently in reference to NCOs than to officers. Although it could be argued that NCOs usually outnumbered officers in operational aircraft and that the imbalance was therefore logical, there runs through the history of this unhappy subject a marked bias in favour of commissioned aircrew. If an officer refused to fly, there was a strong possibility that he would be posted to some quiet job with a note in his records about nervous strain and exhaustion. It's hard to find records of any NCOs being so treated. In some cases, station commanders made abject examples of them, parading them before their squadrons and publicly stripping them of their badges of rank and flying brevets. LMF cases usually went to transit camps or disciplinary units to be remustered to the army or to spend the rest of their service lives washing dishes or cleaning latrines.

The vast majority of aircrew condemned such practices. J. Douglas Harvey, a pilot with 408 Squadron, wrote of LMF cases: "The harsh treatment they received sickened me. Had our commanders shown any compassion or tried in any way to rehabilitate them, they could have continued flying. Professional medical advice was ignored and psychiatric help scorned."[17] The Americans and Australians seemed to have been the most enlightened when it came to dealing with these cases, with extensive use of psychiatric services and rest camps. But in the RAF and RCAF the belief apparently existed that if a single aircrew member managed to get himself taken off flying without suitable disciplinary action being taken, then pilots and navigators, and indeed all aircrew trades, would be quitting in the thousands. It was an inexplicable attitude, for, from the grisly slaughter of the daylight raids in 1939, to the wholesale destruction of hundreds of four-engined bombers and their crews over Germany in 1943 and 1944, the *only* thing the authorities didn't have to worry about was the willingness of their young aircrews to set off for whatever target they were told to bomb, night after night, no matter what the conditions. Of course they were afraid; there would have been something wrong with them if they weren't. Perceptive, intelligent young men, they realized what dangers they faced; they understood how slim their chances were. Only the survivors know what battles they fought within themselves before clambering aboard their Lancasters and Halifaxes. Over heavily defended targets, with searchlights sweeping the sky and flak streaming by, it took a special kind of courage to fly an undeviating bomb run, to sit for hours on end in a turret, watching, waiting, to crouch over a tiny table and work on navigational problems while the world went mad outside. Some found they didn't possess that kind of courage. Or they found that courage was a variable commodity, strong enough for some situations but not all, adequate one night and not another.

Reasons for quitting flying varied. Ralph Green of Regina, a pilot with 424 Squadron, recalls one of the unit's crews that was discovered dropping its bombs in the sea en route to the target, then flying back and forth for several hours before rejoining the bomber stream on the way home. "The whole crew was in on it of course; they all had to 'cook' their logs," Green comments. He says the skipper was married in England with a couple of children; the family had severe medical and other problems.

Many ex-aircrew talk of living in a state of "controlled fear" throughout their operational careers. Green says frankly that one of his best moments in the air force was when he discovered he could control his fear and do the job without flinching. Al Avant, who later commanded 429 Squadron, recalls an air gunner on his crew who was intensely nervous and often physically sick before sorties, yet he always managed to brace his shaky nerves by take-off time. (Unfortunately this gallant man was eventually lost on ops.) Many commanders understood that every airman started off with a certain amount of courage, a sort of bank account of resolve. Inevitably, some had larger accounts than others. "I feel the real heroes were those who pressed on after their accounts were over-drawn," comments Lucien Thomas, who flew with 405 Squadron. "All of us saw examples of people who kept going, realizing that their chances of completing a tour were all but nil. I have heard people in high places say that this was a defeatist attitude. I do not agree. Perhaps the real culprits were those who allowed such individuals to be selected for aircrew duties in the first place."

A former navigator with 408 Squadron, Jim McInerney, writes of the term LMF: "Surely some other terminology could have been applied. I have always violently objected to its use and have expressed sympathy for those to whom it has been applied." The vast majority of aircrew sympathized with those who openly admitted their fears, but were bitterly critical of those who were dishonest. Stuart Leslie, a pilot with 429 Squadron, remembers his crew's original mid-upper gunner, a Canadian from the West, who became too scared to fly: "He covered it as medical but he did not fool the other NCOs in the crew – or we three officers either . . . By chance I saw this particular person many years later and even then he could not look me straight in the eyes . . ."

Ernie Dickson of Toronto, a bomb-aimer with 428 and 433 Squadrons, fortified himself (as did the vast majority of aircrew) with the belief that *it* would never happen to him. He was correct and survived thirty-six ops. But when he returned to Canada, still in his early twenties, he was found to have a duodenal ulcer – caused by the stress of operational flying, according to the doctors. Early in Dickson's tour, his skipper had become incapable of carrying on. It happened en route to Berlin. The skipper announced that the aircraft wouldn't climb. A moment later he jettisoned the bombs in the sea and turned back. The next morning the CO took the aircraft for an air test and found it functioned perfectly. The pilot vanished from the station the same day. The crew was broken up, the members going to various squadrons. Only Dickson, the wireless operator (and, it must be assumed, the original skipper) survived the war. Marcel Beauchamp, formerly a navigator with 425 Squadron, writes that after completing his tour and while he was still in England: "I met a Canadian instructor I had had in Canada. He had evidently refused to fly operationally and quite freely admitted that he had been classified LMF. I was shocked by his candour but it didn't seem to bother him. In retrospect I think it was a courageous thing for him to do."

Joe Hartshorn, a pilot with 419 Squadron, was one of the 6,129 U.S. citizens who joined the RCAF before Pearl Harbor. By early 1944 he had transferred to the USAAF but had obtained permission to complete his tour before leaving the RCAF. He took off on May 27, 1944, headed for Bourg-Léopold, a large military camp in Belgium. Halfway across the Channel, the navigator announced in a shaky voice that the Gee equipment had broken down; the aircraft was lost; the sortie had to be abandoned immediately. Hartshorn told him that he was maintaining the last course he had been given – and he was *not* turning back. No response. A few minutes later, however, the navigator provided Hartshorn with a new course; the sortie was successfully completed and the crew returned to base. But the navigator was badly shaken. Over the next few weeks he became intensely nervous before every op, clearly having difficulty controlling his fear. It was a delicate problem for a young skipper. Should he report a member of his crew because he *appeared* to be scared and *could* be a danger on future ops? Or should he simply hope for the best? Hartshorn chose to hope. It appeared to have been the right choice; in the course of the next few ops the navigator performed his duties adequately.

Then came the trip to Duisburg. The trouble began on the way to the target. Flak scored a direct hit, smashing into the armour-plating behind Hartshorn's head, blowing away most of the cockpit canopy, wrecking the mid-upper turret and hydraulic system. But the target was close at hand and, despite an icy hurricane screaming through the remains of the canopy, Hartshorn pushed on and lined up for his bomb run.

Bombs gone! Relieved of their weight, the Lancaster rose in its buoyant way – whereupon the navigator pushed his way forward, parachute pack clipped to his harness. He had suffered a superficial wound to his hand, apparently the last straw. The aircraft was doomed, he yelled to Hartshorn. Bale out! Immediately! There wasn't a moment to lose! He made for the emergency exit in the nose.

Hartshorn always carried a pistol on ops. The crew claimed that he used it to force them to fly with him; in fact he took it because it might come in handy if he was shot down. With the frigid wind bellowing about him, Hartshorn drew the gun and pointed it at the navigator, ordering him to return to his seat. After a moment's reflection, the man did as he was told. Hartshorn flew the battered Lancaster back to Middleton St. George and landed safely. The navigator immediately went to see the MO and declared himself unfit to fly because of the injury to his hand. To the relief of Hartshorn and the rest of the crew, the MO accepted this and excused the navigator from flying duties.

Soon afterwards, Hartshorn learned that he had been awarded the DFC for his performance over Duisburg. To his astonishment, he discovered that another member of the crew had received the same award – none other than his erstwhile navigator!

It is interesting to compare the treatment of this *commissioned* navigator with that accorded an NCO wireless operator, Wally Loucks, who had survived a tragic crash during training that killed several of the crew. Posted as a "spare bod" to 419 Squadron (by coincidence, Hartshorn's unit), Loucks found himself assigned to a crew that had lost its wireless operator. Loucks flew with the crew on several trips but was dismayed by their lack of professionalism. "They behaved," Loucks says, "as if the whole thing was a joke." Concerned, he went to the adjutant and explained his dilemma. The reaction? Loucks was immediately called "yellow" and threatened with an LMF "branding." Loucks then consulted the MO who authorized a few days' leave. When Loucks returned to Middleton, he was saddened but not surprised to learn that his former crew had gone missing. Assigned to another crew, Loucks completed a tour of thirty-one ops.

The authorities repeatedly demonstrated that they had one set of rules for officers, another for NCOs. Bruce Betcher, also of 419 Squadron, recalls: "I knew of only two cases of LMF while I was at Middleton St. George. A sergeant gunner refused to fly and was given the standard treatment. His rank was reduced to AC2 . . . and he was given permanent latrine duty. A flight commander whose family was alleged to be prominent in Canada did the same. He was returned to Canada and was last heard from touring training bases, lecturing on operational flying." Paul Burden of Fredericton, New Brunswick, a 434 Squadron pilot, recalls a skipper from the unit turning back at the Dutch coast despite the urgings of his crew to continue the sortie. After dumping the bombs the crew returned to Croft. Burden says the pilot, a commissioned officer, was offered a second chance by the CO. He declined the offer and was posted away from the station without delay.

John McQuiston, a 415 Squadron pilot, remembers being ordered to report to his aircraft with his crew, minus the wireless operator. He found the CO at the dispersal, in company with the MO, the Protestant padre, and an uncomfortable-looking sergeant wireless operator.

The CO, Frank Ball, ordered the wireless operator to board the aircraft for a test flight. The sergeant shook his head and said he wouldn't.

Again Ball ordered the sergeant to board the aircraft.

" 'I'm sorry, sir. I can't do that,' was the respectful reply," McQuiston relates. He adds: "Twice more, Frank Ball ordered the sergeant to board the aircraft, and twice more the sergeant refused."

McQuiston later learned that the wireless operator was a "spare bod" and he had become demoralized by his status – an indication of how important a crew was to every operational airman; the crew represented stability, comradeship, and a form of security in a distinctly uncertain world. Categorized as LMF, the unfortunate man soon left the station.[18]

The Canadian Group had its share of men who found themselves incapable of flying – and undoubtedly some were individuals who found the realities of ops far tougher than they had anticipated and who decided to get out of their obligations any way they could. Ralph Green of 424 Squadron remembers a Canadian pilot at his OTU who attempted to be excused from operational flying by complaining of severe "bends" at twelve to fourteen thousand feet in the altitude simulator tank. His ploy was uncovered when the simulator was rigged up to indicate pressure drop when in fact there was none. There seems little doubt, however, that the majority of LMF cases were genuine – genuine in the sense that the men were literally incapable of facing another op with all its attendant horrors and dangers. But any study of such cases indicates how a man's courage might waver after a particularly terrifying trip only to recover later. John Neal, a bomb-aimer with 419 Squadron, remembers how the strain built up as his tour progressed. He admits frankly, "I still wonder how close I came." Jim Northrup of Surrey, B.C., a pilot with 415 Squadron, declares that at the beginning of his tour he was "very close to telling the CO I could not do any more." With Northrup, the problem appears to have been a case of too much too soon: "I did five trips very fast and had difficulties on every one of them. The flak, the fighters and searchlights, seemed endless." Northrup got very little sleep between these trips and his responsibilities as a skipper weighed heavily on him. He recalls, "Fortunately there was a lull in operations and I got three or four nights' sleep and I never experienced that feeling again." He says he has talked to many ex-bomber pilots and "every one of them told me there was a time when they thought they could not go again." John Wullum, a gunner with 434 Squadron, recalls a pilot who had gone on his Second Dickey ride with an experienced crew. At debriefing, the pilot talked to the CO, describing his physical reaction to the buffeting, the lights, and the flak; he candidly declared that he could not function under such conditions and was not capable of being a skipper. Wullum says: "I was deputy gunnery leader that night and happened to be in the CO's office when this chap interrupted us. I was surprised that he would speak out in my presence and I recall thinking that this man had more guts to speak out about his failure than the rest of us who carried on and hid our fears." Wullum's comments typify those of the majority of 6 Group aircrew who kept their misgivings to themselves and, displaying courage of a high order, simply got on with the job.

Unquestionably, the threat of being labelled LMF was a powerful incentive to keep going. Northrup remembers, "I once made an early return and was more worried about being classed as LMF than the fact that my crew and I were very close to 'buying it.'" It is significant that he should have even considered such an eventuality, for he had a very real emergency on his hands. He recalls suffering from a violent headache as the aircraft climbed. At nineteen thousand feet he passed out. The oxygen system had failed. He regained consciousness to find his bomb-laden Halifax in a power-on spin at seven thousand feet. Fortunately, Northrup was more experienced than the majority of 6 Group pilots, having been an instructor before going overseas. He was able to wrestle the big bomber out of the spin while there was still some air left below.

Most skippers, at some point in their tours, had to decide whether to abandon a trip or carry on. Laurie Cormier of Dieppe, New Brunswick, was a Warrant Officer gunner with 427 Squadron; his crew returned early from a sortie one night because the canopy over the pilot's head would not close properly. "We were raked over the coals by Wing Commander Turnbull for turning back," Cormier says, "and told never to do it again." Some time later, while en route to a target, the crew experienced a succession of problems: trouble with one engine followed by interruptions in the oxygen supply system – Cormier himself almost passed out in the rear turret – *plus* technical difficulties with the "Monica" set that warned of enemy aircraft in the vicinity. The skipper decided to turn back, then rapidly changed his mind when he recalled the CO's words. With its engine trouble, the aircraft was unable to keep up with the stream. Doggedly pushing on toward the target, the solitary bomber was a perfect target for the German night fighters. It soon became a casualty, but the crew survived and were taken prisoner. "Ironically," adds Cormier, "when we were preparing to board our aircraft for this mission, Mr. Turnbull came over to our dispersal and told us that this was the aircraft's last trip." The crew's battle-weary old Halifax Mark V was about to be replaced by a new Mark III Halifax, but the airmen never returned to accept delivery.

Nervous reaction to the strain of operation took many forms. Don Saunders, a 424 Squadron pilot, saw a rear gunner who "lost control in his walk. His legs shot out to the sides, his arms were flying all over the place, and he jibbered." Wilbur "Wib" Pierce, a flight commander with 433 Squadron based at Skipton-on-Swale, Yorkshire comments: "One could spot someone getting 'edgy' and give him a rest for a few days. I never had any cases of LMF and never would have. I felt it was an unfair categorization of a perfectly understandable stress situation." Edith Kup, formerly a

WAAF intelligence officer with 405 Squadron, remembers how she came to watch for signs of operational strain among the crews she debriefed after operations – "for if a crew was rested . . . or even grounded for a bit, disaster might be averted." She debriefed one crew who had returned early from their first op and "it became apparent that something had happened with one of the young sergeants." The WAAFs took him into the Ops Room and had him lie down on a cot there, while they concocted a story of engine failure for the crew. Later they sent for the MO: "When he came and they lifted the sergeant, he was as stiff as a board. The MO said we were looking at someone literally scared stiff. He was carted off, never to reappear. No one ever mentioned it outside those in the know and, sadly, the crew was missing a few days later."

The handling of frightened men was never easy. When Toronto's George Rogers had completed his tour of ops with 432 Squadron, he became assistant navigation officer. After one sortie, a young and inexperienced navigator returned badly shaken. He couldn't go on, he told Rogers; he was going to quit no matter what anyone said. Rogers talked to the young man at length, pointing out that most people had the shakes at some time in their operational careers; it was nothing unusual, nothing to be ashamed of. The talk seemed to help. The youngster managed to get his fears under control. He went off with his crew on the next op. His aircraft was shot down and he was killed.

The young airmen of 6 Group had to deal with death on a regular basis. For that reason, the majority seldom made close friends outside their own crews. They reasoned that there was little point in getting too close to other aircrew types who, according to the statistics, stood every chance of getting the chop. Many skippers objected openly to such friendships, knowing how the loss of a close friend could affect an airman's performance. It was all right, however, to become buddies with your bomb-aimer or navigator; if he was killed, there was every likelihood that you would be killed too. Thus was developed a curiously (but seldom callously) offhand attitude to death: ". . . Hard cheese, Ed buying the farm on the last op of his tour, but that's the way it goes." Soon Ed would join the ranks of those whose idiosyncrasies would be remembered far longer than their features.

"Psychologically we suffered from the inability to get close to anyone because we had lost so many close friends," recalls Bruce Betcher of 419 Squadron. Jim Emmerson, a pilot with 424 Squadron, recounts the story of "Fearless" Fraser and his friend, Warrant Officer Cyples, who became the "self-appointed champions of freedom for Canadians" at an OTU in England. "On their arrival at Long Marston," Emmerson writes,

> Fearless and his friend assessed the situation. It was their opinion that the Canadians were a brow-beaten lot and made to suffer the whims of the RAF staff sergeants who, though in a minority, ruled the Sergeants' Mess with an iron hand. Fearless and his friend set to work. Every spare minute they canvassed the Canadian personnel, securing from them a promise to turn out at a monster Mess meeting. What Fearless would propose his friend would second . . . The shackles were to be undone. A veritable Magna Charta of Sergeants' Messes was to be drawn up. The invasion of Europe could not have been awaited with any more suspense than the Mess meeting.

But Emmerson was posted away on the eve of the meeting. Shortly afterwards he heard that Cyples had been killed in a flying accident. Still later, Emmerson encountered Fraser in Edinburgh. "There were the usual salutations," Emmerson recalls, "and then I mentioned it was too bad about his friend. Fearless's countenance changed in an instant from bright cheerfulness to utter gloom. I squirmed uneasily at having mentioned such a tender subject. 'Yes,' agreed Fearless with a heavy sigh, 'and just before the Mess meeting too.'"

The fortunate crews who completed their tours were "screened," their names removed from the readiness lists. After leave, they would be posted to various training units to pass on their hard-won experience to the fledglings before embarking on a second tour. The completion of a tour was a major event in any 6 Group airman's career, particularly in the murderous days of 1943 and early 1944. In spite of the statistics you had come through! You could reasonably expect to be alive this time next week! Even next month! The rest of humanity thought nothing of discussing the future, but it was a luxury that operational airmen couldn't afford. Now, however, like a patient who has recovered from a near-fatal illness, the airman glowed with a brand-new lease on life.

The odd thing was that for countless airmen the completion of their tour proved to be something less than the unalloyed joy they had anticipated. Alan Helmsley, a navigator with 420 Squadron, arrived at the end of his thirty-seven-op tour and found that "it seemed an anticlimax." One overwhelming reality struck home: the crew, the pivotal element in an airman's operational life, was about to disintegrate, its members scattered wherever the air force chose to send them. When Doug Scanlan of Toronto, a 415 Squadron bomb-aimer, got back from the final trip of his tour, he kissed the ground – yet he admits to mixed feelings: "On the one hand I was relieved that I would now be 'stood-down' for a six-month rest period, but sorry that in all likelihood the seven of us who made up the crew would never fly together again." John Campbell of Woodstock, Ontario, an air gunner who flew with 426 and 432 Squadrons, says his worst moment in the air force was when his crew disbanded. J. Douglas Harvey also has vivid memories of the end of his tour: "A bittersweet feeling overcame me . . . I looked around. Far off across the airfield I could see the Lancasters parked. No more raids. No more S-Sugar. Screened. The familiar sights and sounds of squadron life would be no more. No more terrified flights in the dark. I knew I was pleased and yet a tug of regret nagged at me. How could I leave this place? This was where the war was fought. This is what I had come overseas to do. I would have to leave my crew. We would be split up."[19]

Lucien Thomas flew with 405 Squadron in 1942 and early 1943; his crew was one of the few to survive a tour during that period. He says frankly, "My worst moment was sitting in the Leeming Sergeants' Mess waiting for assignment after completing my tour. The sheer dejection of being a non-player, a 'non-person' and everything that went with it was the most depressing thing I have ever experienced. The squadron was 'on' that night, a maximum effort, and there I sat . . . "

D-Day drew near and the campaign against transportation targets intensified. As in April, operational life became a perpetual battle with weather and time. The more ops, the more frenzied the lives of the ground crews; sometimes they would have aircraft ready only minutes before take-off. Consider the loading of bombs. Usually the ground crews had about five hours between the bomb-load warning broadcast and take-off. A typical 6 Group station with two squadrons might have forty aircraft on charge. A typical load would be eighteen 500-pound bombs per aircraft, which meant that 720 bombs had to be prepared, fused, transported to the dispersals, and hoisted aboard the aircraft (although after D-Day, bombs were often stored at the dispersals, eliminating one step from the process). Simultaneously, the stocks in the bomb dump had to be replaced, brought in by road, and stored ready for use another day. For the armourers, the day's work might involve the handling of a thousand bombs – a hard job and one not without danger. The armourers earned every penny of their modest pay, as did all the little-publicized ground crews on whom the aircrews depended. For 6 Group aircrews, it was particularly difficult because the aircraft had further to fly to reach their targets and return; the longer the aircraft spent in the air, the shorter the time available for maintenance and arming. Relations between air and ground crews were excellent – in most cases. Lucide Rioux, an engine mechanic with 405 Squadron, recalls a pilot returning from an air test complaining bitterly about his aircraft; he was sure, he said, that no ground crew would "dare" take the air in that particular Halifax. The CO and the engineering officer were brought into the discussion; meanwhile the ground crew trooped off to the stores and signed out parachutes and helmets. Later, the aircraft took off with a party of ground crew aboard; the complaining pilot handled the controls; the flight commander went as second pilot; Rioux acted as the flight engineer. A short flight revealed that there was nothing of importance wrong with the aircraft. The pilot vanished from the squadron the next day. Always conscious of the enormous contribution of the ground crews, squadron commanders would brook no unfair criticism of their work.

Marshalling yards and coastal gun positions were 6 Group's principal targets during the early days of May. St-Ghislain, St-Valéry, Haine-St-Pierre, Calais, Ghent, Boulogne, Louvain, Le Clipon, Merville . . . one railway yard looked much like another;

steel tracks glinting in the glare of the Pathfinders' markers, freight sheds and repair shops huddled against street after street of civilian homes. Everyone prayed that there would be no more disasters like the attacks on Lille, Ghent, and Noisy-le-Sec, with hundreds of casualties among civilians. But civilians continued to die, although never in the numbers conjured up by Churchill in his gloomy prognostications. He declared that as many as *one hundred thousand* French and Belgian civilians might be killed in the Transportation campaign. The final tally was about twelve thousand.

As far as the bomber aircrews were concerned, most of these sorties were "a piece of cake." Group recognized the fact. In May, the AOC, McEwen, wrote to all stations advising aircrew of the existence of a new point system; no longer was it simply a matter of completing thirty sorties before being screened. Now the goal for those on their first tours was to accumulate 120 points. Sorties to Germany or to heavily defended targets counted for four points each; those to occupied territory or to lightly defended targets counted for three. For those on second tours, the magic number was sixty; German and heavily defended targets counted for three points each, the others two. In case anyone was in doubt as to whether a target was "heavily defended," the AOC himself would decide and would inform the bases the day of the sortie in question.[20] Although Group HQ considered the French and Belgian targets relatively easy, not all were completed without loss. A raid on the marshalling yards at Haine-St-Pierre, for example, cost six of the seventy-five 6 Group aircraft despatched. On the night of May 12, 6 Group sent 108 Halifaxes and Lancasters in company with four Pathfinder Mosquitoes to bomb the railways at Louvain, Belgium. German night fighters shot down five. The *Luftwaffe* was still a formidable force by night even if its day fighters were in disarray. But the widespread nature of Bomber Command's activities made it impossible for the Germans to intercept every sortie. Furthermore, most of the railway targets lacked adequate flak protection. For example, 6 Group crews noted during an attack on Le Clipon that only one gun was firing at them. It failed to score a single hit.

Harris still mounted major area-bombing assaults whenever he could, still convinced that this was the most efficacious way of wrecking the Germans' ability to wage war. On the night of May 22/23, a force of 375 aircraft (twenty-seven of which were despatched by 6 Group) attacked Dortmund, an important industrial target in the Ruhr. The raid could be classified as moderately successful; residential areas in the south of the city suffered the most. The flak proved to be lighter than usual for the Ruhr, although crews saw many searchlights. The raid cost eighteen Lancasters, 4.8 per cent of the force. Three of these Lancasters came from 6 Group, one being piloted by Wing Commander D.S. Jacobs, the CO of 408 Squadron who was midway through his second tour.

On the same night, 112 bombers from 6 Group, accompanied by twenty-one Pathfinder aircraft, delivered a model attack on the Le Mans railway yards and the nearby Gnome & Rhône factory. The Canadians dropped their bombs with commendable accuracy, inflicting serious damage on the target, and injuring only two French civilians. The bombers did not escape unscathed, however. Eddy Collyer, a flight engineer with 425 Squadron, remembers haze over the target making it difficult for the Pathfinders to mark it accurately. The Master Bomber ordered everyone to orbit while he marked, always a hazardous business in the dark and, Collyer writes, "... we were hit by another aircraft which we did not see. We prepared to abandon aircraft and had the escape hatches open when the skipper (Flight Sergeant Paul Lacaille) managed to get back to level flight. The aircraft was vibrating badly but was manageable, so he decided to press on to bomb the yellow TIs which had just gone down. We had lost a bit of altitude and as soon as we bombed, we made for home. The vibration continued and the aircraft was very difficult to handle but we kept our fingers crossed ..." While the battered Halifax was making its difficult way home, the first glimmers of morning light enabled the aircrew to see the damage that the collision had done. It was a shock. About four feet of the starboard wing outboard of the engines was bent up at an angle of some forty degrees. "The controls had been damaged," Collyer recalls, "and the aircraft was crabbing along; stalling speed was high ... We kept going for home but felt that we might have to bale out ..." They managed to get back to their base at Tholthorpe, Yorkshire. "We touched down at about 140 mph. The starboard wing dropped and the undercarriage on the starboard side collapsed, causing the wing to dig in and throw us into a ground loop. When the aircraft slid to a stop with a lot of grinding and bumping, we all clambered out." Lacaille received a DFM; the Halifax he brought back to base was repaired and used by the same crew for the rest of their tour.

The same Tholthorpe-based squadron lost a Halifax that night. The rear gunner, Flying Officer McGowan, remembered the bomb-aimer dropping the bombs on the target then "... we proceeded to the turning point and began to lose altitude as briefed from nine thousand to four thousand feet." From that moment on, McGowan remembered nothing: "I woke up in a room and couldn't move. I don't know how long I had been unconscious but I did not realize where I was for about three days after that." McGowan's aircraft must have blown up and he had been tossed out, his parachute opening without his assistance.[21] Another collision took place over Le Mans, the Halifax of Pilot Officer L.A. Mann hitting another Halifax over the target. The accident smashed several large holes in the fuselage, tore open the bomb doors, ripping chunks away, damaged the port rudder and elevator, and set an engine on fire. After losing a great deal of height, Mann succeeded in getting the battered aircraft under control and managed to fly it back to England despite intense vibration and much reduced airspeed. Mann was awarded the DFC. His two gunners, Sergeants D.C. Harkness and M.R. Burnett, received DFMs for their part in getting the Halifax back to friendly territory. The raid cost two 6 Group aircraft.

On May 24/25, a major force of 442 aircraft, including sixty from 6 Group, attacked the two railway yards at Aachen. Although considerable damage was done, the Main Force crews complained about the accuracy of the Pathfinders' marking, some indicators being positioned at right angles to the approaching bombers. The Germans seemed to have been busy with decoys that night; Wing Commander W.P. Pleasance, the CO of 419 Squadron, saw many "dummy green TIs of the same hue as the authentic ones ... bursting and cascading on both sides of track as far as fifty miles west of the target." Pleasance recognized the markers as decoys by their relatively short burning period; such was the value of experience on operations. The two trips cost five bombers from 6 Group. One was a Halifax of 429 Squadron. Its mid-upper gunner, Pilot Officer H.D. LaPointe, has to be numbered among the luckiest of airmen. Flak hit the aircraft en route to the target and "knocked out the port outer and both turrets." The skipper elected to press on, but he instructed the crew to put on their parachutes because he was uncertain how much damage had been done. After bombing, LaPointe heard the skipper asking the navigator for a course home. "The next thing I knew was that cannon shells were bursting in the aircraft and then I was falling through space. I pulled my chute but nothing happened." His feelings can be imagined. Plunging earthward, he had to grapple with the faulty parachute and "dig it open," as he later said. That was the last thing he remembered ". . . until I came to on the ground eight hours later." He had suffered a broken ankle, a sprained knee, a ripped fingernail, and a shot through the hand. But he was alive.[22]

On the same night, 6 Group sent fifty-five bombers to attack the coastal battery at Trouville. "Visibility fair," reported the 6 Group records. "Target well marked and bombing accurate. Ground defences negligible." Three nights later, forty-three 6 Group aircraft bombed another coastal battery, this one at Le Clipon: ". . . ten explosions in rapid succession were seen." All 6 Group aircraft returned safely from both operations.

Towards the end of the month, on May 27/28, 331 aircraft, including 149 from 6 Group, attacked the military camp at Bourg-Léopold, Belgium. It was a successful attack but it attracted the attention of the German night fighter force. Ten of the bombers went down, 3 per cent of the force; of these, six came from 6 Group squadrons. A Halifax of 424 Squadron commanded by Lieutenant O.J.G. Keys of the USAAF suffered several attacks by an Fw 190 and an Me 410. But the attackers rapidly became the victims. Keys's mid-upper gunner, Sergeant P. Engbrecht, shot down both enemy aircraft. Another 424 Squadron Halifax, operated by the experienced crew of Flight Lieutenant Mallett, carried a pilot on his Second Dickey ride. Suddenly the aircraft staggered – although no one was sure whether the problem had been caused by flak or fighter. The rear gunner, Flying Officer V.G. Poppa, stayed in his turret while the aircraft fell some five thousand feet. He then noticed a parachute going past him, at which point he decided to bale out without delay. But . . . "after two unsuccessful attempts . . . due to fire, heat and flame, I decided to ride the aircraft in. I put my turret dead astern and left my door open. The next thing I knew I was streaming behind the aircraft." Poppa's legs had become entangled in the turret; when the aircraft started to spin, it threw Poppa clear: "I pulled my rip-cord at approximately 1,500 feet." Four of the crew, including the skipper, Mallett, and the Second Dickey, parachuted to safety and managed to evade the enemy.[23]

The crew of a 420 Squadron Halifax commanded by Flying Officer E.M. Aldred saw a German single-engined fighter attacking another bomber. The rear gunner, Sergeant H.W. Robinson, instructed him to corkscrew to starboard; as he did so, Robinson delivered two well-aimed bursts. The fighter spun down in flames: "it hit the ground and exploded," Robinson later reported.[24]

Another 420 Squadron Halifax encountered a German fighter whose fire hit the bomber's starboard inner engine, the wing, the mid-upper turret and the fuselage, setting the aircraft on fire. The rear gunner, Sergeant G.D. Burton, fired a long burst of twelve hundred rounds into the German aircraft, sending it down in flames. The skipper of the damaged Halifax, Flying Officer R.A. Kalle, told the crew to stand by to bale out, after which he succeeded in extinguishing the fire by diving the aircraft. He flew it home safely. He was awarded a DFC; Burton got the DFM.

A Halifax of 425 Squadron, with Flying Officer E.E. Kirk in command, shot down a fighter. The unit had equipped many of their Halifaxes with ventral gun positions sporting half-inch machine guns. In this case, Sergeant L.S. Owen, the mid-upper gunner, spotted the enemy fighter at a range of about seven hundred yards. Both he and the rear gunner, Pilot Officer O.R. Collins, opened fire. The fighter burst into flames. Several members of the crew saw it hit the ground and explode.

Attacks on coastal radio stations and artillery batteries came thick and fast in the last few nights before the long-awaited invasion. It was a period of intense activity and high expectations. Plus a good deal of worry about the weather. Locals said they couldn't recall worse conditions in the first week of June. But the preparations continued. For 6 Group squadrons, the ops came and went, the majority of raids taking place in the Pas de Calais area, to reinforce the fiction that the landings would take place there. In all, the Allied Air Forces dropped three times more bombs east of the Seine than they did to the west; moreover, a brilliantly successful ruse put the non-existent First U.S. Army Group in supposed readiness across the Channel directly opposite the Pas de Calais, with none other than the feisty General George S. Patton in command. Weeks before D-Day it became apparent that the ploy had worked; an intercepted message made reference to "Patton's Group." Hitler, his famous intuition hard at work, seemed unconvinced by the signs pointing to the Pas de Calais; several times during the weeks prior to D-Day he told his commanders that he thought the Allies would land at Normandy. There is little doubt that uncertainty among the senior German commanders about the location of the landings and the best method to fight the American, British, and Canadian armies did much to ensure the success of *Overlord*.

But there is another factor of enormous significance: the virtual destruction of the *Luftwaffe* day fighter force by the Americans. The job was started by the bombers, carried on by the escorting P-38 Lightnings and P-47 Thunderbolts, and completed by a single-engined fighter known originally as the North American NA-73 and later as the P-51 Mustang. A marriage of convenience between an American airframe and the British Merlin engine produced an aircraft of exceptional performance, in many respects superior to the best of the German piston-engined fighters. Most important, however, was the extraordinary range of the Mustang when fitted with drop tanks under its wings. Although the P-47s and P-38s did a workmanlike job as escorts, they could accompany the bombers only part of the way to German targets. Unescorted, the bombers invariably suffered terrible losses. In the P-51 Mustang, the Americans at last had a fighter able to stay with the bombers all the way to the most distant targets and capable of taking on any aircraft the Germans put up. When the P-51s were seen over Hannover for the first time, Göring refused to believe the reports; it was impossible for single-engined fighters to fly such distances, he declared, reprimanding the officer who had dared to initiate such nonsense. In the early months of 1944, the American daylight armadas had provoked the outnumbered German fighters into a series of devastating aerial combats.

Luftwaffe losses mounted alarmingly – and although the aircraft industry performed miracles of production, rapidly making good the losses of aircraft, it could not replace the aircrews. Indeed, hundreds of brand-new fighters emerged from the factories to sit, waiting for pilots and fuel, until they were destroyed in Allied raids or captured. Week by week, the once-invincible *Luftwaffe* day fighter force dwindled to a pathetic shadow of its former self. According to *Luftwaffe* figures, the tally of German aircraft destroyed, missing, or damaged in the first six months of 1944 amounted to a staggering 2,904. In the same period German aircrew casualties, dead, missing, and wounded, totalled 2,008. The vast majority of the experienced pilots and commanders of the *Luftwaffe* day fighter force were by now dead or otherwise out of action. Hastily trained replacements, some of whom had little more than a hundred hours in their log books, found themselves thrown into the battle. Few survived more than a handful of sorties against the confident and superbly equipped Allied fighter pilots.

8

THE INVASION OF EUROPE

"I will never forget the excitement of the D-Day trips, bombing
a gun position on the coast which threatened the invasion fleet ...
we flew back home as dawn was breaking."

Eddy Collyer, flight engineer, 425 Squadron

It had been a routine Gardening sortie. The mines had been
dropped on target. None of the defences in the Le Havre area had
evinced much interest. The 428 Squadron Halifax turned for
home. One of the crew, Glenn Bassett, remembers: "It was an
uneventful night until we crossed the coast a little west of Ports-
mouth and the Isle of Wight just as the sun was rising over the
horizon. Suddenly our pilot yelled, 'Bloody hell, look to starboard!' That meant *port* for me because I was the rear gunner.
And down there before my eyes was the D-Day invasion fleet,
hundreds of ships and craft of all kinds."

A once-in-a-lifetime sight. Aboard the Halifax, no one said anything for a moment, Bassett recalls, then "we all wanted to talk at once." Transports large and small, barges, tank carriers, destroyers, corvettes, cruisers, battleships . . . the vast Allied invasion fleet was ready to go to Normandy. For Bassett and his crew it was truly a day to remember; after gazing wide-eyed at the huge armada, they flew back to their base at Middleton St. George to be greeted by the CO, Dave French, with good news. They were screened, their tour completed.

At last it was happening! The long-awaited invasion of Europe was really taking place! On June 5/6, Bomber Command broke all records, flying more than 1,200 sorties. The Canadian Bomber Group contributed 230 sorties, with every serviceable aircraft being pressed into service. The aircrews and ground crews of 6 Group had little time for rest. The list of targets grew by the hour: the Coutances bridge, the military camp at Condé-sur-Noireau, the Versailles coastal battery, the railway junction at Achères, the Mayenne railway station, the Le Mans airfield, the Versailles/Matelots railway junction, the Arras marshalling yards, the Cambrai railway crossing, the St-Pol railway depot, the port facilities at Boulogne, the Sautrecourt construction works...

Amid such a frenzy of aerial activity, it was unfortunately inevitable that some French – and Canadian – lives would be lost. Gordon Ritchie was a gunner operating with 429 Squadron and has vivid memories of an op against Achères on June 7/8: "As we crossed the French coast at Dieppe, all hell broke loose as the flak guns opened up on us. The pilot (Squadron Leader W.B. Anderson) caught rather a large fragment . . . and gave us the order to bale out – we were at eighteen thousand feet and the aircraft went into a vertical dive as the pilot slumped over the control column." The navigator, bomb-aimer, and wireless operator succeeded in escaping from the Halifax, but the flight engineer, Gilbert Steere, dragged the injured pilot from his seat, took over the controls, and succeeded in wrestling the big aircraft out of its dive. Ritchie and the mid-upper gunner, John Mangione, went forward to lend what assistance they could. Anderson was in pain but alive; his crew-mates gave him morphine and made him as comfortable as possible. They jettisoned the bombs and headed for England, Steere at the controls but squatting deep in the metal bucket seat because he wasn't wearing a seat-type parachute. He couldn't see over the instrument panel; he maintained control by watching the airspeed indicator, altimeter, and artificial horizon – no mean feat for a non-pilot. "It was anything but a smooth flight back," Ritchie recalls. But at last they found themselves over England. Their Mayday call brought forth voices from several stations, although no one seemed to know precisely where the Halifax was. The redoubtable team of the gunners and the flight engineer decided that the only hope was to bale out. They dragged the wounded skipper back to the rear escape hatch. "We attached his 'D' ring to the snap on the static line and prepared to release him out of the escape hatch," Ritchie writes. "I was the last person to speak to him and told him what we were doing. He asked for a little time and then said, 'OK, let me go.' And so we slid him out." The others followed him. Unfortunately, Anderson died of his injuries, but the others survived. A few days later they received their well-deserved decorations: Gilbert Steere, the gallant flight engineer, was awarded the CGM, and the two gunners received DFMs.[1]

The Arras operation on the night of June 12/13 was successful, but German night fighters shot down six of the Group's eighty-nine aircraft. One squadron, 434, lost three that night, including the Halifax skippered by the CO, Wing Commander Chris Bartlett, who was killed. The Cambrai op on the same night cost nine of ninety-two. The raid saw displays of extraordinary courage and self-sacrifice. A Halifax of 432 Squadron commanded by Flying Officer L.R. Lauzon took flak hits at six thousand feet just as it turned away from the target. In moments, fire was roaring through the narrow fuselage. Lauzon ordered the crew to bale out. He held the aircraft steady while they did so. But just as Lauzon himself was preparing to jump, the mid-upper gunner, Sergeant C. Christoff, came forward. His parachute had been damaged by fire. Lauzon offered him his own parachute and said he would crash-land. Christoff refused the offer of the skipper's parachute, saying he would stay aboard and take his chances. While Lauzon concentrated on his approach, Christoff attacked the fire with a portable extinguisher. Then he hurried to the engineer's position immediately behind the pilot to prepare himself for the crash. Lauzon, unable to see the ground through the darkness, put the blazing Halifax down on instruments, a remarkable feat of air-manship. Afterwards he said, "The mid-upper gunner put up a very good show in keeping the fire down sufficiently for the air-craft to be kept under control." Both Lauzon and Christoff escaped through the escape hatch in the roof of the cockpit. Lauzon was captured but Christoff managed to evade the Ger-mans and was back in England by September.[2]

Another of the casualties on that eventful night was A-Able, a Lancaster of 419 Squadron skippered by Flying Officer Art deBreyne. He and his crew were on their thirteenth sortie. Before they reached the target, a Ju 88 night fighter attacked from below, pouring an accurate stream of cannon fire into the port wing and rear fuselage. Three explosions staggered the Lancaster. "I noticed a strong smell of burning," recalls Jim Kelly, the wireless operator. "Smoke started to fill the cabin and the navigator, Bob Bodie, got up and reached for his parachute." A moment later Kelly saw that the port wing was in flames. Both engines on that side had stopped; fire streamed from the No. 2 fuel tank between them. In the pilot's seat, deBreyne glanced in vain at his instru-ment panel. There wasn't much to see; the lights had gone out. Realizing the situation was hopeless, deBreyne ordered the crew to bale out. But the intercom was no longer working. He told the flight engineer, Roy Vigars, to pass the word to the others. Aban-don aircraft! Immediately! He used the emergency warning-light system to convey the message to the gunners. Then, unable to do more than hope the faltering aircraft wouldn't blow up before everyone jumped, he held it as steady as he could. And waited. One by one the crew escaped. By now the Lanc was down to little more than a thousand feet. It was now or never. Art deBreyne heaved himself out of his seat and hurriedly made his way to the emergency exit in the nose while the aircraft was still on an even keel. He jumped, believing that all his crew had jumped.

He was wrong. The rear gunner was still aboard, trapped in his turret when the port outer stopped, since that engine powered the hydraulic system that operated his turret. The turret jammed at an angle to the fuselage. The gunner, Pat Brophy, managed to pry the sliding doors open wide enough to reach into the rear fuselage and grab his parachute pack. Now he tried to hand-crank the turret around to a ninety-degree position, which would enable him to roll out backwards. But the mechanism broke. He would go down with the kite like countless gunners before him. The only hope was that the bombs might go off and blow him to bits. It was preferable to being burned to death. Meanwhile, the mid-upper gunner, Andy Mynarski ("a quiet, cheery guy," remembers Jim Kelly), had extricated himself from his turret and had made his way aft along the fuselage, by now a nightmare of smoke and flame. He opened the main door on the starboard side near the tail unit to make good his escape. An instant before jumping, he happened to glance back – and glimpsed Brophy in the rear turret. Did Mynarski fight a fierce little battle within himself, a tug-of-war between self-preservation and the desire to help a crew-mate in trouble? When a fully loaded Lancaster is on fire, time is in desperately short supply. Mynarski could have jumped. But he didn't. He left the open doorway and struggled back along the narrow aft-fuselage. Fingers of flame clutched at him. Mynarski's flying suit started to burn. He beat out the flames. They sprang up again. Ignoring them, he took the axe from its stowage and attacked the stubborn doors of Brophy's rear turret. In the shuddering, swaying, claustrophic metal tube, there was hardly room to move let alone swing an axe. But Mynarski kept at it, smashing at the stubborn doors as smoke and fire swirled around him. The doors gave a little, but not enough. Furiously he wielded the axe again and again. It was hopeless. Brophy knew that Mynarski had done all he could. He gestured for him to jump while there was still time. Mynarski continued to attack the doors but finally he accepted defeat. Eyes glued on Brophy, he backed away, his flying suit and parachute pack burning. But even now he didn't jump. With magnificent contempt for the flames and smoke, he dragged himself to attention and saluted Brophy. Then at last he leapt from the aircraft, vanishing into the hostile darkness. Trapped in the rear turret, Brophy could do little but await death. It wouldn't take long, he knew. The kite was low when it was hit, so it would dive in...

The din of bombs exploding woke him. He found himself lying in a French field. Somehow, by a shuffling of impossible odds, he had survived the crash of the burning Lancaster with its load of bombs; it had hit the ground on a relatively even keel. The impact had torn the rear turret free of the fuselage and had ripped the turret doors off so that he had tumbled out onto the grass. Incredulous, he got to his feet. He appeared to be uninjured – except for the loss of his hair, which fell out as he tugged off his helmet. He had no right to be alive. But he was. And so was the rest of the crew; except for the gallant mid-upper gunner, Andy Mynarski. Resistance workers had seen his descent, his parachute trailing fire. Mynarski fell into a swamp. Eager hands quickly pulled him out, but the young man died of his terrible burns. When Brophy met up with other members of the crew he was able to relate the story of the gunner's self-sacrifice. In October 1946 Andrew Charles Mynarski of Winnipeg, Manitoba, was posthumously awarded the Victoria Cross, the only VC ever won by a member of 6 Group.

In the immediate post-D-Day period, the bombing of the enemy's synthetic oil industry began to gather momentum. The USAAF had initiated the campaign in May; now Eisenhower ordered Bomber Command's participation. Many of the Allied leaders felt that this campaign was the key to victory, that concentrated bombing of the enemy's facilities could bring his war machine to a complete standstill. But, as far as Harris was concerned, oil was just the latest in the "panacea parade"; predictably, he maintained that Bomber Command should continue and intensify its area-bombing campaign. Supreme Headquarters, Allied Expeditionary Force (SHAEF) didn't agree. And so, on June 16/17, 6 Group despatched one hundred bombers to attack Sterkrade, part of a force of 321 aircraft sent to destroy the synthetic oil plant in this Ruhr town. The weather was poor; thick cloud covered the target. When the Pathfinders dropped their markers, they vanished. For the Main Force it was a question of bombing "on the glows" in the clouds.

The raid did some damage to the facility but proved to be extremely costly to Bomber Command. German night fighters intercepted the bombers as they turned for home, shooting down twenty-one. (A Ju 88 night fighter fell to the gunners of a Halifax of 432 Squadron commanded by Pilot Officer R.F. Anthony; another went down before the defensive fire of a 408 Squadron Lancaster II flown by Pilot Officer W.J. McIntyre.) Flak

First of many: In August 1943, Victory Aircraft workers swarm around the first Canadian-built Lancaster at Malton, Ontario. The aircraft, named the *Ruhr Express*, went on to serve with 419 Squadron before coming to an untimely end in January 1945. (City of Toronto Archives/SC266-86576)

First crew: The Canadian airmen who flew the *Ruhr Express* from Malton to the U.K., with a lengthy stop-over in Quebec. At left, S/L Reg Lane, the skipper; in the doorway, F/S R.K. Burgar, the mid-upper gunner, and Bambi. (DND/PL 19696)

Ashes to ashes: All that was left of the *Ruhr Express* after a collision with a piece of construction equipment had set off an uncontrollable blaze. The crew escaped unhurt. (DND/UK 18259)

Farm hand: On several 6 Group bases, thriving farms helped augment the food supply. (DND/PL 19170)

Convertible: Transportation was a perennial problem for 6 Group personnel. Here, aircrew of 431 Squadron attempt to fashion a makeshift roof for an elderly auto. Left to right, F/O George Kercher, WO Jack Dempsey, F/S Cal McInroy, P/O Al Mills. (DND/UK 14350)

Sports-minded: Canadian airmen organized sports activities whenever possible. At a 6 Group station, a Halifax bomber taxies past an impromptu baseball game. (DND/PL 28521)

WD domesticity: Many members of the RCAF Women's Division served in 6 Group. At the Group's HQ, "Castle Dismal," several WDs make themselves as comfortable as possible in their austere quarters. (DND/PL 26754)

The Legendary Lecomte: W/C Joe Lecomte, highly regarded CO of 425 and later 415 Squadron. Lecomte was one of 6 Group's finest leaders. (DND/UK8867)

Arms and the man: Joe Hartshorn, an American pilot with 419 Squadron, always carried a pistol on ops. Over Duisberg, he had to draw it to spur a reluctant crew member to action. (DND/UK13173)

Peripatetic padre: A familiar sight to all those who served with 419 and 428 Squadrons–Father J. Philip Lardie, the popular padre at Middleton St. George on his first BSA motor-bike. Father Lardie flew on two ops to learn at first hand what his "parishioners" experienced in combat. (Lardie collection)

The Berlin kid: Roger Coulombe of 426 Squadron had an alarmingly eventful operational tour which almost precisely coincided with the duration of the Battle of Berlin. Surprisingly, Coulombe survived, later receiving a watch for having dropped more bombs on the German capital than any other pilot. (Coulombe collection)

Sole survivor: P/O Dick Garrity, seated second from right, was the navigator of a 431 Squadron Halifax crew commanded by P/O George Johnson, standing next to Garrity. The crew returned safely from a sortie to Berlin in January 1944 and are seen during debriefing. On the night of June 16/17, however, flak downed their aircraft. Garrity was the only survivor. He evaded the Germans for nearly three months, aided by many extraordinarily brave civilians in occupied Europe. (DND/PL26434)

Evaders: Bill Gerard's crew at OTU. Back row, left to right, Dave Weib, bomb-aimer, Bill Gerard, pilot, Bill Lastuk, navigator. Front row, Dave McInnes, wireless operator, and Doug Sam, rear gunner. When their aircraft was shot down, all of them, plus P/O K. Beeley, flight engineer, avoided the Germans and returned to England. The mid-upper gunner, T.A. Rogers, was the only casualty. (Sam collection)

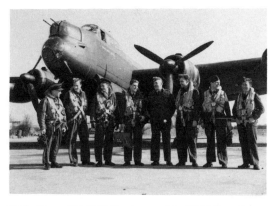

End of tour: W/C Bill Swetman, CO of 426 Squadron, fourth from left, with his crew and, fourth from right, the AOC of 6 Group, McEwen. Swetman's Hercules-powered Lancaster II is seen in the background. (DND/UK9426)

Gallantry on the ground: "Black Mike" McEwen congratulates 425 Squadron personnel for their part in saving the aircrew of a Halifax that crashed at Tholthorpe in June 1944. Left to right, McEwen, F/S J.R.M. St. Germain, LAC M.M. McKenzie, and Cpl. M. Marquet. St. Germain and Marquet won the George Medal. The station commander, A/C A.D. Ross, was badly injured in the incident. He won the George Cross. (DND/UK 16328)

The gunner gonged: Lucien Thomas, an American air gunner with the RCAF, won the DFM during his tour with 405 Squadron. Later he flew several hundred ops with the U.S. Air Force in World War II and Korea. (Thomas collection)

Medal winners: The flight engineer and two air gunners of a 429 Squadron Halifax succeeded in flying the aircraft back to England after their skipper received fatal wounds in an attack on Achères, June 7/8, 1944. Left to right, Sgt. John Mangione, mid-upper gunner, Sgt. Gilbert Steere, flight engineer (RAF), F/S Gordon Ritchie, rear gunner. Steere won the CGM, the two gunners the DFM. (DND/UK 12647)

Hero: Andrew C. Mynarski, 6 Group's sole Victoria Cross winner. Mid-upper gunner on a 419 Squadron Lancaster, the 27-year-old Mynarski lost his life attempting to save the crew's rear gunner from the blazing aircraft. (DND/PL38261)

Home at last: One of the first Lancasters built by Victory Aircraft, KB739 of 428 Squadron survived 56 operational sorties. Here, at Dartmouth, N.S., on June 8, 1945, she poses for the photographer with the crew that flew her home. From left, Les Powell, PR officer, Gord Claire, flight engineer, Doug Miller, bomb-aimer, Cliff Pratt, pilot, Jim Gunn, navigator, Hal Baldock, radar technician, Archie Martin, mid-upper gunner, Ted Dykes, rear gunner, W.A. "Shoes" Magee, wireless operator. (RCAF/PL36550, courtesy Jim Gunn)

Aftermath: Three years after the war, a photographer spotted the remains of KB739 in an Edmonton scrapyard. Minus engines and instruments, she was little more than a hulk, but the proud record of 56 ops still adorned her nose. Shortly after George F. Marks took this picture, KB739 became scrap metal. Today only one Lancaster of airworthy condition exists in Canada, at the Canadian Warplane Heritage Museum in Mount Hope, Ontario. (George F. Marks)

accounted for ten more. Twelve of 6 Group's aircraft were numbered among the casualties, four from 432 Squadron alone. One of the casualties that night was a Halifax of 434 Squadron commanded by Flying Officer F.J. Haldenby. A Ju 88 attacked the bomber close to the target and knocked out one engine, setting the wing on fire. "The aircraft went into a shallow dive and I tried to feather the engine but it ran away," Haldenby later reported. "I then ordered the crew to bale out." The navigator escaped through the front floor hatch. Then the enemy attacked again, killing the flight engineer. The Halifax snapped into a spin. Haldenby was pinned to his seat by the merciless centrifugal force. The blazing wing broke away: "I managed to crawl out of the top hatch. I saw four other chutes in the air." Haldenby made a successful descent and was captured.[3]

Flak smashed into a Halifax of 431 Squadron commanded by Pilot Officer George Johnson. The navigator, Flying Officer Dick Garrity, recalls a "dull-sounding thud." The aircraft caught fire and Johnson gave the bale-out order. "As navigator, I held at that moment an enviable position," Garrity remarks, "for I sat over the escape hatch." He went first, falling through several layers of cloud. His parachute opened perfectly. He remembers the bitter cold: minus thirty degrees Celsius. "As I drifted downward ... I had time to formulate ideas about escaping. I would travel south and east and as it was now fifteen minutes after midnight, I would try to get as far as possible before daylight." Garrity landed safely in a ploughed field. Without delay he set off, beginning an odyssey that would take him well over two months and that would bring him into contact with a succession of remarkable, courageous citizens of Holland, Belgium, and France. Garrity's experiences, while extraordinary, were in some ways typical of the more than three thousand Allied airmen who succeeded in evading the Germans after being shot down. Every one of them recalls with the deepest admiration and affection the members of the Resistance and the uncounted ordinary citizens who had nothing to gain and everything to lose by helping them. Few ever hesitated.

Garrity was sure he had landed in Holland, so he was among friends, a cheering thought. He made good headway at first. Then it began to rain and in the darkness he stumbled into a small river. Soaked, he decided to seek shelter, eventually finding a barn on the outskirts of a village. He slept as well as he could on a pile of faggots. At seven, a boy passed on a bicycle; shortly afterwards, an elderly lady came to the barn to feed her chickens. Garrity took a deep breath and clambered down the wooden ladder. The lady glanced up, displaying commendable self-control as the young, uniformed foreigner emerged from her loft. The two couldn't communicate with one another. A Quebecer, Garrity could speak fair French but no Dutch. It didn't matter; the lady, Gertrudis Schreurs, understood the situation at once and had no hesitation in taking him to her house nearby and giving him a cheese sandwich and a glass of milk. Her husband, Henk, appeared and "he greeted me with a torrent of words," Garrity writes. "A telephone call was made and I waited with some apprehension. Shortly afterwards a young man about my own age, whose name was J. Nijs, entered." Nijs spoke English and assured Garrity that he was a loyal Hollander and would help. Later, he returned with his sister; the two of them guided Garrity to the home of a music teacher, Peter Schmitzeler, and his wife, Martha. The Schmitzelers soon found civilian clothes for Garrity, after which the head of the local Underground arrived to interrogate the Canadian airman. This was a vital step as far as the Dutch were concerned, for the Germans often attempted to infiltrate escape routes with agents pretending to be downed Allied airmen. After Garrity answered the man's questions, he learnt to his dismay and sorrow that he was the sole survivor of the Halifax's crew. The aircraft had apparently exploded moments after he jumped.

A local priest and a policeman, J. Evers, arrived. Evers took Garrity to the next staging point, a large private estate owned by relatives of the late Professor DuBois, the anthropologist of Java Ape Man fame. The professor's daughter, Mrs. E. Hooijer, lived in the main house; nearby was a small caretaker's cottage. Here Garrity met eight more Allied airmen. Six were USAAF, two were RAF who had been shot down over Düsseldorf. The airmen's hostess said their stay at the estate would be brief, but a promised escort failed to appear; the escape line had been broken by the Germans, the airmen learned. They had to be patient. It wasn't easy. Two of the Americans had been on the run for several months; at times tempers became frayed. Food was sparse. The Americans, unaccustomed to the privations of European rationing, seemed to have trouble comprehending what sacrifices the Dutch people had to make in order to find food to feed them. But in comparison with most evaders, Garrity recalls, the airmen were living like kings: "We had a large estate to move about in and there was a lake if one wished to go swimming and fishing. While we caught only minnows, it was a great way to pass an afternoon. Mrs. Hooijer had quite a library and there was no shortage of reading material."

Two weeks after arriving at the estate, Garrity and his companions (now including a French civilian who had escaped from a prison at Düsseldorf) began a strange journey of short, nerve-racking stages by foot, car and tram and train, each under the control of a different individual or group. Six Dutchmen came to escort them on a night hike which ended at a farmhouse near the village of Kelpen. In the morning Garrity met his hosts, Mr. and Mrs. Mooren, a gallant middle-aged couple who permitted the evaders and their French companion to hide in their hen house – despite the fact that they had half a dozen German soldiers from the local flak unit billeted in their home! The following afternoon the journey was resumed, by car, a 1937 Chevrolet that the Germans, with uncharacterisitic generosity, had permitted the villagers to retain for what were described as "official" uses – although it's certain they never intended it to be used to assist Allied airmen. The plan was to cross the Willems Canal by daylight, boldly, under the eyes of the German guards. The Dutchman in charge of this sector of the escape line, Henk Geerdink, carried an automatic pistol and drew it as the car neared the canal. Fortunately the weapon wasn't needed. The guard recognized the car and let it pass. At eleven that night, two new guides appeared to escort the airmen to a rendezvous. They reached the spot in good order but did not find the promised contact. The guides instructed Garrity and his companions to hide again, this time in a ditch. It was a tense wait with German guards nearby.

Not until 4:00 a.m. did the escorts reappear. What was left of the night was spent in a haystack. Then the airmen resumed their journey, now escorted by four men armed with rifles. After hiding in another ditch to evade the police, the march soon resumed, with Liège the objective. The airmen had been organized into two groups. Garrity, the two RAF men, and two Americans, Bob and

Leo, formed the first group to head out. First came a five-kilometre hike, then a journey on a streetcar. Two young female Resistance workers, Alphonsine Vliexs and Josephine Finneke, took command. They demanded to see the airmen's forged identification cards. When Garrity handed his to one girl, she shook her head in exasperation and rubbed it on the dirty floor, pointing out that it was supposed to be several years old. Such errors could lead to disaster! Chastened, the evaders followed their seasoned young guides aboard the streetcar.

"I had never seen a more dilapidated conveyance," declares Garrity. Most of the passengers were factory workers but there were also Germans in evidence. Garrity held his breath as the ancient tram clattered across the Albert Canal. He and the others completed the balance of the journey into Liège by foot to avoid a Gestapo control point. Liège, Garrity soon discovered, was a garrison town teeming with German troops. To his surprise, he found ice cream on sale there; the confection had been unavailable in England since soon after the declaration of war.

Enter Marie. She was to earn the everlasting gratitude and admiration of the airmen. She embodied all the best qualities of the Resistance workers. Her husband was in a concentration camp; she had been tortured by the Gestapo who had tightened a type of mask over her face, breaking her jaw and all her teeth on one side. This savage treatment failed utterly to discourage her from her illegal activities, serving only to stiffen her determination to fight the Germans in every way she could. She took the airmen on another streetcar ride, a harrowing journey with the car full of Germans, none of whom evinced the slightest interest in Garrity or the others. Arriving safely at the railway station, the evaders caught a train to Agimont, the last stop in Belgium before the French border. They spent the night in a small *pension* in Agimont, then set off for the border. In France, another agent was waiting, they were told. Then came the bad news: the Gestapo had broken the escape line and had arrested the airmen's contact. Marie led the evaders to a local café. There, the proprietor's daughter, Rollande, and her friend Elianne Jacques told Marie of a smuggling trail across the border. They suggested following this trail to the village of Foiche in France where Marie could contact the local priest; he could be trusted, they said.

The journey across the border into France went easily. With mounting confidence, Marie knocked on the door of the first farm house and asked where the priest lived. She was told that he had been arrested and sent to a concentration camp; a priest from a nearby town now served the village but he came on Sundays only. Marie then explained to the startled farmer that she had five Allied airmen in tow. Somewhat reluctantly, the farmer agreed to take the group in for the night. Understandably nervous, the farmer gave them a meal. But before they had finished eating, Elianne Jacques burst into the house. She had followed them along the smugglers' trail to tell them that the Germans were in hot pursuit!

Garrity recalls that the news left the farmer "all but hysterical." Remarkably, in spite of his very natural fears, he let the party stay another night in one of his barns. The following day a second farmer made an appearance and took Garrity and the RAF airmen home for dinner. A pleasant interlude, but short-lived. German patrols appeared. The airmen had to escape from the barn and beat a hasty retreat back across the border into Belgium.

"Elianne led us to a field behind her home," Garrity recalls, "where they had built a small shelter in which to take cover in the event of bombing. We were unable to use it as water had seeped in, so we made ourselves comfortable in the midst of a small growth of bushes."

They spent five days there; every afternoon, Elianne came to bring food and visit the airmen. It was a relaxing time – except for Elianne's alarm when she heard Garrity and the Americans saying "yeah"; to her it sounded like the German "ja." Fortunately Garrity's French was equal to the occasion and he managed to convince her that it was simply a North Americanism. On the evening of July 26, Elianne led the airmen through fields and woods to a new hiding place.

"I shall always remember how Elianne looked that evening," Garrity writes. "Barely five feet tall and just brimming with determination and energy, she wore a dark cape to cover her white blouse and skirt." The airmen's admiration for the intrepid Elianne intensified the longer they were in her company. Daily she risked everything to aid these total strangers. "We would have followed her anywhere," Garrity writes.

The airmen's new host was Ernest Dambly, a prosperous Agimont farmer. He told the party to settle down in a small wood for the night; he would be back in the morning with food. "What a night it was! Not just rain but a severe thunderstorm!" recalls Garrity. The next morning, the airmen found slightly more congenial quarters in one of Dambly's barns. They stayed there for several days, emerging in fine weather to pass the time in the nearby estate of the Count de Paris, Pretender to the Crown of France, a magnificent establishment and a pleasant change from the barn. One day they had a visitor: Bill, a member of *L'Armée Blanche*, the Belgian equivalent of the *Maquis*. Would the airmen like to join the organization? The airmen declined the offer. Disappointed, Bill took his leave. On the evening of July 31, Elianne returned. She had become alarmed about the number of people who had learned about the Allied airmen; a new hiding place must be found at once! Garrity and Jim Firth, one of the RAF men, set off with her, following a maze of tiny trails through the hills until they came face to face with Bill once more, now accompanied by a young blond lad. Then it was time to say goodbye to Elianne. "I worshipped her as a saviour," writes Garrity, "a girl of undaunted courage, determination and patriotism. She had encountered us by chance and after a few minutes of conversation had committed herself, without regard for the risks involved, to our well-being."

They trekked north, first on country roads, then on mountain trails. The going got tougher for Garrity and Jim; their shoes began to disintegrate, the soles flapping as they trudged on. Soon their feet were a mass of blisters and cuts. But the journey had to continue. "Darkness fell as we began a treacherous and exhausting climb up the mountainside," Garrity writes. "Finally, limping and gasping for breath, we reached a grass-covered plateau." There, two men met them and took them to a house in a village where a meal was waiting. But as soon as they had eaten, the airmen had to continue their journey. Two new guides took them for another hike through the darkened countryside until, at two in the morning, they reached the village of Onhaye where they met Victor-Jules Hayot, the local schoolmaster. He was a genial man of about forty who made the airmen something to eat and showed them to their room. "That night Jim and I slept in a bed with sheets and blankets – what supreme luxury! With such comforts, we slept until noon . . . "

Later that day they met Hayot's wife, his son and two daughters. This warm and amiable family made the airmen feel at home. But the grim realities of the Occupation kept intruding. At midnight, Hayot slipped a pistol in his coat pocket, kissed his wife goodbye, and beckoned to the airmen to follow. The three of them made their cautious way through the silent village, once hiding in a doorway until a German patrol passed. Then they set off again, striking out across the country, through several hamlets until they met three men, two of them armed, the third a stocky man wearing shorts who saluted them with a clenched fist. He was Victor Willemart, Commandant of the local *L'Armée Blanche*, one of the legendary figures of the Resistance, leader of a force of some four hundred men. His headquarters was a small farm with a number of adjoining buildings. There, Garrity made the acquaintance of an American, a radio operator. The American was overjoyed to learn that Garrity spoke French. He had been in the place for several weeks and had had a difficult time communicating with his hosts. When Garrity and Jim set off with yet another escort for the village of Flavion, the radio man stayed with the Willemart organization to operate their set.

Gustave and Claire Petit were the evaders' new hosts, both utterly fearless freedom fighters. Late in the evening a dark, slim woman named Jeanne Prumont arrived. She was the housekeeper of the nearby Château Flavion. It would be the airmen's home for the next few weeks. The large, thirty-room house was owned by Camille Closen, a businessman who greeted the airmen warmly and wanted to hear all about their adventures as they downed several glasses of his excellent cognac. Then it was off to bed in the small room that had been prepared for them.

Life in the château was tranquil but tedious. About a week after their arrival, the airmen were joined by Taffy, the second RAF man. "Jeanne had scrounged about and now presented us with fresh clothes. We each had three shirts, two pairs of pants and a good pair of shoes or boots. Being six foot three tall, my long legs presented a challenge to a community where no one exceeded five foot eight. Jeanne ingeniously solved the problem by turning my pants into plus fours and outfitting me with long stockings. I cut quite a figure," Garrity recalls, "and would be long remembered as *le golfer.*"

The idyll was rudely interrupted on the afternoon of August 11. A car arrived at the château carrying a civilian from the Gestapo. Fortunately the airmen and their hosts had established emergency procedures. Everyone knew what to do. Garrity and the others hurried upstairs to the laundry room, which contained a fifteen-foot-long reservoir made of galvanized iron with boards on top, some of which had been loosened for just such an emergency. The airmen hopped in, crouching in the chilly water for about fifteen minutes until Jeanne signalled the all-clear. The German had just been asking directions, she said.

A few days later, while the airmen were eating breakfast, a platoon of German troops arrived. Once again it was into the reservoir, to huddle and shiver while the jackboots thudded about downstairs. At last Jeanne arrived to announce that the Germans had departed. Relieved, the airmen clambered out of their damp hiding place – only to hop back again when someone yelled that the Germans had returned. "Stalag, here I come," was the thought that kept thumping through Garrity's brain as he crouched in the tank, waiting. Eventually the Germans left. But Jeanne had unwelcome news: the Germans had been inspecting the château with a view to billeting troops there. It seemed prudent to abandon the place without delay. The ever-resourceful Jeanne then proposed that the airmen move into an empty house that she and her husband owned in the village. It was a tiny place with few amenities but it provided a secure haven for a stay which, though short, had its exciting moments.

For a start, a German regiment arrived and took over the Villa Rose just a thousand yards up the road. Overnight the village had become a garrison town. Every street crawled with field-grey uniforms. To make matters worse, Jeanne's house opened directly onto the street; the airmen had to keep their voices to a whisper in case they were overheard by the Germans who kept striding by only a few feet away. But on the morning of September 1, Jeanne came to them with exciting news: The *Boche* had begun to leave! Delighted, the airmen returned to the château. Their joy was short-lived. At two o'clock in the morning Jeanne burst into their bedroom. The Germans had returned! There was no time to go to the laundry room. Pausing only to throw the covers over their beds, the airmen hastened to Monsieur Closen's quarters where they hid, hardly daring to move. They could do nothing but listen to the Germans as they stomped about the place in their jack-boots, every footfall sounding like a blow from a battering-ram. How long before their fragile sanctuary fell apart about their ears?

"We were living at German Regimental Headquarters, right in their bloody midst!" Garrity recalls. Despite the presence of these unwelcome guests, Monsieur Closen maintained a remarkable *sang-froid*. He told the airmen that the regiment was encamped in the grounds; the Colonel and his officers were in the château. It was vital that the airmen remain in his room; Jeanne would bring food whenever she could. If everyone kept their heads, the crisis would be survived, he maintained. His parting shot was to tell the airmen to stay away from the windows. "We had to creep about on all fours like caged animals," Garrity writes. "Whenever the officers came up the centre stairway we of course heard the tramp of their boots along the hallway but could not be sure if they were walking toward our room or going the other way to their own quarters." Constantly on edge, the airmen agreed that if the Germans entered the room the place to hide would be the two large wardrobes that stood like sentinels against one wall. Taffy and Jim managed to squeeze in one; Garrity eventually succeeded in folding himself into the other. Before long the plan was put to the test. "One afternoon Jeanne burst in to warn us that the Boche were making a security check and entering all rooms. Without hesitation, we scrambled into the wardrobes and with hearts pounding and imaginations running wild, we waited as Jeanne escorted a Jerry in, and we heard him stomp about, comment about how big and attractive a suite it was – and he was gone. But the tense atmosphere began to take its toll. We were now in a constant state of anxiety – tense and irritable – jumping at every unexpected sound. We were cut off from our cherished social visits and desperate for news about the advancing Americans."

A few days later, the airmen had another worry: Allied fighters and bombers began harassing the German forces in the area. Damn them! If the German bivouac was spotted, it would undoubtedly be shot up. Perhaps bombed. How ironic to get the chop at the hands of Allied airmen!

But it never came to that. And on the following Sunday it was all over. The Germans left. All in a matter of fifteen minutes. It was as if they had abruptly dematerialized. After four years of their overwhelming presence, the village was finally, gloriously free. The next day American tanks lumbered into the village. "The reception given the Americans was heart-rending," Garrity remarks, "and tears of joy and happiness were to be seen on most faces. 'What kept you so long, Yank,' I asked. 'Say, you speak good English,' was the surprised reply."

The airmen were treated like conquering heroes. "We were more important even than the Americans," Garrity comments, "for we were a symbol of their resistance – their refusal to bow down to defeat by the hated Boche."

After a tearful and emotional farewell to their fearless hosts, the airmen clambered aboard trucks and were whisked off to corps HQ where the friendly Americans fitted them out with U.S. Army uniforms. Later they made their way to a grass strip and flew back to England on a C-47. It had taken Garrity eighty-two days to return from Sterkrade.[4]

On the same night as the raid on Sterkrade, Bomber Command mounted an attack in the Sautrecourt area which marked the beginning of a new phase in the air war. Some four hundred aircraft participated. The Canadian Group despatched 102 bombers. They all returned safely. Their targets: flying-bomb sites.

Several days earlier, on June 12, the first of Hitler's much-vaunted "V" weapons fell on London. The V-1, soon to be universally known and loathed as the "doodlebug" or "buzz-bomb," was a flying bomb, gyroscopically guided and powered by a pulse jet engine. Not until June 22 did British Home Secretary Herbert Morrison admit to the existence of the pilotless weapons; he provided fellow-citizens with the following helpful hints: "When the engine stops and the light at the end of the machine is seen to go out, it may mean that an explosion will soon follow, perhaps in five to fifteen seconds."[5] Soon the doodlebugs became commonplace, nasty, dangerous contraptions, but not the war-winners that Hitler had counted on. Londoners, and citizens of other towns and cities, learned to live with them as they had learned to live with all the other trials and tribulations of the war. Everyone would look up the moment they heard the distinctive throbbing sound. *Keep going*, was the fervent wish of those in the immediate vicinity. But if it spluttered and stopped, there was a scrambling for cover, any sort of cover, for every buzz-bomb packed a fearful wallop with a ton of high explosive in its cigar-shaped body.

Some ops against the flying-bomb sites were flown at night, others became 6 Group's first major daylight operations, with fighter escorts to protect the bombers against any *Luftwaffe* day fighters that might put in an appearance. Recognizing that Bomber Command crews had never been trained to fly in formation, HQ instructed them to operate "in as compact and cohesive a column as practicable. It should be noted," asserted the order of July 9, "that it is easier for the supporting fighters to cover a broad and reasonably short column of bombers than to cover a proportionately long one." For the most part, 6 Group's sorties against the flying-bomb sites were relatively uneventful, with very little to be seen on the ground and not much opposition to be faced. Many were flown without any casualties. But there were exceptions. The June 21 daylight attack on the sites at St-Martin, for example, cost seven of the 105 aircraft from 6 Group.

Unfamiliar with daylight ops, the airmen of 6 Group found them full of strange and sometimes distressing sights. John McQuiston of 415 Squadron recalls an incident from a daylight operation in which no enemy aircraft were involved. En route for home, he flew close to a Halifax with the identity letter R-Roger:

> The squadron letters were not familiar to me, so I supposed that she was from an RAF outfit. As we flew northward, I stole the odd glance at our companion to see that a safe separation was being maintained. As I watched, I saw a light flare up in the mid-upper gun turret. Not a large flame but about what one would expect from a struck match. An instant later there was a colossal explosion, and a huge, dirty, black and brown boiling mass blotted out R-Roger. I could still see the plastic nose and the rudders in place and intact, but only for an instant before a

bright red glow suffused the pall from which the pitiful fragments fluttered down. In literally one second, a powerful four-
engined bomber flown by seven brave lads had been reduced to a
shower of charred debris. The enormity of what I had seen was
slow to sink in, for I had trouble believing my eyes ... I was
convinced that R-Roger was destroyed by fumes ignited when
the gunner lit a cigarette.[6]

On the night of June 26/27, a raid on the flying-bomb sites at
Forêt d'Eawy took place with 106 aircraft from the Canadian
Bomber Group taking part. "Successful attack," stated the ORB.
The Canadians had suffered no casualties. But when 420 and 425
Squadrons returned to their base at Tholthorpe, Yorkshire, there
occurred one of those dramas which rated no headlines in the
newspapers but which highlighted the dangers faced daily by the
Group's ground crews. The base commander, Air Commodore
A.D. Ross, was walking from the control tower to the interroga-
tion room when A-Apple of 425 Squadron landed on three engines
and collided with another Halifax, U-Uncle. Ross hurried to the
scene and helped Corporal M. Marquet to extricate the injured
pilot of A-Apple, Sergeant M.J.P. Lavoie, with the assistance of
Flight Sergeant J.R.M. St. Germain, a bomb-aimer who had just
landed, and two ground crew, LACs M.M. McKenzie and R.R.
Wolfe. They had no sooner dragged Lavoie clear of the wreck,
when ten 500-pound bombs exploded, hurling the rescuers to the
ground. As the din and debris subsided, a cry could be heard from
the rear turret of A-Apple which was by now blazing furiously.
Ignoring the very real possibility of the wrecked aircraft blowing
up, Ross, St. Germain, McKenzie, and Wolfe smashed a hole in
the turret to pull the gunner free. But another bomb went off.
Shrapnel hit Ross in the right arm and virtually severed his hand.
In spite of the injury, he walked quietly to an ambulance which
took him to Sick Quarters where doctors later amputated his
hand. McKenzie and Wolfe were also injured but not seriously.
Ross was awarded the George Cross, St. Germain and Marquet
the George Medal; McKenzie and Wolfe received the British
Empire Medal.

The last op of the month, on the night of June 28/29, was an
attack by one hundred bombers of 6 Group on the railway yards at

Metz. The crews found clear conditions over the target and had no trouble identifying the yards. But seven 6 Group aircraft were lost, all shot down by fighters. Two fighters attacked the Halifax flown by Flying Officer Eric Brown of 424 Squadron. The first set a wing on fire. The second sent a cannon shell slicing through Brown's leg and blowing the instrument panel to pieces. "Woke up at the controls," Brown later reported, "and couldn't keep rudder control because my foot was off." He looked around and saw no one left in the aircraft. As rapidly as possible, he baled out, hitting a gun turret and the tail unit, knocking himself unconscious. He came to when his parachute opened. "The pilot was splendid," reported Flying Officer H.R. Weller, the navigator. Warrant Officer H.J. Branch, the rear gunner, agreed: "The pilot stayed at the controls so long that he had to get out of the escape hatch and was hit by machine guns. I thought the pilot did a splendid job [and] deserves some award."[7]

Two more 6 Group squadrons, 427 and 432, also lost aircraft, although Halifaxes from 433 Squadron scored several victories. One 433 Squadron aircraft, C-Charlie, commanded by Warrant Officer H.G. McVeigh, survived four attacks by fighters. McVeigh successfully evaded them all – until his Halifax sustained hits in the tail unit and wing. The damage was serious: starboard fin and rudder shot away, starboard elevator and wing badly damaged. C-Charlie snapped into a spin at thirteen thousand feet. McVeigh ordered his crew to bale out. Two of them escaped from the violently revolving bomber. Then McVeigh managed to regain control. The crippled Halifax had plunged seven thousand feet. McVeigh set course for England only to have his port inner engine fail. The aircraft was by now virtually uncontrollable, remaining in the air only because of the pilot's exceptional skill and determination. Fighting the Halifax every foot of the way, McVeigh succeeded in getting across the Channel. The landing presented problems; only relatively high speed kept the Halifax aloft. Any reduction in speed resulted in an immediate dropping of the starboard wing. A standard approach would be fatal. McVeigh chose to alight on an emergency strip with a couple of miles of runway. He touched down at more than 150 mph, bringing the battered aircraft to a halt at the end of the runway, the crew unharmed. McVeigh received a well-deserved DFC.

One of two 426 Squadron Halifaxes lost that night had Flying Officer Bill Gerard in the pilot's seat. His crew had been selected as one of the backers-up for the two Pathfinder aircraft on the operation. But Ju 88 night fighters intercepted the bombers en route to the target. Gerard's aircraft took hits in the wing which quickly became a mass of wind-beaten flame. Gerard gave the bale-out order and all the crew escaped with the exception of T.A. "Pop" Rogers, the mid-upper gunner, who had been killed in the fighter attack. Two members of the crew, Gerard himself and his rear gunner, Pilot Officer Doug Sam, landed beside an airfield near Reims, although neither was aware of the other's presence. Gerard set off without delay, heading west toward the advancing Allied armies. Sam, a Canadian of Chinese descent, gathered his parachute and found a bushy area in which to hide while he decided what to do. Early in the morning, a German observation aircraft flew low overhead. Was it looking for him and the others who had been shot down? Sam lay low for a few hours. At dusk he ventured out of his hiding place and made his cautious way to a house on the outskirts of a nearby village. He knocked on the door. A middle-aged couple opened the door – but, taking one look at his uniform, they yelped at him to go away. *Vite!* Sam hurried back to his hideout in the bushes. Questions pounded through his head. Had the couple informed on him? Should he run for it? Or wait? He waited. No one appeared. Another night passed. As dawn broke he observed half a dozen men beginning the day's work in a field two hundred yards away. It seemed to Sam that the direct approach might be the best; he stood up and walked into the field. If the workers were alarmed, they managed not to show it. They told Sam that they were fishermen from Boulogne pressed into farm work. One asked him where his parachute was. Sam showed him. The men buried it and told Sam to stay hidden. Someone would come for him, they added.

Doug Sam's skipper, Bill Gerard, had also found himself involved in farm work. After walking through the darkened countryside for three nights, he had encountered an RAF gunner limping along on an injured ankle. The airmen joined forces. Soon they encountered two French youths who took them to an abandoned flour mill. Here the airmen were interrogated by three burly men, two in their thirties, one about sixty. After a day's wait in the mill, the airmen were taken to a tiny hut in a wood near Chamuzy, some fifteen miles southwest of Reims. It would be their home for the next three weeks during which they assisted the Resistance in an attack on German communications. Five men, including Gerard, ventured out on bicycles one night and planted plastic explosives on the legs of three high-tension towers, secured one-minute acid fuses, pinched them . . . and ran. "All three towers came down," Gerard recalls, "cutting the power supply for more than three weeks. Unfortunately, seven cows were barbecued by the falling wires."

The raid set off an angry flurry of searches by the Germans. Alarmed, the Resistance leader decided to disperse the airmen. Gerard found himself billeted at a farm near Chamuzy owned by Jules Trucheon and his wife, another of the splendid couples who never hesitated to put their lives on the line to aid Allied airmen. Gerard, in civilian clothes, worked the Trucheons' fields, harvesting, while improving his French with the assistance of one of the local girls. But the business of the Resistance didn't stop. "After three or four weeks we were instructed (by radio from London) to blow up a German underground communication installation somewhere near Reims. We did this by lowering yellow plastic-type dynamite down the air vents," Gerard recalls. But the Germans had heard the saboteurs at work. They emerged from an underground door. Gerard and the others fired their Sten guns. Strobe-like flashes from the guns showed the Germans darting back inside. Then the explosives blew. Half a dozen Germans died instantly.

Gerard remembers that a few nights later, a Resistance leader and one of his hosts' sons were busy throwing tire-puncturing jacks on the road when a quartet of SS troops appeared. The saboteurs shot them. Gerard comments: "This and our underground job caused all hell to break out. The farms all around were being searched so I decided to leave . . . I made my way to a little farm near Montmirail, some thirty miles from Chamuzy." There Gerard met a girl, a member of the Resistance. She took him to another farm where he hid; it was too dangerous to go further. The Germans were retreating and not taking prisoners. Gerard stayed at this farm for six days during which the booming of artillery was almost constant; shells passed overhead in both directions. Then the Germans pulled back still further. Suddenly Gerard found himself in American territory. The nerve-pounding days of evading and engaging in guerrilla warfare were over. Later, at the home of the Resistance girl, Marcelle Pomier, he enjoyed a lively party to celebrate the liberation.

Some weeks earlier, his rear gunner, Doug Sam, had himself been contacted by the FFI. Two men appeared on bicycles. One, named Raoul, had brought civilian clothes for the gunner; Sam put them on although he retained his RCAF identity discs. Then, sitting uncomfortably on the crossbar of Raoul's bicycle, he journeyed to the man's home, gratefully consumed hot soup and bread and went to bed. He awoke to the familiar but incongruous strains of "The Beer Barrel Polka." Raoul, a boisterous type, was happily pounding out the tune on his piano. After breakfast and formal introductions to Raoul's wife and two daughters, Sam was taken to the windowless attic of a church on a quiet country road. There Sam met an RAF sergeant who had been in the place for no less than six months. The two men spent a couple of days in the attic while their names and service numbers were checked through London. Then Raoul and another man arrived at the church in an ancient "gasohol"-powered Citroën to take Sam to Epinay. There he met a distinguished-looking Frenchman who spoke excellent English. Hospitably, he produced vintage champagne and a tin of Craven "A" cigarettes. Immediately following this visit, Sam was driven to Reims and deposited at the Café-Bar de l'Univers, 65–67 rue de Courcelles. Marcel Lacour, who ran the place, had been a corporal in the Great War; like Raoul, he had a wife and two daughters. He made Sam welcome.

By this time Sam's mother in British Columbia had received word that her son was missing. The news had also made the papers at home, since Sam was the first Chinese-Canadian to appear in the casualty lists. But the authorities refused to release the fact that he was alive and well. MI9 (the British Intelligence escape organization) in London was keenly interested in Sam's Chinese heritage, convinced that he could be useful in France by pretending to be from Indo-China. It is unlikely that the irony was lost on Sam. Early in the war, he had volunteered for the air force but had been turned down. Apologetically, the RCAF recruiting officer had pointed to a long-forgotten dictum that all recruits had to be of Caucasian background. Sam had gone back to work at his father's whaling station at Rose Harbour in the Queen Charlotte Islands. Not until 1942 were the regulations altered. Sam at last donned air force blue. Now MI9 asked: Was he willing to stay in France and work with the Resistance? Sam agreed despite Marcel Lacour's gloomy prognostications; in his opinion, the Canadian's French wasn't good enough and he would never fool anyone; the Germans would see through him in no time. Undeterred, Sam went to work to brush up his high school French, study the geography of Reims and district, and become familiar with local customs. Particularly important, he learned, was the way he held his cigarettes and knives and forks. If he forgot and performed these simple, everyday actions the North American way he would immediately be spotted by the Germans. He assumed a new identity with documents provided by the Resistance.

Sam's job was to maintain a liaison between the various groups of Resistance fighters, setting up escape routes for Allied servicemen and distributing arms and other equipment dropped by RAF aircraft. It was even more hazardous work than flying on ops – and far lonelier. But Sam tackled the job and did it well. In the following months he was twice trapped in Gestapo round-ups and his forged documents scrutinized by experts. But he told his story convincingly and the Germans accepted it. Sam became involved in the ambushing of German convoys and the summary execution of German agents and collaborators. It was pitiless, the work of the Resistance. Sam was saddened to hear of the death of the boisterous Raoul. The first reports indicated that the Germans had killed him after catching him in the act of cutting down telephone wires. But Sam heard later that the Resistance had killed Raoul because he had become a security risk, talking too freely after a few drinks.

The U.S. Third Army was hard on the heels of the retreating Germans. London ordered the Resistance to do everything to hinder the enemy's withdrawal and to help maintain law and order during the transition from occupation to freedom. On September 1, Sam witnessed a curious little ceremony when a group of German officers and other ranks came into the café and solemnly shook hands with the Lacours, saying goodbye and promising to return as tourists after the war.

The next day a solitary American tank entered Reims and was directed to the Café-Bar de l'Univers. A major from Boston emerged – and was intrigued to find a Chinese-Canadian airman in charge. The Third Army would arrive in Reims in two days, the major announced. There was much to do. Roadblocks. Barricades. Trenches. Weapons had to be taken from secret caches and distributed to Resistance fighters who now proudly sported FFI arm bands. Lacour dug up his Great War pistol from the back yard. Pitted with rust, the pistol looked as if it would blow up if fired. Prudently, Sam gave Lacour a 9 mm Browning pistol.

Fighting flared up in Reims at 0700 hours on September 3, the fifth anniversary of the declaration of war on Germany. German patrols ran into blockades guarding the escape routes to the east. The crackle of gunfire rang through the streets. For Sam, it was the most hazardous phase of the war, for the French Resistance fighters tended to blaze away in all directions at once. Fortunately the fight didn't last long. At 1500 hours it was over. Trapped between the American Army and the trigger-happy Resistance, the small German force surrendered. That night Sam was the guest of honour at a dinner held at the Town Hall; he was made an Honorary Citizen of the Prefecture of Marne and presented with a silver cigarette case bearing the official coat of arms.

Sam said his farewells and headed off to London. At last he could send a telegram to his mother, telling her that he was alive and well. The news didn't surprise Sam's grandmother. A devout Anglican, she had visited the Chinese Temple in Victoria and a reading of joss sticks had convinced her that he was safe.

For his services to France, Pilot Officer Kam Len Douglas Sam was later awarded the *Croix de Guerre*.

Remarkably, the other four surviving members of Bill Gerard's crew also managed to avoid capture by the Germans: Pilot Officer K. Beeley, the flight engineer; Flight Sergeant Dave Weib, the bomb-aimer; Flying Officer Bill Lastuk, the navigator; and Flight Sergeant Dave MacInnes, the wireless operator.[8]

June had been an extraordinarily busy month for 6 Group. McEwen and his staff could be well satisfied with the performance of their aircrews, who had demonstrated a greater versatility than perhaps even they knew they possessed. The majority of targets attacked by 6 Group in recent weeks had been small, many of them artfully camouflaged or concealed in woods. To hit such targets demanded professional skill and discipline of a high order, and the Canadians proved themselves equal to the task. Immediately prior to the D-Day landings, 6 Group had been called upon to bomb a heavy coastal battery. The Army later signalled: "Three of the four large guns received direct hits while the fourth had its barrel twisted by blast. This raid undoubtedly saved many lives for which the Army is very grateful."[9]

The Canadian Group had come of age. No longer was it the problem child of Bomber Command, consistently suffering the highest casualties and registering the worst early-return and the lowest serviceability rates. Indeed, in certain important respects the Group was showing the way to the rest of Bomber Command. The Canadians had long been dissatisfied with traditional take-off and landing procedures; as far back as 1942, Johnny Fauquier, then CO of 405 Squadron based at Pocklington, Yorkshire, had experimented with various methods of speeding up the process. Conventional wisdom called for an aircraft taking off to be completely clear of the runway before the next aircraft started its roll. Fauquier said no. When aircraft No. 1 was three-quarters of the way on its take-off run, aircraft No. 2 should already be rolling. But what if aircraft No. 1 had to abort or even crashed at the end of the runway? Then aircraft No. 2 would take off and swerve past the problem, was the response. In the early days of 6 Group, bombers landed at a rate of eight to twelve per hour. By mid-1944, the rate had risen to an average of one aircraft every 1.75 to two minutes. The use of tracer ammunition was another traditional feature of the night air war that the Canadians questioned. The basic idea behind tracer ammunition was sound enough; the trailing sparks provided the gunner with some means of checking where his bursts were going. But at night there were disadvantages. The Canadians felt that, on balance, the use of tracers probably did more to attract the attention of night fighters than to help destroy them. Henceforth no tracer rounds were to be found in 6 Group's aircraft.

Ops at the beginning of July were little different than those in June. The Group attacked flying-bomb installations, railway yards, road junctions, and tactical battlefield sites such as gun emplacements and troop positions. Many were difficult to find and equally difficult to hit, requiring a number of return trips, some by day, others by night. Sorties in direct support of the armies were seldom dull. Eddy Collyer flew with 425 Squadron during this period and recalls:

> The close support attacks in cooperation with the army on the ground gave us a lot of satisfaction. When we learned that a successful attack had allowed the army to advance without too many casualties, we felt that we had played a useful part in the operation. On one occasion we took part in a low-level bombing attack on enemy troops and armour in cooperation with the Canadian army, a close support effort calling for extremely accurate timing and bombing. The weather deteriorated as we neared the target, with the Master Bomber calling the aircraft lower and lower below the cloud base. We had been briefed to bomb from 5,000 feet – breaking cloud at around 2,000 feet, still descending, we finally bombed at 1,600 feet, the blast from exploding bombs giving us a very rough ride and throwing mud up into the bomb bay of our aircraft.

Frank Hamilton, a pilot with 424 Squadron, also has vivid recollections of "the amount of dust and dirt thrown up" – invisible at night but disconcertingly noticeable in daylight. During these attacks on enemy positions, 6 Group used a variety of fusings on their bombs to create different types of craters. For example, when bombing targets over which Allied armour would soon advance, instantaneous fusing was usually employed to blast shallow but broad craters. When the purpose of the bombing was to deprive the enemy of the use of a certain area of terrain, .025-second fusing was common. Its use resulted in large, deep craters.

On July 7, the Army asked for Bomber Command's assistance in neutralizing a number of fortified village strongpoints around Caen which had held up the advance of the First Canadian and the Second British Armies. The Canadian Group despatched eighty-eight bombers to join 379 aircraft from RAF groups. The raid took place in the early evening under the supervision of a Master Bomber, Wing Commander Pat Daniels of 35 Squadron.

With his assistance, the Oboe Mosquitoes marked the aiming points meticulously. In minutes, more than two thousand tons of bombs fell in concentrated patterns. "All crews enthusiastic over success of this raid," was the cheerful summation in the 6 Group ORB. The army seemed equally pleased; a signal to Bomber Command read: "Heavy bomber attack just taken place. A wonderfully impressive show and was enormously appreciated by the Army. The Army would like their appreciation and thanks sent to all crews."[10] But some soldiers complained that the raid had been *too* efficient; the bombs had virtually demolished the town, creating enormous piles of rubble which had hindered the advancing troops. All 6 Group aircraft returned safely from this operation, but an RAF Lancaster fell to flak.

This was the first of a series of attacks on the environs of Caen. On the eighteenth, 6 Group sent ninety-nine aircraft to join more than eight hundred bombers from RAF groups in a massive dawn attack, dropping more than five thousand tons of bombs on elements of two German divisions. After the first wave of bombers had bombed, the target was obliterated by smoke and dust. At that point, one of the Master Bombers on the raid, Squadron Leader E.K. Cresswell, took over control of the raid; the bombing was devastatingly accurate, wiping out several villages below the Bois de Bavent and the Colombelles steelworks. According to eyewitnesses, the attack was probably "the heaviest and most concentrated ever attempted in support of ground forces." The aircraft bombed from between five thousand and nine thousand feet. Six were lost, including two from 6 Group. One of the RCAF losses was a Halifax of 429 Squadron, LW217, which took a hit by a "friendly" bomb dropped by a higher-flying Halifax. The bomb neatly removed LW217's starboard tailplane. A photographer snapped the scene as the bomber staggered, half its tail surfaces already fluttering earthward. The shot appeared in countless newspapers, one of those "our bombers get home no matter what damage is inflicted" items that the press of the period loved so dearly. In fact, LW217 crashed in the target area. Its skipper, Flight Lieutenant G.W. Gardiner, had been holding the aircraft steady while the camera recorded his bombs hitting the ground. The mid-upper gunner, Sergeant E. McGregor, suddenly spotted bombs falling from above. He called: "Bombs! Corkscrew starboard!"

But it was too late. Before Gardiner had time to react, the bombs hit the aircraft. The bomber had been bombed. Gardiner lost all elevator control. The Halifax dropped like a stone. Gardiner ordered the crew to jump. Fortunately the aircraft plunged almost vertically without spinning. Everyone but the flight engineer escaped.[11]

Close to seven hundred bombers constituted the force sent on the third assault on the Caen area on July 30. Ninety-nine 6 Group bombers participated in this daylight operation aimed at destroying German strong points in the Amaye-sur-Seulles and Villers-Bocage area. Unfortunately, cloud moved in as the bombers approached: "Eight-tenths cloud, base down to 1,500 feet, tops 8,000 feet. Defences nil," stated the 6 Group ORB. The Master Bomber directed the force to bomb from below the clouds but only about half the bombers hit the targets. Four Lancasters failed to return from the operation; none was from 6 Group.

It was a period when the Group's losses would be nil for days on end; then the bombers would encounter accurate flak or swarms of night fighters and casualties would soar. The attack on the railway yards at Villeneuve-St-Georges on July 4/5 was typical. A force of 102 bombers from the Canadian Group encountered German night fighters near Rouen. Nine 6 Group aircraft, 8.8 per cent of the force, went down. Three of the lost aircraft came from 419 Squadron. One crew reported being attacked by a captured B-17 Flying Fortress. Pilot Officer W. R. Gibson, the rear gunner of a Lancaster commanded by Flying Officer L.W.A. Frame reported: "I saw a Fortress II on our starboard quarter at eight hundred yards ... it had a black nose and no turret. As it edged over to a position dead astern at seven hundred yards, I gave the order to corkscrew and the Fortress followed us through all combat manoeuvres." Gibson opened fire and the enemy aircraft banked away at ninety degrees and "fell away to the starboard quarter down." After eluding the Fortress, the Halifax was attacked by no less than three Ju 88s in succession and finally shot down. The crew survived.[12]

The pilot and flight engineer of a Halifax of 433 Squadron also enjoyed exceptionally good luck that night. After a fighter set the aircraft on fire, the skipper, Pilot Officer G. A. Wolstencroft, ordered the crew to bale out. The flight engineer, Sergeant Chambers, came forward with two parachute packs. But they were useless, having been damaged in the attack. He tossed them overboard. By this time the aircraft was full of smoke and fires were burning fiercely. Wolstencroft had no choice but to attempt a crash landing. He later reported: "I kept the aircraft level and flew into the ground at 130 mph, landing in a soft field with no damage to either of us." Ironically, the wireless operator, Flight Sergeant Brewer, might have survived had he stayed with the aircraft; he chose to jump with a burning parachute. He plunged to his death, the only casualty from this crew.[13]

The Group's bombers accounted for at least two German fighters: a Ju 88 shot down by Sergeant P.F. Hunt, the rear gunner on Flying Officer D.A. McNaughton's crew of 429 Squadron, and an unidentified fighter destroyed by Flight Sergeant E.A. Snider, rear gunner on Pilot Officer H.A. Kirby's crew of 424 Squadron.

The month saw a modest increase in the number of Bomber Command attacks on synthetic oil facilities. The Canadian Group participated in most of them. On the night of July 18/19, the target was the synthetic oil plant at Wesseling in the Ruhr. With the *Luftwaffe* night fighter force still a potent threat, Bomber Command's planners decided to experiment with new tactics. The plan called for the force to cross the English coast at about nine thousand feet, then drop to altitudes of between two thousand and three thousand feet over enemy territory. At briefing, many crews shook their heads in dismay. Did those dumbbells at Group know how tough it was to wrestle a fully loaded Lanc or Hally around at low level? Did they have any idea how lethal light flak could be? Did they even comprehend how tough it was to *see* anything at night?

The Main Force of 194 aircraft consisted largely of 6 Group bombers; the RAF provided only forty-one. In spite of the crews' misgivings, the new tactics worked well, apparently fooling the fighter controllers; only one aircraft was lost and that to flak over the target. Although the crews encountered the usual Ruhr haze, plus a smoke screen sent up by the defences, visibility was generally good. "Target visually identified," was the ORB comment. "Explosions seen 0113 hrs. and 0129 hrs. Oil tank exploded 0115 hrs., smoke rising to 11,000 feet." The Pathfinders marked the target accurately and, although the Master Bomber's radio transmissions were unintelligible due to jamming, the attack was successful. About a thousand bombs landed in the plant area in twenty minutes. The bombing put the facility out of action for some time. It was a memorable op for a Lancaster of 419 Squadron commanded by Hal Calder. Arthur Angus was the navigator: "We went to within thirty miles of the target at 5,000 feet and then climbed to 12,000 feet to bomb." But the Lancaster was suddenly coned. Halder escaped "by losing about 7,000 feet in seconds," Angus recalls. "I thought the aircraft was going to break in two coming out of the dive."

Even when the Germans were nowhere near, the aircrews often faced dangerous situations. At Tholthorpe, a Halifax of 425 Squadron with Flight Sergeant Paul Lacaille in the skipper's seat began its take-off run, bound for Wesseling. But the starboard outer engine lost an oil seal on the propeller. Oil spewed back on the hot engine and caught fire. It was too late to abort the take-off. As the wheels left the ground the crew feathered the offending engine and managed to extinguish the fire. The bomber, loaded to capacity, struggled to stay in the air. Only the remarkable airmanship of the pilot averted disaster. He managed to coax the aircraft up a few precious feet, then headed in the direction of the North Sea. He couldn't advise Tholthorpe of his problem; radio silence had to be maintained because the transmission would become an advance warning to the Germans that a raid had been mounted. Witnesses to the incident anticipated a crash but, after jettisoning the bombs in the sea and flying around to use up fuel, Lacaille brought the three-engined bomber in for a perfect landing.

The Canadian Group contributed forty-two bombers to the total of over six hundred attacking Kiel on the night of July 23/24, the first raid on the port city since April 1943. On the same night, one hundred aircraft from the Canadian Bomber Group attacked an oil refinery and storage facility at Donges, near St-Nazaire. Walter Miller was skipper of Halifax MZ828 of 433 Squadron which participated in the operation. The aircraft took a flak hit that caused little damage to the aircraft but injured Miller in the knee. It was not particularly painful but, on the way home, Miller was conscious of the wound and could feel his flying boot filling up with blood, a thoroughly disquieting sensation. When he landed back at Skipton-on-Swale, he examined the wound. It was a scratch with only a trickle of blood. His imagination had provided all the gruesome details!

The following night, July 24/25, forty 6 Group bombers joined over four hundred RAF aircraft to bomb Stuttgart; it was the first of two assaults on this city on successive nights. The second op saw 175 aircraft from the Canadian Group participating in a force of 550. This raid, which completely destroyed the centre of the city, cost the Canadians five aircraft. A third raid on Stuttgart took place on the night of July 28/29 but 6 Group did not participate, virtually the entire force being involved in an attack on Hamburg. The two raids were a stinging reminder of how dangerous the *Luftwaffe* night fighter arm could still be. Over Stuttgart the RAF lost thirty-nine Lancasters, 7.9 per cent of its 496 aircraft. Proportionately, 6 Group suffered an even greater loss over Hamburg with twenty-two of its 234 aircraft being shot down, 9.4 per cent of the force, the highest loss ever recorded by the Canadian Group on a single operation. The bombers had been distributed over a four-thousand-foot height band between seventeen thousand and twenty-one thousand feet over the target. The plan called for a descent to eight thousand feet at the second turning point, followed by another descent to the level of the cloud tops. At briefing, the crews had been instructed to use cloud cover if attacked. But the elements, contrary as ever, failed to cooperate. The cloud turned out to consist of thin, broken layers that provided little protection. This fact discouraged many crews from descending as rapidly as ordered. Thus they were several thousand feet above the nearest cloud cover and extremely vulnerable to attack. Unfortunately this happened to be a night of intense activity by *Luftwaffe* night fighters. The first fighters had been seen over the target and they continued to harry the homeward-bound Canadians as far as Heligoland. One 6 Group squadron, 431, lost five aircraft on the raid; 408 lost four. The raid was far from successful, the bombing being badly scattered. Wilbur "Wib" Pierce, a pilot with 433 Squadron, remembers the op well: "It was a particularly tiring raid as we had been to Stuttgart on the 25th (an eight-and-a-half-hour trip) and landed at Ford on the south coast with about twelve minutes of gasoline left – and very late to bed. We flew home the next day and then went to Hamburg the following night. Cloud cover was supposed to be available at ten to twelve thousand feet coming home. It wasn't. Those who stayed up were in trouble, those who went down to four thousand feet were better off. It was quite a trip!" Frank Hamilton of 424 Squadron lost his crew that night; he was away from the base at Skipton-on-Swale for a few days and when he returned he learned that the CO, Don Blane, had gone on the Hamburg op. He had taken Hamilton's crew. The CO's aircraft didn't return.

An RAF flight engineer, Rowland Hughes, flew on the Hamburg operation with the 432 Squadron crew of Sergeant Franco; he recalls being informed at the briefing that the raid's purpose was to break German morale. Bob Marshall was the mid-upper gunner on a Lancaster X of 428 Squadron and remembers the briefing officer telling the crews that people had started to move back into Hamburg ". . . and it was our job to move them out again." It was an eventful sortie for the Marshall crew: "We got picked up by fighters on the way home and came within a few feet of colliding with an Fw 190." The navigator and wireless operator of a 433 Squadron Halifax were astonishingly fortunate when their aircraft was hit by flak and set on fire. The outer panel of one wing broke away and the aircraft whipped into a vicious spin. Flying Officers W.A. Martineau and J.A. Robertson found themselves immobilized by centrifugal force, pinned to the floor of the revolving aircraft, unable to do anything but wait for it to hit the ground. The suicidal plunge continued. Then, with a shattering roar, the bomber blew up. Both men lost consciousness momentarily. They came to in mid-air, tumbling earthward in the darkness. They pulled their rip cords. Nothing happened. Neither man's parachute opened. Helplessly they plummeted, unable to see each other. Frantically the two airmen clawed at their parachute packs, trying to rip them open. Incredibly, both succeeded. Two sharp cracks signalled the delayed but successful opening of the parachutes. Both men survived, among the luckiest of 6 Group's airmen.[14]

Luftwaffe night fighters exhibited great determination that night. Doug Penny was the rear gunner on a 432 Squadron Halifax commanded by Squadron Leader M.W. Pettit. The Hamburg op was Penny's twenty-third. He recalls the long trip home and the gradual descent as the Halifax approached the English coast. Penny himself was beginning to relax, about to enjoy a cup of coffee from the thermos flask now that the Hally was down to four thousand feet and oxygen masks could, thankfully, be taken off. Suddenly he glimpsed a movement in the blackness. A fighter! Penny and the fighter opened fire at the same instant. The German hit the Halifax's tail unit; but Penny's fire was lethal. The fighter dived straight into the sea, its end witnessed by several crews. Penny received a DFM and was later commissioned.

Flying Officer J.D. Burns was the navigator on a 424 Squadron Halifax which took flak hits in the port wing when about ten miles from the coast on the way home. Fires broke out. "The engineer, Sergeant McAlpine, was at work at once," Burns later reported, "and got both fires under control and also assisted Flight Sergeant Mylehurst, who was wounded, from his turret. The coolness and efficiency with which Sergeant McAlpine worked are worthy of recommendation. I'd like to see him get the DFM." Ironically, when McAlpine was later questioned, he could remember nothing of the incident.[15]

In spite of a costly and disappointing raid at the end of the month, July had been further confirmation of 6 Group's newly won reputation as one of the best in Bomber Command. During June, an average of 93 per cent of the Group's aircraft had bombed their primary targets, a Bomber Command record. In July, the figure rose to 95 per cent. Among aircrew, the word was spreading that 6 Group was no longer a chop outfit. A Group report noted with obvious satisfaction: "During the past several months the change in attitude of crews arriving from OTUs for operational duties has been particularly noticeable. Aircrews are now requesting posting to the Group where heretofore the feeling existed that the chances of surviving a tour of operations was infinitely better in other Groups in the Command."[16]

During the month, the Canadian Group finally achieved its ultimate strength. The fourteenth squadron, 415, joined 6 Group after three years as a Coastal Command unit flying a remarkable variety of aircraft, starting with Beauforts and then Hampdens converted to carry torpedoes, followed by Wellingtons and Albacores. In its new role as a heavy bomber unit, 415 Squadron flew Halifax IIIs. The costly July 28/29 operation against Hamburg was 415 Squadron's baptism of fire in the bombing war.

By mid-1944, eleven of 6 Group's squadrons were equipped

with the Hercules-powered Halifax; one, 408, was about to give up its Lancaster IIs (also Hercules-powered) for Halifaxes; two, 419 and 428, both based at Middleton St. George, operated the excellent Canadian-built Lancaster Xs. Many crews preferred the later marks of the Halifax over the Lancaster because of its strength and its reputation for being the easier heavy bomber to escape from in emergencies. But the Lanc had no equal as a lifter and transporter of high explosives and incendiaries. To Harris, tonnage was all-important; if he had had his way, all his squadrons would have flown the Lancaster. It's easy to see why. The Halifax III's maximum range without overload tanks was 1,300 miles; the Lancaster could carry the same load 1,850 miles. Thus a force of Lancasters could carry a 62 per cent greater weight of bombs 1,300 miles. On longer trips, the Halifax had to be equipped with overload tanks which blanked off several bomb installation points, reducing its load by up to 33 per cent. Consider an operation involving a trip of 1,625 miles. The Halifax, with five bomb stations blanked off, could carry only 4,500 pounds of bombs. The Lancaster could do the same trip with all fifteen bomb stations clear, carrying some 11,000 pounds of bombs, or a 145 per cent greater load than the Halifax.

The Canadian Bomber Group was still operating as a support force for the Allied armies in France, still coming under the direct orders of the supreme commander, Eisenhower. Tactical sorties to the battlefields as well as attacks on flying-bomb sites, railway yards, and oil storage depots continued to be the Group's principal duties in the first days of August. Most of these were low level operations by relatively small forces. Bois de Casson, Bois d'Amont, St-Leu d'Esserent, Chantilly, Pourville, Forêt de Croc ... day after day 6 Group's aircraft set out to find these tiny pinpoints on their maps. It was demanding but not particularly dangerous work. Casualties were light. But airmen still died, sometimes far from their targets. Walter Miller, the 433 Squadron pilot who believed his life blood was filling his flying boot after an op on Donges on July 23, recalls being briefed for the Forêt de Chantilly op on August 4. He and his crew rode out to the dispersals with Flying Officer "Junior" Harrison and his crew. This was to be Harrison's first op since breaking his foot. Miller (inevitably known as "Dusty") writes: "During this truck ride he complained that he had been given aircraft G-George which was noted for being heavy on the controls and he was concerned as to how his recently mended foot would hold up. 'Junior' and I switched aircraft without advising Admin." When Miller returned from the op he encountered the adjutant who yelped, "Dusty, you're dead!" It transpired that something had gone terribly wrong with Halifax D-Dog. The aircraft, with Harrison at the controls, had crashed in the village of Skipton-on-Swale; he and Dennis Whitbread, the flight engineer, were killed, as well as one civilian.

Early in the afternoon of August 8, Bomber Command received a request from the Admiralty to lay some forty mines in the inner harbour of Brest as soon as darkness fell. The U.S. Seventh Army was closing in on Brest and it had become apparent that the Germans intended to evacuate their submarines and surface craft that night. By this stage of the war, 6 Group was widely regarded as Bomber Command's experts in Gardening. At 1400 hours the order went to Skipton-on-Swale, home of 424 and 433 Squadrons: Prepare twelve aircraft with four sea mines each. Such orders hit the stations like thunderbolts. In this case the aircraft had already been bombed-up for the night's ops. It's not hard to imagine the reaction of the armourers when informed that they were required to remove the bombs that they had spent much of the day installing and replace them with mines. As the official report put it:

Eventually, as a result of extraordinary efforts by the Armament Section at Skipton, all twelve aircraft were loaded up with four mines apiece and forty-seven mines were successfully laid in Brest harbour. (The forty-eighth mine failed to release due to the accidental cutting of an electric lead during bombing-up. The fault was discovered before take-off but there was no time to correct it.) It has since been learnt from Intelligence sources that the results of this operation were most satisfactory and contributed in a very large degree to the loss to the enemy by scuttling of a large number of naval units which would have been of the greatest use to them elsewhere.

The Admiralty and Bomber Command Headquarters expressed their satisfaction for the job having been well done on such short notice.[17]

On the night of August 12/13, 6 Group sent sixty-nine aircraft to join 310 bombers from RAF groups in an attack on Brunswick. The raid, experimental in nature, employed only H2S-equipped aircraft. The intention was to discover how well they would perform without Pathfinders to mark their target. Although the 6 Group crews seemed to feel the experiment was a success – "Good concentration of fires over large area," stated the ORB – Bomber Command was not impressed. *Luftwaffe* night fighters made it a costly night, accounting for twenty-seven bombers; five were 6 Group aircraft. The combats were fierce. Sergeant D. Hache, rear gunner in the 434 Squadron Halifax commanded by Flight Lieutenant B. Imrie, shot down an unidentified twin-engined fighter. The crew saw it crash and explode. Flight sergeants H.S. Smith and R.W. Pettigrew, gunners in the Halifax flown by Flying Officer R.C. Penrose, destroyed an Me 410. Another 410 and an Me 109 fell to the guns of Sergeants Engbrecht and Gillanders aboard the 424 Squadron Halifax commanded by Lieutenant O.J.G. Keys of the USAAF. Gillanders won the DFM. A Ju 88 attacked the Canadian-built Lancaster X commanded by Flying Officer J.A. McGregor near the target. McGregor had to contend with a fire and serious damage to his controls. He ordered his crew to bale out, then held the crippled aircraft steady while his crew escaped. When they had all gone, he attempted to follow them. Like so many pilots in similar circumstances, he found that the instant he let go of the controls, the aircraft fell away in a spin. "I was thrown to the starboard side," McGregor reported. "The aircraft stalled and spun again and I was thrown into the nose." It must have seemed to McGregor that this would be the pattern all the way to the ground. But: "At the next stall and spin I was thrown clear." He survived to become a POW.[18]

In mid-August, the Canadian Group was involved in operations against German troop positions in the Caen/Falaise area. The tragic consequences are still a source of bitter disagreement among the planners, the participants, and the surviving victims. Ever since the Normandy invasion, heavy bombers of Bomber

Command and the USAAF had been used in a tactical role, performing much the same sort of function as the immense artillery barrages of the Great War, which pulverized the enemy's positions, clearing the way for advancing troops. The Army's senior officers, all veterans of the Western Front, were ever-conscious of the necessity of avoiding the ghastly slaughters of that war. What better way than to have the heavies soften up the enemy from the air before sending a single soldier in? So far the concept had been a singular success. But Harris was never enthusiastic. He repeatedly warned the Army of the dangers of using heavy bombers for such tasks; errors were always a very real possibility – and once heavy bomber attacks had started it was usually difficult to stop or redirect them. He pointed out that his crews had never been trained for this type of work; they were accustomed to navigating by radar and radio aids at night and to dropping their bombs in large areas delineated by TIs which showed up well in the darkness. He felt that the performance of his crews on daylight ops had been remarkably good to date, *in spite of*, rather than because of, their experience and training. Although the Army expressed its willingness to accept the risks in question, Harris was still concerned; it would be all too easy for something to go catastrophically wrong.

On August 14 something did.

The Army had asked Bomber Command to bomb six targets in the Quesnay-Fontaine-le-Pin-Bons-Tassilly area. A force of 144 aircraft set off. The majority, 105, were provided by 6 Group. As Harris later pointed out:

> The circumstances of war being what they are operations such as the one under discussion are inevitably laid on ad hoc at the shortest possible notice, never allowing adequate time for any practice or even for extended discussion and instruction. On this occasion details of the operation were brought over to this Headquarters late on the evening of the 13th. On studying the proposals it became at once clear to me that the necessity to bomb the targets in succession from north to south in order to meet the timetable essentials postulated by the Army was inviting a dangerous situation if the wind, as predicted (and as it turned out to be) was northerly.[19]

Harris was particularly concerned about the possibility of smoke drifting across the target area and confusing the bomb-aimers. He refused to direct his aircraft over the enemy's lines: "I was not prepared to subject my crews to this additional risk in order solely to lessen the risk of bombing our own troops."

The crews had been provided with stop-watches. Their orders were explicit: Do a timed run from the coast and do not bomb before the elapsed time.

The planners must have thought they had considered every eventuality. They hadn't. In the early afternoon of the fourteenth, Canadian troops heard the sound of engines and looked up to see scores of heavy bombers approaching with bomb doors open. Alarmed, the troops set off yellow flares – the standard recognition signals for forward troops to indicate their positions to friendly aircraft. Therein lay the tragic weakness of the plan. Unaccustomed to working in the army cooperation role, Bomber Command crews were not familiar with the various pyrotechnics commonly used by the Army. No one had thought to brief the crews on their use; neither had the airmen thought to tell the Army that the Pathfinders would be dropping *yellow* TIs. Crouched over their sights in the bombers, the bomb-aimers were confused and uncertain. Had the situation changed since take-off? Why the yellow smoke *here*? Were *these* the TIs to bomb? Had the timed run been abandoned? Or changed? Had every other aircraft received a radio message about it? It took only one man to set the deadly process in motion; when the others saw him dropping his bombs, many more followed suit. Although the instructions were to stick to the timed run, scores of airmen came to the conclusion that they couldn't ignore the evidence of their own eyes. The others were bombing, so it had to be all right . . .

The bombing errors occurred in four distinct phases: From 1441 to 1459 hours, nine 6 Group aircraft, one Pathfinder, and four 4 Group aircraft bombed in the vicinity of St-Aignan. From 1514 to 1518 hours, twelve more 6 Group aircraft and one Pathfinder bombed the same area; this part of the tragedy seems to have been caused by a Pathfinder back-up aircraft carrying ground TIs. The bomb-aimer saw what he thought were yellow target indicators burning on the ground amid much smoke from the bombs that had already fallen. At that moment, the Master Bomber several miles further on was instructing the Main Force to bomb on the yellow TIs. Undoubtedly more than one of the bomb-aimers now over St-Aignan heard the Master Bomber's voice in their earphones and thought the instructions were directed at them. There was no time to ask questions. The decision had to be immediate. In the Services wasn't it always best to *obey* no matter what? In this sad case it wasn't.

From 1514 to 1520 hours, twenty-three aircraft of 6 Group bombed the quarry at Haut Mesnil. Two 428 Squadron Lancasters bombed first, apparently confusing the smoke drifting over from St-Aignan for smoke that they had been briefed to expect from Aiming Point 21. The Master Bomber was busy directing the forward crews to bomb the yellow TIs that could be found "when you have passed the first column of smoke." By awful coincidence the instructions fitted the situation over the quarry almost perfectly. When the 428 Squadron aircraft dropped their bombs, many others released theirs.

From 1532 hours on, more bombs fell on the Canadians in the Haut Mesnil quarry, this time from twenty-six aircraft of 1 Group. Crews reported seeing red markers – undoubtedly red flares fired from an Auster. The tiny army cooperation monoplane had taken off in an apparent attempt to halt the bombing; unfortunately its presence only added more confusion to an already bewildering scene.

Harris's worst fears had been realized. Sixty-five Canadian soldiers had been killed outright; more than three hundred were wounded or missing. The miracle was that the casualties weren't far greater.

"It was a sad day for us, particularly when the trip was a 'milk run,'" writes Bob Marshall, an air gunner with 428 Squadron then on his second tour of operations. "There was no enemy opposition; it was one of the very few trips I experienced without being shot at."

Marcel Beauchamp was a navigator with 425 Squadron who recalls delightful summer weather with just a little haze. The bomb-aimer aboard Beauchamp's Halifax was beset by the same doubts that affected many of his confrères. To his surprise, Beauchamp heard the bomb-aimer directing the skipper in preparation for bombing: "Luckily I caught the bomb-aimer in time ... My

ETA on the target was still some minutes away and since I had just taken a visual fix on crossing the coast I couldn't see how I could be in so much error." There followed a brief conference among the crew members in the narrow confines of the Halifax; they agreed to go on to Falaise and to turn back if it was found out that this was indeed the right place. Such conferences took place on many 6 Group aircraft that day.

Squadron Leader Don Lamont was skipper of a 428 Squadron Lancaster and recalled that his crew "had quite a discussion about where to bomb but decided to stay with the timed run."

On the other hand, Jim Mossman, a bomb-aimer with 429 Squadron, claims the directions given to the crews were straight-forward. He observed in his log: "Saw bombs prang target. But some bastards dropped five miles short even after Master Bomber gave clear instructions."

Doug Scanlan, a bomb-aimer with 415 Squadron, recalls the careful planning that went into the August 14th operation. When the squadron's crews returned to East Moor, they were instructed not to remove the film magazines from their cameras; ground staff took care of that chore. Scanlan was relieved to learn later that his aircraft's photographs showed that he had bombed correctly. "I recall visiting a friend in a hospital in Scotland some time after and as I passed through the open ward, a couple of bed-ridden Canadian soldiers, seeing my air force uniform, started cursing and accused me of having ... 'bombed us, you bastards!'"

The controversy flourishes still. Who was to blame? The crews who obeyed the Master Bomber's directions and abandoned the timed run? The troops who fired yellow warning flares? The senior Army and RAF staff who failed to communicate with each other about signals procedures? The "brass hats" who expected heavy bomber crews to perform army cooperation and close assault duties without the necessary training and experience? Perhaps all of them, perhaps none of them. Perhaps it was just the war, that exercise in international lunacy that daily placed men and women in impossible situations and "gonged" them if they succeeded and court-martialled them if they didn't. In any event, the senior commanders lost no time in putting pen to paper to absolve themselves of any culpability. The bomb-aimers had been told to do the timed run. Some had failed to adhere to it. Yes, there had been certain extenuating factors but that didn't excuse anyone for failing to obey orders.

The whole question of signals troubled Harris, however. He pointed out:

> No information had been given to this Command to the effect that this system of marking was in use and in fact my Senior Air Staff Officer, who had in the very short time available hurriedly arranged this operation with the First Canadian Army in France the previous day, had particularly sought information on the subject of possibly confusing pyrotechnics and been assured that none would be used. To that extent, therefore, the First Canadian Army themselves subscribed to the errors which were made. Furthermore, AEAF [Allied Expeditionary Air Force] and/or First Canadian Army should have informed this Command of the common use of these pyrotechnics.[20]

Predictably, the Army expressed suitably righteous astonishment that the airmen weren't aware of the signalling instructions that had been delineated in SHAEF Operational Policy Memorandum No. 19 of March 27, 1944 – "the recognition, or identification, procedure ordered to be observed by the three services of all nationalities." General Crerar observed: "I submit that the surest and swiftest preventative of any future mistakes of a similar nature is for the RAF to forbid the use of yellow target markers in any bombing operation carried out in proximity to our forces on the ground."[21] Many of the crews who bombed too soon found themselves in London at a Court of Enquiry. They did their best to explain their actions: "Air bomber thought that the quarry looked like military field works. Target had been stated to be a dug-in position" ... "When there was approximately one minute to go before ETA, air bomber saw columns of smoke on the port side which he assumed to be from the attack on AP 21. He then heard the Master Bomber instruct, 'Bomb centre of smoke and overshoot by one second.' A column of smoke was seen ahead, to which he assumed Master Bomber to be referring ... After bombing, the Master Bomber was heard to say, 'Do not bomb quarry'. Now having seen the quarry, they did not know whether this referred to them, though they were suspicious because some aircraft were seen continuing ahead with bomb doors still open" ... "The quarry was mistaken for a triangular mark at AP 28."[22]

The outcome was never in doubt. The Pathfinder crews involved had to relinquish their PFF badges and their acting ranks and were reposted to ordinary crew duties. The squadron and flight commanders involved lost their commands and their acting ranks. All the guilty crews were to operate at least thirty miles from Allied troops until they were "reassessed" by their AOsC. They were the scapegoats. They had been punished. Officialdom could now close the file.

At this stage of the war, 6 Group was able to send close to three hundred Lancasters and Halifaxes into battle. But seldom were so many aircraft employed on a single target. On August 16, for example, 144 bombers from 6 Group joined 204 aircraft from other groups in an attack on Kiel. The same night twenty-seven 6 Group aircraft formed part of a force of 461 aircraft raiding Stettin.

Over Kiel, flak smashed into the 429 Squadron Halifax commanded by Pilot Officer N.C. Muir; it seriously injured the navigator, Flight Sergeant E.J. Lafave, in the abdomen and leg. Despite acute pain, Lafave continued to navigate and told no one of his injuries until the aircraft landed. He was awarded a DFM. Flying Officer J. Wagman was the skipper of a Halifax of 434 Squadron which also suffered a direct hit from flak. In spite of the fact that fuel was streaming from the aircraft, Wagman pushed on and bombed; on the way home, however, he had to ditch some forty miles from the coast. The crew survived. Wagman received a DFC.

Of the two operations carried out that night, the attack on Stettin was probably the more destructive; according to local reports, many of the bombs dropped on Kiel landed wide of the city. Three 6 Group bombers did not return from Kiel; one was lost over Stettin.

Two nights later, on August 18/19, 6 Group participated in a raid on Bremen, contributing one hundred of the 288 aircraft employed. Although by earlier standards the force was not large, the operation was a singular success, probably the most destructive raid of the entire war on this city. "Marking very accurate and concentrated," reported the 6 Group crews. "Bombing appeared concentrated and fires quickly took hold. Mushrooms of thick black smoke rose to 12,000 feet." According to German sources, a form of firestorm took hold and hundreds of people were incinerated in public shelters. Nearly ten thousand houses and apartment buildings were destroyed, plus many industrial and commercial structures. Only one aircraft was lost, a Lancaster of 428 Squadron. The same night, small forces of 6 Group bombers attacked a variety of minor targets without loss.

On August 25/26, thirty-four 6 Group Lancasters joined nearly four hundred Lancasters from 1, 3, and 8 Groups in an attack on the Opel plant at Russelsheim on the Main river near Mainz. The bombing was notably accurate with only a few bomb-aimers fooled by the decoy fires ten miles to the south. The Canadian Group's crews reported much ground haze but said the bombing was "spot-on" – provided the markers had been correctly placed, an indication of how everything so often depended on accurate work by the Pathfinders. The raid cost fifteen aircraft, but only one from 6 Group, a Lancaster of 419 Squadron which collided with another aircraft over the target. The sole survivor was the skipper, Flying Officer H.D. Witwer. The squadron suffered more fatalities that night while the bombers were landing. When E-Easy attempted an overshoot due to poor visibility, all four engines cut out and the Lancaster crashed into trees near the field. Four of the seven crew members died.

Four nights later, thirty-six 6 Group aircraft constituted a small part of the force of 402 Lancasters and one Mosquito that launched a successful attack on Stettin. "Large fires which merged into one conflagration," stated the Group's ORB. The fire could be seen one hundred miles away, according to returning crews. It was a costly raid, however, with twenty-three Lancasters lost, 5.7 per cent of the force. But only one 6 Group Lancaster failed to return.

Airfields, stations, docks, shipping, coastal batteries, and rocket installations were 6 Group's targets for the second half of August. Losses were light, but being shot down was just as traumatic for the aircrew involved whether one aircraft was involved or one hundred. On a notably successful daylight raid against the airfield at Soesterberg, for example, 6 Group lost one Lancaster. It came from 428 Squadron and was commanded by Warrant Officer A.P.A. Jakeman who was on his seventeenth op. He encountered "heavy, concentrated flak" over the target and later reported: "The last bomb had just gone when we were hit." The damage was serious, affecting the Lancaster's controls and engines. "The aircraft immediately went into a spiral dive ... I gave the order to bale out and the engineer, who was in the bomb-aimer's compartment dropping Window, reached up with my chute. Meanwhile I was trying to regain control before feathering the engines. However, in a matter of seconds, before I could trim, it was in a violent spin." He was still strapped in his seat when the aircraft blew up, tossing him out without a scratch, to parachute to safety.[23]

On the thirty-first, 165 of 6 Group's bombers carried out a low-level daylight assault on the Île de Cezembre, a heavily fortified island near St-Malo. Bombing from between twelve hundred and three thousand feet, the Canadians achieved deadly accuracy and completely silenced all the batteries on the island. The Germans promptly surrendered. All 6 Group aircraft returned safely.

August had been a remarkable month for 6 Group. The Canadians had completed no less than 3,704 sorties, a record never equalled by any other group in Bomber Command. During the month 6 Group had attacked seventy-four different targets and had dropped 4,735.7 tons of bombs by night and 8,315.8 tons by day, plus more than three hundred mines, a further 222.9 tons. Casualties totalled twenty-two aircraft, a percentage loss of 0.6 per cent – a far cry from the heart-rending figures of only a few months earlier and the lowest loss by any group during the month. It was an astonishing performance from the group that, a few months before, had been regarded as an inefficient chop group.[24]

As September began, the tempo of 6 Group's operations slackened, reflecting the changing military scene. After the weary weeks of battle in and around the beachheads, the Allied armies had broken free and were advancing on every front. Paris was liberated on August 25; a few days later British troops crossed the border into Belgium and captured the important port of Antwerp. The First Canadian Army entered Rouen and American troops reached the German border near Aachen. To many it seemed that the end was in sight; soon the victorious Allied armies would be thrusting through Germany itself. Surely it would all be over by Christmas. Perhaps even earlier. To a large extent, the work of Bomber Command seemed to be done. It had performed an extraordinarily effective tactical function in France and Belgium. But what now? The Command had reached its awesome pinnacle of efficiency; its technical troubles were all but solved; it could find any target in Germany and hit it with what in those pre-atomic days seemed to be cataclysmic power. But what targets? Some men in high places were questioning whether Harris should be permitted to revert to his systematic demolition of Germany's cities. What was to be gained by destroying the very areas that would soon be occupied territory? Others, perhaps having personal knowledge of the Germans' tenacity and superb fighting qualities, demanded a continuation of the bombing until the enemy surrendered. The Germans might be reeling but they were by no means out for the count.

Although Bomber Command would be released from SHEAF's control during the month, it was on the understanding that the bombers were to be made available for tactical missions as required. But such ops would employ only a fraction of the Command's strength. Harris now had at his disposal more than eighty heavy bomber squadrons with about fifteen hundred Halifaxes and Lancasters; thousand-bomber operations could now be mounted as a matter of course. The question was: How best to employ Bomber Command in this, the last phase of the war? Oil or transportation? These were the targets favoured by senior Allied commanders. Predictably, Harris favoured neither. As far as he was concerned, oil and transportation belonged in the detested "panacea" category. Perhaps still clinging to the hope that Bomber Command might win the war with a series of devastating blows, he claimed that his Command was best employed in the task of destroying the Germans' means of production and will to keep fighting. Although this stage of World War II is largely remembered in terms of armies, it was in fact Bomber Command's most active period; in these last nine months the Lancasters and Halifaxes would drop close to half the tonnage of bombs dropped by the Command throughout the entire war. In September, Harris laid on a few token raids on the enemy's synthetic oil facilities, but he soon reverted to massive area attacks on German cities. With the inestimable benefit of hindsight, it is easy to see how every Allied bomber should have been employed in attacks on oil plants and supplies. The Germans were already desperately short of fuel. It seems not unreasonable to claim that if the full weight of Bomber Command had been brought in alongside the Americans in round-the-clock attacks on oil targets, the war may well have been brought to an end before 1945. But Allied Intelligence failed to plumb the depth of the enemy's desperation; the Germans managed with extraordinary efficiency to continue the battle with their dwindling supplies.

For 6 Group, the month was characterized by a preponderance of daylight operations, a number of repeat visits to the same targets, and gratifyingly low losses. Only six aircraft went missing in September and three of these ditched in the North Sea with the crews being saved. In total, then, 6 Group's losses amounted to a remarkably low .001 per cent of the crews despatched. The Group undertook twenty raids in September. Nineteen were flown by day; only one, Kiel on September 15/16, was flown by night. Eleven of the targets could be classified as tactical, three were strategic; and six were synthetic oil plants. In addition, the Group undertook three Gardening operations.

On the third, 105 Halifaxes of 6 Group helped to make up a force of 675 aircraft delivering a highly effective series of attacks on six airfields in Holland: Gilze-Rijen, Eindhoven, Venlo, Soesterberg, Deelen, and Volkel. The attacks had been designed to neutralize these fields in preparation for Operation *Market Garden*, an imaginative strategic operation which might have shortened the war but which, because of a string of misfortunes, succeeded only in destroying the British First Airborne Division. Volkel was 6 Group's assigned target. The Canadians dropped some eight hundred bombs on the airfield, destroying both runways as well as assorted aircraft, hangars, and other buildings. A Halifax of 425 Squadron commanded by Flight Lieutenant R.J.M. Langlois took flak hits as it approached the field. One engine cut out. Undaunted, Langlois pressed on to the target, and completed his attack. He won a DFC.

Three days later, on September 6, 139 aircraft of the Canadian

Group constituted most of the force attacking Emden in daylight, the first time the port city had been bombed since 1942. A strong escort of Spitfires and Mustangs accompanied the Canadian bombers but encountered no *Luftwaffe* fighters. Flak scored a direct hit on the Lancaster of the Deputy Master Bomber, Flight Lieutenant Granville Wilson, killing him instantly. 6 Group suffered no losses in this successful raid but it was a near thing for Walter Miller and his crew of 433 Squadron. Their Halifax was the last in the stream – and they had to do a second run-up to the target, thus receiving the full attention of the flak. "I will never forget the quiet courage of our rear gunner," Miller writes. The gunner, George Cracknell, provided Miller with a running commentary on the flak, keeping him informed about the range of the bursts, whether they were high or low and when to evade, all in a quiet, emotionless voice. For a few moments it looked as if the crew would escape unscathed. But just after the bombs fell, flak struck the Halifax. The aircraft dived. Miller had to wedge his feet against the instrument panel to haul the plunging bomber back to level flight. Somewhat to his surprise, he found it still flew. He got back to base in good order – to be greeted by criticism of his target photos; the CO complained that they showed nothing but a good view of the horizon!

Emden was a "mass of flames," according to the 6 Group ORB. The "thick, black, oily smoke rising to ten thousand feet" could be seen 150 miles away. The engineering shops of the U-Boat builder, *Nordsee Werke,* had been seriously damaged, as had the shipbuilding yards of *Berkamer Kleinbohn.* The attack sank or wrecked several ships in the harbour. Flying Officer A.L. Lakeman, a 419 Squadron bomb-aimer, suffered head wounds during the run-in to the target. Despite his injuries, he directed his skipper to a successful attack and earned a DFC.

The ninth saw the beginning of a series of tactical attacks on pockets of enemy resistance: three trips each to Le Havre and Domburg, four to Calais, one each to Boulogne and Cap Gris Nez. Not all were successful; poor weather forced a cancellation of the Le Havre attack on the ninth; the crews had to bring their bombs home (so intense had been the aerial activity in recent months that demand was outstripping supply). Not until the eleventh was Bomber Command able to deliver the final assault on the German positions around Le Havre. 6 Group contributed fifty-five of the more than two hundred aircraft involved. After a devastating attack, the garrison surrendered.

On the same day, more than a hundred 6 Group bombers joined 274 aircraft from other groups in a raid on the synthetic oil plant at Castrop-Rauxel. Squadron Leader B.S. Imrie's 434 Squadron Halifax took several flak hits before and during his bomb run which stopped the two starboard engines. Losing height, the Halifax staggered as more shells scored direct hits; nevertheless, Imrie maintained control and brought the battle-scarred aircraft back to base. It bore more than forty holes. The following day, some two hundred bombers of the Canadian Group were part of a force of over five hundred aircraft attacking synthetic oil production plants at Wanne-Eickel and Dortmund. "Many fires with explosions," reported the Canadians' ORB of the former, although the target lay under a dense smoke screen. One 6 Group aircraft was lost, the first of the month. "Bombing reported as being well concentrated, numerous fires developed, with black billowing smoke. Large explosions with numerous smaller ones," reported the Group ORB of the Dortmund op.

A 428 Squadron crew distinguished themselves. Over Dortmund, flak hit the Lancaster of Flight Lieutenant Russel E. Curtis, an American with the RCAF. Curtis sustained a compound fracture of the skull but he remained at the controls and continued his bomb run. When the bombs had gone, he finally asked for assistance and collapsed. Crew members got him back to the rest position amidships. Meanwhile, Flying Officer Dougal A. McGillivray, the bomb-aimer, took over the Lancaster's controls and kept it on course for home. Assisted by several crewmen, particularly Sergeant J.W. Rose, the RAF flight engineer, McGillivray succeeded in landing the bomber, although it ground-looped because of a tire blow-out. Curtis, already a DFM winner, was awarded the DSO, as was the resourceful bomb-aimer, McGillivray.

On the thirteenth, in fine weather, 6 Group attacked the railway lines around Osnabruck. Flak hit the Halifax of Flight Lieutenant J.Y.A. Coté of 425 Squadron. Coté completed his attack, however, and returned to base. He was awarded a bar to his DFC. The next day, eighty-five 6 Group bombers set off for Wilhelmshaven, only to be recalled mid-way across the North Sea because of deteriorating weather.

A major force attacked Kiel on the fifteenth, with 6 Group providing two hundred of the 405 aircraft involved. "TIs well backed up and formed thoroughly good concentration. Bombing well concentrated. Several fires and one particularly large explosion," declared the Group ORB. To the crews involved it seemed to be a highly successful raid, but local reports indicate that many of the bombs fell outside the town. Two 6 Group aircraft, Halifaxes from 420 and 432 Squadrons, failed to return from this, the Group's only night raid of the month. Wally Loucks, the wireless operator on Jack Bell's 419 Squadron Lancaster crew, recalls the op well. A curious incident occurred while his aircraft, KB722, was en route to the target. Loucks could hear a female German radio operator directing the fighters; a moment later an Me 410 was observed flying straight and level two hundred yards above. Both gunners, Buff Strain and Chuck Murphy, wanted to open fire. But Bell, with true democratic instincts, asked the rest of the crew for their opinion. Most agreed with the gunners. Loucks didn't. Everything depended on the gunners getting the fighter with their first shots, he pointed out, by no means a sure thing. What if the gunners missed? Wouldn't the night fighter immediately attack and probably shoot the Lanc down? "Our business is dropping bombs not dog-fighting." This seemed to sway the rest of the crew. They changed their minds; meanwhile the Me 410 had disappeared in the darkness.

One of 428 Squadron's Lancasters carried a passenger on this trip, the Catholic padre from Middleton St. George, Father J. Philip Lardie. Squadron Leader J.G. Edwards had invited Father Lardie to fly with his crew so that he might learn at first-hand what his "parishioners" were experiencing on ops. This was actually Father Lardie's second sortie; he had flown with Flight Lieutenant Lloyd Gonyou's crew on the unhappy Falaise operation a month before. The Kiel trip had its moments, Father Lardie recalls. Approaching the target, Edwards turned to his passenger and said, "You're going to enjoy this, Father," as he flew into the dazzle of flares and tracers. After bombing, Edwards banked away. A fighter appeared. The rear gunner immediately called for a corkscrew, whereupon the padre, who had been standing between the skipper and the flight engineer, found himself airborne inside the aircraft. He walloped his head on the canopy roof. A moment later, as the aircraft climbed, he was flat on the floor. Disquieting though the manoeuvre may have been, it enabled the Lancaster to escape in the darkness. Of the sorties, Father Lardie says, "I wasn't looking for thrills but for a better understanding of what it meant to fly on operations – and afterwards I had an entirely different outlook. I felt much closer to the airmen." It's hardly surprising that the padre was so highly regarded at Middleton St. George. His operational career was brief, however. Wing Commander Chester Hull, the CO of 428 Squadron, found him reading a newspaper in the Mess the day after the Kiel op. Father Lardie remembers a large, authoritative hand appearing and lowering the newspaper, after which the face of the CO materialized. "Padre," Hull declared, "you're screened!"

For the balance of the month, 6 Group's principal activity was in tactical operations: repeated attacks on airfields at Boulogne, Domberg, and Calais, and batteries in the Cap Gris Nez area. All were daylight ops and incurred just one loss, a Lancaster of 419 Squadron with Flying Officer B.D. Walker in command. All the crew died when the aircraft was shot down.

In addition to its tactical operations, 6 Group mounted attacks on synthetic oil plants at Bottrop on the twenty-seventh and at Sterkrade on the thirtieth, both only moderately successful because of heavy cloud. One aircraft was lost from these two ops, a Halifax of 426 Squadron commanded by Flying Officer T. Frederickson. Flight Sergeant D.E. Turnquist was the navigator; he recalled the bombs being dropped; a moment later flak hit the aircraft and it blew up before anyone had time to bale out. Frederickson was knocked out and woke up tumbling through the air. Fortunately he was wearing his parachute and had time to tug at the rip-cord. Only one other member of the crew survived.

The value of the tactical ops flown during September was acknowledged in a signal from Lieutenant General H.D.G. Crerar, General Officer Commanding First Canadian Army, to Harris:

> Our total casualties in the capture of Calais and Gris Nez were under three hundred and over eleven thousand prisoners were captured. Considering the strength of the defences such a suc-

cess would have been impossible but for the accurate, consistent and timely effort of Bomber Command. I hope you will accept my sincere appreciation of all you did for us and pass on to your staff and aircrews and ground staffs my thanks for their indispensable share in this very satisfactory operation. I hope your casualties were light.[25]

9

WHIRLWIND

"Everyone knew we had a job to do and we did it
to the best of our ability."

Allan Caine, DFC, pilot, 420 Squadron

The rumble of aero-engines drifted across the farmlands of Yorkshire and Durham, just one or two at first, then others picked up
the theme. Quickly, it became a thundering, insistent chorus. A
procession of aircraft took off and turned as they passed beyond
trees that had already begun to display their autumn colours. The
bombers vanished in the distance, leaving a rumbling echo. Soon
they reappeared, black-winged, purposeful, banking over diminutive villages as they lined up to land. Nose-high, the big aircraft
approached, undercarriages reaching for terra firma like the claws
of enormous birds. A puff of smoke as the long-suffering tires

took the impact of twenty tons of airplane touching down. Another smear of black on the runway. A rocking of great wings and a waggling of rudders, a self-satisfied trundling down the runway.

Ops would be on that night, the locals concluded. They knew the signs. Air tests. Fuelling-up. Bombing-up. Not a single airman to be seen outside the aerodrome. Everyone in *there*, getting ready for the ordeal ahead.

Linton-on-Ouse, East Moor, Tholthorpe, Leeming, Skipton-on-Swale, Middleton St. George, Croft: it was the same on all the operational airfields of 6 Group. They readied every available aircraft. This operation, on the night of October 6/7, would be 6 Group's biggest effort of the war, with 293 Canadian bombers making up well over half of the 523 aircraft participating. Afterwards, it would be a source of some irritation to many Canadian airmen that the British newspapers and the BBC would make no mention of their involvement, describing the force as "RAF."

That morning Harris had selected Dortmund as the target. Located at the eastern edge of the Ruhr, a city of about half a million, Dortmund had twenty-nine heavy industrial plants plus fourteen engineering and armaments works, a municipal gas-works, ten power stations, a number of railway marshalling yards, and an inland harbour.[1]

The attack was to commence at 2025 hours with Mosquitoes of 8 Group dropping TIs triggered by barometric fuses to burst at five thousand feet above the aiming point and emit bright red lights. Pathfinder backer-up aircraft would keep re-marking the aiming point with green TIs for the benefit of the bomb-aimers in the Main Force. If unexpected cloud obscured the target and the TIs, the Pathfinder aircraft would use another marking method, Emergency Wanganui, radar-directed sky-marking employing flares suspended under parachutes.[2] By now, Bomber Command had the means to cope with virtually any combination of conditions. The prospects of an accurate raid were vastly improved by the presence of Oboe stations on the Continent. Poor visibility presented few difficulties because of new, modified H2S equipment. With a wide range of bombs and some fifteen hundred heavy bombers, Lancasters and the latest Halifaxes, to deliver them, Bomber Command was capable of inflicting catastrophic damage on any target in

Germany in all but the most horrific weather and against all but the most determined enemy resistance.

Four waves of bombers would attack Dortmund, the first from 2025 to 2029 hours, the second from 2028 to 2032, the third from 2032 to 2036, the fourth from 2035 to 2039. The Lancasters of 3 Group would lead each wave, the Lancasters and Halifaxes of 6 Group following them. Bomber Command planners sent the bombers over liberated French territory at low level to delay detection by radar as long as possible.

The extent of the diversionary activities planned for the night of October 6/7 is an indication of the size and versatility of the force that Bomber Command had become. No less than 253 aircraft from 1 and 5 Groups would attack Bremen, the first bombs dropping at the same moment as those over Dortmund. In addition, other aircraft would bomb Berlin, Ludwigshafen, and Saarbrücken while intruder patrols attacked fighters and their bases. As an extra security measure, 100 (Special Duties) Group provided jamming cover.[3]

During the early afternoon of October 6, the crews filed into briefing rooms and took their places. On many stations, the briefing rooms became chapels on Sundays; to accommodate the congregation, the long tables were removed but the aircraft identification models still revolved on the wires suspending them from the ceilings and the posters still adorned the walls exhorting one and all not to talk to strangers or to indulge in sexual intercourse without due precautions. The briefing began. The curtains parted with a rattle of rods and rings. The airmen's eyes narrowed at the sight of the map and the red ribbon snaking its way into Germany. The Ruhr. Dortmund. Mouths became suddenly dry. No milk run, this. The intelligence officers explained the importance of the target, described the defences, warned of decoy fires, drawing the airmen's attention to a particularly notorious site half a mile south of the city. The route had been planned to avoid the heaviest flak concentrations so it was important to stay "bang on track." Aircraft that strayed would risk fire from the heavy flak concentrations at Cologne, Koblenz, Münster, and half a dozen other areas.[4]

For some 6 Group airmen, area-bombing was a new experience. So intense had been the summer schedule of invasion-support ops that scores of crews had completed their tours without flying a single area-bombing sortie. Now the tactical jobs had largely been done. As Harris saw it, this was the time to hit Germany's cities again, to keep up the pressure on the enemy's means of production and the morale of the people. Unfortunately his bosses, Portal and Tedder, didn't agree. The senior air commanders would spend much time in the next few weeks arguing with one another, trying in vain to assert their various points of view, a ludicrous state of affairs which made a mockery of the chain of command.

But arguments among the brass were of no concern to the aircrews. They clambered aboard their aircraft and set off for the target. Conditions were perfect. A measure of the vastly increased efficiency of 6 Group's maintenance is indicated by the fact that every one of the 293 bombers detailed took off, although Flight Lieutenant W.P. Scott and his crew of 426 Squadron had to take the standby aircraft because their Halifax became unserviceable at the last minute.[5] On airfield after airfield, the hardstandings were deserted, the "frying pan" dispersal areas looking oddly forlorn without Lancasters or Halifaxes parked on their oil-stained concrete surfaces. The ground crews watched the last aircraft disappear in the distance, then returned to their huts to begin the familiar vigil.

The bombers flew under a cloudless sky, a great stream of aircraft some ten miles long. They encountered little flak on the outward journey. Near the target, however, the flak increased in intensity. And fighters began to put in an appearance. One approached a 428 Squadron Lancaster X with Flying Officer G.R. Pauli in the pilot's seat. At 2024, a minute before the first bombs were due to go down, Pauli's mid-upper gunner, Sergeant W. Harper, spotted the fighter, identifying it as an Me 410. When the fighter closed from the starboard quarter above, Pauli hurled the Lancaster into a corkscrew to starboard. At the same instant Harper and the rear gunner, Sergeant A.G. Scott, opened fire. The 410 broke away, the pilot apparently disinclined to press the attack. Scott and Harper fired some two hundred rounds but neither claimed to have inflicted any damage on the fighter.[6]

Dead on time, the Pathfinders' TIs burst, spilling droplets of colour over the darkened city. For the bomb-aimers in the Main Force aircraft, the aiming point was vividly outlined in red and green, another surreal design in a sky slashed by searchlights and punctuated by flak and darting tracer. The bombs streamed earthward.

A Halifax VII of 408 Squadron flown by Pilot Officer T.V. Barber had just bombed and was turning homeward when a single-engined Me 109 attacked from astern. The mid-upper gunner, Sergeant G.L. Humphrys, opened fire; an instant later the enemy fighter exploded and crashed.[7]

Flight Lieutenant W.P. Scott of 426 Squadron, who had been obliged to take the standby aircraft at Linton-on-Ouse, had difficulty in climbing to bombing height over the target. According to the bomb-aimer, Flying Officer A.F. Livingstone, "the a/c had to be coaxed up from 13000'. We got to 17500 feet and the skipper said she wouldn't have climbed very much higher. On the bombing run we did an S-turn to port because of another a/c directly above us. Flak was very heavy and we just bounced across the target." As the bombs fell away, the Halifax staggered as flak thudded into the fuselage and wing. The flight engineer suffered a terrible wound from a chunk of flak ". . . which took a good piece of the side of his head with it," Livingstone reported. Before he could be restrained, the unfortunate man grabbed Flying Officer J.H. Mack, the wireless operator, around the neck and yanked his oxygen mask off. Livingstone and Mack tried to make the mortally wounded engineer as comfortable as possible while Scott descended to eleven thousand feet to enable everyone to breath without oxygen. Livingstone recalls: "I moved from the nose to the cockpit and just then the kite lurched and we weren't getting any use out of the port engines." Scott throttled the starboard engines back to keep the aircraft level; now the airspeed indicator and altimeter began to unwind steadily, ominously. Fire broke out in the port inner engine. Scott ordered the crew to bale out. Livingstone left after the navigator and wireless operator: "I seemed to stay in the slipstream for a long time and did three complete flips. The chute opened and hit me on the forehead as it went up. Then there was a bright reddish orange flash on the ground which lasted for a second or two then died down to a small glow. I presumed this was the a/c. In a short time which seemed less than a minute I landed in a field of cattle." Four of the seven-man crew survived to become POWs.[8]

Another 6 Group bomber was a victim of flak, a Halifax III of 433 Squadron flown by Flying Officer V.G.B. Valentine who was on his first operational sortie. Approaching the target at twenty thousand feet, the Halifax took a flak hit which stopped both port engines. Gamely, Valentine pressed on after feathering the damaged engines and trimming the aircraft: "Even so considerable pressure was needed on the aileron controls to keep it level." The aircraft rapidly began to lose height: a thousand feet per minute at first, gradually easing to five hundred feet per minute. Valentine reported, "The target was very near . . . so I decided to bomb the target, turn due west and then bale the crew out over Allied lines." By the time he reached the target, his Halifax was down to between seven thousand and eight thousand feet and still descending, a perfect target for light flak. Indeed, the batteries scored several more hits on the wings, tail, and fuselage. After bombing, Valentine turned west. By this time the Halifax's altitude had slipped to five thousand feet and, "I levelled the aircraft off and it promptly stalled at 125 mph." Although Valentine managed to recover from the stall, he was dangerously low over Duisburg and he believes he hit a factory chimney. "Four members of the crew were in crash positions when we crashed and two others were going into their positions. The four in position were killed whereas the other two were badly injured but saved."[9]

The attack on Dortmund devastated the city. Most of the 6 Group crews bombed between 2027 and 2037 hours, aiming at the centre of the red and green TIs. Damage was particularly heavy near the goods yard and the main passenger station. Five engineering works and fifteen factories were destroyed or extensively damaged. At Bomber Command, the analysts gleefully estimated that the built-up areas of Dortmund were 70 per cent wrecked and half the entire city had been demolished. The death toll in the city was 191 dead, 418 injured, and 38 missing.[10]

Airmen of the Canadian Group earned several decorations that night. A navigator with 433 Squadron, Flying Officer W.J.N. Burnett, won the DFC. An incendiary bomb dropped by another bomber hit Burnett's Halifax, smashing through the nose and seriously injuring Flight Sergeant N.D. Dixon, the bomb-aimer. A 200 mph gale screamed through the wrecked fuselage, taking Burnett's instruments, log, and charts and whipping them out into the night. "Despite great difficulties and aided only by a small pilot's chart, this officer continued to navigate the damaged aircraft and the mission was successfully completed. Throughout the return flight he also rendered first aid to the injured air bomber," the citation reported. For his "devotion to duty" Dixon received a DFM.[11]

Flying Officer T.A. Shore, a 431 Squadron skipper, won the DFC when flak severely damaged his Halifax over Dortmund. The aircraft became almost impossible to control but he managed to return safely to base. In addition, a Bar to the DFC went to 425 Squadron's Flight Lieutenant M.J. Belanger. Pilot Officer G. Avranettes of 425 Squadron, an air gunner aboard Halifax LW381, won the DFC.[12]

The returning bombers encountered foggy conditions north of the Wash. Most of 424 Squadron's Halifaxes were diverted to the USAAF base at Mendelsham, Suffolk. Although the crews were unamimous in their praise of the hospitality of the Americans, they criticized their radio procedures, which bore little relation to those used by the RAF and RCAF, caused much confusion and uncertainty, and vastly increased the risks of crashes in the unfamiliar surroundings. (Despite the obvious dangers of having different procedures in effect at various fields, the two air forces continued to operate in their own ways throughout the war.) Fortunately, on this occasion the Canadian bombers landed without incident, bringing to an end a highly successful operation that many refer to as the opening blow of the "The Second Battle of the Ruhr."[13]

Bomber Command had finally realized the aims set forth by the Air Staff between the wars. It had been a lengthy and costly process – and, ironically, it was too late. The job was all but done. The enemy was in full flight, his fuel production brought almost to a standstill, his factories able to continue production of war materials only by dint of extraordinary efforts and innovation.

Time had run out on Harris. The summing-up was at hand. The historians would soon be ferreting through the files, weighing the evidence and counting the costs. Harris had desperately wanted Bomber Command to be the decisive weapon of victory; now it appeared that its contribution, significant though it undoubtedly was, would be seen as relatively minor in the context of the invasion of Europe, the great land battles – and particularly the spectacular successes of the American aerial armadas that, with relatively little help from Bomber Command, had decimated the *Luftwaffe*'s day fighter force and destroyed Germany's oil facilities. Harris, like all the British commanders, had been obliged to undergo the uncomfortable process of diminution. Without enthusiasm, he had to accept the steady shrinkage of his significance in the giant scheme of things as the Americans acquired both experience and incalculable strength in men and *matériel*. It had all happened in two short years. In the fall of 1942, Harris had been the master, the all-wise guru of strategic bombing to whom the eager Americans had come seeking counsel. Now the tables were turned. Irreversibly.

But Harris, as might have been expected, refused to accept the inevitable. There might still be time. No matter that Portal kept on bleating about the need to concentrate on oil targets or that Tedder was equally insistent about transportation. Both of them had been caught up in the insidious mania for finding panacea targets. Harris, as usual, knew better. Bomber Command could still be the decisive weapon that would bring the Third Reich to its knees. Thus began a period of extraordinarily intense bombing. Whether it was necessary or even advisable is still a subject for the polemics of historians. The disagreements between Harris and Portal became the stuff of legend. Harris simply wouldn't obey orders. Although Portal kept requesting – almost pleading – for him to attack oil targets, Harris continued to employ the bulk of his massive force on area-bombing operations. During this period 53 per cent of operations were area attacks, compared with 14 per cent against oil targets, 15 per cent against transportation targets, 13 per cent against military, and 5 per cent against naval and other targets.[14] In fact, Harris was now attacking oil targets less frequently than he had in the early days of 1944. Between January and May 1945, 26 per cent of Harris's attacks had been directed against oil targets and only 37 per cent against cities. It seems incredible that Portal did nothing about it except write more memos. True, Harris was immensely popular; true, his departure would have been a shock. But would that have mattered so much at that stage of the war? Fighter Command didn't collapse when Air Chief Marshal Dowding left so soon after he had won the Battle of Britain. Bomber Command wouldn't have collapsed if Harris had gone and been replaced by, for example, Cochrane of 5 Group or Bennett of the Pathfinders.

Unaware of these controversies, the airmen of 6 Group continued to obey orders and fly wherever they were sent. Three days after the Dortmund operation, on the night of October 9/10, 209 crews set off for another Ruhr target, Bochum. Again the Canadians contributed about half the total force of bombers. It was not a particularly successful attack; poor visibility and intense fighter activity made the bombing scattered and ineffective. Only minor damage was caused in the south of the city. 6 Group lost three crews that night, of the five lost by the total force. Wing Commander G.A. Roy, CO of 424 Squadron, was shot down; he and five members of his crew survived to become POWs. An experienced crew from 434 Squadron, that of Flying Officer R.C. Diamond, was lost when their aircraft was struck by falling bombs over the target. With three engines and most of the instruments out of action, half the tail unit gone and a massive hole through the fuselage at the flight engineer's position, the Halifax fell out of the sky. Diamond managed to pull out of the dive and turned west. None of the crew was hurt – the flight engineer had not been at his station when the bombs hit – and Diamond hoped to limp as far as the Allied lines. But the worse-for-wear Halifax was a prime target for flak as it limped over the heavily defended Ruhr. It faltered, taking more hits. Diamond ordered the crew to bale out over Duisburg. All landed successfully and were captured. In contrast, only one member of Pilot Officer A.I. Cohen's 419 Squadron crew survived when their Lancaster was shot down.[15]

Harris ordered a daylight raid on the synthetic oil refinery at Wanne-Eickel for October 12. It was a modestly proportioned attack, presumably a sop for Portal, an operation that Harris could point to if Portal ever said that his orders were being completely ignored. The force consisted of 137 aircraft, 111 of which were 6 Group Halifaxes. Although the crews saw a good deal of smoke and fire, it seems probable that it emanated not from the oil refinery but from a nearby chemical plant which was demolished. All the Group's aircraft returned safely but one airman had been killed and several injured by flak.[16]

Two days later came a notable operation in the annals of 6 Group: the "Double Whammy" on Duisburg during the day on October 14 and again on the night of October 14/15. The Canadians comprised about a quarter of the force that Harris despatched to destroy Duisburg in this unusual attack. More than a thousand aircraft bombed the city in daylight, flew back to base, refuelled and re-armed and then returned for a night raid. Designed to demonstrate Bomber Command's indisputable air superiority, the operation delivered more than nine thousand tons of bombs on Duisburg, slightly more than fell on Hamburg in July and August 1943 and about the same tonnage as was dropped on London during the Blitz. It is interesting to compare this operation with the thousand-bomber raids of May and June 1942. Only by using hundreds of instructors and crews under training was Harris able to muster the vital thousand bombers in those dark days. Now, two and a half years later, he could mount *two* thousand-bomber raids in one twenty-four hour period without using a single training aircraft – in fact, without using about a third of his force.

In the first attack, 6 Group contributed 260 aircraft: 40 Lancasters from 419 and 428 Squadrons and 220 Halifaxes from 408, 415, 420, 424, 425, 426, 427, 429, 431, 432, 433, and 434 Squadrons. The aircraft arrived over Duisburg soon after 0900 hours. Cloud obscured the target. The Pathfinders' TIs quickly vanished from sight, having been seen by only a few of the crews. The Master Bomber instructed the force to bomb "targets of opportunity." Most 6 Group crews bombed the built-up area between the Rhine and the marshalling yards. They later described the bombing and the fires as "very scattered" but they saw "several large explosions." The German defences consisted of "extremely accurate predicted heavy flak" which ranged from "moderate to intense" during the run-up to the target. Over Duisburg, the Canadian crews encountered "moderate heavy flak in loose barrage form." Only one *Luftwaffe* fighter appeared on the scene; it sensibly disappeared, confronted by scores of RAF escorts.

The Canadian Group lost four bombers in the operation (of the fourteen lost by the whole force). Flight Lieutenant J. Galipeau and his crew from 425 Squadron were on their twentieth operation. Approaching the target, Galipeau encountered heavy flak and saw five large explosions ahead – which he took to be aircraft exploding. Then he saw two Halifaxes spinning down, one in flames. Just after he released the bombs, his aircraft received a direct hit in the starboard wing ... the shell going through without exploding. "Then the m/u [mid-upper gunner] spotted a fire in the wing and told me so. The engineer told me one tank was draining fast. After that I tried to feather the propellers without success. We could not put out the fire." In desperation Galipeau put the big aircraft in a steep dive, hoping to extinguish the fire without ripping off the damaged wing:

> I expected the a/c to blow up at any time so reduced the speed to about 160 mph and told the crew to do an emergency bale-out so as to be out as soon as possible. The two starboard props were just windmilling and made the aircraft very hard to control and we were losing height fast. After I saw the b/a [bomb-aimer] leaving, I checked the intercom to see that everybody was out. Having no answer, I started to get out of my seat. I looked back and there was quite a bit of smoke . . . I could not see anyone so I baled out. I saw the aircraft go into a spiral and enter a thin layer of cloud . . . I went thru [sic] the clouds after which I saw two or three other chutes. When I got down fairly close to the ground the Germans opened fire on me with light machine pistol and rifle. I spilled air out of my chute and luckily enough I reached the ground without being hit. I was captured immediately on reaching the ground.

Three other members of the crew were also captured. Three more were killed.[17]

The Lancaster of Flying Officer A.M. Roy of 419 Squadron was lost in a similar manner. Flak hit the starboard wing while Roy was on his bomb run, knocking out the two engines on that side and starting a fire in a pierced fuel tank. All too aware of the danger of the bomber blowing up, Roy ordered the crew to abandon aircraft. They didn't have time. A violent explosion knocked Roy unconscious; he came to in mid-air, tumbling earthward at about six thousand feet, having been blown clear of the doomed bomber. He pulled his rip-cord and landed unhurt to be captured by German troops, the only member of his crew to survive.[18]

Back at the bases, the ground crews awaited their charges, eager to get on with the work of servicing, refuelling, re-arming, and bombing up the aircraft for the night's operation. For every squadron involved, the mounting of a second operation so soon after the first created immense difficulties – but for none more so than for those of 6 Group. With their airfields in Yorkshire and Durham, the Canadian units had to spend longer in the air than most of the RAF groups; thus they had less time on the ground for servicing and readying their aircraft for the night op. The Canadians amazed the rest of Bomber Command when they trained clerks, cooks, and other trades to assist on the flight line. With their help, the job was done on time.

For the aircrews it was equally tough. They returned from Duisburg expecting to have the rest of the day off. Jim McInerney, a navigator with 408 Squadron recalls it as "quite an experience." He writes that his crew was "hardly back from the day trip and in bed when we were recalled for briefing for the night trip. Members of the crew were provided with 'wakey-wakey' pills to offset drowsiness."

For Bill Hutchins, a 426 Squadron pilot, the Duisburg daylight op was the first of his career. He flew as Second Dickey to Flying Officer Mann. Over the target one of the 1,000-pound bombs "hung up" in the bomb bay despite the energetic efforts of the crew to release it. It remained there all the way home. But at the instant of touch-down, it finally broke free of its shackles, smashed through the closed bomb bay doors and went bounding along the runway. The Halifax's tailwheel bounced right over it. Over the intercom the crew heard the rear gunner's alarmed voice telling everyone that the bomb was following them down the runway! Fortunately it did not explode. Hutchins recalls being tired and nervous after the raid – and aghast when he was ordered to take part in *another* op that night. He appealed to his flight commander, Russ Cowans. Didn't he think it "a bit much" to have to do one's first and second ops all in the same day? "Cowans and I had been good friends in Canada," Hutchins remarks. "We were both flying instructors at No. 17 EFTS at Stanley, Nova Scotia. I was sure he would excuse me from this one." Hutchins was to be disappointed. Cowans replied that everyone was tired and "If I'm going, you're going." On Hutchins's second trip of the day he flew with Flying Officer Beeker and crew. He remembers seeing the flames of Duisburg from a hundred miles away. The flak seemed horrendous to him, but when he commented on it after the op, the members of Beeker's crew – perhaps taking advantage of Hutchins's lack of operational experience – informed him that it was much lighter than usual. After the raid, Hutchins slept for ten hours.

Jim Northrup, a 415 Squadron pilot, flew both Duisburg trips early in his operational career. "The morning raid seemed very successful to me," he writes, "and when we got there in the evening the city was burning fiercely." He remembers the visibility being good even at twenty thousand feet, the flames outlining the pattern of the streets: "A very large area of the city was on fire and I could see it from miles away."

The 1,005 aircraft on the night raid flew in two waves two hours apart. The Canadians again represented about a quarter of the force: 40 Lancasters from 419 and 428 Squadrons and 212 Halifaxes from the balance of 6 Group's units. They found varying conditions over the target, the cloud cover ranging from 30 to 100 per cent with tops up to ten thousand feet. In general, however, visibility remained excellent. The attack commenced on time. Returning crews reported that the Pathfinders' TIs were "clearly visible and accurately placed." A "good carpet of fires took hold." Crews saw five large explosions. There is little doubt that Duisburg took a grim pounding that night. Two hundred miles away, homeward-bound crews could still see the fiercely burning city. They described the flak as "moderately heavy"; they saw many searchlights but rated them as not very effective. A few enemy fighters put in an appearance and some inconclusive combats took place. The flak defences scored all the victories that night.

Bomber Command lost seven aircraft. One came from 6 Group, a Halifax of 425 Squadron with Flying Officer C.T.L. Pidock in the pilot's seat. Moments after its bomb fell away, the Halifax lurched, struck by flak in one wing. Fire broke out in the starboard outer engine. The crew tried, but couldn't extinguish it. Pidock ordered them to bale out. Five made it but Pidock and Flight Sergeant F. P. Cartan didn't get out in time. They died when the Halifax crashed. Back in England, a returning 434 Squadron Halifax crashed, killing five of the crew and injuring the other two. Compared with earlier forays over the Ruhr, however, the losses were minuscule.

In sixteen hours, the Canadians had despatched 501 bombers

and had dropped more than twenty-one hundred tons of bombs. The two raids created chaos in Duisburg with severe damage throughout the city; areas that had previously escaped the effects of bombing were now devastated. The bombers had destroyed about half of Duisburg's key industries, all but demolished the railway station and dock facilities, and seriously damaged the airport.[19]

The day after the Duisburg operation, on October 15/16, 134 aircraft from 6 Group joined 372 from RAF Groups in an attack on Wilhelmshaven; three Canadian bombers didn't come back – almost inconsequential losses by the standards of an earlier day, but still horrific for the crews and unspeakably tragic for their families. Three more crews failed to return from raids on Essen on the night of October 23/24 and the 25th. Close to two thousand aircraft pounded the much-bombed city with some seventy-five hundred tons of bombs, virtually eliminating it as a productive centre.

Then it was Cologne's turn. More than seven hundred bombers hit the battered city in two waves on October 28. Sixty-four 6 Group aircraft participated in the first wave, 167 in the second. Aided by generally good visibility, the bombers shattered the districts of Mülheim and Zollstock, demolishing more than two thousand residential buildings as well as fifteen industrial premises and a number of power stations and dock facilities. One 6 Group bomber was lost; it may have been the one seen by John Wullum, a rear gunner with 434 Squadron: "There was an aircraft behind us at a somewhat higher altitude; I saw it as I did my continual fifteen-second sweep to both sides and the rear. Just before we reached the target, there was suddenly no aircraft! Just a huge ball of smoke!" A moment later Wullum's Halifax was also in trouble, taking a flak hit and losing two engines; however, the crew made it back to England. (Some eighteen months later Wullum went to a movie theatre in Canada where wartime footage was being shown – and he saw the bomber being blown up again. "I'd swear it was the same one," he declares. "I was shaken up for a week.")

On the night of the thirtieth, 243 bombers from the Canadian Group joined 662 from RAF groups in yet another assault on what remained of Cologne. A local newspaper wailed: "Districts of the city have sunk like islands in a natural catastrophe and Cologne has acquired new areas of silence and death. By day and night the enemy continuously spreads destruction over us. He had deprived us of gas, water and communication. Bread has become increasingly scarce and a helping of soup is regarded as a gift from heaven..." One source claimed that the population of the city, normally some 800,000, had dwindled to a few thousand, most of them municipal workers.[20]

The pattern continued into November: massive assaults on the cities that constituted the heart of industrial Germany. On the night of November 1/2, it was Oberhausen's turn. Two hundred and fifty 6 Group bombers formed the bulk of the force. The following night, 222 aircraft from the Canadian Group joined more than seven hundred from RAF groups in an attack on another familiar target: Düsseldorf. Six of the twelve casualties were 6 Group aircraft. Returning crews reported "several outstanding explosions" in the city. On the night of November 4/5, 214 aircraft from 6 Group formed part of the force of 749 bombers that hit Bochum, another Ruhr target. The raid demolished more than four thousand buildings, according to local reports. Five bombers from the Canadian Group failed to return. One was flown by Ray Mountford of Toronto, a 433 Squadron pilot on his twenty-third op. He believes he was shot down by a night fighter fitted with upward-firing *schräge Musik* guns, but neither he nor the gunners saw their attacker. Within moments, two of the Halifax's engines were ablaze. The fire spread with alarming rapidity. Mountford told the crew to bale out. Well-trained in emergency procedures, the airmen escaped from the burning bomber – although Mountford somehow knocked himself out getting clear of the aircraft. The sound of screaming woke him up. He opened his eyes and realized that he was hurtling earthward. The "screaming" was the sound of the wind in his ears. He hastily tugged at his rip-cord. All the crew survived.

Another aircraft lost that night was Halifax MZ831 of 425 Squadron commanded by Flying Officer Donald Smith. Flak knocked out the starboard inner engine. In an instant, the wing was aflame. Four of the crew jumped. Smith's intention was to jettison the bombs over the target but the aircraft became uncontrollable, snapping into a vicious spin. It then blew up. Smith lost consciousness with his helmet, oxygen mask, and earphones still in place. But when he came to in mid-air, moments later, those items of equipment had vanished. He attempted to pull his rip cord but his right arm would not respond. (He later found it was broken.) An additional problem was that the gauntlets of his flying gloves had turned inside out, trapping his fingers. After plunging more than fifteen thousand feet, he succeeded in hooking a gloved finger through the ring and tugging it. His parachute opened in the nick of time. He thumped down in a field of cabbages, breaking a rib, but alive. Dazed and in considerable pain, Smith wandered for about a mile. He came across what looked like a tree stump. He found himself talking to it, saying that he was hurt and needed medical attention: "After standing there a few feet apart, staring in the dark at the object for what seemed several minutes, the object moved off into the bush without speaking." Smith adds: "Two or three years later, I was relating the incident to my navigator (Flying Officer Jamie Jamieson) who, greatly surprised, said, 'My God, was that you? I didn't recognize your voice.' I guess we were both a bit more stunned than usual." Shortly afterwards, the Germans picked Smith up.

Six of the seven airmen aboard MZ831 survived, but Flight Sergeant Wallace Clowes, the RAF flight engineer, died, almost certainly killed by the flak that struck the Halifax. Smith said: "Because he was standing beside me, he prevented the shell splinters hitting me."

A daylight attack on the synthetic oil plant at Gelsenkirchen on November 6 cost two 6 Group aircraft. Ten days later, on the sixteenth, the Canadian Group participated in a tactical operation at the request of the U.S. Army, a reversion to the type of trip flown in the period immediately following D-Day. Three towns stood in the path of the proposed advance by the American First and Ninth Armies in the area between Aachen and the Rhine. More than two hundred 6 Group aircraft bombed the town of Jülich in good weather, virtually wiping out the place. No aircraft were lost but several suffered flak damage. Then it was Münster, the Castrop-Rauxel synthetic oil refinery, Neuss, and back to Duisburg on the last day of November. Despite Portal's pleas, Harris kept up the pressure on Germany's cities, hitting them with gigantic tonnages of bombs. In the final three months of 1944,

Bomber Command dropped more bombs than in the whole of 1943. Urban Germany became a world of blackened rubble, of jagged remains of walls, of tottering shells of buildings, a world without services or supplies, a world reeking with the sour smell of death and defeat. In December, it was Hagen, Karlsruhe, Soest, and Osnabrück – the latter memorable for the crew of one 426 Squadron Halifax. The rear gunner, Flying Officer Harry Schmuck, witnessed a collision soon after take-off involving a Pathfinder aircraft. He remembers the sight as "beautiful yet horrible" with a grotesque "Christmas tree effect" as the pyrotechnics exploded, dripping bright colours into the darkened sky. Fourteen airmen died instantly but they were not counted among the operational casualties of the night because the crash took place over England. Only a few minutes later, a Lancaster nearly demolished Schmuck's turret: "I could almost have reached up and scratched his belly as he went over," he recalls. Schmuck's aircraft dived so violently that all four engines cut out. The Halifax plunged three thousand feet before the engines could be restarted.

Flying Officer Bob Thompson, another 426 Squadron air gunner, remembers that op because he saw "a bright ball of light" appear below the cloud layer. It was two or three miles to the left and travelling at great speed in the same direction as his aircraft. Moments later, the light zoomed up through the cloud, climbing at incredible speed. It was an Me 163, the *Luftwaffe*'s new rocket fighter. "The rear gunner gave the 'Port go' as it came up and started in to attack," he recalls. "There was a single half-second burst of fire by the rear gunner and the attacker rolled over to the right and dived straight down through the cloud and exploded on the ground." A few minutes later another Me 163 appeared and was also shot down. At debriefing, several crews reported the appearance of the Me 163s. Intelligence officers discounted the claims, not believing that the Germans were using these fighters at night.

Later in the month, the Canadians participated in more heavy raids on familiar targets – Ludwigshafen, Duisburg, Cologne, and Düsseldorf. Two 6 Group bombers didn't get back from the raid on the Düsseldorf airfield; one may have been the aircraft that collided with the Halifax flown by Harry Shotton of 420 Squadron. Shotton remembers that the point of impact seemed to be on one engine – and a piece of a wing brace smashed through the canopy and hit him in the chest. "I was completely winded and knocked out for the moment," he says. "I came to and found the wireless operator apparently about to stab me!" In fact the stabbing was directed at Shotton's Mae West. The flying fragment of engine had hit Shotton's carbon dioxide bottle, instantly inflating his life jacket and almost throttling him. A quick jab with the knife solved the problem. Shotton and the crew managed to get the shuddering, badly damaged Halifax back to England on three engines without benefit of radio or radar. They landed on the emergency strip at Manston on England's south coast.

On Boxing Day, 1944, sixty-three 6 Group bombers joined over two hundred from RAF groups to attack St-Vith in support of U.S. forces engaged in the fierce Battle of the Bulge. Bob Thompson, the 426 Squadron gunner who had seen the Me 163s over Osnabrück, was now a member of 433 Squadron. He remembers the "fierce and accurate" flak encountered on this daylight op. Some bombers climbed rapidly to loftier – and safer – altitudes. But Thompson's skipper stayed at the briefed height. Thompson then watched in horror as bombs came hurtling down. He saw one pass between his aircraft's wing and tail unit – his worst moment of the war, he declares.

Two of the 150 Canadian bombers involved in a raid on Opladen on the night of December 27/28 didn't get back. Two more failed to return from an attack on an oil refinery at Scholven on the 29/30th. They were the last 6 Group aircraft lost in 1944; the final raids of the year – on the railway yards at Troisdorf and yet another assault on Cologne – were completed without casualties in the Canadian Bomber Group.

Thus ended 1944. Most members of 6 Group had expected the war to be over by now. In the heady days of early fall, the end had seemed so near; rumours of imminent surrender kept surfacing like rays of sunshine after a storm. But they came to nothing. The battles ground on – and the Germans had astounded everyone in mid-December by mounting a vigorous and highly effective counter-attack in the Ardennes; a fortnight later, on New Year's morning, while Allied airmen of the Second Tactical Air Force were recovering from the jollities of the night before, some nine hundred fighters, practically the entire fighter force of the

Luftwaffe in the West, attacked and shot up their airfields, destroying more than two hundred aircraft. The operation, *Bodenplatte*, cost the Germans about three hundred *Luftwaffe* aircraft, but it was further proof that the enemy had still not admitted defeat. In the Allied camp, heads were shaken. How long would the war drag on? What would it take to make the Germans realize that the end was near? Or was it? People were beginning to wonder. In the fall Jerry had followed up his V-1 with the frightening V-2s (known to the Germans as A-4s), rocket-propelled missiles carrying 2,200-pound warheads. Fighters and flak had been able to account for a healthy proportion of the V-1s; but there was no protection against these weapons, the direct antecedents of the space vehicles of the second half of the century. To add to Allied disquietude, jets and rocket-powered fighters had appeared on the scene. John McQuiston, a 415 Squadron skipper, spotted an Me 262 during a November raid on Düsseldorf: "Suddenly one shot across our nose, about five hundred feet below. It travelled at terrific speed, and I caught a brief impression of bulbous, underslung engines – one under each wing. No one else had seen it and I wondered if my eyes or nerves were playing tricks. Nothing flew that fast!"[21] Neither the RAF nor the USAAF had any aircraft to compare with the amazingly speedy fighters. Then there was evidence of a new type of U-Boat capable of remaining submerged for weeks at a time, thanks to the *Schnorkel* device that enabled the vessels to charge their batteries under water. What other technological tricks did the Germans have up their sleeves?

The Canadian Group's first operation of 1945 was a successful raid on the I.G. Farben chemical plants at Ludwigshaven on the night of January 2/3. A total of 389 aircraft carried out the attack; 156 were from 6 Group. None was lost. On the same night fifty-four 6 Group Lancasters made up part of a force of over five hundred aircraft that delivered a devastating attack on Nuremberg, that scene of Bomber Command's greatest defeat nearly a year before. The weather was good, the marking excellent and the bombing accurate. Although four aircraft were lost, none came from 6 Group. But, returning from the raid, a Lancaster of 419 Squadron, Z-Zebra, caused furrowed brows among its crew as it approached to land at Middleton St. George. The undercarriage indicator showed only one wheel down and locked, although a visual check seemed to indicate that all was well below. The skipper, Flight Lieutenant A.G.R. Warner, decided to proceed with the landing. The aircraft's hydraulic system had long been troublesome; now it wouldn't hold the ten degrees of flap on the crosswind leg. Turning on to final approach, Warner selected full flap. The aircraft's change of attitude seemed to indicate that this time the flaps had functioned correctly. "However, I think we must have lost the flap on our round-out," comments Warner, "because even though we were well above stall speed there was a 'clunk' and we sank and hit runway 240 a hell of a smack – the worst landing I ever made." The Lancaster bounced violently and Warner had to use power to renegotiate its return to terra firma. But in so doing, he soon ran out of runway, finally coming to a halt fifty feet beyond the end of the concrete. Quickly Warner swung the aircraft ninety degrees and looked back along the runway. Another Lancaster was speeding down the strip. "This was my twenty-second op," says Warner. "I was fully familiar with the regulation that a 'bogged' aircraft had to wait to be towed away. But I was also aware that we were in direct line with incoming aircraft." He opened up the throttles with the aim of reaching the perimeter track. He didn't make it. His starboard outer propeller hit a ditch-digger that had been left by civilian workers repairing a dispersal. In moments Z-Zebra was on fire, ammunition exploding, smoke filling the cockpit: "I can remember, as though it just happened, thinking, 'What a helluva way to go, in a fire, sitting on the ground, at your own base.' I felt myself losing it, a prelude to going under. But the opening of the window on the left let the smoke out – or the air in – and I unharnessed and I went out head first." The accident caused no casualties but it wrote off a famous aircraft, the first Canadian-built Lancaster, KB700, the *Ruhr Express*, at the conclusion of her forty-ninth op. Only her tail unit remained intact after the fire had burned itself out. Ironically, plans had been made to retire the famous Lanc after her fiftieth op and fly her back to Canada.[22]

On the night of January 5/6, 133 bombers from the Canadian Group constituted about 25 per cent of a force attacking Hannover. *Luftwaffe* night fighters intercepted the bomber stream over the German coast and harried the bombers all the way to the target and much of the way home. Ten 6 Group Halifaxes became casualties, in addition to twenty-one RAF bombers. One unit, 425 Squadron, lost three aircraft.

As far as the Allied leaders were concerned, Germany's eventual collapse was certain, jets, rockets, and *Schnorkel* submarines notwithstanding. What was uncertain was *when*. While the battered, beleaguered enemy fought on, tenaciously, skilfully, the Air Ministry re-examined Operation *Thunderclap* which had first been broached the previous July, a suggestion for "a series of overwhelming raids" that might finally wreck German morale and end the war. The plan had been rejected a month later. Now, the Allied leaders mused, perhaps the time was right. The Soviets had advanced across the eastern borders of Germany, a development both heartening and worrisome. On the one hand, it was proof of the impressive progress of the Russians. On the other, it conjured up fearful images of an unstoppable red tide sweeping westward. So might not the American and British bomber forces perform a vital duty both tactical and political in nature? In the Red Army's path lay several cities through which the Germans supplied their forward lines with both troops and *matériel*. Refugees attempting to escape the advancing Russians had flooded into the area. Massive bombing attacks would thus serve two purposes: they would assist the Soviets by disrupting German troop and supply movements and, perhaps even more importantly, they would demonstrate to the Russians the awesome strength of the Allied air forces. They would, in fact, be a not-so-subtle hint that the westward advance could be permitted to go so far and no further.

Which city would be the main target? Berlin had obvious attractions but Portal was not enthusiastic. Memories of the ghastly losses of a year earlier were too fresh in his mind. The Germans could be expected to defend Berlin to the last fighter and flak gun. Rather than a demonstration of might, an assault on Berlin could turn out to be a humiliating defeat. Harris agreed, favouring attacks on Chemnitz, Leipzig, and Dresden, key locations in Germany's network of communications and supply for the Eastern Front. The Soviets said they wanted the Allies to bomb Berlin and Leipzig. But not Dresden.[23] So why was Dresden selected? According to Harris, the city was a communications centre "of the first importance" and the attack was intended to render it "useless as a controlling centre for the defence." Although the popular image of the place is that of a lot of plump and jolly folk in *lederhosen* spending their days making china figurines and drinking beer, the truth is that the ancient city, Germany's seventh largest, had become a significant target – the "largest Reich city still intact." The city's population, normally about 630,000, had at this stage of the war burgeoned to some 1.25 million, principally because of the huge influx of refugees from the East. The capital of Saxony, Dresden sat astride the river Elbe, with the *Altstadt* (old town) on the left or west bank and the *Neustadt* (new town) opposite. The *Altstadt*, the largest part of the city, contained public buildings and commercial and residential areas. Pre-war Dresden could hardly have been described as a major industrial centre. But the war had changed the city's industrial face. By early 1945, Dresden had two companies engaged in aircraft and engine repairs plus twenty-four engineering and armaments firms. Products included small arms and ammunition, machine tools, electric gauges and measuring instruments, radio receivers and transmitters for ships and aircraft, electric generators and motors for U-Boats, gear wheels and differentials for vehicles, firefighting equipment, grinding wheels, small steam turbines for minesweepers, cameras and lenses for U-Boat periscopes, anti-aircraft and artillery weapons, tank landing and assault craft, chemicals, and explosives. The city had long been an important railway centre with many repair shops and yards. Through Dresden passed the lines that connected Berlin with Prague and Vienna and that linked eastern and southern Germany. The city was also a freshwater port, the Elbe being a much-used artery for freight traffic.[24]

Despite all this, few historians have defended the bombing of Dresden, claiming that there was no good reason for attacking the city, indeed no need for area-bombing in the winter of 1944/45 with the end of the war in Europe only a matter of weeks away. But such criticism enjoys the comforting foundation of hindsight. In order to understand the Dresden raid, it is necessary to consider the historical context in which it took place. By early 1945, World War II had dragged on for almost six years, a bitter war of attrition that had killed millions and had threatened the very survival of western civilization. At this stage of the conflict, the Allies were in no mood to show mercy to the perpetrators of such horrors as Auschwitz, Belsen, and Dachau. The pressure had to be maintained. Besides, in those pre-atomic days, the defeat of Japan still lay ahead, a formidable proposition that some claimed might take five years and cost a million Allied dead. The aim was to defeat Germany first, then to turn to Japan. The Allies had already suffered far too many casualties in the invasion of Europe. The bloodletting had to be brought to a halt as rapidly as possible. Against Germany, the combination of ground attacks by the Allied armies and a continuation of the Combined Bomber Offensive seemed, to the Allied leaders, to be the best way to accomplish this goal. If they had known how desperate the enemy's fuel situation was, they might well have arrived at a different conclusion.

Time has wrought the myth that the purpose of the raid on Dresden was to kill civilians in the largest possible numbers and in particularly horrible ways. The truth is that the attack was a routine operation; the city had become a target because it was strategically and politically important; the huge death toll was the result of a freak, catastrophic firestorm just like the one that devastated Hamburg during the summer of 1943. The mix of high explosive to incendiary bombs was typical of the raids of the period. The critics of the operation usually do their best to cast Harris as a sort of modern-day Genghis Khan gleefully devising every phase of the demolition of Dresden. In fact, Harris was simply doing what he had been doing, with the enthusiastic and grateful support of the Allied nations, for three years, and Churchill's later attempts to disavow any involvement in the operation will forever tarnish his memory. The Dresden raid was planned and carried out in precisely the same manner as hundreds of operations before and dozens after. Bomber Command ordered up 796 Lancasters and nine Mosquitoes. The Canadian Group's involvement in the raid was relatively minor; the sixty-seven Lancasters from 419, 424, 428, 431, 433, and 434 Squadrons constituted less than 10 per cent of the Main Force. A further 115 aircraft from the Canadian Group – all Halifaxes – joined 253 aircraft from 4 and 8 Groups in a diversionary raid on the Braunkohle-Benzin synthetic oil plant at Böhlen near Leipzig.

The plan called for the bombers to attack Dresden in two waves three hours apart. The first wave would consist entirely of 5 Group aircraft with the job of marking the target, using their low-level techniques. Their job was to start the fires that would become a beacon for the Main Force in the second wave. The aiming point selected was a sports stadium in the *Altstadt*. The second wave of bombers from 1, 3, 6, and 8 Groups, using standard Pathfinder marking methods, were to "start new fires," "scatter burning debris," "spread the flames," and "blow in windows and roofs" – typical area-bombing objectives. The aiming point for the second wave was the marshalling yards.[25]

The aircrews who filed into the briefing rooms on February 13 had no idea that they would be participating in a raid which would become infamous, a symbol of the immorality of war. As far as the crews were concerned, they had a challenging job ahead, a long and hazardous flight of ten to eleven hours in mid-winter, much of it across enemy territory. They settled down in their chairs and the briefing officers informed them of Dresden's industries and its strategic importance. At Middleton St. George, home of 419 and 428 Squadrons, the intelligence officer told the crews that Soviet Marshal Koniev had pushed the front line to within seventy-five miles of the city and that Dresden had become a military HQ and supply base for the Germans. He added that untold numbers of refugees had swarmed into the city and that a successful attack would "add to the turmoil and the administrative difficulties of the civil authorities." At Skipton-on-Swale, the message to the crews was blunt: Their job was the destruction of Dresden's built-up area, plus the railway and industrial targets. But, they were told, the Germans had established three POW camps in the area, less than ten miles from the aiming point. Accurate bombing was therefore vital. Moderate to heavy flak could be expected.[26]

At 2215 hours, 244 Lancasters of 5 Group began the attack, dropping more than eight hundred tons of bombs and setting in motion fourteen hours of unmitigated hell for the citizens of the charming Baroque city. The first wave reported a "fine concentration" of both marking and bombing. One crew thought the city looked "very beautiful ringed with searchlights . . . and fires in its heart were of different colours. Some were white, others of a pastel shade outlined with trickling orange flames. Whole streets were alight." Then the second wave attacked, 529 Lancasters, including sixty-six from 6 Group. A further eighteen hundred tons of bombs went down on the reeling city. The result was horrific.[27]

The second great firestorm of World War II began as many individual fires quickly merged, creating a vast conflagration that sent immeasurable volumes of rapidly heated air up into the chilly sky above the city. Instantly, greedily, the fires sucked in air from the surrounding area. The frightful blast furnace went to work just as efficiently and horribly as it had done in Hamburg. Starved of oxygen, the voracious fires pulled in more air, creating screaming winds that tore through the city, carrying burning trees, bits of buildings, men and women, and flinging them into the blaze. The firestorm began at approximately 2300 hours and eradicated about eleven square miles of the *Altstadt*. As in Hamburg, the temperatures in the vicinity of the fire reached fantastic levels. In tunnels under the main railway station, rescue workers found hundreds of people "who had apparently fallen asleep, slumped against the station walls." Poisonous fumes and smoke had killed them in the unventilated tunnels. The same fate befell countless others who had taken refuge in their cellars. Most of those who tried to escape fared no better; on the streets they encountered "jets of flame forty to fifty feet long" and heavy furniture hurtling through the air "like matchsticks," carried on the hurricane-force gales. "Many people died alone; their shrivelled corpses littered the streets, glued to the surface where the tarmac had melted and then solidified."[28]

Above the city, the aircrews saw several massive explosions including "an orange one and two huge red ones." Columns of smoke rose to thirteen thousand feet. Some crews described "a sea of fire with the glow visible for 160 miles." The German defences were "negligible," the crews declared. There was little flak and few searchlights. It is a measure of the desperate state of Germany's fuel supplies that on that night only twenty-seven German fighters were airborne – and they were "spread all over eastern and central Germany."[29] The raid was agonizingly frustrating for the *Luftwaffe* night fighter pilots based near Dresden. They could see the hideous effects of the bombing but they could take no action; their aircraft sat silent, tanks empty. Wilhelm Johnen, the German night fighter pilot who had been so bewildered by the first use of Window over Hamburg, later wrote of the appalling carnage among Dresden's citizens:

> Hundreds remained stuck in the melting asphalt and were burnt alive like flaming torches. Hundreds jumped with their clothes on fire into the icy waters of the Elbe or into the nine-foot-deep water basins from which they could not clamber out. Those who could swim were dragged down into the depths by nonswimmers. The Exhibition Grounds in the Dresden gardens were filled with refugees who had taken cover there when the sirens wailed. But even the lawns with their centuries-old trees were sprayed with bombs and phosphorus canisters until a forest fire was raging ... The human remains were placed on huge steel platforms, sprinkled with petrol and burnt in the open air.[30]

The raid was catastrophic. Bomber Command estimated that about 85 per cent of the built-up area had been destroyed. The *Altstadt* was "almost completely wiped out" and the majority of the structures in the inner suburbs, together with many industrial works, had been "gutted." After the shattering Bomber Command assault, more than three hundred USAAF B-17s flew over the pyre the following day. They concentrated on the railway yards. Mustang fighters then flew at low level, machine-gunning any traffic still moving.

Precisely how many people died that night in Dresden will probably never be known because of the presence of so many refugees. Estimates range all the way from 50,000 to 150,000, with 135,000 being the widely accepted number.[31] Certainly the raid had the sickening distinction of killing more people than any other in history, exceeding even those in which the first atomic bombs were dropped in August of 1945.

The war in Europe began to wind down. In the remaining weeks of the conflict, 6 Group was involved in a variety of operations: area-bombing cities, tactical strikes in support of ground forces, attacks on oil and transportation targets and sea-mining.

Although devastating casualties and an almost total drying-up of fuel supplies had decimated the German fighter force, from time to time it still demonstrated its ability to cause severe losses among Allied bombers. On the night of February 21/22, 349 aircraft, including 111 Halifaxes from the Canadian Group, attacked the Rhenish town of Worms in clear weather. More than a thousand tons of bombs fell, destroying an estimated 40 per cent of the built-up area. "Streets and buildings seen in light of fires..." declared the 6 Group ORB with evident satisfaction. But the bombers met vigorous opposition: seachlights, flak, and fighters. Six of the 6 Group Halifaxes went down, most of them destroyed by fighters. Particularly hard hit was 432 Squadron which lost three Halifaxes. One of them was commanded by Flying Officer F.D. Baxter; his rear gunner, Flight Sergeant S.E. Waterbury, recalled the night's events vividly:

> It was a normal trip 'til we got up to the target, the flak was light and we hit the target bang on. When we were about one minute out of the area I reported a twin-engined fighter dead astern and gave evasive action to starboard. We both fired at the same time; he did not get us. Then he came in from port again, I gave corkscrew to port and we were firing. The third attack came from starboard, the fighter got us and we were in flames. The fourth attack came from port and the fighter shot away our controls. The skipper gave the order to bale out. The aircraft rolled over on its back and I was in the top of my turret and couldn't get my doors open. It rolled over again and the side of the turret collapsed and I was thrown out, dazed from a bang on the head. When my head cleared I was falling through the air, so I pulled my rip-cord and the 'chute opened. It was only fastened by one hook. I landed in some trees, OK but scared.

Baxter, Waterbury, and, Flight Sergeant G.E. Armstrong survived but four other members of the crew were killed. 408 Squadron lost two aircraft and 427 Squadron one. The skipper of this latter aircraft, Pilot Officer W.R. Wilson, was remarkably lucky. Hit during the bomb run, the aircraft caught fire in both wings. Wilson found his controls immovable. He had no choice; he ordered the crew to bale out. Almost at the same instant, the

Halifax blew up, hurling Wilson clear. Dazed but unhurt, Wilson found himself falling free; he reached for his rip-cord and pulled it. He landed safely but all his crew died.[32]

At this period of the war, the weather sometimes proved more dangerous than the enemy. In the late afternoon of March 5, 185 bombers from the Canadian Group prepared to take off, part of a force of 760 aircraft attacking Chemnitz in a continuation of Operation *Thunderclap*. It was a disaster. Six aircraft from the Canadian Group were lost over the target – but eleven more crashed in England, most of them at the beginning of the operation, the victims of icing. At Linton-on-Ouse, three of 426 Squadron's Halifaxes plunged to earth within minutes of take-off, cocooned in thick ice that had been lurking in the clouds. It quickly coated wings, tail units, propellers, and cabins. One Halifax, LW210, flown by Flight Lieutenant I. Emerson, crashed in York, killing several civilians. 420 Squadron also lost three aircraft, two of them immediately after take-off. The Halifax flown by Pilot Officer R.F. Sollie, NA190, crashed near Church Fenton. One of Sollie's gunners, Flight Sergeant Harry Waugh, had a remarkable escape from death that afternoon. He jumped from the plunging, iced-up aircraft. But he was too low and his parachute had not opened fully. The ground rushed up at terrifying speed. Death seemed certain. Then the aircraft hit the ground immediately beneath him. The blast of rising air from the explosion filled Waugh's parachute and flung it upward with Waugh bouncing at the end of the lines. The parachute collapsed but now enough precious height had been regained. After a fall of about four hundred feet, Waugh's parachute opened fully and he landed unhurt, the only survivor of the unfortunate crew. Two 425 Squadron Halifaxes were also victims of the icing, one crashing near Ousebourne, the other near Linton; 419, 428, and 429 Squadrons each lost one aircraft.

At the time of take-off the weather was described as: "7/10 to 10/10ths variable SC [strato-cumulus cloud], base between 2,000 and 3,000 feet, in layers to 8,000 to 9,000 feet. Thin medium layers between 10,000 and 20,000 feet. Freezing level 5,000 feet. Icing index moderate." The official report added: "Somewhere between Tholthorpe and Linton and south of Tholthorpe was a cloud formation approximately ten miles in diameter. It was indistinguishable from the remainder of the cloud, except that to ground observers it was somewhat darker though not markedly so. The top of this cloud was flat and comparable with the surrounding cloud. Holes could be seen north of this cloud."

The crashes occurred at approximately 1700 hours; all the lost aircraft took off between 1628 and 1648. The severe icing seems to have occurred in a "localized area near Linton and Tholthorpe." Two of the lost aircraft may have collided: "425/J and 426/A crashed close together and at the same time. The story of the survivor in 425/J brings out the possibility of a straight collision or 426/A icing up and falling on top of 425/J. 425/S crashed only a short distance away and within a half-minute of these two, apparently from icing only." A final note pointed out: "The dispersals in which the crashed aircraft normally were parked are widely separated from each other on both airfields. This reduces the likelihood of sabotage, though it does not entirely rule it out."[33] Those aircraft that made it to the target encountered ferocious winds, far stronger than predicted. Jim Gunn was the navigator of a 428 Squadron Lancaster commanded by Flight Lieutenant Cliff Pratt; he remembers the winds being so strong that on the return journey fuel began to run low and that it was necessary to eliminate an enormous "dog-leg" in order to make it home. Doug Goodwin was an air gunner on a 420 Squadron Halifax which also ran low on fuel while homeward-bound and which he attempted to land at Juvincourt; descending in poor visibility, the aircraft hit a mast atop a hill. The Halifax was demolished but the crew escaped.

In addition to the grim loss of life caused by the weather, a 432 Squadron Halifax, RG475, with Squadron Leader E.A. Hayes in command, was shot down by British anti-aircraft fire on its return to England. The aircraft crashed at Walton near London; the crew, including a Second Dickey, were killed.[34]

Two nights later, one hundred 6 Group aircraft joined nearly two hundred bombers from RAF groups in an attack on the Deutsche Erdoel oil refinery at Hemmingstedt, some sixty miles northwest of Lübeck. A 420 Squadron pilot, Harry Shotton, remembers the op well: "It was probably the most unsatisfactory trip of my tour. The opposition was fierce with flak and fighters but that wasn't the problem. It all went wrong when the Master

Bomber was shot down. His aircraft crashed a few miles outside the town, his TIs going off and creating what looked like ground marking. Most of the crews bombed on the wreckage of his aircraft. Hardly any damage was done to the refinery."

Two 6 Group aircraft, one from 408 Squadron, the other from 425, failed to return from Hemmingstedt, out of a total Bomber Command loss of five. Three more 6 Group bombers were lost that same night in the course of a highly successful attack on Dessau. Two of the crews were from 424 Squadron, the other from 419 Squadron. The following night eighty-five 6 Group bombers were part of a force of 312 aircraft attacking the Hamburg shipyards in which the new Type XXI *Schnorkel*-equipped U-Boats were being assembled. The only casualty was a Halifax of 415 Squadron commanded by Warrant Officer A.F. McDiarmid; fortunately, the entire crew survived to become POWs for the last few weeks of the war.

By now the Germans armies were in disarray, retreating on all fronts. Harris kept up the pressure. Close to two hundred 6 Group bombers joined more than eight hundred aircraft from RAF Groups in a massive daylight raid on Essen during the afternoon of March 11. It was to be the last Bomber Command raid on the ruined city. Most of the population had abandoned the place and many of the heavy industrial plants were inactive. Air power had virtually eliminated a major centre of German war production. But the notorious defences, though much depleted, were still capable of inflicting casualties on the attackers. Three aircraft failed to return, two of them 6 Group bombers. 431 Squadron lost its CO, Wing Commander R.F. Davenport, when his Lancaster fell victim to flak; the crew were killed. A 434 Squadron Lancaster was also shot down by flak; its skipper, Flight Lieutenant R.J. Fern, and five of the crew died in the crash. Only the rear gunner, Flight Lieutenant J.A.H.B. Marceau, survived.

The pounding of Germany continued, immense swarms of bombers flying almost unhindered over cities that had once been veritable death traps for Allied aircrew. Dortmund, Wuppertal, Zweibrücken, Castrop-Rauxel ... not one 6 Group aircraft was lost on these early spring raids. But on the night of March 15/16, 6 Group's run of luck ended abruptly. A force of 267 aircraft attacked the Ruhr town of Hagen; 6 Group provided 142 bombers, more than half the force. Eight were lost, four over the target, four on the trip home, all victims of night fighters. Flak hit a 425 Squadron Halifax near Hagen; moments later a fighter attacked. The skipper, Flight Lieutenant J.R.S.Y. Laporte, was wounded in both elbows. One starboard engine burst into flames and a fire took hold in the fuselage. Although one of the crew managed to extinguish the fuselage fire, the flames from the engine couldn't be quelled. Laporte gave the order to abandon aircraft. Despite his wounds, he remained at the controls until all the crew had baled out. But, as he began to extricate himself from the fiercely burning bomber, a massive explosion shook the aircraft. It hurled Laporte to the floor. He was lucky. He managed to scramble to the escape hatch and jump clear. All but one of the crew survived. Laporte was later awarded a Bar to his DFC. Two more 6 Group aircraft were lost on the night of March 18/19 in an attack on Witten in the Ruhr. The Canadian Group provided about a quarter of the 324 aircraft involved in this highly destructive operation carried out in exceptionally clear weather. But flak, searchlights, and fighters made it a costly night for the attackers. Eight bombers failed to return; two of the lost aircraft came from 425 Squadron, and one from 420 Squadron.

On the night of March 20/21 a force of 160 Lancasters returned to Hemmingstedt, the scene of the disappointing raid two weeks before. Two-thirds of the force consisted of 6 Group aircraft. This time the attack was successful, the oil refinery being virtually demolished. A Lancaster of 419 Squadron went down; the skipper, Flight Lieutenant R.W. Millar, was on the thirty-sixth and last trip of his operational tour. Only one member of the crew, Flight Sergeant J.W. Aitken, survived. A falling bomb struck a Lancaster of 431 Squadron over the target. A huge hole appeared in the port wing and one engine was badly twisted in its mounting and had to be feathered. The skipper, Flight Sergeant F.G.K. Saunders, found the aircraft almost uncontrollable. It dived, vibrating violently, but Saunders managed to pull out and, astonishingly, brought it back to base. He was awarded a well-deserved DFM.

This was the last night attack of the month for 6 Group. Eight daylight operations followed in eleven days. Only two resulted in losses of 6 Group aircraft, an attack on the marshalling yards at Hildesheim (two lost) and a raid on Münster (three lost). On

March 31, two hundred 6 Group bombers were part of a force of 469 aircraft delivering a heavy attack on the U-Boat assembly facilities at Hamburg. An unpleasant surprise was in store for the Canadian crews: the new jet fighters of the *Luftwaffe*. Solid cloud obscured the target. The Master Bomber called for sky-marking. The first waves of aircraft bombed without interference, but the final, third wave of Canadian Lancasters arrived over the target ten minutes late and lacked fighter support. Testing out a new "gaggle formation," the 6 Group aircraft came under lively attack from Me 262s which "rocketed up from the cloud banks" below. RAF Mustangs sped back to help the bombers but it was too late. About thirty in number, the jets were "skilfully directed by ground controllers."[35] Flying Officer Don Saunders, a 424 Squadron pilot, was amazed by their speed: "I felt as if we were standing still. The gaggle closed in and were wing tip to wing tip ... creating the closest formation of bombers I have ever seen! Each time the jets came the gunners were at work." He saw five bombers shot down. "Our bombing operations would not have been as successful if the Germans had had the Me 262 at an earlier date," he asserts. On the way back to England after the raid, Saunders witnessed a mid-air collision between a Halifax and a Lancaster near Heligoland. One aircraft broke in two, Saunders recalls. Three parachutes opened but it is believed that the airmen drowned. Over the target, Flying Officer John Campbell, a wireless operator with 426 Squadron, looked out of his window and saw several bombers on fire as the jet fighters sped through the formation. "I then turned my attention to the screen of the 'Fishpond' which was my responsibility." "Normal evasive action was quite useless," recalls Flying Officer Neil Fletcher who was on the op with 420 Squadron. On the other hand, Flying Officer Bill Hutchins, of 426 Squadron, says: "We never saw the jets and never saw any of our fighters make a move." For Hutchins, the Hamburg op completed his tour.

Eleven bombers went down, eight of them from 6 Group. The jets seemed to concentrate on 433 Squadron. It suffered sixteen attacks on seven of its ten aircraft. Two Me 262s attacked the Lancaster of Squadron Leader P.D. Holmes, one from the port quarter, the other from behind. The Lancaster's rear gunner, Warrant Officer E.J. Ash, took on one jet while the mid-upper gunner, Warrant Officer V.M. Ruthig, fired at the other, a few moments later joining Ash who was still engaging the first Me 262. Members of the crew saw hits on one jet, "striking it on the wing, engines and nose." The fighter broke away, "shedding debris" and "trailing smoke." Ruthig earned a DFC.

Three of the jets attacked a 431 Lancaster flown by Flying Officer C.E.G. Heaven. His rear gunner, Flight Sergeant William Kuchma, blazed away at one as it "closed from 700 yards." His fire was devastatingly accurate. The German pilot pulled up to starboard at fifty yards as "smoke and fragments streamed from the fighter." The jet's "tail assembly tore away," as the fighter fell "end over end" into the clouds below. Two other Me 262s attacked the Lancaster, and both were driven off, one trailing smoke. Both Heaven and Kuchma were decorated for their performance over Hamburg. Flying Officer J.W. Watson of 424 Squadron was fortunate to survive an attack by two jets. One of his gunners, Flight Sergeant C.K. Howes, couldn't fire; his guns had jammed. But the jet's cannon fire missed the bomber. Watson's other gunner, Flight Sergeant S.J.O. Robinson, opened up on the second jet directly behind the Lancaster. One of the fighter's engines belched black smoke and the aircraft went out of control. Robinson saw flames "along the underside of the fuselage."

The jets launched nine attacks on the newly issued Lancasters of 429 Squadron. Flying Officer H.A.M. Humphries and his crew claimed a probable after an encounter with an Me 262. Both the rear and the mid-upper gunner, flight sergeants D.H. Lockhart and R. Jones respectively, opened fire. But Lockhart's guns jammed after discharging twenty rounds. It didn't matter; the job had been done. The jet fighter "went out of control" and "fell into the clouds" with "pieces flying off the starboard wing." Another of the squadron's aircraft, with Flying Officer S.F. Avis in the pilot's seat, received serious damage; the jet wrecked the aircraft's starboard aileron, damaged the mid-upper turret, and blew a large hole in one wing. The jet fighters damaged two 427 Squadron Lancasters. One, flown by Flying Officer D.L. McNeill, took holes in the fuselage and tail unit, but the rear gunner, Warrant Officer J.G. Jarvis, saw hits on the enemy fighter; it rolled over and plunged vertically, trailing black smoke. Another Lancaster from the same squadron got back to England less five feet of one wing. The skipper, Flight Lieutenant J.L. Storms, displayed exceptional airmanship, maintaining control all the way home, then bringing the crippled bomber in to a safe landing.

The Canadian Bomber Group's losses were five Lancasters and three Halifaxes. Twenty-six aircrew lost their lives.[36] It had been a costly encounter for the Canadians, all of whom had the greatest respect for the jets with their top speed of over 500 mph and their armament of four 30 mm MK108 cannons, a powerful arsenal capable of blowing a heavy bomber apart in the air. On some Me 262s, the Germans added even more firepower in the form of R4M rockets of 50 mm calibre.

By now, after the setbacks of the winter, the Allied Armies were advancing everywhere, pursuing the exhausted, outnumbered German troops. In late March, British and Canadian forces surrounded the Ruhr after crossing the Rhine. Patton's Third Army was thrusting into southern Germany. A few days later, the U.S. Ninth Army reached the Elbe. The Russians closed in on Berlin. The end was at last in sight. The air war had one more month to run, a month in which twelve 6 Group aircraft would be lost, a month of unreliable weather and many scrubbed ops, a month in which the Group's activity would decline as its once-familiar targets were occupied one by one. Bomber Command was now at the peak of its power. Hundreds of newly trained aircrew waited, hoping to get "an op in" before the end. The vast majority didn't. Losses had been so low and the training establishments so efficient that, by early 1945, trained aircrew were already being diverted to other duties, never having an opportunity to serve on an operational squadron. (Many hoped to be involved in the fight against Japan; at this period one of the authors, as an ATC cadet at Pocklington, Yorkshire, was told by Air Commodore Gus Walker that it would take five years to beat Japan and that the cadets present would "get their chance." None did.)

In April, 6 Group aircraft took part in twelve bombing operations. Two were cancelled, the aircraft recalled soon after take-off. Three struck naval and shipyard targets, Hamburg, Kiel, and Heligoland; three concentrated on railway targets, Mockau and Engelsdorf and Schwandorf; two were against oil targets, Merseburg and Harburg; and the final op of the war was directed against Wangerooge. In addition, 6 Group completed four sea-mining operations.

On the night of April 4/5, 105 bombers from the Canadian Group constituted part of a force of more than three hundred aircraft attacking the Leuna synthetic oil plant at Merseburg in poor weather with thick cloud and icing conditions. Most crews bombed on sky-markers, resulting in little new damage to the facility. Flying Officer J.W. Watson and his crew of 424 Squadron had been lucky in late March when they encountered a jet fighter over Hamburg on March 31; but, returning from this operation, they crashed on landing. All seven men died.

On the same night, ninety 6 Group Halifaxes were part of a force of 327 aircraft attacking the Rhenania synthetic oil plant at Harburg. The weather was good and concentrated bombing resulted in two huge explosions and black smoke rising to six thousand feet. The flak was classified as "moderate" but *Luftwaffe* fighters put in an appearance, intercepting the bombers over the target and engaging them on their way home. They shot down four bombers, including one from 6 Group, the 408 Squadron Halifax of Pilot Officer A.K. Brown.

An operation against Hamburg on the night of April 8/9 cost two 6 Group aircraft. Nearly two hundred Halifaxes and Lancasters of the Canadian Group comprised about half the force attacking the battered city for the last time in World War II. Flak hit a 408 Squadron Halifax just after it bombed. The skipper, Flying Officer A.P. Jensen, and all but one of his crew were killed. A 419 Squadron Lancaster commanded by a second-tour man, Flying Officer H.R. Cram, had engine trouble on the way to the target. He bombed with one engine out; on the way home a second engine caught fire. The Lancaster lost height with alarming rapidity; Cram ordered the crew to bale out. All landed safely behind the lines and were back in Britain in a few days.

The following day, some two hundred 6 Group bombers set out for the marshalling yards near Leipzig in support of U.S. Army operations. Two aircraft didn't get back, a Lancaster from 433 Squadron commanded by Pilot Officer R.J. Grisdale, and a Halifax of 415 Squadron with Flying Officer R.S. Evans at the controls. On the night of April 13/14, more than two hundred 6 Group aircraft formed the majority of a 377-bomber force attacking the U-Boat yards at Kiel. It was not successful; most of the bombs fell on nearby suburbs, some bomb-aimers undoubtedly confused by the many decoy markers employed by the Germans during the raid. Fighters appeared on the scene and shot down a Lancaster of 419 Squadron. The crew died. Flak hit the 428 Squadron Lancaster of Flying Officer D.M. Payne during the bomb run. Payne was hit in the legs and in his left arm and hand, but pushed on to unload on the target, before turning for home. On the way, flak again smashed into his aircraft. With three of his engines out, Payne got away from the target area and set off across the North Sea. He didn't get far. The remaining engine failed. Payne ditched the Lancaster but hit his head on the windshield at the moment of impact. Only two of the crew were uninjured and Flight Sergeant Vardy died when the aircraft sank. For the next twelve days, the survivors huddled in their raft, Payne drifting in and out of consciousness. The navigator, Flying Officer G.C. Riley, took command and

> organized the sailing of the dinghy as well as attending to the injuries of the crew . . . With coolness, calm courage and splendid example he kept up the spirits of the crew by reading passages from a pocket Bible and by organizing diversions such as card games. He was instrumental in preventing the crew from drinking sea water when the fresh water supplies were running low and he organized the distribution of emergency rations on an economical basis. Eventually the dinghy grounded on some sand flats near Bremerhaven and the crew were taken prisoner. Without this officer's direction, guidance and example, it is doubtful if the members of his crew would have survived this very trying ordeal

declared the official citation when Riley received the MBE.[37]

Flying Officer Reg Moase, a 426 Squadron pilot from St. Catharines, Ontario, was on the second trip of his tour with his own crew. He recalls the op vividly because his navigational equipment failed shortly after take-off. Nevertheless, the crew proceeded to the target and "to us, as amateurs, it seemed to be well defended..." After dropping their bombs, the crew set off for home "...mostly on guesswork, by flying west and then north." Moase remarks that they didn't travel westward far enough, for they soon found themselves over Heligoland. "The enemy gunners there were delighted to have a lone bomber as target. However, we quickly flew west again to get out of the flak. Eventually we returned to England . . . " A couple of nights later, Moase was in a bar in York with a friend from another squadron. "He asked if we had been to Kiel and if we had seen the 'stupid bugger' who flew over Heligoland on the return trip." Moase says, "I felt pretty good to be able to tell him that I was the 'stupid bugger.' "

On the sixteenth, 6 Group bombers made up the majority of the 167 aircraft attacking the marshalling yards at Schwandorf. Conditions were excellent and the bombing accurate, virtually demolishing the yards, effectively disrupting German military traffic through this major junction north of Regensburg. The same night, twenty 6 Group Halifaxes attacked the airfield at Gablingen, near Augsburg. All aircraft returned safely from these raids, the last night operations of the war for the Canadian Group.

On the 18th, 112 Halifaxes from 6 Group joined 857 bombers from RAF Groups in a devastating assault on the town, the airfield, and the naval base of Heligoland. In clear weather the bombers attacked in two waves, and the entire island was soon invisible beneath huge palls of smoke and dust. No fighters appeared on the scene, but flak scored hits on several aircraft, one of which blew up and damaged the 426 Squadron Halifax of Pilot Officer J.A.H. Whipple. Whipple won the DFC for bringing the crippled aircraft safely back to base. The 408 Squadron Halifax flown by Pilot Officer A.J. Cull was hit over the target and crashed. A 420 Squadron Halifax commanded by Flight Sergeant W.J. Dunningan crashed into the sea en route to the target. All aboard both Halifaxes were lost.[38]

Two hundred 6 Group bombers set off for Bremen on April 22, part of a total force of 767 aircraft attacking the port to assist the British XXX Corps. The first waves of bombers were able to identify their aiming points, but by the time the 6 Group aircraft were ready to bomb, heavy cloud had moved in. The Master Bomber ordered the operation cancelled. Don Saunders, the 424 Squadron pilot who had been impressed by the speed of the jet Me 262s over Hamburg on March 31, was wounded during this abortive raid. It was the last trip of his tour – and, as it turned out, very nearly his last ever. Flak struck his Lancaster, a chunk slicing through his left-hand window, just missing his head before departing through the windscreen. Hit in the eye by a fragment of Perspex, Saunders was momentarily stunned: "The next thing I remember is being at 6,000 feet in a dive..." Saunders managed to pull the plunging Lancaster out and jettisoned the bombs into the sea. He spent the next two weeks in Northallerton Hospital, having bits of flak and Perspex removed from his eyes and face, after which "the Group Captain specialist gave me the only recommendation I have ever heard of for an RCAF pilot to wear a monocle!" He was awarded the DFC for getting the aircraft and crew safely back to base in spite of his injury.

Three days later came 6 Group's last offensive operation of World War II, an attack on two coastal batteries on Wangerooge Island at the eastern end of the Frisian chain. The Canadian Group contributed 192 of the 482 aircraft participating, ninety-two Halifaxes from 408, 415, 425, 426, and 432 Squadrons, plus one hundred Lancasters from 419, 424, 427, 428, 429, 431, 433, and 434 Squadrons. Ten squadrons of Spitfires from 11 Group escorted the bombers in cloudless weather. The crews heard the Master Bomber's instructions clearly and were able to place their bombs in a well-concentrated pattern until dust and smoke obscured the target area. Thereafter the Master Bomber directed the Main Force to "bomb the edge of the smoke." Crews saw many fires and observed a huge explosion at 1722 hours. The bombs appear to have done enormous damage to the area surrounding the batteries although the concrete gun positions themselves suffered little damage. A nearby "camp for forced workers" was hit, as were a Catholic church and a holiday resort, including some hotels, guest houses, and two unoccupied children's holiday homes. More than three hundred people were killed on the island.

Flak damaged three aircraft but the day's losses were the result of a tragic error. One aircraft hit the slipstream of another and lurched into a third. Within moments, six bombers had become a tangle of wreckage. All crashed into the sea. Four were 6 Group aircraft, two Lancasters from 431 Squadron, and two Halifaxes from 408 and 426 Squadrons. Despite the reported sighting of as many as nine parachutes, all twenty-eight occupants of the Canadian aircraft died.

The last bomber to return to base was a Lancaster from 428 Squadron, D-Dog, with Flying Officer D.R. Walsh at the controls. It touched down at 2036 hours. The Canadian Bomber Group's shooting war had ended.[39]

In the last days of conflict, 6 Group's Halifaxes and Lancasters turned to the congenial task of flying 4,329 liberated prisoners of war to Britain in Operation *Exodus*.[40]

Even before the Third Reich had capitulated, the planners were busy organizing the VLR (Very Long Range) bomber force, usually known as "Tiger Force," which was to join the Americans in the Far East. Consisting of 408, 419, 420, 425, 428, 431, and 434 Squadrons as well as 405 Squadron, which was due to be transferred to 6 Group from the Pathfinders, the force lost no time in making preparations to fly home to Canada. On May 31, Harris and McEwen journeyed to Middleton St. George to witness the departure of the first contingent.

Harris told the Canadians, "You leave this country, after all you have done, with a reputation that is equal to any and surpassed by none. We in Bomber Command have always regarded our Canadian Group and Canadian crews outside the Group as among the very best."[41] Did he recall his early misgivings about 6 Group as he uttered those words? One wonders.

The exodus began with fourteen Lancasters from 428 Squadron, the first aircraft commanded by Flight Lieutenant S.V. Eliosoff. Over the next few weeks, 165 Canadian-built Lancaster Xs set off for home. The journey was not without incident. One Lancaster had to ditch off the Azores but the crew was rescued. A far more tragic accident occurred on June 15 on the airfield at Terceira in the Azores. Lancaster X, KB936 of 425 Squadron, landed there after a flight of six hours and thirty minutes from Tholthorpe. The skipper, Flying Officer G. Halle, parked the aircraft in the dispersal bay near the south end of the runway. "As it was intended that we should continue on to Newfoundland later that night," writes the wireless operator, Bernard Marcoux of Alliston, Ontario, "we grabbed some food and a few hours of sleep before reporting to the briefing room in early evening. After the usual weather reports, flight preparations and radio instructions, the crew returned to the plane which had been refuelled and serviced by local ground crews."

Darkness had fallen by the time the Lancasters were ready to take off. Halle took up his position immediately behind another 425 Squadron aircraft, KW-I, commanded by Flying Officer H. Chappel. The crew were excited at the prospect of being back in Canada in a matter of hours.

"But," says Marcoux, "it was not to be, for in the next fateful instant, our elation, excitement and euphoria vanished."

Taxying to take off, Halle was suddenly blinded by dust and sand driven by wind and prop-wash. With a sickening crunch, his starboard inner propeller hit the rear of KW-I.

"Our pilot quickly shut down all engines and ordered the crew out," Marcoux recalls. "Meanwhile . . . KW-I's wireless operator fired a red distress flare . . ."

The rescue personnel arrived and, by the glare of headlamps, tended to the occupant of KW-I's rear turret, Flight Sergeant N.J. Holowaty, rushing him to the base hospital while the two damaged aircraft were being towed out of the flight line.

"In the flight van which drove us to the base, distraught and overwhelmed by emotion, we sat in silence and listened to the roar of our Lancasters above, going home without us."

Flight Sergeant Holowaty died on Sunday, June 17. The next morning, "after a profoundly moving funeral service attended by all Canadians on the station, he was buried in a small cemetery adjacent to the base." He was 6 Group's last casualty.

An enquiry into the accident attributed no blame. A few days later, when repairs had been completed, the aircraft resumed their journey. KW-G encountered bad weather and was diverted to Argentia, Newfoundland, where the Americans on the base accorded the crew "memorable" hospitality. The next day, the crew took KW-G for the one hour, twenty-five-minute flight to Gander, before the final leg to Scoudouc, New Brunswick.

The Canadian Bomber Group had flown more than 40,000 operational sorties and had dropped 126,122 tons of bombs and mines. In the course of operations, the Group's aircraft had had 1,312 encounters with enemy aircraft – 116 of which were shot down.

Another twenty-four enemy fighters were claimed as "probably destroyed." The cost had been grievous. No fewer than 814 aircraft from 6 Group, Wellingtons, Halifaxes, and Lancasters, had not come back from operations. Of the approximately 5,700 airmen aboard those aircraft, 4,272, or almost 75 per cent of them, lost their lives. Hundreds more died in non-operational accidents.[42]

6 Group was a unique formation. It played a major role in one of the most controversial campaigns of the war against Germany. Some historians delight in denigrating the contribution of the Combined Bomber Offensive, dragging out reams of statistics to demonstrate that Bomber Command failed to achieve this or that. Rather than proving Bomber Command's inadequacies, these figures merely indicate that the enemy's productive capacity and morale were much tougher and more resilient than the experts had predicted.

Strategic bombing was – and is – a cruel way to wage war. But half a century ago it was the only way the Allies had to hit the enemy repeatedly and effectively. Harris was undoubtedly wrong in expecting "his boys" to win the war alone. His force simply wasn't large enough. But the bombers' contribution to victory cannot be denied. They destroyed vast acreages of German industry, ensuring that immense amounts of war *matériel* never came to be used against the Allies. They prepared the way for D-Day with the highly effective Transportation Plan. They put Germany on the strategic defensive, forcing the switch from bomber to fighter production. They laid sea mines in such profusion that they sank more enemy shipping than the RN. But perhaps their greatest contribution was they they tied down immense numbers of troops and airmen who might have been employed to deadly effect elsewhere.

The Germans came close to taking Moscow in 1941 and Cairo in 1942. They might have succeeded – and the war might have taken a different turn – if the Nazi forces had been a million men stronger. But those million Germans were busy flying fighters and operating flak and searchlight batteries, defending the Fatherland against the bombers of the Allies. The Canadians of 6 Group were a major part of that force.

10

THE REUNION OF JUNE 1990

"It's important that we get together from time to time
to refresh the memories of the most stirring,
most traumatic period of our lives."

Robert L. Kift, CD, air gunner, 429 Squadron

They're stockier now. Some of their blazers are a trifle over-stressed amidships. Their locks, once so meticulously Bryl-creem'd, are thinner and greyer. There are some walking sticks to be seen. And the occasional hearing aid. The years, indifferent as ever, have been kind to some, cruel to others. Most of the 6 Group veterans have accumulated close to three score and ten years; some have already passed that particular milestone. But their eyes light up like those of youngsters when, at the RAF Museum at Hendon, just outside London, they come face to face with the aircraft that were once such a big part of their lives. They approach them with oddly cautious steps, as if anxious not to disturb them.

The aircraft possess features as familiar as those of close friends. The Lancaster's lean good looks, the assured tilt of her nose, the beautiful symmetry of her elliptical vertical tail surfaces. A classy lady, the Lanc. Everyone has heard of the Lanc. Everyone admires her. But what of the Halifax? More 6 Group aircrew flew in Hallies than in Lancs. Once the fields of Yorkshire and Durham were home to hundreds of them. Handley Page, English Electric, Rootes, and others built more than six thousand Hallies. Now there is only one left. She reposes at Hendon after spending some thirty years at the bottom of Lake Hokingen in Norway. They dragged her out of the depths and put her on display. As is. Poor old girl, she lies flopped on her belly, glumly enduring the indignity of being scrutinized when she is most definitely not looking her best. Her cabin framework is skeleton-like; the blotches on her battered metal flanks look like liver spots; her propeller blades, amputated in the crash-landing decades ago, are just four splintered stumps. She looks as if she is still decaying, rotting away, slowly returning to the elements from which men made her half a century ago. A workmanlike airplane, the Halifax, a no-nonsense job with slab-sided fuselage and square-tipped wings, about as subtle as a cart horse. She possessed an evil reputation in her early days but, modified almost out of recognition, she became a favourite of 6 Group aircrews.

At Hendon, there's another old comrade of many a battle, even more venerable than the Lanc and the Hally. It's the Wellington, known to all those who flew and serviced her as the Wimpy. Two engines. Fabric-covered body made from countless strips of metal in a sort of basketweave pattern. Geodetic, the experts called it. The Brits built more Wimpies than any other bomber, over eleven thousand in all. The sight of her evokes memories of the Canadian bomber squadrons' earliest days. Of Johnny Fauquier and Moose Fulton. Of Dudley Burnside and George Brookes. Of lonely wanderings over darkened Europe in the amateurish days before Gee, Oboe, and H2S, with everyone trying to convince each other that, yes, that really was Essen below, wasn't it? The Wimpy sits in a comfortable way, like a favourite uncle digesting a hefty Sunday dinner.

There are technical data to be perused: wing spans, bomb loads, speeds, weights; although the 6 Group vets know them by heart. They are reluctant to turn their backs on the aircraft; and even when they move away, they glance back as if expecting a response, a hint of recognition.

One veteran is blind, but still he revels in the presence of the aircraft, their smell, their feel. A comrade guides his hand; he runs it along the side of the fuselage, traces the shape of a propeller blade. He nods, smiling, remembering. The airplanes are much more than machinery; they are companions of youth, proof positive that the memories don't lie. The planes are just as they always were. They represent those fantastic years that were packed to capacity with sights that couldn't be believed, with emotions that all too often couldn't be explained.

The 6 Group reunion coincides with the forty-fifth anniversary of the end of the war in Europe. Predictably, everyone expresses astonishment. Has it really been that long? Where has the time gone? It's surprising how many veterans say they spent the first few post-war years trying to forget the whole thing. But now, after all this time, there's a vigorous resurgence of interest in that era. Like many 6 Group veterans, Bob Marshall, who now lives in Fergus, Ontario, had no involvement with the air force for some thirty-five years after the war: "Even my old crew lost contact with one another," he writes. "But, I think in common with others, the wartime bonds are coming back again." Father Lardie, the Catholic padre at Middleton St. George who flew on two "semi-authorized" ops with 428 Squadron, agrees; for thirty-five years he "never mentioned the war to anyone," but then the memories would be denied no longer. He began to look up old comrades. He attended association meetings. Since then, his interest in those distant days has continued to intensify. Now retired, he lives in Kitchener, Ontario. A native of Medicine Hat, Alberta, now resident in Calgary, Jack McIntosh was a pilot with 419 Squadron. He says he went back to work at a bank after the war and "...put all my stuff in a trunk and I told no one I had even been in the service, neither did I join any veterans' organization. And so it stayed until about 1985." McIntosh found that nostalgia nagged at him; it had to be satisfied. Like so many ex-6 Group airmen, he discovered that the passing of the years lent a new urgency to tracing old crew-mates, to rehashing ancient points of controversy – preferably, it sometimes seems, those to which there is no definitive answer. Meeting old comrades is a way of reliving some of those extraordinary moments. Like precious souvenirs from an attic trunk, the stories come out for yet another airing. They are pieces of an enormous puzzle that is always tantalizingly close to completion: "So *that's* what happened to Jake." "Always wondered about *that*." Bit by bit the little mysteries are solved. But there will always be more questions. And that's the way it should be.

The veterans of 6 Group are wary of the "experts" who've seen *The Dambusters*, *Twelve O'Clock High*, and *The Memphis Belle*, and think they know all there is to know about the bombing campaigns of World War II. Most of the ex-airmen have had to put up with the self-righteous with their accusing stares, the kids who were not even born when the last Lancaster was struck off charge, who demand to know how decent Canadians could have brought themselves to drop bombs on civilians, putting Dresden to the torch, blowing Berliners to bits. Why didn't they refuse to fly on such missions? In vain it is explained that you really had to be there at the time, you had to experience the bitterness of the struggle, the total commitment to defeat the enemy by any means at hand. However much one may mourn the fact, declarations of brotherly (and sisterly) love are not notably effective protection against the ambitions of despots. The kids will have to discover this for themselves, and one can only hope that it will be *history* that teaches them.

Many of the veterans still dream of flying. All too often the experiences are relived again and again in nightmares. Being "coned" by searchlights. Attacked by fighters. Unable to control a crippled aircraft. Spinning in, trapped by centrifugal force in a metal coffin, incapable of moving a muscle, feeling the searing heat of hungry flames, beaten into a frenzy by the slipstream. Then waking up, heart thumping, fingers clutching at nothing. Repeated over and over, the dreams are as fresh as ever. They seem to be permanent now, a sort of appendage firmly and irreversibly implanted by the years. Something to learn to live with, like a limp.

The scene shifts to York. The RCAF flag flies over the Royal York Hotel; a banner welcomes the Canadians back to the area that remembers them so well. And so fondly. The Canadians' memories of the Yorkshire folk are equally affectionate, unspoiled by encounters with a few disagreeable publicans and cab drivers. At Betty's, the manager nods before you've finished asking your question. An elegant forefinger points the way. Downstairs. There it is, the wall panel on which so many of the Canadian aircrew scribbled their signatures. Now it is protected by a sheet of glass, but you can decipher the signatures and you shake your head as the memories flood back.

The tireless committee has arranged trips. Allerton Hall, near Knaresborough, once "Castle Dismal" and the HQ of 6 Group, is on the list. The imposing structure is now the property of a Miami doctor who is spending untold sums on renovating the old place. The basement is a sort of shrine to 6 Group, containing an operations room, offices, equipment, uniforms. Some of the veterans remember it as it was in the war years, with plywood panels protecting the elaborate woodwork, with bare walls because the priceless paintings had been removed for storage, with stalactites of bare wires where now hang magnificent chandeliers.

At Elvington, a bomber airfield during the war, a 6 Group Memorial is dedicated in gale-force winds; the salute is taken by Reg Lane and Chester Hull, both wartime flyers, now retired generals. The Central Band of the Canadian Armed Forces contributes its talents. At Elvington, two survivors of the same Halifax crew, Canadian Bob Kift of Peterborough, Ontario, and Englishman Stan Boustead from Bristol, meet again after forty-five years. Shot down during the notorious Night of the Big Winds, the Berlin raid of March 24/25, 1944, they shook hands more than a year later when liberated from POW camp and promised to keep in touch. They did. But somehow they never managed to get together – until Elvington. Despite fears that they might not recognize one another, neither experiences the slightest hesitation when the moment comes. The years fall away as if they had never intervened.

There are old airfields to be visited. Some, like Leeming, are still in use, much changed to accommodate Tornado jet fighters. A cheer goes up when the veterans see that the Willow Tree pub still stands just outside the gates. The pink-cheeked RAF officers assigned to each bus point out a venerable structure, the camp chapel: "*That* was probably there in your time." Your time. Another era. A prehistoric period to young men who have never flown anything but jet-powered aircraft. At other fields, Tholthorpe for one, the farmlands are gradually resuming ownership, weeds and grass pushing up through the remnants of runways and hardstandings. It's a slow process. Hundreds of workmen laboured months to build those airfields, and they built them to last. In some cases, the old buildings have been turned over to farmers or local businesses in need of space to store equipment and supplies. A former crew room contains lumber. Bags of fertilizer fill a wobbly old hut that once accommodated an armaments section. A tractor stands where the CO used to park his car. Off to one side, a sagging monument to a time that is long gone, is the control tower. Or what's left of it. Its windows have been empty of glass for four decades. The doors fell off before Korea. The bricks have a defeated look, as if a strong wind would reduce them to dust. At one corner many of them are missing, leaving a great gash, the sort of wound that an exploding shell would inflict. But this wasn't a shell's work, it was Father Time's. Less spectacular, but just as final in the end.

The bus trundles past the New Inn, a landmark familiar to all who were stationed here. The old place has had a face-lift; the blackboards with the dismal NO BEER signs have gone, one hopes for ever. A passenger boards the bus, a local farmer who was a boy when the Canadians occupied the airfield. The farmer is a jovial fellow who regales the visitors with one anecdote after another of the wartime goings-on at the airfield. Hilarious stuff, to judge by his frequent splutters of mirth. Sad to say, most of the punch-lines fall a bit flat on the Canadians; the rural Yorkshire accent is a trifle too thick after all these years. But the visitors chuckle good-naturedly. The farmer means well, even if he is almost incomprehensible.

The airfield at Middleton St. George is still in use. But it's become Teesside International Airport. The vets who were stationed there point to hangars and other buildings. That small hill in the distance, once the bomb dump, is now just a small hill in the distance. Gerry Gill, operations director of the airport, welcomes the 6 Group vets: "We are ever conscious of the debt we owe to thousands of young Canadians who volunteered to join the grim struggle for freedom in dark days of the 1940s. At the same time we remember many of your friends who did not return..."

The ranks keep thinning. Gus Edwards, Johnny Fauquier, George Brookes, Black Mike McEwen, Joe Lecomte, Doug Sam, Russ Curtis, Pat Brophy, Don Lamont...

But most ex-6 Group airmen are still hale and reasonably hearty. And most can look back on successful careers. A large number took advantage of the government's offer of financial assistance for those who wanted a university education. The bureaucrats managed to keep a tight lid on the country's gratitude to the ex-airmen; but the assistance was undeniably better than nothing. Roger Coulombe became a dental surgeon and prosthodontist and lives in Lachine, Quebec; Ken Shedden became an architect and lives in Calgary; Harry Shotton an engineer, Joe Hartshorn a professor of geology; John McQuiston, John Neal, and Joe Widdis all became chemical engineers; Arthur Bishop took a law degree. George Rogers and Donald Smith obtained degrees in geology; George Wilson chose forestry; Bob Marshall graduated from the Ontario Agricultural College, then stayed on staff for the next twenty years. Stanley Fletcher became an aircraft engineer and had a distinguished career in the British aerospace industry. Others simply treated war service as an interlude. Joe Foley was a pharmacist before going into the Service and serving as a navigator with 419 Squadron; after the war, he resumed his practice and now lives in Ajax, Ontario. Another 419 Squadron navigator, Arthur Angus, was an optometrist in civilian life and returned to his profession after the war. Dick Garrity had been a teacher before the air force; he went back to teaching and recently retired as a principal. He now devotes a good deal of time to his involvement in the Royal Air Forces Escaping Society. This organization has some 150 Canadian members who haven't forgotten the selfless courage of the men and women in occupied Europe who risked their lives to help such 6 Group airmen as Garrity, Bob Furneaux, Bill Gerard, Doug Sam, Stuart Leslie, Jim Moffat, and many others. The Society's members maintain contact with these remarkable people, bringing up to ten of them to Canada every year for reunions with the airmen they helped so nobly.

Jerry Fultz worked for the post office before his air force service; he considered university at the end of the war, but "two tours had convinced me that what I needed most was a little peace and quiet." He went back to the post office, eventually becoming director general of operational systems and the man who devised the Canadian postal code. He lives in Pleasantville, Nova Scotia. Harry Schmuck became a Catholic priest. Doug Scanlan went into real estate, as did Harry Waugh and Russell McKay. Jim Moffat and Jack McIntosh both worked for financial institutions. Ray Mountford became an executive in the printing business in Toronto, Jim Emmerson, a reporter with the Toronto *Telegram*, later the *Star*. Wally Loucks went into construction after the war; Bill Gerard had a career in sales. Jim Kelly worked for Air Canada's accounting division. Bruce Betcher joined the U.S. Federal Aviation Administration.

Several ex-6 Group airmen stayed in the Service. Reg Lane had a distinguished career, becoming deputy commander of Norad, retiring as a lieutenant general, as did Chester Hull. Bill Swetman also stayed in the Service and retired as a group captain in 1967. Denis Jennings remained in the RAF and retired a squadron leader. American-born Lucien Thomas transferred to the USAAF after a tour with 405 Squadron. He served throughout World War II and later in Korea, completing an astonishing total of more than four hundred operational sorties. He writes: "405 was unique. It was the *people*. I can truly say that it was an honour to be associated with them."

Some 6 Group veterans went into politics. Gilles Lamontagne, who was shot down in a 425 Squadron Wellington in March of 1943, became mayor of Quebec City in 1965. In 1977 he was elected Liberal member of parliament; soon afterward he became a cabinet minister, finally becoming Canada's minister of national defence in 1980. He is currently lieutenant-governor of Quebec. Frank Hamilton, formerly a 424 Squadron pilot, also went into politics after running the family farm, becoming the MP for Swift Current–Maple Creek, Saskatchewan.

As a youngster, Don Lamont had decided to teach history; when he became a pilot in the RCAF, he little realized that he had found a career for life. After the war, he joined Trans-Canada Airlines (later Air Canada), and eventually retired as a captain. He recalled seeing Black Mike McEwen on many flights in the immediate post-war period when the former AOC of 6 Group was connected with the airline. McEwen always made a point of joining Lamont on the flight deck to talk, not about airline business, but "about the good old days at Allerton Park."

The veterans of 6 Group who contributed their memories and their views to this book are, almost to a man, unanimous in their admiration of, and respect for, the late Sir Arthur Harris, who drove them all so hard. "He did a tremendous job," says Ernie Dickson. "And if he had had his way, the war would have been finished a year earlier." They remember the politicians with far less affection. "They did not appreciate the sacrifices of so many of my generation of friends," comments Stuart Leslie of Mississauga, Ontario, who, like many others, is deeply resentful of the failure of the authorities to create a campaign medal to recognize those who fought in Bomber Command. "It just goes along with the policy of our Canadian government to mistreat its war veterans," asserts Roger Coulombe. "They act as if we Canadian airmen never existed! Where do you see Canadian airmen veterans being honoured anywhere, any place, even during Armistice Day celebrations? The Canadian government created the Order of Canada not to honour its war veterans ... but to honour business successes, intellectual or political achievements..." "Sorry, shabby, and shameful," comments Jim Emmerson. "I think it's a disgrace," declares Jerry Fultz. "They made one for the 8th Army and one for the Battle of the Atlantic ... But what else could you expect from politicians?"

A few of the 6 Group veterans who contributed to this history had moments of doubt about the rightness of the bombing campaign. Bill Hutchins, now of Etobicoke, Ontario, remembers a period of self-questioning when he saw a Spanish newspaper that someone had brought in to the Officers' Mess at Linton-on-Ouse: "It showed dead civilians in a bus . . . in Hamburg, all dead from lack of oxygen after the firestorm – not a mark on them." John McQuiston of Don Mills, Ontario, was also troubled by the morality of bombing cities, adding that the feeling intensified in later years: "Our aircraft had a jettison toggle on the pilot's instrument panel so that he could drop the bombs in an emergency. I always had my bomb-aimer leave the last bomb for me to drop. I guess I wanted to share in the responsibility (and the guilt)." John Neal recalls no such feelings during the war – "but a lot of guilt has plagued me since the war."

Most of the 6 Group veterans see the bombing war as a nasty, dangerous job that had to be done. "I am of the firm opinion that the war could not have been won without it," declares Jim Emmerson. Roger Coulombe says, "We had no choice. Someone had to protect and defend civilization." Ted Radford adds, "Bomber Command dished out the dirt when no one else on our side could."

Many 6 Group veterans feel that if Harris had been given the four thousand heavy bombers he asked for, Bomber Command could have won the war and the invasion would never have been necessary.

Time is gradually easing the sting from the memories. There are still injustices to be condemned and stupidities to be analysed. But the passing years are blending those memories, imbuing them with a certain smoothness, a homogeneity that merges bitterness and anger. Only one emotion remains as bright and fierce as ever. It is pride. Perhaps Jerry Fultz put it best: "I had the honour and pleasure of serving in the finest force that this country ever raised . . ."

THE END

APPENDIX A

The Operational Squadrons of 6 Group

405 (Vancouver) Squadron, formed April 23, 1941
408 (Goose) Squadron, formed June 24, 1941
415 (Swordfish) Squadron, formed August 20, 1941
419 (Moose) Squadron, formed December 15, 1941
420 (Snowy Owl) Squadron, formed December 19, 1941
424 (Tiger) Squadron, formed October 15, 1942
425 (Alouette) Squadron, formed June 22, 1942
426 (Thunderbird) Squadron, formed October 15, 1942
427 (Lion) Squadron, formed November 7, 1942
428 (Ghost) Squadron, formed November 7, 1942
429 (Bison) Squadron, formed November 7, 1942
431 (Iroquois) Squadron, formed November 11, 1942
432 (Leaside) Squadron, formed May 1, 1943
433 (Porcupine) Squadron, formed September 25, 1943
434 (Bluenose) Squadron, formed June 13, 1943

APPENDIX B

6 Group Operations

These statistics do not include those aircraft involved in attacks on alternate targets or those that were unable to find the aiming point and returned with the bomb-load. Consequently, the number of aircraft despatched on a given date may be greater than the total number of aircraft represented in the other three columns.

Date	Target/purpose	Despatched	Attacked primary	Early return or aborted	Lost
January 1943					
3/4	Gardening	6	3	3	0
9/10	Gardening	40	34	6	1
14/15	Lorient	14	11	2	1
14/15	Gardening	6	6	0	0
15	Norden	6	1	5	0
15/16	Lorient	38	36	1	1
21/22	Gardening	39	35	3	2
23	Esens	6	0	1	0
23/24	Lorient	15	15	0	0
26/27	Lorient	55	50	4	1
27/28	Gardening	6	3	1	0
29/30	Gardening	4	1	3	0
29/30	Lorient	69	42	25	2
30	Oldenburg	11	0	6	2

Date	Target/purpose	Despatched	Attacked primary	Early return or aborted	Lost
February 1943					
2/3	Gardening	13	5	8	0
3/4	Hamburg	46	19	25	2
4/5	Turin	15	12	3	0
4/5	Lorient	60	55	4	1
6/7	Gardening	38	26	10	2
7/8	Lorient	69	61	7	1
9/10	Gardening	4	3	1	0
11/12	Gardening	24	17	7	0
12/13	Gardening	12	10	1	0
13/14	Lorient	95	78	16	1
14/15	Cologne	55	47	7	1
16/17	Lorient	80	78	2	0
18/19	Wilhelmshaven	4	3	1	0
18/19	Gardening	30	26	1	1
19/20	Wilhelmshaven	83	79	3	1
20/21	Gardening	20	17	2	1
24/25	Wilhelmshaven	98	88	10	0
25/26	Gardening	20	6	14	0
26/27	Cologne	85	69	11	3
27/28	Gardening	34	28	4	1
28/1	St-Nazaire	74	66	6	2
March 1943					
1/2	Berlin	21	14	3	2
1/2	Gardening	17	14	3	0
2/3	Gardening	18	9	8	1
3/4	Hamburg	75	61	11	1
5/6	Essen	77	65	8	3
8/9	Gardening	17	10	1	0
8/9	Nuremberg	19	18	1	0
9/10	Gardening	20	17	2	1
9/10	Munich	18	14	4	0
11/12	Stuttgart	35	24	5	5
12/13	Essen	93	73	17	3
13/14	Gardening	19	13	5	1

Date	Target/purpose	Despatched	Attacked primary	Early return or aborted	Lost
22/23	St-Nazaire	38	33	5	0
23/24	Gardening	25	23	2	0
26/27	Duisburg	114	101	12	1
27/28	Berlin	31	23	6	2
28/29	St-Nazaire	106	94	11	1
29/30	Berlin	23	6	15	2
29/30	Bochum	75	43	22	6

April 1943

2/3	St-Nazaire	9	8	1	0
2/3	Lorient	10	9	1	0
3/4	Essen	22	14	3	4
4/5	Kiel	128	108	13	4
6/7	Gardening	10	9	0	1
8/9	Duisburg	75	49	20	4
10/11	Frankfurt	108	90	16	4
11/12	Gardening	10	9	0	1
14/15	Stuttgart	109	86	15	8
15/16	Gardening	6	6	0	0
16/17	Pilsen	27	22	1	4
16/17	Mannheim	90	65	19	5
20/21	Stettin	21	19	1	1
20/21	Gardening	6	5	1	0
26/27	Duisburg	81	71	6	4
27/28	Gardening	36	21	15	0
28/29	Gardening	37	25	7	3
30/1	Essen	20	13	7	0

May 1943

4/5	Dortmund	70	55	9	6
12/13	Duisburg	60	40	10	8
13/14	Bochum	60	47	6	6
16/17	Gardening	21	20	1	0
18/19	Gardening	4	4	0	0
21/22	Gardening	24	17	6	1
23/24	Dortmund	76	65	8	3

Date	Target/purpose	Despatched	Attacked primary	Early return or aborted	Lost
25/26	Düsseldorf	58	49	6	2
27/28	Essen	50	43	3	4
28/29	Gardening	6	6	0	0
29/30	Wuppertal	82	63	12	6

June 1943

Date	Target/purpose	Despatched	Attacked primary	Early return or aborted	Lost
1/2	Gardening	9	8	1	0
3/4	Gardening	8	4	4	0
11/12	Düsseldorf	101	80	14	7
12/13	Bochum	37	28	5	3
12/13	Gardening	8	4	4	0
13/14	Gardening	6	6	0	0
14/15	Gardening	6	5	1	0
19/20	Le Creusot	42	38	3	1
21/22	Krefeld	72	57	7	8
22/23	Mülheim	48	34	8	6
22/23	Gardening	10	8	2	0
23/24	Gardening	3	2	1	0
24/25	Wuppertal	62	48	5	7
25/26	Gelsenkirchen	36	31	2	3
26/27	Gardening	8	4	3	1
28/29	Cologne	51	42	8	1

July 1943

Date	Target/purpose	Despatched	Attacked primary	Early return or aborted	Lost
2/3	Gardening	16	14	2	0
3/4	Cologne	68	52	10	6
6/7	Gardening	8	4	4	0
8/9	Gardening	6	4	2	0
9/10	Gelsenkirchen	42	37	2	3
12/13	Gardening	6	5	1	0
13/14	Aachen	69	55	7	7
24/25	Hamburg	72	66	6	0
25/26	Essen	66	56	8	2
27/28	Hamburg	78	67	9	2
29/30	Hamburg	83	74	7	2
30/31	Remscheid	33	30	1	2

Date	Target/purpose	Despatched	Attacked primary	Early return or aborted	Lost
August 1943					
2/3	Hamburg	73	26	42	4
3/4	Gardening	12	10	0	0
6/7	Gardening	6	6	0	0
9/10	Mannheim	39	32	6	1
10/11	Nuremberg	41	40	0	0
11/12	Gardening	7	5	1	0
12/13	Milan	47	42	4	1
12/13	Gardening	8	5	2	1
15/16	Gardening	8	8	0	0
17/18	Peenemünde	62	47	3	12
22/23	Leverkusen	62	52	9	1
23/24	Berlin	68	50	11	5
24/25	Gardening	12	12	0	0
25/26	Gardening	14	10	3	0
26/27	Gardening	6	5	0	0
27/28	Nuremberg	66	57	7	2
27/28	Gardening	12	11	1	0
30/31	Mönchengladbach	76	63	9	3
31/1	Berlin	58	43	8	7
September 1943					
2/3	Gardening	33	23	10	0
3/4	Berlin	3	3	0	0
3/4	Forêt de Raismes	8	8	0	0
4/5	Gardening	9	5	4	0
5/6	Mannheim	55	46	5	3
5/6	Gardening	9	8	0	0
6/7	Munich	53	36	11	5
8/9	Boulogne	12	12	0	0
15/16	Montluçon	63	55	7	1
16/17	Modane	56	42	13	1
22/23	Hannover	89	77	8	4
23/24	Mannheim	64	57	3	4

Date	Target/purpose	Despatched	Attacked primary	Early return or aborted	Lost
27/28	Hannover	81	56	18	7
29/30	Bochum	39	30	3	3
October 1943					
2/3	Gardening	24	14	10	0
3/4	Kassel	75	62	8	5
4/5	Frankfurt	59	52	2	5
7/8	Stuttgart	28	22	4	1
7/8	Gardening	10	5	5	0
8/9	Hannover	100	86	8	6
17/18	Gardening	6	5	1	0
18/19	Hannover	26	24	2	0
18/19	Gardening	6	6	0	0
20/21	Leipzig	28	21	5	0
22/23	Kassel	107	68	26	12
22/23	Gardening	7	7	0	0
November 1943					
3/4	Düsseldorf	115	88	14	4
11/12	Cannes	20	20	0	0
18/19	Ludwigshafen	94	58	15	7
18/19	Berlin	29	23	6	0
19/20	Leverkusen	66	49	8	3
22/23	Berlin	110	93	11	4
23/24	Berlin	19	14	3	1
25/26	Frankfurt	88	73	8	6
26/27	Stuttgart	56	51	4	1
26/27	Berlin	39	33	4	2
December 1943					
2/3	Berlin	35	25	8	2
3/4	Leipzig	97	70	20	7
16/17	Berlin	40	31	4	4
20/21	Frankfurt	116	93	11	10

Date	Target/purpose	Despatched	Attacked primary	Early return or aborted	Lost
24/25	Gardening	20	17	2	0
29/30	Berlin	129	109	15	5
January 1944					
1/2	Berlin	31	29	2	0
2/3	Berlin	28	21	4	3
2/3	Gardening	4	3	1	0
4/5	Gardening	18	16	1	0
5/6	Stettin	35	34	1	0
6/7	Gardening	12	12	0	0
14/15	Brunswick	46	41	1	4
20/21	Berlin	144	117	17	9
21/22	Magdeburg	114	86	13	14
27/28	Berlin	48	38	2	8
28/29	Berlin	124	101	14	9
30/31	Berlin	47	44	2	1
February 1944					
2/3	Gardening	22	20	2	0
3/4	Gardening	12	10	2	0
5/6	Gardening	11	10	1	0
10/11	Gardening	6	6	0	0
11/12	Gardening	8	8	0	0
12/13	Gardening	6	4	1	1
15/16	Berlin	150	136	10	4
19/20	Leipzig	129	92	15	18
20/21	Stuttgart	66	56	8	1
21/22	Gardening	10	10	0	0
24/25	Schweinfurt	143	122	16	5
24/25	Gardening	16	15	1	0
25/26	Augsburg	65	52	7	6
25/26	Gardening	50	35	12	2
March 1944					
1/2	Stuttgart	30	26	4	0
2/3	Meulan-les-Meureaux	63	61	2	0

Date	Target/purpose	Despatched	Attacked primary	Early return or aborted	Lost
3/4	Gardening	19	18	1	0
4/5	Gardening	10	10	0	0
6/7	Trappes	119	117	2	0
7/8	Le Mans	140	85	55	0
11/12	Gardening	24	17	7	0
13/14	Le Mans	110	104	6	0
15/16	Amiens	54	49	4	0
15/16	Stuttgart	130	109	21	1
16/17	Amiens	50	49	1	0
18/19	Frankfurt	119	106	11	0
18/19	Gardening	39	35	3	0
22/23	Frankfurt	99	87	5	0
22/23	Gardening	74	69	5	0
23/24	Laon	51	27	24	0
24/25	Berlin	113	85	13	13
25/26	Aulnoye	73	71	2	0
26/27	Courtrai	47	46	1	0
26/27	Essen	105	99	5	1
29/30	Vaires	49	46	2	1
30/31	Nuremberg	118	94	8	13
30/31	Gardening	29	29	0	0
April 1944					
1/2	Gardening	22	21	0	0
8/9	Gardening	8	8	0	0
9/10	Lille	53	50	3	0
9/10	Villeneuve-St-Georges	107	101	6	0
10/11	Laon	24	23	1	0
10/11	Ghent	122	118	4	0
11/12	Gardening	15	13	2	0
12/13	Gardening	15	24	1	0
13/14	Gardening	6	6	0	0
17/18	Gardening	12	11	0	1
18/19	Gardening	44	41	2	1
19/20	Noisy-le-Sec	137	133	0	4

Date	Target/purpose	Despatched	Attacked primary	Early return or aborted	Lost
20/21	Lens	154	152	1	1
20/21	Gardening	4	4	0	0
21/22	Gardening	20	19	0	0
22/23	Düsseldorf	136	122	6	8
22/23	Laon	40	38	1	1
23/24	Gardening	37	34	2	1
24/25	Karlsruhe	137	123	8	6
24/25	Gardening	18	16	2	0
26/27	Essen	117	111	5	1
26/27	Villeneuve-St-Georges	47	45	2	0
26/27	Gardening	6	0	0	0
27/28	Aulnoye	90	89	1	0
27/28	Friedrichshafen	19	19	0	0
27/28	Montzen	54	42	2	10
27/28	Gardening	8	8	0	0
29/30	Gardening	18	17	1	0
30/1	Somain	114	111	2	1
30/1	Gardening	30	28	2	0
May 1944					
1/2	St-Ghislain	115	103	9	2
1/2	Gardening	18	18	0	0
3/4	Gardening	22	22	0	0
4/5	Gardening	8	8	0	0
5/6	Gardening	10	10	0	0
6/7	Gardening	8	8	0	0
7/8	St-Valéry	56	55	1	0
7/8	Gardening	18	17	1	0
8/9	Haine-St-Pierre	75	67	2	6
8/9	Gardening	22	22	0	0
9/10	Calais	53	53	0	0
9/10	St-Valéry	52	50	2	0
9/10	Gardening	16	16	0	0
10/11	Ghent	104	102	2	0
10/11	Gardening	12	11	0	1

Date	Target/purpose	Despatched	Attacked primary	Early return or aborted	Lost
11/12	Boulogne	106	92	12	2
11/12	Gardening	6	5	1	0
12/13	Louvain	108	84	19	5
12/13	Gardening	17	15	2	0
14/15	Gardening	10	9	0	0
15/16	Gardening	12	10	2	0
19/20	Le Clipon	58	58	0	0
19/20	Merville	57	56	1	0
19/20	Gardening	4	4	0	0
20/21	Gardening	11	10	1	0
21/22	Gardening	23	21	2	0
22/23	Dortmund	27	21	3	3
22/23	Le Mans	112	100	10	2
22/23	Gardening	2	2	0	0
23/24	Gardening	4	4	0	0
24/25	Aachen-Rothe Erde	60	56	0	4
24/25	Aachen-West	30	27	2	1
24/25	Trouville	55	54	1	0
26/27	Gardening	6	5	0	0
27/28	Le Clipon	43	42	1	0
27/28	Bourg-Léopold	149	143	0	6
27/28	Gardening	21	21	0	0
28/29	Gardening	6	5	0	0
29/30	Gardening	3	3	0	0
31/1	Au Fèvre	125	118	7	0
31/1	Gardening	7	5	2	0

June 1944

Date	Target/purpose	Despatched	Attacked primary	Early return or aborted	Lost
1/2	Gardening	10	10	0	0
2/3	Neufchâteau	70	69	1	0
2/3	Gardening	24	24	0	0
3/4	Gardening	25	25	0	0
4/5	Calais	69	68	1	0
5/6	Merville	99	80	19	0
5/6	Houlgate	106	102	3	1

Date	Target/purpose	Despatched	Attacked primary	Early return or aborted	Lost
5/6	Longues	25	24	1	0
6/7	Coutances	132	125	7	0
6/7	Condé-sur-Noireau	115	106	9	0
7/8	Versailles	20	19	0	1
7/8	Achères	100	89	7	4
7/8	Gardening	8	8	0	0
8/9	Mayenne	70	70	0	0
8/9	Gardening	12	5	0	0
9/10	Le Mans	100	100	0	0
9/10	Gardening	14	13	0	0
10/11	Versailles	100	91	6	3
10/11	Gardening	12	12	0	0
11/12	Gardening	5	5	0	0
12/13	Arras	89	79	4	6
12/13	Cambrai	92	79	4	9
12/13	Gardening	4	4	0	0
14/15	Cambrai	94	91	1	2
14/15	St-Pol	61	58	3	0
15/16	Boulogne	162	153	8	1
16/17	v-bomb sites	102	100	2	0
16/17	Sterkrade	100	82	6	12
17/18	v-bomb sites	102	101	1	0
17/18	Gardening	4	4	0	0
18/19	Gardening	5	5	0	0
21	v-bomb sites	204	112	85	7
23/24	v-bomb sites	104	103	1	0
23/24	Gardening	4	4	0	0
24	v-bomb sites	99	97	2	0
24/25	v-bomb sites	103	102	0	1
24/25	Gardening	6	6	0	0
25	v-bomb sites	101	100	1	0
26/27	v-bomb sites	106	105	1	0
26/27	Gardening	8	8	0	0
27/28	v-bomb sites	104	98	6	0
27/28	Gardening	6	6	0	0

Date	Target/purpose	Despatched	Attacked primary	Early return or aborted	Lost
28/29	Metz	100	86	7	7
28/29	Gardening	8	8	0	0
July 1944					
1	V-bomb sites	101	99	2	0
4	V-bomb sites	99	98	1	0
4/5	Villeneuve-St-Georges	102	91	2	9
5/6	V-bomb sites	99	99	0	0
5/6	Gardening	6	6	0	0
6	V-bomb sites	150	147	2	1
7	Caen	88	87	1	0
8/9	Gardening	8	8	0	0
9	V-bomb sites	100	98	2	0
10/11	Gardening	8	7	1	0
12	V-bomb sites	91	89	2	0
12/13	V-bomb sites	99	98	1	0
14/15	V-bomb sites	50	50	0	0
15/16	V-bomb sites	91	91	0	0
17/18	Gardening	8	8	0	0
18	Caen: 1st op	98	97	0	1
18	Caen: 2d op	99	97	0	2
18	Vaires	28	25	1	2
18/19	Wesseling	153	146	3	1
19/20	Gardening	6	6	0	0
20	V-bomb sites	99	97	2	0
21	V-bomb sites	48	47	1	0
23/24	Donges	100	99	1	0
23/24	Kiel	42	41	1	0
24/25	Stuttgart	40	37	2	1
24/25	V-bomb sites	100	64	35	1
24/25	Gardening	4	4	0	0
25/26	Stuttgart	175	153	8	4
25/26	Gardening	4	4	0	0
28/29	Hamburg	234	209	3	22
28/29	Gardening	5	4	0	0

Date	Target/purpose	Despatched	Attacked primary	Early return or aborted	Lost
30	Caen	99	97	2	0
31	v-bomb sites	76	73	2	1
31/1	Gardening	4	4	0	0
August 1944					
1	v-bomb sites	151	0	151	0
3	v-bomb sites	261	251	9	0
4	v-bomb sites	211	206	2	2
5	v-bomb sites	248	230	1	1
5/6	Gardening	3	3	0	0
7/8	Caen	235	133	101	1
7/8	Gardening	6	6	0	0
8	Forêt de Chantilly	191	189	1	0
8/9	Gardening	6	6	0	0
9	v-bomb sites	67	66	0	1
9/10	v-bomb sites	165	161	3	0
10/11	La Pallice	138	130	8	0
12	Forêt de Montrichard	104	99	5	0
12/13	v-bomb sites	40	38	2	0
12/13	Brunswick	69	60	4	5
12/13	Falaise	48	44	4	0
12/13	Gardening	10	10	0	0
13/14	Gardening	10	10	0	0
14	Falaise	225	214	7	0
15	Soesterberg	104	101	2	1
15	Melsbroek	101	98	2	1
15/16	Gardening	6	6	0	0
16/17	Kiel	144	138	3	3
16/17	Stettin	27	23	1	1
16/17	Gardening	18	13	2	3
17/18	Gardening	6	6	0	0
18	v-bomb sites	16	14	2	0
18/19	Connantre	102	99	3	0
18/19	Bremen	100	94	5	1
18/19	Gardening	7	7	0	0

Date	Target/purpose	Despatched	Attacked primary	Early return or aborted	Lost
24/25	Gardening	6	6	0	0
25	V-bomb sites	14	8	6	0
25/26	Brest-Pte-Robert	36	27	9	0
25/26	Russelsheim	34	32	1	1
25/26	Brest-Fort-des Cornouailles	38	38	0	0
25/26	Brest-Pte-de-St-Mathieu	38	34	4	0
25/26	Brest-Kervinieu	37	34	3	0
25/26	Kerandieu	37	35	2	0
26/27	Gardening	4	4	0	0
27	V-bomb sites	200	197	3	0
28	V-bomb sites	77	70	7	0
28	Ile de Cezembre	23	22	1	0
28	Brest	23	23	0	0
28/29	Gardening	6	6	0	0
29/30	Stettin	36	35	0	1
31	Ile de Cezembre	165	165	0	0

September 1944

Date	Target/purpose	Despatched	Attacked primary	Early return or aborted	Lost
3	Volkel	105	101	4	0
6	Emden	139	139	0	0
9	Le Havre	104	0	104	0
10	Le Havre	207	201	6	0
11	Le Havre	55	25	30	0
11	Castrop-Rauxel	105	103	1	0
11	Gardening	18	17	1	0
12	Wanne-Eickel	107	100	2	1
12	Dortmund	74	70	4	0
12/13	Gardening	12	1	11	0
13	Osnabrück	98	98	0	0
14	Wilhelmshaven	85	0	85	0
15/16	Kiel	201	190	8	2
15/16	Gardening	20	19	0	0
17	Boulogne	210	197	9	1
18	Domburg	60	0	60	0

Date	Target/purpose	Despatched	Attacked primary	Early return or aborted	Lost
19	Domburg	55	0	55	0
20	Calais	108	105	3	0
23	Domburg	34	33	1	0
24	Calais	31	29	1	1
25	Calais	253	242	11	0
26	Calais	164	161	3	0
27	Sterkrade	143	74	9	0
27	Bottrop	142	127	3	0
28	Cap Gris Nez	252	162	91	0
30	Sterkrade	108	15	2	1

October 1944

4	Bergen	128	109	1	0
4	Gardening	12	10	0	1
5/6	Gardening	10	10	0	0
6/7	Dortmund	293	273	12	2
9/10	Bochum	209	201	5	3
12	Wanne-Eickel	111	105	3	0
14	Duisburg	258	238	8	4
14/15	Duisburg	243	225	17	1
15/16	Wilhelmshaven	134	129	2	3
15/16	Gardening	10	8	1	1
19/20	Stuttgart	42	41	1	0
21/22	Hannover	101	0	101	0
22	Gardening	10	9	0	0
23/24	Essen	272	251	11	2
24/25	Gardening	9	8	1	0
25	Essen	46	45	0	1
25	Homberg	199	190	5	0
28	Cologne	231	151	8	1
28/29	Gardening	6	0	1	0
30/31	Cologne	243	237	6	0

November 1944

1/2	Oberhausen	250	239	3	6
2/3	Düsseldorf	222	209	7	6

Date	Target/purpose	Despatched	Attacked primary	Early return or aborted	Lost
4/5	Bochum	214	204	4	5
6	Gelsenkirchen	215	130	7	2
11	Gardening	12	6	0	0
16	Jülich	204	193	11	0
18	Münster	200	196	4	0
21	Gardening	12	12	0	0
21/22	Castrop-Rauxel	230	220	6	4
24/25	Gardening	13	10	0	1
27/28	Neuss	225	220	5	0
27/28	Gardening	6	4	0	0
30/1	Duisburg	243	231	9	2

December 1944

Date	Target/purpose	Despatched	Attacked primary	Early return or aborted	Lost
2/3	Hagen	199	190	6	1
4/5	Karlsruhe	200	196	4	0
5/6	Soest	195	184	9	2
6/7	Osnabrück	199	182	13	4
15/16	Ludwigshafen	51	51	0	0
17/18	Duisburg	232	215	12	2
21/22	Cologne	50	49	1	0
21/22	Gardening	11	9	0	0
24	Düsseldorf	150	144	4	2
24/25	Gardening	12	12	0	0
26	St-Vith	63	61	2	0
27/28	Opladen	150	144	4	2
28/29	Gardening	16	15	0	1
29/30	Scholven/Buer	48	43	3	2
29/30	Troisdorf	149	142	3	0
29/30	Gardening	6	6	0	0
30/31	Cologne	200	198	1	0
31/1	Gardening	16	16	0	0

January 1945

Date	Target/purpose	Despatched	Attacked primary	Early return or aborted	Lost
2/3	Ludwigshafen	156	156	0	0
2/3	Nuremberg	54	53	1	0
5/6	Hannover	190	177	2	10

Date	Target/purpose	Despatched	Attacked primary	Early return or aborted	Lost
6/7	Hanau	189	185	1	2
7/8	Munich	30	28	2	0
12/13	Gardening	12	8	1	3
13/14	Saarbrücken	140	139	1	0
14/15	Grevenbroich	136	134	0	0
14/15	Leuna	53	50	0	3
14/15	Gardening	11	10	0	0
16/17	Magdeburg	125	109	9	7
16/17	Zeitz	51	49	1	1
16/17	Gardening	12	11	1	0
28/29	Stuttgart	179	158	17	4

February 1945

1/2	Mainz	86	83	3	0
1/2	Ludwigshafen	60	57	3	0
2/3	Wanne-Eickel	107	97	9	1
2/3	Wiesbaden	65	60	3	2
4/5	Osterfeld	100	97	3	0
4/5	Bonn	100	96	2	2
4/5	Gardening	12	12	0	0
7/8	Goch	200	48	152	0
8/9	Wanne-Eickel	98	89	8	1
13/14	Dresden	67	66	1	0
13/14	Böhlen	115	110	4	0
14	Gardening	19	14	2	3
14/15	Chemnitz	118	112	3	3
15/16	Gardening	12	11	1	0
17	Wesel	110	2	108	0
19	Gardening	10	10	0	0
20/21	Dortmund	84	82	0	2
20/21	Monheim	112	109	1	2
21/22	Duisburg	85	85	0	0
21/22	Worms	111	105	0	6
23	Essen	119	117	2	0
23/24	Pforzheim	50	50	0	0
23/24	Gardening	12	11	0	0

Date	Target/purpose	Despatched	Attacked primary	Early return or aborted	Lost
24	Kamen	110	108	1	1
24/25	Gardening	10	8	2	0
25/26	Gardening	10	8	1	1
27	Mainz	187	182	4	0
28	Neuss	60	0	60	0
March 1945					
1	Mannheim	160	159	1	0
2	Cologne	182	177	4	1
2/3	Gardening	9	8	1	0
5/6	Chemnitz	183	170	9	6
7/8	Dessau	82	78	1	3
8/9	Hamburg	85	82	2	1
8/9	Gardening	27	26	1	0
9/10	Gardening	10	9	1	0
11	Essen	196	194	0	2
12	Dortmund	192	191	1	0
12/13	Gardening	9	7	1	1
13	Wuppertal	100	97	3	0
14/15	Zweibrücken	196	192	4	0
15	Castrop-Rauxel	70	70	0	0
15/16	Hagen	142	139	0	3
16/17	Gardening	12	11	1	0
18/19	Witten	83	81	0	2
20/21	Hemmingstedt	110	109	0	1
21	Rheine	90	80	1	0
22	Hildesheim	88	84	1	2
22	Dorsten	100	96	4	0
24	Gladbeck	100	95	4	0
24	Bottrop	75	73	0	0
25	Münster	99	92	2	3
25	Hannover	100	97	2	0
31	Hamburg	200	189	3	8
April 1945					
4/5	Harburg	90	89	1	0
4/5	Merseburg	105	104	1	0

Date	Target/purpose	Despatched	Attacked primary	Early return or aborted	Lost
4/5	Gardening	15	14	1	0
8/9	Hamburg	190	184	5	1
9/10	Gardening	20	18	2	0
10	Leipzig	200	188	8	2
11/12	Plauen	4	0	4	0
13/14	Kiel	210	204	4	2
13/14	Gardening	20	20	0	0
16/17	Gablingen	19	17	2	0
16/17	Schwandorf	120	116	2	0
18	Heligoland	112	108	2	2
21/22	Gardening	20	20	0	0
22	Bremen	200	0	200	0
25	Wangerooge	192	184	2	4

Sources: Historical Review No. 6 (RCAF) Heavy Bomber Group, European Theatre, 1943–1945, and 6 Group Operational Record Book.

NOTES

Although the bibliography lists secondary sources almost exclusively, most of the research materials used in the preparation of this book consist of primary documents from archives and museums in Canada and England. In Ottawa the Directorate of History (DHist), the Department of National Defence, possesses most of the extant RCAF files. DHist also has significant quantities of photocopied documents from English sources. The National Archives of Canada (NAC), also in Ottawa, holds numerous RCAF files, in addition to the Mackenzie King papers and his diaries. The Power papers, which DHist has photocopied extensively, are located at Queen's University in Kingston, Ontario. In England, the Public Record Office (PRO) at Kew retains the Air Ministry and RAF files, much of which DHist has photocopied. Two other sources of documentation are the RAF Museum at Hendon (Harris papers) and Christ Church Library, Oxford (Portal papers). Again, DHist holds large photocopied portions of both collections.

Data pertaining to all the operations of 6 Group have been obtained from the 6 Group Operations Book (ORB) in the National Archives of Canada (NAC), as well as from individual squadron operations record books, also held at the NAC, in the National Defence record group (RG) 24, E7. Additional information on the operations is provided by Martin Middlebrook and Chris Everitt in *The Bomber Command War Diaries* (New York: Viking, Penguin Inc., 1985).

INTRODUCTION

1. Toronto *Globe*, 28 May 1917.
2. Philip Moyes, *Bomber Squadrons of the RAF* (London: Macdonald & Co., 1964), p. 326.
3. Sir Charles Webster and Dr. Noble Frankland, *The Strategic Air Offensive Against Germany, 1939-1945*, 4 vols (London: HMSO,

1961), vol. 4: app. 13, "Report by Mr. Butt to Bomber Command on his Examination of Night Photographs, 18th August 1941," p. 205.

4. Charles Messenger, *"Bomber" Harris and the Strategic Bombing Offensive, 1939-1945* (London: Arms & Armour Press, 1984), p. 39.

5. Ibid, p. 49.

6. Webster and Frankland, *Strategic Air Offensive*, vol. 4. app. 8, Directive No. xxii, 14 February 1942, p. 144.

7. Sir Arthur T. Harris, *Bomber Offensive* (New York: Macmillan, 1947), p. 90.

CHAPTER 1: INTO BATTLE

1. Letter from the town of Schwerte, reference 41-35-01/13, 30 March 1990.

2. C.P. Stacey, *A Date with History* (Ottawa: Deneau Publishing, n.d.), p. 76.

3. "Losses of Halifax Aircraft: July 1941-June 1942," Report No. 48, 30 July 1942, pp. 5-8, Public Record Office (PRO) Air 14/1794.

4. Brookes to Harris, McEwen papers (uncatalogued), Canadian War Museum (CWM).

5. Edwards, McEwen papers, CWM.

6. 1 December 1942, Harris papers, File H81, DHist.

7. 13 August 1942, Harris papers, File H81, DHist.

8. Harris to Portal, September 1942, Harris papers, File DHist.

9. Edwards to Breadner, Report No. 9, 30 October 1942, p. 1, Power papers, Box 64, File No. D1084.

10. Edwards to Breadner, 28 January 1943, Directorate of History (DHist) 181.003(D1290).

11. "Curriculum Vitae," pp. 1-2, DHist, Biog "B." No file number.

12. Night Raid Report No. 235, p. 1, 23 February 1943, PRO Air 14/3409.

13. Edwards to Breadner, Report No. 6, 11 August 1942, p. 5, Power papers, Box 64, File No. D1084.

14. Brian J. Rapier, *White Rose Base* (Lincoln: Aero Litho Co., 1972), pp. 28, 57, 81.

15. George Sweanor, *It's All Pensionable Time: 25 Years in the Royal Canadian Air Force* (Toronto: Gesnor Publications, 1981), pp. 78-80.

16. "Historical Review No. 6 (RCAF) Heavy Bomber Group. European Theatre 1943-45." 6 Group Headquarters, n.d., p. 14., DHist 181.009(D550).

17. Station Operation Order No. 361, January 9/10, 1943, DHist 181.009(D4376).

18. Alfred Price, *Instruments of Darkness: The History of Electronic Warfare* (Los Altos: Peninsula Publishing, 1987), pp. 98–104; Webster and Frankland, *Strategic Air Offensive* 4:4–6.

19. Webster and Frankland, *Strategic Air Offensive*, vol. 4, app. 8, Directive No. xxvii, 14 January 1943, pp. 152–53.

20. *The RCAF Overseas,* 3 vols (Toronto: Oxford University Press, 1944), vol. 1: *The First Four Years*, p. 191.

21. Messenger, *"Bomber" Harris*, p. 102.

22. "Historical Review," attached list of operations, p. 2.

23. Nora Bottomley, *424 Squadron History* (Belleville, Ont.: Hangar Bookshelf, 1985), pp. 34–35.

24. Webster and Frankland, *Strategic Air Offensive*, 2:98.

25. Harris, *Bomber Offensive*, p. 137.

26. *RCAF Overseas* 1:193–94; and Leslie Roberts, *There Shall Be Wings* (Toronto: Clarke, Irwin & Co., 1959), p. 163.

27. Ray Jacobson, *426 Squadron History* (Belleville, Ont.: Hangar Bookshelf, 1985), p. 11.

28. *RCAF Overseas* 1:196.

29. Jacobson, *426 Squadron*, p. 11.

30. "Historical Review," attached list of operations, p. 3.

31. Brookes diary, 25 February 1943, DHist, Biog "B." No file number.

32. "Historical Review," attached table, n.p.

CHAPTER 2: PATRIOTISM AND PARSIMONY

1. J. Douglas Harvey, *Boys, Bombs, and Brussels Sprouts* (Toronto: McClelland & Stewart, 1981), pp. 72–73.

2. W. A. B. Douglas, *The Official History of the Royal Canadian Air Force* (Toronto: University of Toronto Press, 1985), vol. 2, *The Creation of a National Air Force*, pp. 191–92.

3. C. P. Stacey, *Arms, Men and Governments* (Ottawa: Queen's Printer, 1970), pp. 305, 290.

4. Douglas, *Official History* 2:209.

5. Stacey, *Arms*, Appendix 'D,' "British Commonwealth Air Training Plan Agreement, 17 Dec 1939," pp. 540–53.

6. King to Campbell, 12 September 1939; in *Documents on Canadian External Relations* (hereafter cited as DCER), vol. 7, *1939–1941*, D. R. Murray, ed. (Ottawa: External Affairs, 1974), pt. 1, Document No. 1015, pp. 855–56.

7. Stacey, *Arms*, p. 21.

8. Campbell to Skelton, 6 September 1939; in DCER, Vol. 6: *1936–1939*, J.A. Munro, ed. (Ottawa: External Affairs, 1972), Document No. 1073, p. 1305.

9. Chamberlain to King, 26 September 1939, in Murray, DCER, vol. 6, Document No. 688, p. 550.

10. Minutes of meetings held by the British War Cabinet, PRO, CAB65: II/113(39)8, 13 December 1939, p. 409, on microfilm at McMaster University; and Skelton to King, 13 December 1939; in Murray, DCER, vol. 6, Document No. 754, p. 648.

11. Minutes of meetings held by the British War Cabinet, PRO, CAB 65: II/113(39)8, pp. 408–9.

12. Brian Nolan, *King's War: Mackenzie King and the Politics of War 1939–1945* (Toronto: Fawcett Crest Books, 1989), pp. 30, 168.

13. Stacey, *Arms*, p. 265.

14. "Note of a Meeting Held at the Air Ministry, 8 July, 1941," pp. 5–6, DHist 181.009(D897).

15. Balfour to Sinclair, 23 May 1942, PRO Air 20/2978.

16. Hollinghurst, 23 May 1942, PRO Air 20/2978.

17. Harris to Freeman, 29 July 1942, PRO Air 20/2978; and Freeman to Harris, 3 August 1942, PRO Air 20/2978.

18. Hollinghurst to Freeman, 5 August 1942, PRO Air 20/3798.

19. F. J. Hatch, *Aerodrome of Democracy* (Ottawa: Canadian Government Publishing Centre, 1983), pp. 200, 206.

20. Harvey, *Boys*, pp. 69, 70.

21. Ibid., p. 70.

22. Max Hastings, *Bomber Command* (New York: Dial Press/James Wade, 1979), p. 199.

23. Portal to Courtney, 24 December 1942, Harris papers, File H81.

24. John H. McQuiston, *Tannoy Calling* (New York: Vantage Press, 1990), pp. 8–9.

25. Ibid., p. 9.

26. Leslie McCaig, unpublished diaries, copyright Michael LeBlanc and Ted Wright.

CHAPTER 3: THE BLOODY RUHR

1. Harris, *Bomber Offensive*, p. 23.

2. Ibid., p. 25.

3. Ibid., p. 26.

4. Ibid., p. 10.

5. John Bushby, *Gunner's Moon* (London: Ian Allan, 1972), pp. 116–17.

6. Biographical data principally from Harris, *Bomber Offensive*, and from Dudley Saward, *"Bomber" Harris: The Story of Marshal of the Royal Air Force Sir Arthur Harris* (London: Cassell, 1984), p. 187.

7. Webster and Frankland, *Strategic Air Offensive* 2:10–11.

8. Ibid., vol. 4, app. 8, Directive No. xxviii, 21 January 1943, p. 153.

9. Martin Middlebrook, *The Nuremberg Raid* (Harmondsworth: Penguin Books Ltd., 1986), p. 23.

10. Webster and Frankland, *Strategic Air Offensive*, vol. 4, app. 8, Directive No. xxviii, 21 January 1943, pp. 153–54.

11. Webster and Frankland, *Strategic Air Offensive* 2:10–11.

12. Saward, *"Bomber" Harris*, p. 187.

13. Webster and Frankland, *Strategic Air Offensive* 2:15.

14. Ibid., p. 214; and Harris, *Bomber Offensive*, pp. 220–23.

15. Harris, *Bomber Offensive*, p. 144.

16. Webster and Frankland, *Strategic Air Offensive* 2:14–15.

17. Harris, *Bomber Offensive*, p. 162.

18. "Historical Review," pp. 29–30.

19. Webster and Frankland, *Strategic Air Offensive* 4:7; Brian Johnson and H.I. Cozens, *Bombers: The Weapons of Total War* (London: Methuen, 1984), pp. 208–9; Price, *Instruments*, p. 123; and R.V. Jones, *Most Secret War* (London: Coronet Books, 1979), p. 352.

20. Webster and Frankland, *Strategic Air Offensive* 2:111.

21. Webster and Frankland, *Strategic Air Offensive* 4:8–10; and Harris, *Bomber Offensive*, p. 159.

22. Webster and Frankland, *Strategic Air Offensive* 2:131, 135.

23. "Historical Review," attached list of operations, p. 4; RCAF *Overseas* 1:202; and Webster and Frankland, *Strategic Air Offensive* 2:114–18.

24. RCAF *Overseas* 1:202; and "Gunnery Report," 8 March 1943, DHist 181.003(D53).

25. Webster and Frankland, *Strategic Air Offensive* 2:125–26.

26. "Secret and Personal" memo from Air Commodore C.M. McEwen, base commander, RCAF Topcliffe, 13 May 1943, ref. AOC/DO, McEwen papers, CWM.

27. "Historical Review," attached list of operations, p. 4; and RCAF *Overseas* 1:203–4.

28. RCAF *Overseas* 1:203–4.

29. "Questionnaire for returned aircrew: Loss of Bomber Aircraft," 30 April 1945, DHist 181.001(D23).

30. RCAF *Overseas* 1:206; and "Historical Review," attached list of operations, p. 4.

31. RCAF *Overseas* 1:207–8.

32. Edwards to Breadner, Report No. 14, 21 April 1943, pp. 3–4, 8–9, Power papers, Box 64, File No. D1084.

33. "Historical Review," attached list of operations, p. 5; and *RCAF Overseas* 1:210-11.
34. *RCAF Overseas* 1:210-11.
35. Ibid., p. 211; and Jacobson, *426 Squadron*, p. 14.
36. "Historical Review," attached list of operations, p. 6; and *RCAF Overseas* 1:215-16.
37. Ibid.
38. *RCAF Overseas* 1:216-17.
39. Webster and Frankland, *Strategic Air Offensive*, vol. 4, app. 8, Directive No. xxxii, 10 June 1943, p. 158.
40. Webster and Frankland, *Strategic Air Offensive* 2:23-24, 30.
41. "Historical Review," attached table, n.p.
42. Bufton, 15 March 1945, p. 3, PRO Air 14/1847.
43. "A Note on 6 Group Losses," Report No. B.147, 15 July 1943, PRO Air 14/1794.
44. Edwards to Power, Report No. 15, 19 July 1943, p. 6, Power papers, Box 64, File No. D1084.
45. "Historical Review," attached list of operations, p. 7; Webster and Frankland, *Strategic Air Offensive* 2:130-31; and Jacobson, *426 Squadron*, p. 15.
46. Jacobson, *426 Squadron*, p. 15.
47. "Historical Review," attached list of operations, p. 8; and *RCAF Overseas* 1:225-26.
48. Combat Report, 21 June 1943, DHist 181.003(D53).
49. "Loss of Bomber Aircraft," 11 May 1945, DHist 181.001(D23).
50. "Historical Review," attached list of operations, p. 8; and *RCAF Overseas* 1:230-31.
51. "Loss of Bomber Aircraft," 27 May 1945, DHist 181.001(D23).
52. Harris, *Bomber Offensive*, p. 148.
53. Webster and Frankland, *Strategic Air Offensive* 2:108.
54. Harris, *Bomber Offensive*, p. 148.
55. Martin Middlebrook, *The Battle of Hamburg* (Harmondsworth: Penguin Books, 1984), p. 30.
56. Saward, *Harris*, pp. 195-96, 206.
57. Williamson Murray, *Luftwaffe* (Baltimore: Nautical & Aviation Publishing Co. of America, 1985), pp. 171, 180-82.
58. Alastair Revie, *The Lost Command* (London: Corgi Books, 1972), p. 182.
59. Webster and Frankland, *Strategic Air Offensive* 2:141, 136.
60. Ibid., p. 110.
61. "Historical Review," attached table, n.p.
62. Messenger, *"Bomber" Harris*, p. 83.
63. "Historical Review," attached table, n.p.

CHAPTER 4: THE BATTLE OF HAMBURG

1. Wilhelm Johnen, *Duel Under the Stars* (London: New English Library, 1975), p. 62.
2. Middlebrook and Everitt, *Diaries*, p. 411.
3. "Bomber Command Operation Order No. 173," DHist 181.009 (D6792).
4. Middlebrook, *Hamburg*, pp. 82–83.
5. Price, *Instruments*, pp. 116–17.
6. Norman Longmate, *The Bombers: The RAF Offensive Against Germany, 1939–1945* (London: Arrow Books, 1988), p. 259.
7. Price, *Instruments*, p. 120.
8. Middlebrook, *Hamburg*, p. 69.
9. Harris, *Bomber Offensive*, pp. 132–33.
10. Price, *Instruments*, pp. 140–41, 149.
11. Ibid., p. 152.
12. Longmate, *The Bombers*, p. 164.
13. "Historical Review," attached list of operations, p. 8.
14. Webster and Frankland, *Strategic Air Offensive* 2:124.
15. Webster and Frankland, *Strategic Air Offensive* 4:11.
16. Middlebrook and Everitt, *Diaries*, p. 335.
17. Ibid., p. 410.
18. Webster and Frankland, *Strategic Air Offensive* 2:150–52.
19. Harris, *Bomber Offensive*, p. 173.
20. *RCAF Overseas* 1:232; Price, *Instruments*, pp. 155–58; Middlebrook, *Hamburg*, pp. 129, 140; Harris, *Bomber Offensive*, p. 175; and Alfred Price, "The Duel Over Germany," *History of the Second World War* (Part 59), p. 1646.
21. Combat Report, 26 July 1943, DHist 181.003(D53).
22. Ibid.
23. Price, *Instruments*, p. 160; "Historical Review," attached list of operations, p. 9; and Middlebrook, *Hamburg*, p. 243.
24. Middlebrook and Everitt, *Diaries*, p. 411.
25. Middlebrook, *Hamburg*, pp. 259–61, 264–67, 277, 280.
26. *RCAF Overseas*, 1:232.
27. Middlebrook, *Hamburg*, pp. 239, 245; and Price, *Instruments*, p. 160.
28. Middlebrook, *Hamburg*, pp. 65–67; Price, *Instruments*, p. 145; R. F. Toliver and T. J. Constable, *Horrido!* (New York: Bantam Books, 1979), p. 193; Murray, *Luftwaffe*, p. 173; Hastings, *Bomber Command*, p. 271; and Harris, *Bomber Offensive*, pp. 179–80.
29. Middlebrook, *Hamburg*, p. 248.
30. Ibid., p. 287; "Historical Review," attached list of operations, p. 9; and Webster and Frankland, *Strategic Air Offensive* 2:153–54.

31. "Loss of Bomber Aircraft," 7 May 1945, DHist 181.001(D23).
32. "Loss of Bomber Aircraft," 29 April 1945, DHist 181.001(D23).
33. Combat Report, n.d., DHist 181.003(D53); and RCAF Overseas 1:233.
34. "Historical Review," attached list of operations, p. 9.
35. RCAF Overseas 1:235.
36. "Loss of Bomber Aircraft," 26 April 1945, DHist 181.001(D23); and Middlebrook, *Hamburg*, p. 311.
37. RCAF Overseas 1:235; and Middlebrook, *Hamburg*, pp. 313, 319.
38. Harris, *Bomber Offensive*, p. 175.
39. Middlebrook, *Hamburg*, pp. 11, 323.
40. Longmate, *Bombers*, p. 272; Middlebrook, *Hamburg*, p. 238; and Hans Rumpf, *The Bombing of Germany* (London: Muller, 1963), pp. 80–81.
41. Albert Speer, *Inside the Third Reich* (New York: Avon Books, 1971), p. 370; Louis P. Lochner, ed., *The Goebbels Diaries, 1942–1943* (Garden City: Doubleday & Co., 1948), p. 419; Longmate, *Bombers*, pp. 272–73.
42. Rumpf, *Bombing*, p. 85.
43. Toronto *Globe and Mail*, 7 August 1943.
44. Ibid.
45. C. Frank Turner, "The Ruhr Express," *Airforce*, vol. 6, no. 3 (September 1982), pp. 4, 5, 16, 17.
46. "The Effects of Operational Experience in No. 6 Group," 15 August 1943, DHist 181.003(D4840).
47. Jean Pouliot, Toronto *Globe and Mail*, 14 November 1984, p. 7.
48. Hollinghurst to ACAS(P), 23 September 1942, PRO Air 20/3799; Harris to McEwen, 26 June 1944, PRO Air 14/1144; and "Final Minutes of Meeting to Consider Future Use of the Halifax in Bomber Command and the Possible Switch of Halifax to Lancaster Production," 21 December 1943, p. 2, PRO Air 8/836.
49. William S. Carter, *Anglo-Canadian Wartime Relations, 1939–1945: RAF Bomber Command and No. 6 (Canadian) Group* (New York: Garland Publishing, 1991), pp. 63–64.
50. Martin Middlebrook, *The Peenemünde Raid* (London: Allen Lane, 1982), p. 61.
51. Ibid., p. 71.
52. Ibid., p. 79.
53. John Searby, *The Everlasting Arms* (London: William Kimber, 1988), p. 157.
54. Middlebrook, *Peenemünde*, p. 130.
55. Ibid., p. 130.
56. Ibid., p. 167.

57. Ibid., p. 168.
58. Ibid., p. 169.
59. Searby, *Arms*, p. 160.
60. Middlebrook, *Peenemünde*, p. 233.

CHAPTER 5: THE "COLONIAL" BOYS

1. Norman Longmate: *How We Lived Then: A History of Everyday Life During the Second World War* (London: Hutchinson, 1971), p. 470; and Middlebrook, *Nuremberg*, p. 50.
2. Larry Milberry, ed., *Sixty Years: The RCAF and CF Air Command, 1924-1984* (Toronto: Canav Books, 1984), p. 176.
3. Donald Fraser, *Live to Look Again: Memoirs of a Canadian Pilot with the RAF during World War II* (Belleville, Ont.: Mika Publishing, 1984), pp. 51-52.
4. Stacey, *Arms*, Appendix 'K,' "Air Ministry Letter on 'Canadianization' of the RCAF Overseas, 19 Feb. 1943,'' p. 579.
5. "Carbon Copy of Pamphlet Prepared for the Information of RCAF Personnel Proceeding Overseas from Canada," 10 September 1941, DHist 181.009(D1096).
6. C.P. Stacey and B.M. Wilson, *The Half-Million: The Canadians in Britain, 1939-1946* (Toronto: University of Toronto Press, 1987), p. 62; and Report No. C.7. "RCAF Personnel in Britain," May 1941, pp. 1-2, DHist 181.009(D283), vol. 1.
7. 13 February 1941, DHist 181.009(D283), vol. 1; and HQ No. 26 (Signals) Group to Tait, 10 April 1941, DHist 181.009(D283), vol. 1.
8. Report No. C.7, p. 1; and Report No. C.10, "RCAF Personnel in Britain," n.d., p. 1, DHist 181.009(D283), vol. 2.
9. "Morale survey for RCAF Personnel in U.K., September–December 1942," n.d., p. 6, DHist 181.003(D3456).
10. Edwards to Deke, 6 January 1942, DHist 181.002(D406).
11. Hastings, *Bomber Command*, p. 340.
12. No. 6 Group to Stations, Satellites and Squadrons, 26 March 1943, DHist 181.009(D2932).
13. Ibid.
14. Extracts No. 60, 20 March 1941, and No. 57, 19 March 1941, Report No. C.7.
15. Stacey and Wilson, *Half-Million*, pp. 62, 40; Robert Collins, *The Long and the Short and the Tall: An Ordinary Airman's War* (Saskatoon: Western Producer Prairie Books, 1986), p. 97; and Hugh Halliday, "Six Group," *Roundel*, vol. 15, no. 3 (April 1963), p. 17.
16. Collins, *Ordinary Airman's War*, p. 86.

17. Jean Ellis, with Isabel Dingman, *Face Powder and Gunpowder* (Toronto: S. J. Reginald Saunders & Co. Ltd., 1947), p. 53.
18. Jean Hibbert, ed., *The War Brides* (Toronto: PMA Books, 1978), pp. 156–57; and Stacey and Wilson, *Half-Million*, p. 136.
19. Edward Smithies, *Crime in Wartime: A Social History of Crime in World War II* (London: George Allen & Unwin, 1982), pp. 137–38; and Sutton to Saunders, 5 August 1943, PRO Air 2/5995.
20. Ellis, *Face Powder*, p. 133; Harris to AOsC, 9 January 1943, PRO Air 2/5995; and Richards to Harris, 19 July 1943, PRO Air 2/5995.
21. J.K. Chapman, *River Boy at War* (Fredericton: Fiddlehead Poetry Books, 1985), p. 70; and Stacey and Wilson, *Half-Million*, p. 62.
22. Chapman, *River Boy*, p. 70.

CHAPTER 6: THE BIG CITY

1. Harris, *Bomber Offensive*, pp. 220–24.
2. Saward, *Harris*, p. 218.
3. London *Evening Standard*, 12 October 1943.
4. "A Further Comment on 6 Group Losses," 7 October 1943, PRO Air 14/1794.
5. "A Review of Bomber Losses on Night Operations with Special Reference to No. 6 (RCAF) Group," n.d., pp. 3–5, DHist 181.003 (D4223).
6. Harris to Sinclair, 30 December 1942, pp. 1–2, PRO Air 14/3512.
7. Turner, "The Ruhr Express," *Airforce*, vol. 6, no. 4 (December 1982), pp. 4–6, 16.
8. Toronto *Telegram*, 28 November 1943.
9. Alan Cooper, *Bombers Over Berlin* (London: William Kimber, 1985), p. 91.
10. Ibid., p. 97.
11. Sweanor, *Pensionable Time*, p. 90.
12. Cooper, *Berlin*, p. 119.
13. McEwen, 6 Group Summary of Operations, McEwen papers, CWM.
14. Russell McKay, *One of the Many* (Burnstown: GSPH, 1989), pp. 29–30.
15. Harris to Portal, 10 January 1943, PRO Air 20/3096.
16. McKay, *Many*, p. 46.
17. McCaig diaries.
18. Cooper, *Berlin*, p. 134; and *RCAF Overseas* 2:53.
19. "Loss of Bomber Aircraft," 30 May 1945, DHist 181.001(D23).
20. Cooper, *Berlin*, p. 143.
21. "Loss of Bomber Aircraft," 16 May 1945, DHist 181.001(D23).

22. Ibid., 10 May 1945, DHist 181.001(D23).

23. *RCAF Overseas* 2:58.

24. "Loss of Bomber Aircraft," 14 May 1945, DHist 181.001(D23).

25. Cooper, *Berlin*, p. 164.

26. Ibid.

27. "Historical Review."

28. Moyes, *Bomber Squadron*, p. 328.

29. McKay, *Many*, p. 25.

30. Ibid., p. 27.

31. Middlebrook and Everitt, *Diaries*, pp. 477–84.

32. Nigel West, *Unreliable Witness: Espionage Myths of the Second World War* (London: Grafton Books, 1986), pp. 160, 146–66; and Middlebrook, *Nuremberg*, p. 299.

33. Middlebrook, *Nuremberg*, pp. 284–85, 301–2.

CHAPTER 7: PREPARATION FOR INVASION

1. Ronald Heiferman, *World War II* (London: Octopus Books, 1973), p. 184.

2. Sir David Fraser, *Alanbrooke*, p. 397, quoted in Hastings, *Overlord* (New York: Simon & Schuster, 1984), p. 19.

3. Saward, *"Bomber" Harris*, pp. 247–48.

4. "Loss of Bomber Aircraft," 11 May 1945, DHist 181.001(D23).

5. Ibid., 12 May 1945, DHist 181.001(D23).

6. Ibid., 10 May 1945, DHist 181.001(D23).

7. Ibid., 27 May 1945, DHist 181.001(D23).

8. Ibid., 12 May 1945, DHist 181.001(D23).

9. Ibid., 18 May 1945, DHist 181.001(D23).

10. Ibid., 14 May 1945, DHist 181.001(D23).

11. McKay, *Many*, p. 62.

12. *RCAF Overseas* 2:87.

13. "Loss of Bomber Aircraft," 28 May 1945, DHist 181.001(D23).

14. Ibid., 12 May 1945, DHist 181.001(D23).

15. "Report on Mining in Bomber Command," by Wing Commander T.V. Stokes, RAAF, OHQ, January 1945.

16. "Historical Review," p. 17.

17. Harvey, *Boys*, p. 163.

18. McQuiston, *Tabnoy*, p. 203.

19. Harvey, *Boys*, p. 196.

20. McEwen to Bases and Stations, 19 May 1944, pp. 1–2, DHist 181.009(D4243).

21. "Loss of Bomber Aircraft," 17 May 1945, DHist 181.001(D23).

22. Ibid., 17 May 1945, DHist 181.001(D23).

23. Ibid., 15 May 1945, DHist 181.001(D23).
24. *RCAF Overseas* 2:93.

CHAPTER 8: THE INVASION OF EUROPE

1. Bruce Halpenny, *To Shatter the Sky: Bomber Airfield at War* (Cambridge: Patrick Stephens, 1984), pp. 163–68.
2. "Loss of Bomber Aircraft," 12 May 1945, DHist 181.001(D23).
3. Ibid.
4. Based on interviews and an unpublished narrative by Garrity.
5. Longmate, *How We Lived*, p. 490.
6. McQuiston, *Tannoy*, p. 47.
7. "Loss of Bomber Aircraft," 10 February and 15 May 1945, DHist 181.001(D23).
8. Based on correspondence with Gerard and an interview with Sam's family.
9. "No. 6 (RCAF) Group – Summary of Operations for AOC-in-C (RCAF) Overseas Headquarters," p. 2, McEwen papers, CWM.
10. *RCAF Overseas* 2:210.
11. "Loss of Bomber Aircraft," n.d., DHist 181.001(D23).
12. Ibid., 12 May 1945, DHist 181.001(D23).
13. Ibid., n.d., DHist 181.001(D23).
14. Ibid., 16 May and 28 May 1945, DHist 181.001(D23).
15. Ibid., 28 May 1945, DHist 181.001(D23).
16. "Summary of Operations, No. 6 (RCAF) Group," McEwen papers, CWM.
17. Memorandum from 6 Group HQ to Breadner, 4 September 1944, McEwen papers, CWM.
18. "Loss of Bomber Aircraft," n.d., DHist 181.001(D23).
19. Harris, 25 August 1944, File no. 87/51, Harris papers.
20. Ibid.
21. Crerar to Harris, 29 August 1944, Harris papers, File H81, DHist.
22. Reports of Court of Enquiry, PRO Air 14/862.
23. "Loss of Bomber Aircraft," 17 May 1945, DHist 181.001(D23).
24. 6 Group HQ report to Breadner, 4 September 1944, McEwen papers, CWM.
25. *RCAF Overseas* 3:16.

CHAPTER 9: WHIRLWIND

1. "The Bomber's Baedeker (Guide to the Economic Importance of German Towns and Cities)," p. 1, 2d ed. (1944), pp. 142–53, DHist 181.003(D3993).
2. Command Operational Order, 6 October 1944, PRO Air 14/3126.

3. Ibid.; Interception/Tactics report no. 249/44, Part 2 – "Night 6th/7th October 1944," 12 October 1944, p. 3, PRO Air 20/5960; and Night Raid Report No. 734, 15 February 1945, p. 3, DHist 181.003(D1518).

4. Intelligence Briefing Notes, 6 October 1944, pp. 1–2, DHist 181.009(D2466).

5. "Loss of Bomber Aircraft," 16 May 1945, DHist 181.001(D23).

6. Combat Report, n.d., pp. 1–2, DHist 181.003(D53).

7. Ibid.

8. "Loss of Bomber Aircraft," 16 May 1945.

9. Ibid., 8 May 1945, DHist 181.001(D23).

10. Handwritten Raid Reports, 7 October 1944, DHist 181.003(D5124); and Interpretation Report No. K.3272, 15 October 1944, p. 1, DHist 181.003(D1826).

11. *RCAF Overseas* 3:30.

12. Ibid.

13. Night Raid Report, p. 1; and Handwritten Raid Reports.

14. John Terraine, *A Time for Courage: The Royal Air Force in the European War, 1939–1945* (New York: Macmillan, 1985), p. 675.

15. *RCAF Overseas* 3:30–31.

16. Ibid., pp. 31–32.

17. "Loss of Bomber Aircraft," 29 May 1945, DHist 181.001(D23).

18. Ibid., 17 May 1945.

19. Roberts, *Wings*, p. 192; and *RCAF Overseas* 3:33.

20. *RCAF Overseas* 3:43.

21. McQuiston, *Tannoy*, p. 91.

22. C. Frank Turner, "The Ruhr Express," *Airforce*, vol. 6, no. 4 (December 1982), p. 16.

23. Longmate, *Bombers*, pp. 331–33; Frankland, *Bomber Offensive: The Devastation of Europe* (New York: Ballantine Books, 1970), pp. 145, 148; and Hastings, *Bomber Command*, p. 398.

24. Harris, *Bomber Offensive*, p. 242; Hastings, *Bomber Command*, p. 399; Revie, *Lost*, p. 251; and "Baedeker," pp. 154–61.

25. *RCAF Overseas* 3:116; and Longmate, *Bombers*, pp. 334–36.

26. "Briefing Notes – Dresden – 13/14th Feb/45," DHist 181.009 (D3312); and "S.I.O.'s Briefing Notes," DHist 181.009 (D3313).

27. Longmate, *Bombers*, p. 336.

28. Ibid., pp. 337–39.

29. Ibid., p. 336.

30. Johnen, *Duel*, p. 149.

31. Middlebrook and Everitt, *Diaries*, p. 663; and Longmate, *Bombers*, p. 341.

32. *RCAF Overseas* 3:124–25.

33. "Report on Crashes during Operational Take-off in No. 6 Group Area, March 5th, 1945," by Air Commodore R.E. McBurney, Senior Air Staff Officer, 7 March 1945, McEwen papers, CWM.

34. Ibid.

35. *RCAF Overseas* 3:152–53; and Roberts, *Wings*, p. 192.

36. *RCAF Overseas* 3:153–56.

37. Ibid., p. 166.

38. Ibid., p. 168.

39. *The RCAF Overseas* 3:169–70; and "Base Summary of Operations," 25 April 1945, Nos. 62 and 64 Bases, DHist 181.003(D719).

40. "Historical Review," p. 46.

41. Ibid.

42. Ibid.

BIBLIOGRAPHY

Bekker, Cajus. *The Luftwaffe War Diaries*. London: Macdonald and Co., 1966.

Bomber Command: The Air Ministry Account of Bomber Command's Offensive Against the Axis, September 1939 – July 1941. London: HMSO, 1941.

Bomber Command Continues: The Air Ministry Account of the Rising Offensive Against Germany, July 1941 – June 1942. London: HMSO, 1942.

Bomber's Battle: Bomber's Command's Three Years of War. London: Duckworth, 1943.

Bottomley, Nora. *424 Squadron History*. Belleville, Ont.: Hangar Bookshelf, 1985.

Brookes, George E. "Not Enough WD in 6 Group." *Airforce*. Edited by C. Frank Turner. Vol. 8, No. 2 (Jun–Jul–Aug, 1984): 23.

Bush, E. F. "Room With a View: A Bomb Aimer's War." *High Flight*. Vol. III, No. 1 (Spring, 1983), pp. 35–40; Vol. III, No. 2 (Summer, 1983): 69–76.

Bushby, John. *Gunner's Moon*. London: Ian Allan, 1972.

Caidin, M. *The Night Hamburg Died*. New York: Ballantine Books, 1960; reprint ed., 1979.

Campbell, James. *The Bombing of Nuremberg*. London: Futura Publications, 1974.

The Canadians at War. 2 vols. N.p.: Reader's Digest, 1976.

The Canadians in Britain 1939–1944. Ottawa: King's Printer, 1945.

Carter, William S. *Anglo-Canadian Wartime Relations, 1939–1945: RAF Bomber Command and No. 6 (Canadian) Group*. New York: Garland Publishing, 1991.

Chapman, J.K. *River Boy at War*. Fredericton: Fiddlehead Poetry Books, 1985.

Charlwood, Don. *No Moon Tonight*. Australia: Angus and Robertson, 1956; London: Goodall Publications, 1986.

Collins, Robert. *The Long and the Short and the Tall: An Ordinary Airman's War*. Saskatoon: Western Producer Prairie Books, 1986.

Cooke, Owen A. *The Canadian Military Experience: A Bibliography*. Ottawa: Ministry of Supply and Services, 1979.

Cooke, R.C., and R.C. Nesbit. *Target: Hitler's Oil*. London: William Kimber, 1985.

Cooper, Alan. *Bombers Over Berlin*. London: William Kimber, 1985.

Coughlin, Tom. *The Dangerous Sky: Canadian Airmen in World War Two*. Toronto: Ryerson Press, 1968.

Douglas, W.A.B. *The Official History of the Royal Canadian Air Force*. Vol. II: *The Creation of a National Air Force*. Toronto: University of Toronto Press, 1986.

Douglas, W.A.B., and B. Greenhous. *Out of the Shadows: Canada in the Second World War*. Toronto: Oxford University Press, 1977.

Dzwonchyk, W.M. "Fateful Pathway Clearly Marked." *World War II*. Vol. 2, No. 5 (January 1988): 18–25.

Eayrs, James. *In Defence of Canada*. Vol. II: *Appeasement and Rearmament*. Toronto: University of Toronto Press, 1967.

Ellis, Jean. *Face Powder and Gunpowder*. With Isabel Dingman. Toronto: S.J. Reginald Saunders and Co. Ltd., 1947.

Feasby, W.R., ed. *Official History of the Canadian Medical Services, 1939–1945*. 2 vols. Ottawa: Her Majesty's Printer, 1953 and 1956.

Foulds, Glen. *419 Squadron History*. Burnaby, B.C.: Crosstown Printers, n.d.

Frankland, Dr. Noble. *Bomber Offensive: The Devastation of Europe*. New York: Ballantine Books, 1970.

_____. *The Bombing Offensive Against Germany*. London: Faber and Faber, 1965.

Fraser, Donald. *Live to Look Again: Memoirs of a Canadian Pilot with the RAF during World War II*. Belleville, Ont.: Mika Publishing, 1984.

Gaffen, F. "Hamburg Raid Most Costly for 6 Group." *Airforce*. Vol. 8, No. 3 (Sep–Oct–Nov, 1984): p. 43.

Galland, Adolf. *The First and the Last*. London: Methuen and Co., 1955.

Galland, A., et al. *The Luftwaffe at War, 1939–1945*. London: Ian Allan, 1972.

Granatstein, J.L. *Canada's War: The Politics of the Mackenzie King Government, 1939–1945*. Toronto: Oxford University Press, 1975.

Green, William. *Warplanes of the Third Reich*. London: Macdonald and Co., 1970.

Halliday, H.A. "Six Group." *Roundel*. Vol. 15, No. 3 (April, 1963): 16–23.

Halpenny, Bruce. *Action Stations 4: Military Airfields of Yorkshire*. Cambridge: Patrick Stephens, 1982.

_____. *To Shatter the Sky: Bomber Airfield at War*. Cambridge: Patrick Stephens, 1984.

The Hangar Bookshelf. *408 Squadron History*. Belleville, Ont.: Hangar Bookshelf, 1984.

_____. *433 Squadron History*. Belleville, Ont.: Hangar Bookshelf, 1985.

_____. *434 Squadron History*. Belleville, Ont.: Hangar Bookshelf, 1984.

Harris. Sir Arthur T. *Bomber Offensive*. New York: Macmillan, 1947.

Harvey, J. Douglas. *Boys, Bombs, and Brussels Sprouts*. Toronto: McClelland & Stewart, 1981.

_____. *Laughter-Silvered Wings: Remembering the Air Force II*. Toronto: McClelland and Stewart, 1984.

_____. *The Tumbling Mirth: Remembering the Air Force*. Toronto: McClelland and Stewart, 1983.

Hastings, Max. *Bomber Command*. New York: Dial Press/James Wade, 1979.

_____. *Overlord*. New York: Simon and Schuster, 1984.

Hatch, F. J. *Aerodrome of Democracy: Canada and the British Commonwealth Air Training Plan," 1939-1945*. Ottawa: Canadian Government Publishing Centre, 1983.

_____. "The British Commonwealth Air Training Plan." *The CAHS Journal*. Vol. XIX, No. 1 (Winter, 1981): pp. 100–109, 123.

Heiferman, Ronald. *World War II*. London: Octopus Books, 1973.

Henry, Mike. *Air Gunner*. London: G.T. Foulis and Co., 1964.

Hibbert, Joyce, ed. *The War Brides*. Toronto: PMA Books, 1978.

Hilliker, J.F., ed. *Documents on Canadian External Relations*. Vol. IX: *1942-1943*. Ottawa: External Affairs, 1980.

Hillmer, Norman. "Vincent Massey and the Origins of the British Commonwealth Air Training Plan." *Canadian Defence Quarterly*. Vol. 16, No. 4 (Spring, 1987): pp. 49–56.

Irving, David. *The Destruction of Dresden*. London: William Kimber, 1963; New York: Ballantine Books, 1973.

_____. *The Mare's Nest*. London: William Kimber, 1964; rev. ed., London: Panther/Granada 1985.

Jacobson, R., ed., *426 Squadron History*. Belleville, Ont.: Hangar Bookshelf, 1985.

Johnen, Wilhelm. *Duel Under the Stars*. London: New English Library, 1975.

Johnson, B., and H.I. Cozens. *Bombers: The Weapons of Total War*. London: Methuen, 1984.

Johnson, B. and T. Hefferman. *A Most Secret Place*. London: Jane's, 1982.

Jones, Don. *405 Squadron History*. Winnipeg: Craig Kelman and Associates, n.d.

Jones, R.V. *Most Secret War: British Scientific Intelligence, 1939–1945*. London: Coronet Books, 1979.

Keegan, John. *The Second World War*. London: Penguin, 1989.

Kostenuk, S., and J. Griffith. *RCAF Squadron Histories and Aircraft, 1924–1968*. Toronto: Samuel Stevens Hakkert and Co., 1977.

Lamontagne, J. Gilles. "Souvenirs du 425ième Escadron." *Canadian Defence Quarterly*. Vol. 11, No. 1 (Summer, 1981): p. 41–43.

Lochner, Louis P., ed. *The Goebbels Diaries, 1942–1943*. Garden City: Doubleday and Co. Inc., 1948.

Longmate, Norman. *The Bombers: The RAF Offensive Against Germany 1939–1945*. London: Arrow Books, 1988.

_____. *How We Lived Then: A History of Everyday Life During the Second World War*. London: Hutchinson, 1971.

McBurney, R.E. "Bombing of Canadian Troops at Haut-Mesnil Quarry, 14 Aug 1944." *Airforce*. Vol. 8, No. 1 (Mar–Apr–May, 1984): pp. 4–5.

McKay, Russell. *One of the Many*. Burnstown, Ont.: GSPH, 1989.

McKee, A. *Dresden 1945*. N.p.: Souvenir Press Ltd., 1982; London: Granada, 1983.

McQuiston, John H. *Tannoy Calling: A Story of Canadian Airmen Flying Against Nazi Germany*. New York: Vantage Press, 1990.

Messenger, Charles. *'Bomber' Harris and the Strategic Bombing Offensive, 1939–1945*. London: Arms and Armour Press, 1984.

Middlebrook, Martin. *The Battle of Hamburg*. Harmondsworth: Penguin Books Ltd., 1984.

_____. *The Berlin Raids*. New York: Viking, 1988.

_____. *The Nuremberg Raid*. London: Allen Lane, 1973; rev. ed., Harmondsworth: Penguin, 1986.

_____. *The Peenemünde Raid*. London: Allen Lane, 1982.

Middlebrook, M., and C. Everitt. *The Bomber Command War Diaries*. New York: Viking, 1985.

Milberry, L., ed. *Sixty Years: The RCAF and CF Air Command 1924–1984*. Toronto: Canav Books, 1984.

Milberry, L., and H.A. Halliday. *The Royal Canadian Air Force at War, 1939–1945*. Toronto: Canav Books, 1990.

Mitcham, Samuel. *Men of the Luftwaffe*. Novato, Calif.: Presidio Press, 1988.

The Moose Squadron: 1941–1945, The War Years of 419 Squadron. Winnipeg: CFTMPC, 1980.

Morris, Jerrold. *Canadian Artists and Airmen, 1940–1945*. Toronto: Gilchrist-Wright, n.d.

Morrison, L.C. "The Missing Air Force." *Airforce*. Vol. 9, No. 4 (Jan–Feb–Mar, 1986): pp. 2–4.

Morton, Desmond. *A Military History of Canada*. Edmonton: Hurtig Publishers, 1985.

Moyes, Philip. *Bomber Squadrons of the RAF*. London: Macdonald and Co., 1964.

Munro, J.A., ed. *Documents on Canadian External Relations*. Vol. 6: *1936-1939*. Ottawa: External Affairs, 1972.

Murray, D.R., ed. *Documents on Canadian External Relations*. Vol. 7: *1939-1941*. Ottawa: External Affairs, 1974.

Murray Williamson. *Luftwaffe*. Baltimore: Nautical and Aviation Publishing Co. of America, 1985.

_____. *Strategy for Defeat: The Luftwaffe, 1933-1945*. Secaucus, N.J.: Chartwell Books, 1986.

Musgrove, Gordon. *Operation Gomorrah*. London: Jane's, 1981.

Nolan, B. *King's War: Mackenzie King and the Politics of War, 1939-1945*. Toronto: Fawcett Crest Books, 1988.

Overy, R.J. *The Air War 1939-1945*. New York: Stein and Day, 1981.

Pariseau, Jean. "Alouette, Je Te Plumerai – L'Histoire du 425ième Escadron de L'A.R.C." *Canadian Defence Quarterly*. Vol. 11, no. 1 (Summer, 1981): 31-40.

Peden, Murray. *A Thousand Shall Fall*. Stittsville, Ont.: Canada's Wings, 1981.

Pickersgill, J.W. *The Mackenzie King Record*. Vol. 1: *1939-1944*. Toronto: University of Toronto Press, 1960.

Pouliot, Jean. ["Letter to the Editor"] *The Globe and Mail*. 14 November 1984.

Price, Alfred. *Battle Over the Reich*. London: Ian Allan, 1973.

_____. "The Duel Over Germany." *History of the Second World War*. Part 59, pp. 1644-52.

_____. *Instruments of Darkness: The History of Electronic Warfare*. Los Altos: Peninsula Publishing, 1987.

_____. *Luftwaffe Handbook, 1939-1945*. New York: Charles Scribner's Sons, 1977.

_____. *Pictorial History of the Luftwaffe, 1933-1945*. London: Ian Allan, 1969.

Rapier, Brian J. *White Rose Base*. Lincoln: Aero Litho Co., 1972.

The RCAF Overseas. 3 vols. Toronto: Oxford University Press, 1944, 1945, 1949.

Revie, A. *The Lost Command*. London: David Bruce and Watson, 1971.

Richards, Denis. *Portal of Hungerford*. London: Heinemann, 1977.

Rigby, V. "Air Marshal Harold (Gus) Edwards and the Canadianization of the RCAF Overseas, 1941-1943." *Canadian Defence Quarterly*. Vol. 16, No. 3 (Winter, 1986-1987): pp. 41-45.

The Rise and Fall of the German Air Force, 1933–1945. London: Arms and Armour Press, 1983.

Roberts, Leslie, *C. D.: The Life and Times of Clarence Decatur Howe.* Toronto: Clarke, Irwin and Co., 1957.

_____. *Canada's War in the Air.* 2 vols. 3d ed. Montreal: Alvah M. Beatty, 1943.

_____. *There Shall Be Wings.* Toronto: Clarke, Irwin and Co., 1959.

Rumpf, Hans. *The Bombing of Germany.* London: Muller, 1963.

Saward, D. *"Bomber" Harris: The Story of Marshal of the Royal Air Force Sir Arthur Harris.* London: Cassell, 1984.

Searby, John. *The Everlasting Arms.* London: William Kimber, 1988.

Sheard, T. "The BCATP and Defense Policy." *International Journal.* Vol. II, No. 1 (Winter, 1946–1947): pp. 37–46.

Sigson, M. "Bombing Wangerooge." *Sentinel.* Vol. 21, No. 2 (1985): pp. 8–9.

Smithies, Edward. *Crime in Wartime: A Social History of Crime in World War II.* London: George Allen and Unwin, 1982.

Speer, Albert. *Inside the Third Reich.* New York: Avon Books, 1971.

Stacey, C. P. *Arms, Men and Governments: The War Policies of Canada, 1939–1945.* Ottawa: Queen's Printer, 1970.

_____. *A Date with History.* Ottawa: Deneau Publishing, n.d.

Stacey, C. P., and B. M. Wilson. *The Half-Million: The Canadians in Britain, 1939–1946.* Toronto: University of Toronto Press, 1987.

Sweanor, George. *It's All Pensionable Time: 25 Years in the Royal Canadian Air Force.* Toronto: Gesnor Publications, 1981.

Terraine, John. *A Time for Courage: The Royal Air Force in the European War, 1939–1945.* New York: Macmillan, 1985.

Thompson, Walter. *Lancaster for Berlin.* London: Goodall Publications, 1985.

Toliver, R. F., and T. J. Constable. *Horrido!* New York: Bantam Books, 1979.

Tubbs, D. B. *Lancaster Bomber.* New York: Ballantine Books, 1972.

Turner, C. Frank. "The Ruhr Express." *Airforce.* Vol. 6, no. 3 (September, 1982): 4, 5, 16, 17.

_____. Vol. 6, no. 4 (December, 1982): 4, 6, 16.

Verrier, A. *The Bomber Offensive.* London: B.T. Batsford, 1968.

Webb, G.W. "Nuremberg: A Night to Remember." *Airforce.* Vol. 6, no. 1 (March, 1982): 4, 12–14, 41.

Webster, Sir Charles, and Dr. Noble Frankland. *The Strategic Air Offensive Against Germany, 1939–1945.* 4 vols. London: HMSO, 1961.

ACKNOWLEDGEMENTS

This book could not have been written without the generous cooperation of those who served in 6 Group and in other formations of the Allied air forces. The authors wish to acknowledge their deep appreciation of the following ex-airmen and airwomen, Canadian, British, and American, who dug deeply into their storehouse of memories and patiently provided answers to countless questions about 6 Group and its times. This is their book.

Arthur G. Angus, Kitchener, Ontario; Robert Armstrong, Stockton-on-Tees, England; Al F. Avant, Surrey, British Columbia.

Frederick G. Banbury, Cheddar, England; Glenn Bassett, Calgary, Alberta; Marcel Beauchamp, St. Lambert, Quebec; Paul W. Benson, Toronto, Ontario; Bruce E. Betcher, Grand Forks, North Dakota; Arthur A. Bishop, Calgary, Alberta; Bert Bond, Southport, England; Stan Boustead, Bristol, England; Norman Bullock, Stowmarket, England; Paul E. Burden, Fredericton, New Brunswick; John Burke, Sault Ste. Marie, Ontario; Dudley Burnside, Windsor, England.

Allan M. Caine, Scarborough, Ontario; John Campbell, Hamilton, Ontario; Dennis Clark, Warley, England; Eddy G.W. Collyer, Slough, England; John Cooper, Oakville, Ontario; J. Laurie Cormier, Dieppe, New Brunswick; Roger Coulombe, Lachine, Quebec; James H. Coventry, Nipawin, Saskatchewan; Kenneth Culpin, Spalding, England.

William I. Davies, Toronto, Ontario; Ernest D. Dickson, Cambridge, Ontario; Les Dring, Wirral, England; David Dworkin, Calgary, Alberta.

Doris Ellis, London, England; James W. Emmerson, Brampton, Ontario; R. N. Flaherty, Scarborough, Ontario; Neil Fletcher, Kelowna, British Columbia; Stanley Fletcher, Staines, England; Joe Foley, Ajax, Ontario; Reg J. Fuller, Watford, England; Jerry G. Fultz, Pleasantville, Nova Scotia; Robert V. Furneaux, London, Ontario.

Richard Garrity, Pointe Claire, Quebec; Stuart (Bill) W. Gerard, Richmond, British Columbia; Douglas H. Goodwin, Ottawa, Ontario; J. Douglas Gray, Toronto, Ontario; Ralph W. Green, Regina, Saskatchewan; Keith E. Greenwood, Etobicoke, Ontario; Bruce Grey, Calgary, Alberta; James H. Gunn, New Bern, North Carolina.

Frank F. Hamilton, Mazenod, Saskatchewan; Joseph H. Hartshorn, St. Petersburg, Florida; John Harvey, Willowdale, Ontario; E. J. Hawn, Lethbridge, Alberta; Alan F. Helmsley, Prescott, Ontario; Harry W. Holland, Mississauga, Ontario; Peter Holt, Peterborough, England; Len Hossie, Mississauga, Ontario; John W. Huggins, Ossett, England; Rowland A. Hughes, Coate, England; A. William Hutchins, Etobicoke, Ontario.

Richard Jackson, Hythe, England; Norman James, London, England; Denis Jennings, Marlborough, England; Bill Johnson, Milford, England.

W. James Kelly, Willowdale, Ontario; Robert L. Kift, Peterborough, Ontario; Edith Kup, Ilkley, England.

Don W. Lamont, Brampton, Ontario; J. Gilles Lamontagne, Sillery, Quebec; Rev. J. Philip Lardie, Kitchener, Ontario; Stuart M. Leslie, Mississauga, Ontario; Felicia Locke, Wickford, England; Wally Loucks, Etobicoke, Ontario; James C. Lovelace, Sydney, Nova Scotia.

Harvie W. MacDonald, Willowdale, Ontario; Bernard V. Marcoux, Alliston, Ontario; Robert Marshall, Fergus, Ontario; Thomas M. McCammon, Newmarket, Ontario; Joseph P. McCarthy, North York, Ontario; Alex McFall, Par, England; James E. McInerney, Islington, Ontario; John McIntosh, Calgary, Alberta; Russell McKay, Richmond, Ontario; John H. McQuiston, Don Mills, Ontario; Walter H. Miller, London, Ontario; Albert E. Mills, Cambridge, Ontario; Reg Moase, St. Catharines, Ontario; Jim Moffat, Lachine, Quebec; Ed A. Moore, Calgary, Alberta; Jim Mossman, Scarborough, Ontario; Ray Mountford, Scarborough, Ontario; John J. Murphy, Agincourt, Ontario.

John A. Neal, Calgary, Alberta; James (Nick) Nicholas, Tenby, England; James R. Northrup, Surrey, British Columbia.

Doug R. Penny, Calgary, Alberta; Wilbur C. (Wib) Pierce, Mississauga, Ontario; Jim Poulter, Teignmouth, England; Harvey Powell, Hamilton, Ontario; Steve Puskas, Waterdown, Ontario.

Edward M. Radford, Mississauga, Ontario; G. Regelous, Saffron Walden, England; Mac Reilley, Port Coquitlam, British Columbia; Lucide Rioux, Fredericton, New Brunswick; John F. Roberts, Willowdale, Ontario; George Rogers, Calgary, Alberta.

Douglas L. Sample, Ville St-Laurent, Quebec; Don R.W. Saunders, Bexhill-on-Sea, England; P. Douglas Scanlan, Willowdale, Ontario; Reg Scarth, Swindon, England; Rev. Harry J. Schmuck, Scotland, Ontario; Ken Shedden, Calgary, Alberta; Harry Shotton, Burlington, Ontario; Donald E. Smith, Scarborough, Ontario; Jack Summers, Harrow, England; George Sweanor, Colorado Springs, Colorado; W.H. (Bill) Swetman, Tottenham, Ontario.

Lucien Thomas, Scottsdale, Arizona; Robert J. Thompson, Cultus Lake, British Columbia; John B. Trout, Mississauga, Ontario.

David van Vlymen, Portland, Oregon.

A.B. (Tet) Walston, Saskatoon, Saskatchewan; Fred J. Ward, Trenton, Ontario; J. Harry Waugh, Truro, Nova Scotia; Phil G. Weedon, Westerose, Alberta; Robert Welsh, Edinburgh, Scotland; Howard F. West, Tillsonburg, Ontario; Ken H. Westrope, Southwold, England; Joe L. Widdis, Nepean, Ontario; Ross C. Wiens, Ville D'Anjou, Quebec; George Wilson, Calgary, Alberta; John A. Wullum, Surrey, British Columbia.

Of all the people who contributed to this book, none is more deserving of the authors' thanks than that remarkable Canadian airman, Reg Lane. By volunteering to read this book in manuscript form, he demonstrated that his courage and tenacity have not diminished with the years! His comments and counsel on a number of technicalities were of the greatest value and were deeply appreciated.

In addition, the authors thank the following for their invaluable help in research, writing, and production:

W.A.B. Douglas, B. Greenous, S. Harris, O. Cooke, C. Christie, and N. Hillmer of the Directorate of History, Department of National Defence.

P. Robertson, G. Wright, and Barbara Wilson of the National Archives of Canada.

R. Malott and Hugh Halliday of the Canadian War Museum.

Bill Cooper, Ruby and E. Reed and Cathy Gill of the 6 Group Association. Capt. Earl Hewison, RCAF Memorial Museum, Trenton, Ontario.

"Gus" Edwards's daughter, Sue; "Black Mike" McEwen's daughters, Beth, Joyce, and Phyl; Doug Sam's widow, Ruby, and their son, Trevor.

Michael LeBlanc and Ted Wright for their help in making Leslie McCaig's wartime diaries available.

G.W. Boon, R. Clarke, and R. Gurney of the Aircrew Association; F. Houison, B. Konig, and R. Silver of the POW Association; N. Emmott of the Allied Air Forces Association; Ken Cothliff of the Yorkshire Air Museum; H.T.N. Ling of the Bomber Command Association; the Panichellis of the Stirling Aircraft Association; Arthur Somerton, Robert Atkinson, and George F. Marks for their help in unearthing photos.

Mac Johnston of *Legion* Magazine, Marsha Dorge of *Sentinel* Magazine, Douglas Stuebing of *Airforce* Magazine.

Jack Evans of the Canadian Warplane Heritage Museum; Ann Melvin of the Royal Canadian Military Institute; Peter G. Murton and

Michael C. Tagg of RAF Museum, Hendon; John Wing of Christ Church Library, Oxford; and the staff of the Public Record Office, Kew, England.

The Ontario Arts Council whose financial assistance helped to defray the cost of research across Canada and in the U.K.

The staff of the Lucinda Vardey Agency.

Lastly, special thanks to Doug Gibson, Publisher, McClelland & Stewart, whose enthusiasm for this project was the catalyst that set it all in motion, and to Lynn Schellenberg, our editor, whose patience, diligence, and creativity were of so much help in bringing the book together in its final form.

INDEXES

Index of Groups and Squadrons

General Index